HIEROGLYPHIC MODERNISMS
Writing and New Media in the Twentieth Century

Jesse Schotter

EDINBURGH
University Press

For Molly and Hattie

Edinburgh University Press is one of the leading university presses in the UK. We publish academic books and journals in our selected subject areas across the humanities and social sciences, combining cutting-edge scholarship with high editorial and production values to produce academic works of lasting importance. For more information visit our website: edinburghuniversitypress.com

© Jesse Schotter, 2018

Edinburgh University Press Ltd
The Tun – Holyrood Road, 12(2f) Jackson's Entry, Edinburgh EH8 8PJ

Typeset in 10/12.5 Sabon by
Servis Filmsetting Ltd, Stockport, Cheshire

A CIP record for this book is available from the British Library

ISBN 978 1 4744 2477 6 (hardback)
ISBN 978 1 4744 2478 3 (webready PDF)
ISBN 978 1 4744 2479 0 (epub)
ISBN 978 1 4744 5243 4 (paperback)

The right of Jesse Schotter to be identified as the author of this work has been asserted in accordance with the Copyright, Designs and Patents Act 1988, and the Copyright and Related Rights Regulations 2003 (SI No. 2498).

CONTENTS

List of Illustrations	iv
Acknowledgements	v
Series Editors' Preface	vii
Introduction: A Hieroglyphic Civilisation	1
Part I	
1 Misreading Egypt	25
2 The Hieroglyphics of Character	62
3 Sound Enclosures	92
Part II	
4 The 'Essence' of Egypt	127
5 Solving the Problem of Babel	165
6 Matrices and Metaverses	199
Coda: The Rosetta Stone	239
Bibliography	242
Index	257

LIST OF ILLUSTRATIONS

1.1	Image from *The Last Laugh* (dir. F. W. Murnau, 1924, Germany)	40
2.1	Advertisement from *The Adelphi* (1924)	67
2.2	Advertisement from *The Adelphi* (1924)	68
3.1	Publicity photo for Orson Welles's planned adaptation of *Heart of Darkness* (1939)	114
4.1	Image from *al-Mummia* (dir. Shadi abd al-Salam, 1969, Egypt)	155
5.1	Folio 19v from the Book of Kells	182
6.1	Image from *The Matrix* (dirs. Lana and Lilly Wachowski, 1999, USA)	209
6.2	Image from *The Matrix* (dirs. Lana and Lilly Wachowski, 1999, USA)	209
7.1	The Rosetta Stone	240

ACKNOWLEDGEMENTS

I would like to thank Pericles Lewis and Peter Brooks for their unflagging attention to the progress of my work and for their support and enthusiasm throughout the ups and downs of the past ten years. Barry McCrea, Wai Chee Dimock, Jessica Pressman and R. John Williams also provided invaluable feedback to the large-scale argument and the specific chapters of this project. Sam See and Janice Carlisle lent their help to the job-seeking process. I'm also thankful for the opportunity to present portions of this book at forums at the MSA, MLA and ACLA, and through Yale's 20/21-c Colloquium and British Studies Colloquium. I am particularly grateful to the suggestions received from the members of the Yale Dissertation Writing Group over the years: Sam Cross, Colin Gillis, Sam Alexander, Michaela Bronstein, Matt Mutter, Emily Setina and Tony Domestico. Andy Heisel provided invaluable help throughout the process of writing, and I also appreciate the feedback I've received from David Currell, Sarah Novacich, Julia Fawcett, Liz Appel, Hilary Menges, Laura Miles and Dan Gustafson. At Ohio State, the Film Studies Committee provided a forum for me to present my work, and a whole host of my colleagues have helped shepherd this project from dissertation to book: Tommy Davis, Ryan Friedman, Brian McHale, Pranav Jani, Maggie Flinn, Sean O'Sullivan, Jared Gardner, Beth Hewitt, Christa Teston, Jim Phelan and Mira Kafantaris. For the last push, I'm grateful for the extremely helpful suggestions provided by the Edinburgh series editors, Tim Armstrong and Rebecca Beasley.

From letting me read drafts of their own writing to spouting speeches from

Othello, my parents, Richard and Roni Schotter, fostered my love of literature and have given me so much love and encouragement. I am constantly delighted and inspired by my daughter Hattie. And most of all, this book would not have been possible without Molly Farrell's love, support and advice. She has brightened my life each and every day: 'This heart that flutters near my heart / My hope and all my riches is.'

SERIES EDITORS' PREFACE

This series of monographs on selected topics in modernism is designed to reflect and extend the range of new work in modernist studies. The studies in the series aim for a breadth of scope and for an expanded sense of the canon of modernism, rather than focusing on individual authors. Literary texts will be considered in terms of contexts including recent cultural histories (modernism and magic, sonic modernity, media studies) and topics of theoretical interest (the everyday, postmodernism, the Frankfurt School), but the series will also re-consider more familiar routes into modernism (modernism and gender, sexuality, politics). The works published will be attentive to the various cultural, intellectual and historical contexts of British, American and European modernisms, and to interdisciplinary possibilities within modernism, including performance and the visual and plastic arts.

Tim Armstrong and Rebecca Beasley

Edinburgh Critical Studies in Modernist Culture
Series Editors: Tim Armstrong and Rebecca Beasley

Available

Modernism and Magic: Experiments with Spiritualism, Theosophy and the Occult
Leigh Wilson

Sonic Modernity: Representing Sound in Literature, Culture and the Arts
Sam Halliday

Modernism and the Frankfurt School
Tyrus Miller

Lesbian Modernism: Censorship, Sexuality and Genre Fiction
Elizabeth English

Modern Print Artefacts: Textual Materiality and Literary Value in British Print Culture, 1890–1930s
Patrick Collier

Cheap Modernism: Expanding Markets, Publishers' Series and the Avant-Garde
Lise Jaillant

Portable Modernisms: The Art of Travelling Light
Emily Ridge

Hieroglyphic Modernisms: Writing and New Media in the Twentieth Century
Jesse Schotter

Forthcoming

Modernism, Space and the City
Andrew Thacker

Slow Modernism
Laura Salisbury

Primordial Modernism: Animals, Ideas, Transition (1927–1938)
Cathryn Setz

Modernism and the Idea of Everyday Life
Leena Kore-Schröder

Modernism Edited: Marianne Moore and The Dial *Magazine*
Victoria Bazin

Modernism and Mathematics: Modernist Interrelations in Fiction
Nina Engelhardt

Modernisms and Time Machines
Charles Tung

Visit our website at: edinburghuniversitypress.com/series-edinburgh-critical-studies-in-modernist-culture.html

INTRODUCTION: A HIEROGLYPHIC CIVILISATION

In his vision of the utopian possibilities of the cinematic medium, *The Art of the Moving Picture*, first published in 1915 with a revised edition in 1922, the American poet and film critic Vachel Lindsay claims that 'American civilization grows more hieroglyphic every day'. As Lindsay explains, 'The cartoons of Darling, the advertisements in the back of the magazines and on the bill-boards and in the street-cars, the acres of photographs in the Sunday newspapers, make us into a hieroglyphic civilization far nearer to Egypt than to England.'[1] For Lindsay, this 'hieroglyphic civilization' is defined by the rise of new visual media – ads, photographs and cartoons – with *The Art of the Moving Picture* presenting the pictorial 'hieroglyphs' of the movies as a language of direct, unmediated expression. Lindsay's comments thus seem to fit with the larger modernist desire to reform or remotivate language by rendering it more visual.[2] Ezra Pound's 'Imagism' – a movement that influenced Lindsay – was famously inspired in part by the supposedly visual language of Chinese ideograms, and T. E. Hulme defined true poetry as 'not a counter language, but a visual concrete one. [. . .] It always endeavours to [. . .] make you continuously see a physical thing.'[3] To be truly new, Hulme claims, language must be made visual.[4]

Lindsay seems to emphasise the importance of this new 'aspect of visual life' and the dominance of visual media like film (p. 14). But the examples he chooses – cartoons, advertisements and photographs in newspapers – are, like film, not purely visual media. Rather, they are hybrid forms that blur the divide between images and texts, juxtaposing words with photographs or drawings. In his *Art of the Moving Picture*, Lindsay seems to celebrate images but actually expresses the interconnection between pictures and letters.

Hieroglyphic Modernisms contends that this logic is characteristic of how British and American writers and theorists understood writing and new media in the modernist period. Through the comparison to Egyptian hieroglyphs, twentieth-century commentators and creators like Lindsay defined the basic characteristics of any form of inscription – whether writing, film or phonography – in relation to each other.[5] Novelists and theorists in the early twentieth century took for granted what N. Katherine Hayles would call comparative media studies: treating text as a medium in dialogue with other competing media.[6] Rather than attempting to combine media – as in Picasso's collages or André Breton's use of photographs in his novels – writers and theorists defined the uniqueness of any medium by its hybridity, its ability to enclose or embody the sonic, visual or semantic characteristics of other media forms.

By showing how novelists and filmmakers as diverse as Sergei Eisenstein, D. W. Griffith, James Joyce and Virginia Woolf portrayed their respective medium as a hieroglyphic amalgam of letters, images and sounds, *Hieroglyphic Modernisms* recaptures the fertile interplay among media in the early twentieth century, when the characteristics and possibilities of media old and new still seemed fluid and overlapping. At the same time, by situating conceptions of hieroglyphics within the historical context of Egypt in the 1920s and in relation to the novels of Tawfiq al-Hakim and Naguib Mahfouz, the book insists on the fundamental connection between theories of new technologies on the one hand and colonialism, nationalism and the universalist desire to bridge linguistic and cultural boundaries on the other.

Hieroglyphs are everywhere in modernist novels and in early twentieth-century discussions of silent film and sound recording, appearing at moments when writers and theorists seek to understand the similarities or differences between writing and new recording technologies. Filmmakers and inventors from Thomas Edison to Sergei Eisenstein, from Vachel Lindsay to Orson Welles, from D. W. Griffith to Hollis Frampton, invoked hieroglyphs to claim their particular medium as superior to and more embodied than written words. But they defined that superiority partly by its similarity to writing itself. Film or photography was better than but the same as writing. Lindsay, for instance, characterised film's 'photoplay hieroglyphs' in the silent era as textual as well as visual, grammatical as well as depictive (p. 287). And in the sound era theorists like Eisenstein increasingly came to see film as a hybrid of spoken words and visual images. Thomas Edison likewise mentions hieroglyphs to present phonography both as a more direct and motivated form of writing and as a replacement for writing.[7] As one of the prime emblems of intermediality, hieroglyphics in turn served as a natural tool for later twentieth-century writers and theorists to conceive of the newest of new media: digital code.

For their part, modern novelists – from England to America to Egypt – responded to the rise of new media by likewise appealing to the metaphor of hieroglyphics. James Joyce, Virginia Woolf, Joseph Conrad, Naguib Mahfouz and others invoke Egyptian writing to emphasise the hybrid quality of their own written words. Like new media such as film, writing possesses for them a visual and oral form as well as a semantic meaning.[8] These writers point to the multiple ways in which a written text can communicate: through its material form as well as its phonetic signification.[9] Their arguments anticipate the claim of W. J .T. Mitchell that 'Writing, in its physical, graphic form, is an inseparable suturing of the visual and the verbal, the "imagetext" incarnate.'[10] Borrowing from the popular cultural authority of hieroglyphs, these novelists annex new media technologies to the domain of print. They make film or phonography only new and limited iterations of writing itself. Writing is better than but the same as film, better than but the same as phonography.

While Rebecca Walkowitz and Douglas Mao have helped to define the new modernist studies through its focus on technologies of 'media transmission', I argue that the importance of new media to modernism was far more sweeping. The overlap between literature, film and other new media in the modernist period is deeper than a matter of transmission, adaptation or shared techniques.[11] Film makers did not merely take up the subject matter of nineteenth-century novels, and modern novelists did not simply imitate the cross-cutting of early film. The process of media interrelation that Jay David Bolter and Richard Grusin call 'remediation' – the 'representation of one medium in another' – becomes the constitutive ontological basis of all media in the twentieth century, not simply a tactic within particular media texts.[12] Though I do not want to deny that there are fundamental differences among communication technologies, I seek to broaden the focus on media and modernism beyond cross-media comparisons between, say, film and writing.[13] By looking at the broader media ecology of the early twentieth century, *Hieroglyphic Modernisms* re-captures surprising intermedial connections, discovering links among modern novels and film theory, articles on sound recording and, later, conceptions of digital code. Through the imaginative invocation of ancient Egypt and its writing, old media are always understood as akin to new media, and new media are always simultaneously cast as old.

Egyptian Writing in the 1920s

The attention of Britain and America in the 1920s was persistently turned towards Egypt. Unlike other scholars, I do not apply the 'hieroglyph' as my own metaphor for the far-reaching desire to link the visual with the linguistic.[14] Rather, I look directly at the numerous references to Egyptian writing in the works of writers and media theorists of the twentieth century, including those in Egypt, tracking the ways in which they used hieroglyphs to understand the primary media form they sought to master. From Melville's 'mystic hieroglyphics' on the back of whales to Proust's 'hieroglyph of life'; from Woolf's 'spindly and hieroglyphic' furniture to Joyce's 'highpriest's hieroglyphs'; from Djuna Barnes's 'hieroglyphics of sleep and pain' to Freud's comparison of dreams to 'ancient hieroglyphic scripts', Egyptian writing recurs at central moments in many of the most influential works of the early twentieth century.[15]

Yet these references to hieroglyphs did not merely appear in the form of metaphors for the increasing visuality of the world. Especially after the 1922 discovery of King Tutankhamen's tomb, the American, European, English and Egyptian publics came face to face with actual hieroglyphics, as Egypt was in the news not only because of its ancient past, but also because of its contested present. Egypt won independence from Britain in the same year – that literary *annus mirabilis* of 1922 – as King Tut's tomb was unearthed. While British writers were using hieroglyphs as a metaphor for media, Egyptian critics in the mid-1920s persistently associated the discovery of the tomb and its inscriptions with national independence; as Israel Gershoni and James Jankowski write, 'The national significance of the discovery of the tomb of Tut-Ankh-Amon appears best in the ceremonial opening of Tut's tomb in March 1924. The event was deliberately timed to coincide with the inauguration of independent Egypt's first elected Parliament in March 1924.'[16] The 1920s witnessed a movement among Egyptian intellectuals like the essayists Salama Musa and Muhammad Husayn Haykal and the novelists Tawfiq al-Hakim and Naguib Mahfouz to reclaim their ancient legacy in an effort to forge a nationalist future, at the same time as the widespread global focus on Egypt created an interest in hieroglyphics and all things Egyptian throughout Europe and America.[17]

The most famous instantiation of this Egyptian vogue – even though it predates by a few months the 4 November discovery and 26 November opening of King Tutankhamen's tomb by Howard Carter – was Sid Grauman's Egyptian Theatre in Hollywood, which opened on 18 October 1922. As described in newspaper accounts, the theatre featured 'a high wall decorated with Egyptian hieroglyphics' and 'over all broods the spell cast first by the Nile by worshippers of Osiris and Isis who have left the record of their love in hieroglyphics'.[18] The Egyptian Theatre cemented the uncanny relationship between film and Egyptology that had persisted since film's invention.[19] While the link between Egypt and film seems particularly American – given Lindsay's remark about the hieroglyphic civilisation of America and the prevalence of the Hollywood system – the presumed model for the Egyptian architecture of Grauman's theatre was the 'famous Egyptian Hall' that had stood in London in 'Piccadilly for nearly a century'.[20] Indeed, the divides between America and Britain break down in discourses about media forms in this period. While Lindsay, Terry Ramsaye and other American theorists were persistently invoking the model of hieroglyphics in their early considerations of film, Virginia Woolf in 1920s London was living on the same street as the offices of the Egypt Exploration Fund (the former vice-president of which was her godfather the American writer James Russell Lowell) as she reacted to Lindsay's ideas in her 1926 essay 'The Cinema'. And Woolf's essays, and others like them, were published in transnational journals like *Vogue*, *Vanity Fair*, *transition* and the *Little Review* that often included ads for books about King Tut and ancient Egypt. The divides between American and British writing, between film and literature, between poetry and fiction, that we today take for granted simply did not exist in the 1920s and 1930s. Instead, writers and directors incessantly invoked other media as well as other nations as they sought to define the most essential qualities and capabilities of their own. And in attempting to understand the characteristics both shared between and unique to film and writing, these figures persistently turned to the ready symbol with which popular culture confronted them: the Egyptian hieroglyph.

Hieroglyphs were so appealing to those seeking to understand media because of their long history of misinterpretation in the West. Over centuries of speculation about their meaning, hieroglyphs had come to be seen as potentially mystical or sacred visual signs. Each hieroglyph supposedly directly depicted the object it signified. Like film and other emerging technologies of inscription, Egyptian writing promised to render the images of the natural world directly into recorded form. This continued insistence on the quasi-sacred properties of hieroglyphs outlasted the 1822 decipherment of the Rosetta Stone by Jean-François Champollion, who proved that hieroglyphs were phonetic and not primarily visual. They were actually similarly hybrid as Western alphabets, which likewise combine a phonetic meaning with a visual form. Hieroglyphs were not a pure or mystical language of images, but rather an alphabet akin to any other.

In the work of the modernists, hieroglyphs stand for the hybrid nature of all writing and media, even as they continue to evoke these mystical possibilities of universality and direct reference. For theorists of silent film, photography and sound recording, new technologies of inscription would resemble writing but would open up access to a primal union between image or sound and material reality that the mystic interpretations of hieroglyphics had for so long promised.[21] And when it came to their own medium of written words, modern novelists used hieroglyphs to emphasise the hybridity of written letters, how, through their combination of oral and visual elements, they could incorporate the characteristics of film and phonography. Through the metaphor of hieroglyphs, these writers demonstrate a renewed attention to how even printed alphabetical text can be imagined as visual, material and embodied.

Visual Languages, Narrative, Character

Critics like Hugh Kenner have famously placed the fascination with visual languages – Chinese ideograms in particular – at the centre of modernism. By shifting the focus from ideograms to hieroglyphs, however, I argue that this interest in visual languages was not simply about re-making language. As opposed to searching for a new language that might communicate more purely and directly, modern novelists used hieroglyphs to re-affirm the value of writing and of narrative when faced with the rise of new media technologies. *Hieroglyphic Modernisms* exposes the pivotal importance of narrative against a critical tradition that has focused exclusively on poetry. From Kenner up through Marjorie Perloff and Johanna Drucker to contemporary studies like Christopher Bush's *Ideographic Modernism* and Eric Hayot's *Chinese Dreams*, the concern with the conjunction of image and text has been seen as predominately the province of poetry and the avant-garde.[22] These critics have constructed genealogies starting with Mallarmé and ranging through the typographical experiments of Futurism and Dada and the experimental films of Duchamp and René Clair before concluding with American and Latin-American Concrete poets, with pride of place given to Ezra Pound and Ernest Fenollosa's theories of the Chinese ideogram.[23] To take one characteristic example, the 2012 Museum of Modern Art exhibit 'Ecstatic Alphabets/Heaps of Language' featured the works of artists and writers who, in the words of curator Laura Hoptman, 'concentrate on the material qualities of written and spoken language – visual, aural, and beyond'.[24] And yet, by focusing on poetry and the avant-garde, the exhibit yields a drastically limited sense of modernism and the twentieth-century interest in visual languages, emphasising how these artworks and texts resist meaning and communication.[25] Hoptman writes, 'It has been cut loose from the burden of description or commentary. It can be meaningless or can exist in an ambiguous state between meaning and non-meaning. [. . .] It is autonomous and therefore connected to poetry.' Freeing language from the burdens of meaning, or bringing language closer to material reality: these are the usual stories of modernism and the avant-garde. As a result, these histories of modernism leave out narrative altogether; language will communicate not at all or totally, without the need for narrative processes of 'description' or 'commentary'.

Yet interest in hieroglyphics is not confined to poetry and need not exclude narrative forms. By restoring a fuller sense of the modernist interest in visual languages, and by turning from Chinese ideograms – with their association with Ezra Pound – to Egyptian hieroglyphs, I show how that fascination serves as a catalyst for, rather than an alternative to, narrative. Indeed, the very idea of hieroglyphics in the Western imagination is fundamentally linked with narrative itself. As Michel Foucault describes in *The Order of Things*, the hieroglyph is essential to the belief, prominent in the sixteenth and seventeenth centuries, that 'the face of the world is covered with blazons, with characters, with ciphers and obscure words – with "hieroglyphics"'.[26] This idea of the 'Book of Nature' leads to a complex epistemology in which 'language exists first of all, in [. . .] the simple, material form of writing [. . .] a mark imprinted across the world [. . .] Above it, there is commentary [. . .] and below it, the text, whose primacy is presupposed by commentary to exist hidden beneath the marks visible to all' (p. 42). In other words, the material trace or mark – the 'hieroglyph' – serves as a potential access point to a hidden underlying text or truth, and provides the spur for narrative interpretation which tries to grasp but can never ultimately reach that central text. The hieroglyphs of the material world, be they the marks of language or features of a human face, require an effort of 'commentary' and decipherment through the means of narrative.

Given the associations between hieroglyphics and decipherment in the wake of millennia-long attempts to make sense of their meaning, modern novelists and theorists emphasise how the world and its hieroglyphic texts require an arduous process of decoding through the means of narrative itself. Discourses about new media persistently use hieroglyphs to link writing and identity, conceiving of Egyptian writing as both the new language of film and the visual language of our psyches or of our faces, both of which must be deciphered through narrative. New understandings of media and language thus go hand in hand with new notions of character and new forms of narrative. If novelists and film theorists in this period emphasise how writing or other media can 'embody' or emulate the qualities of other media, that 'embodiment' is often a literal one, tied to the human form itself. As Béla Balázs contends about the 'gestural' language of the close-up: 'The new language of gestures that is emerging at present arises from our painful yearning to be human beings with our entire bodies, from top to toe and not merely in our speech. [. . .] The new language arises from our yearning for the *embodied human* being.'[27] In this view, film will be a new and more embodied language, rendering readable our faces, and thus hieroglyphs – with their persistent associations with the Book of Nature – provided a particularly appropriate metaphor.

In turn, novelists sought to re-claim that 'embodied', 'gestural' form by assigning those same physical and material properties to their words and their characters' minds, often through invocations of Egyptian writing.[28] By pointing to the visual and material aspects of words, writers were able to conceive of the world itself or the human body as similarly constituted by a visual writing akin to hieroglyphs. If 'on or about December 1910', as Woolf famously wrote, 'human character changed', then that change goes hand in hand with the changes in media that were occurring simultaneously, which transformed the objects of perception themselves – sights and sounds – into forms of hieroglyphic writing that needed to be deciphered in narrative.[29]

Joyce, Proust, Woolf and Thomas Pynchon all conceive of the essence of character as a material form of writing, with hieroglyphs becoming an emblem of perception more generally, of how the world etches its 'impressions' onto our minds.[30] The hieroglyph serves as a metaphor for human character itself, given the connection between character – etymologically 'A distinctive significant mark of any kind; a graphic sign or symbol' (*OED*) – and written characters or letters. Indeed, this pun is repeatedly invoked by twentieth-century writers. Hieroglyphics become for modern novelists the more embodied language of our characters.

Of course, throughout the nineteenth century writers had self-consciously tried to 'read' others either through their societal type or their household furnishings or the features of their faces.[31] Yet in the twentieth century the basis for perception and for identity in fiction becomes less semiotic than linguistic; faces or furniture are not merely signs, they are actual writing – 'spindly and hieroglyphic' – that contains the promise, however unreachable, of being made legible.[32] The writer, like Champollion, must attempt to translate the 'characters' of the self from an illegible hieroglyphic script into a readable, phonetic one, and this process takes place through the narrative mode of the novel itself. Just as writers and directors emphasise how their own medium incorporates the qualities of other media, so writing itself – and the novel in particular – comes to embody visual perception and human character.

The Hieroglyphic Turn

Hieroglyphs occupy a liminal zone between hyperlegibility and indecipherability, between picture and language, in their twentieth-century use as metaphors for media. This modernist conception of writing as hybrid, as poised among image, sound and text, reveals just how deeply notions of the 'pictorial' and the 'linguistic' are intertwined, in philosophy and linguistics as well as in literature. Richard Rorty has famously argued that the twentieth century witnessed a 'linguistic turn', defined in philosophy by the belief 'that philosophical problems are problems which may be solved (or dissolved) either by reforming language, or by understanding more about the language we presently use'.[33] In response, W. J. T. Mitchell argues for a 'pictorial turn': a growing interest over the course of the twentieth century in images and in the 'material traces' of writing itself (pp. 11, 12).

Hieroglyphics play a central role in both of these 'turns', which were interrelated from the very beginning. Indeed, Michael North and W. J. T. Mitchell trace the linguistic and pictorial turns, respectively, back to the same source: Ludwig Wittgenstein's *Tractatus*.[34] And in the midst of establishing the ground rules of a new universal form of symbolic logic, Wittgenstein in the *Tractatus* claims that 'in order to understand the essence of the proposition, consider hieroglyphic writing, which pictures the facts it describes. And from it came the alphabet without the essence of the representation being lost'.³⁵ In pushing philosophy towards questions of language, Wittgenstein turns paradoxically to images, implying that hieroglyphics are not merely universal, but perfect. Like his logical system, a hieroglyph 'pictures the facts it describes'.³⁶

Now certainly Wittgenstein's use of the word picture (*Bild*) here is more complex than a pre-Sausserean belief that language is natural or motivated; in the context of the argument he means that propositions provide an accurate description of the everyday facts and objects they denote.³⁷ Yet Wittgenstein's rhetoric runs away from him. Not only does he invoke hieroglyphics and their pictorial qualities; he states explicitly that propositions are literally depictive:

> At the first glance the proposition – say as it stands printed on paper – does not seem to be a picture of the reality of which it treats. But nor does the musical score appear at first sight to be a picture of a musical piece; nor does our phonetic spelling (letters) seem to be a picture of our spoken language. And yet these symbolisms prove to be pictures – even in the ordinary sense of the word – of what they represent. (4.011)

Wittgenstein blurs the gap between alphabetical, phonetic letters and hieroglyphic characters – just as the modern novelists do – turning our letters into 'pictures – even in the ordinary sense of the word'. Rather than looking for mystic meanings in hieroglyphics, Wittgenstein searches for their 'ordinary sense'. Yet even in focusing on this 'ordinary sense' of hieroglyphs, Wittgenstein cannot resist implying that they remain, as they were seen before Champollion's decipherment, actual images. Linguistic reform and linguistic philosophy seem inseparable from hieroglyphs, which represent both the ultimate dream of perfect communication and the reality of the hybrid nature of all forms of language and media.³⁸

Hieroglyphs thus have occupied a privileged place in many of the most important twentieth-century theories of language. In his *Course in General Linguistics*, for instance, Ferdinand de Saussure defines the arbitrary and differential nature of the sign by opposing alphabetical languages – which represent only sounds, what Saussure sees as central to language – with the ideogram and the hieroglyph. Saussure writes, 'In an ideographic system each word is represented by a single sign that is unrelated to the sounds of the word itself [. . .] The system commonly known as "phonetic" tries to reproduce the succession of sounds that make up a word.'³⁹ The ideogram is 'unrelated to the sounds of the word itself', but that unrelatedness does not seem to be merely a reminder that the sign is arbitrary, as it is in phonetic languages, but that it is has nothing to do with sound at all. The sign stands for the word and the idea without the intrusion of speech. By depriving ideographic languages of their oral aspects, Saussure more effectively sets up a contrast with 'phonetic' systems, which 'reproduce the succession of sounds'.

In resisting Saussure's phonocentrism, Jacques Derrida in *Of Grammatology* returns to the hieroglyph, making it a privileged emblem of writing itself, of all that exceeds Saussure's linguistics. Breaking down Saussure's binaries, Derrida declares, 'If one considers [. . .] the uncertainty of the frontiers between so-called pictographic, ideographic, and phonetic scripts, one realizes [. . .] the unwiseness of the Saussurian limitation.'[40] Such a view echoes the beliefs of the modernist fiction writers I am discussing, who saw phonetic script as akin to hieroglyphics. Yet Woolf, Proust, Joyce and Mahfouz are not simply anticipating Derrida's insight here. For those novelists are actually more perceptive about the hybrid nature of writing than Derrida, who often falls victim to a mystical view of writing, privileging writing above speech so fervently that he ends up ignoring Champollion's decipherment and implying that hieroglyphs actually directly represent what they denote. As Derrida writes, 'Direct or hieroglyphic pictography represents the thing or the signified. The ideo-phonogram already represents a mixture of signifier and signified. It already paints language' (p. 299). For Derrida here, 'hieroglyphic pictography' is 'direct'; it represents the 'thing' itself. Only once we have made the move into sound, into the 'ideo-phonogram', do we fall into the curse of representation and lose the idea of 'the concept' in favour of only the 'phonic signifier'.[41] Derrida emerges as the mirror of Saussure, arguing for the importance of writing over speech while attempting to minimise the ways in which writing and speech are always already intertwined. Thus Derrida praises Ezra Pound for championing the Chinese ideogram as a purely visual model for poetry, calling his 'irreducibly graphic poetics [. . .] the first break in the most entrenched Western tradition' of logocentrism, but disregards Pound's fundamental misconception of the Chinese (and the Egyptian) language as non-phonetic (p. 299). As Rey Chow writes, 'The East is preserved in an essentialist, unchanging condition in Derrida's text.'[42] This book seeks to challenge those essentialist assumptions on which Derrida's argument rests, looking at Egyptian writers like Naguib Mahfouz who insist on the phonetic nature of hieroglyphs as part of their valorisation of the Egyptian nation.

Derrida thus does not fully dispense with what Foucault calls 'the oldest oppositions of our alphabetical civilization: to show and to name; to shape and to say; to reproduce and to articulate; to imitate and to signify; to look and to read'.[43] Far more than Derrida – or, even, than Apollinaire's Calligrams or the paintings of Magritte, the subjects of Foucault's essay *This Is Not a Pipe* – the European and American modern novelists reveal through their understanding of hieroglyphics how fundamentally blurred the line is between letters and pictures, between visual and textual modes of understanding. All media is intermedial. Language always seems to exist – either as an unreachable dream or as a present reality – in a dynamic, complex and not merely oppositional relationship to images. Language is already visual, and the world of nature, the world of images, the world of character, is already partly constituted by language.

This sense of the conflict between images and language and the impossibility of fully separating one from the other is just as important to twentieth-century film theory as it is to philosophy, linguistics and literature. Debates about the status of film in relation to language have raged from film's invention onward, emblematised in the second half of the twentieth century by the competing theories of Christian Metz and Peter Wollen. While Metz is careful to distinguish the cinema from language, he still uses language as the guiding rubric for forging a film semiotics.[44] By contrast, Peter Wollen in *Signs and Meaning in the Cinema* applies Charles Sanders Pierce's notions of the 'iconic' sign to cinema, emphasising the pictorial elements of film rather than turning to language as a model.[45]

But this conflict between language and image, between icon and symbol, disappears if we return to the theorists of the silent and early sound cinema, whose invocations of hieroglyphics and universality Metz casually dismisses. Despite the fuzziness of many of their ideas, these early writers, from Lindsay to Eisenstein to Terry Ramsaye, are far more attuned to the hybridity of film form than their more doctrinarian descendents. Indeed, Béla Balázs and Vachel Lindsay equate the 'revolution' of film with Gutenberg's invention of the printing press, with Lindsay claiming, 'Edison is the new Gutenberg. He has invented the new printing.'[46] As is characteristic of early twentieth-century understandings of media, the visual language of film surpasses writing by being *like* writing.

The hieroglyphs to which these writers so frequently allude express both sides of the linguistic/pictorial debate, both Metz and Wollen: hieroglyphs have an iconic, pictorial form, but they also function as symbolic elements within language. Rather than emphasising one side or the other, the early theorists of film found the perfect way to embody the contradictions that always have been and always will be inherent to film form. In touching upon the use of hieroglyphs and cuneiform in D. W. Griffith's films, Miriam Hansen thus concludes that 'the model of hieroglyphic writing seems useful here because of its emphasis on the irreducibly composite character of the hieroglyphic sign (consisting of pictographic, ideogrammatic, and phonetic elements) and its constitutive plurality of meanings'.[47] Discourses about hieroglyphs and film short-circuit the fruitless debates about the primacy of icon or language in cinema: like a hieroglyph, film is revealed as always both.

The much discussed 'pictorial turn', or the increased importance of visual media, in the twentieth century is thus not, for the novelists and filmmakers I discuss, a fundamental 'problem' or challenge, as W. J. T. Mitchell puts it, describing the 'turn' as 'a postlinguistic, postsemiotic rediscovery of the picture as a complex interplay between visuality, apparatus, institutions, discourse, bodies, and figurality' (p. 16). The modern novelists demonstrate that writing is just as much constituted by 'visuality, apparatus, institutions, discourse, bodies, and figurality' as images, and hieroglyphs encapsulate for them this essential interrelation. Acknowledging the fundamental structuring work of language and attempting to reform or revivify contemporary languages, literary or otherwise, necessitates an attention to how writing as a concrete, material trace blurs the line between language and the visual. The linguistic turn, in other words, implies the pictorial turn, and vice versa. You can't have one without the other.

My focus on the interconnection between visual languages and debates about writing and new media thus leads to a more expansive sense of modernism and media. This book argues that modernism is defined by the embrace of and engagement with radical media hybridity against W. J. T. Mitchell's contention that 'the impulse to purify media was one of the central utopian gestures of modernism' (p. 5). In the complex relationship among the media of the early twentieth century, writers and directors assert the unique capacity of their own medium for meaning and communication but predicate that capacity on that medium's incorporation of the qualities of other media forms. In traversing media borders, these writers – and this project – traverse national borders as well, with the supposedly 'universal language' of media technologies new and old used to establish commonalities and differences among the cultures of the world. And for both Egyptian and European writers, ancient Egypt becomes the locus for these questions: the origin point for linguistic and medial and cultural development.

Egypt and Egyptomania

For these aesthetic debates about the properties of writing and media cannot be separated from the material and political realities that underlie the widespread fascination with hieroglyphics in the West, particularly the anticolonial struggles simmering at the same time new media technologies began to take hold. The challenge of new media involves an increased attention to and revision of the master narratives that seek to explain the origins of language, race and nation, just as it leads to new conceptions of writing, character and narrative. Racial and cultural differences become a central issue not only in media representations, but also in the very ways in which new media are conceptualised. This book traces the interconnection between two encounters: that between old and new media and that between the West and East. Ancient Egyptian writing – a language itself in a liminal space between African and European, as well as between image and text – became associated in the late nineteenth century with the possibility of a 'universal language' like Esperanto that might bridge different cultures. I situate the rise of new media within what commentators on languages in the early twentieth century like C. K. Ogden and Wyndham Lewis called the problem of Babel: how, in a newly globalised world, different nations and language groups might best communicate with one another.[48] Such a desire to reassert linguistic purity and cross-cultural legibility is characteristic of periods of rapid global encounter; the popularity of universal logical languages like those of Leibniz in the sixteenth and seventeenth centuries coincided with the beginnings of colonialism.[49]

The transnational linkage between alphabetical writing, new media and hieroglyphics can complicate our understanding of modernist politics, capturing the peculiar dance between an embrace of cultural and linguistic difference and a desire to find the common roots or the universal language of all of humanity. Benedict Anderson has argued in tying the rise of nationalism to print culture that the civilisations of the mythic past – including Egypt – were often viewed as lacking spoken language: 'Yet if sacred silent languages were the media through which the great global communities of the past were imagined, the reality of such apparitions depended on an idea largely foreign to the contemporary Western mind: the non-arbitrariness of the sign.'[50] The 'communities of the past' are defined by the motivated character of their writing, and that motivation is tied to the 'silence' of that writing, to its lack of phoneticism. Hieroglyphics, as a silent, sacred language, are defined as other and 'foreign' to the Western present. Indeed, as I discuss in Chapter 1, this is just how Ezra Pound famously sees Chinese writing: as natural and non-phonetic and thus different from Western alphabets. Pound's interest in Chinese, frequently seen as the prime example of modernist primitivism and Orientalism, serves to confine China to a timeless past and render it incompatible with modern nationhood.[51]

Western writers like Joyce, Woolf and others paint a more complicated picture of the twentieth-century use of non-Western languages. By treating alphabetical characters as just as hybrid as hieroglyphs, they refuse to see ideographic and pictographic languages as fundamentally different or more primitive, as 'sacred' and 'silent'. Instead, the hieroglyph becomes a means of universalising languages without privileging one over another, of pointing to the common roots among all languages and cultures. By eliding the differences between alphabetical and ideographic languages, however, these writers occlude the cultural specificity of each language, confusing hieroglyphic and cuneiform writing, Chinese and Japanese scripts. By focusing exclusively on the past – either on dead languages or long-dead poets – they likewise neglect the literature of their contemporaries in Egypt. The modernist interest in hieroglyphs, despite its universalist emphasis, can represent a form of discursive imperialism, a way of reclaiming imaginative control over Egypt at a time when England had finally begun to cede its political control. Yet we might also see the new interpretation of hieroglyphs as similar to modern languages as an implicit acknowledgement, anticipating Anderson, that Egypt has moved away from its 'sacred', 'silent', ancient past and must be considered, both linguistically and culturally, a nation on an equal footing with those of Europe.

When Egyptian nationalist writers in the 1920s and 1930s like Salama Musa, Tawfiq al-Hakim and Naguib Mahfouz turned to their ancient Egyptian heritage, they likewise used the history of Egyptian writing for political ends, similarly straddling the line between nationalism and universalism. This project places twentieth-century Egyptian and British writers and filmmakers side by side, disrupting the usual imperialist temporality of the Western fascination with hieroglyphics and ancient Egyptian civilisation.[52] In so doing, it moves beyond Orientalist formulations of postcolonial writers responding to metropolitan discourses, arguing for the commonality between the political concerns and aesthetic strategies of British and Egyptian writers in the 1920s and 1930s. This juxtaposition exposes not only an engagement with the ancient past on the part of Egyptian writers, but also the political and national implications of references to hieroglyphs in modern British novelists. The literary and cultural interest in ancient Egypt is not a one-way street of co-optation and appropriation, but rather a contested engagement with a distant past that was almost as alien for contemporary Egyptians as it was for twentieth-century Europeans.

For the 'Pharaonic' writers of the 1920s, reclaiming the glories of the Egyptian past was key to forging a new Egyptian nation; as Muhammad Husayn Haykal writes, 'All mankind owed its civilization and progress to the example of ancient Egypt. Pharaonic Egypt had laid the foundations for advanced civilizations elsewhere.'[53] Through the appeal to a Pharaonic past, Musa and Haykal and later novelists like Tawfiq al-Hakim and Naguib Mahfouz argue for the continuity between Egypt and Europe but simultaneously stake a claim for a uniquely Egyptian national identity. As with Joyce and other modernists, an appeal through linguistic and cultural origins to the universal links among nations counterintuitively validates the importance of a particular nation, in this case Egypt. Just like in debates about media in which film becomes both better than but the same as writing, Egypt becomes both better than but the same as Europe. Over the course of centuries, and whether for Egyptian novelists or canonical British modernists, discourses about ancient Egypt, hieroglyphics and new media in the West inevitably expand beyond mere aesthetic grounds, turning into claims about the nature and sources of present-day divisions among languages, races and nations. In promising a mode of inscription or communication that might reach beyond national boundaries, new media inevitably involve a renewed attention to those boundaries themselves.

The first chapter of *Hieroglyphic Modernisms* exposes the complex history of Western misconceptions of Egyptian writing from antiquity to the present. Hieroglyphs bridge the gap between modern technologies and the ancient past, looking forward to the rise of new media and backward to the dispersal of languages in the mythical moment of the Tower of Babel. The contradictory ways in which hieroglyphs were interpreted in the West come to shape the differing ways that modernist writers and filmmakers understood the relationship between writing, film and other new media. On the one hand, poets like Ezra Pound and film theorists like Vachel Lindsay and Sergei Eisenstein use the visual languages of China and of Egypt as a more primal or direct alternative to written words, as a poetic form to be aspired to. But Freud, Proust and the later Eisenstein conversely emphasise the phonetic qualities of Egyptian writing, its similarity to alphabetical scripts. The chapter concludes by arguing that even avant-garde invocations of hieroglyphics depend on narrative form, examining how these two interpretations of the relationship between image and language animate Hollis Frampton's experimental film *Zorns Lemma*.

The second chapter, 'The Hieroglyphics of Character', examines how hybrid conceptions of language and media come to challenge representations of literary character and narrative in the modernist period. Understanding Virginia Woolf as a film theorist situated within the ferment of avant-garde film culture in London in the mid-1920s – a period which saw the formation of the journal *Close-Up* and the London Film Society – I argue that Woolf's engagement with film and its 'hieroglyphs' in her essay 'The Cinema' transforms her understanding of language and character in *To the Lighthouse*. Throughout the late 1920s, Woolf imagines writing as emulating the material and visual form of hieroglyphs, revealing the inscriptions graven upon the 'sacred tablets' of the minds and hearts of her characters.

If Woolf seeks to collapse the gap between perception, character and language, then Joseph Conrad and Orson Welles call attention to the ways in which innovative narrative structures can expose the hybrid nature of all media forms. Moving from theories of film to film itself, my third chapter, 'Sound Enclosures', contends that *Citizen Kane* employs the same narrative form as the novel Orson Welles wanted to adapt when he went to Hollywood, Conrad's *Heart of Darkness*. Both works revolve around the attempted decipherment of a deathbed phrase by multiple narrators. But Welles also derives from Conrad his concern with the relationship among speech, writing and image, a relationship transformed by new technologies of sound recording, frequently described as akin to hieroglyphs. The innovative plot structures of Conrad and Welles seek to call attention to the ways in which the medium of the novel or of film, respectively, can uniquely express the visual and the oral, without seeking to mediate between the two.

The second half of *Hieroglyphic Modernisms* argues that an attention to Egyptian history and Egyptian novelists reveals the political implications of theories of media centred around hieroglyphs. The book moves from aesthetic discussions about hieroglyphs and their associations with language, character and narrative to an examination of how invocations of hieroglyphs intervene in debates about nation, race and colonialism. The fourth chapter, 'The "Essence" of Egypt', exposes how hieroglyphs were not simply a metaphor appropriated by the West in novels and early films by restoring them to their historical and cultural context in post-Revolutionary Egypt. I explore how interpretations of the Pharaonic past and its hieroglyphs intervened in Egypt's twentieth-century struggles for cultural and national identity, in the process complicating a binary between colony and metropole, Egypt and England. The first novels by Naguib Mahfouz and Tawfiq al-Hakim, from the 1920s and 1930s, draw on the 'Pharaonicist' movement of the period, co-opting the European Orientalist discourses with which Egypt was defined in order to forge their own definitions of the racial and cultural 'essence' of Egypt. Yet these national concerns remain linked with an interest in the ontology of media forms, with Mahfouz in particular turning to hieroglyphs to draw connections between the languages of ancient and modern Egypt. Indeed, new media, the Egyptian nation, and the Pharaonic past were inseparable from the start, with the first film made by Egyptians – *In the Land of Tutankhamen* (1923) – coinciding with the discovery of King Tut's tomb and Egypt's independence. The chapter concludes by focusing on Shadi Abd al-Salam's film *al-Mummia*, from 1969, which looks back to early twentieth-century Pharaonicism and connects its attempt to reclaim the past with film's ability to record and preserve Egyptian hieroglyphs and artefacts.

Chapter 5, 'Solving the Problem of Babel', continues to explore how hieroglyphs serve as a way of understanding the possibility for linguistic, cultural, national and racial unity and interconnection. By situating James Joyce within a larger discourse about the problem of Babel, I show how hieroglyphs were used to make arguments for the origin of linguistic differences. The journal *transition* – in which Joyce's work was serialised – served as a clearinghouse for ideas about how a new linguistic unity might be forged: either through Joyce's *Wake*-ese and other avant-garde experiments or through the philosopher C. K. Ogden's universal language of Basic English. Fascinated by these theories of universal language and drawn to the anti-imperialist politics underlying them, Joyce in *Ulysses* and *Finnegans Wake* turns to visual and gestural languages – film, hieroglyphs and illuminated manuscripts – in an effort to subvert theories of 'Aryan' language and imagine a more inclusive origin for the world's cultures. The commonality of writing and new media becomes in Joyce a political gesture: a way of insisting on the unity of all races and languages in a mythic past against Nazi claims for racial purity.

The final chapter, 'Matrices and Metaverses', contends that the association of hieroglyphs with universal languages and mixtures of media gets passed down to the newest of new media, digital code. I examine post-war American fiction and the imaginative connection forged, in theory and in fiction, between hieroglyphs and code, computers, and electronic writing. From the novels of

Thomas Pynchon through the literary-inflected sci-fi of William Gibson and Neal Stephenson, from the Afro-Futurist works of Ishmael Reed to the mass-market novels of Dan Brown, this pairing of hieroglyphs and digital code recurs across genre and style. By linking code with Egyptian writing, these writers emphasise the performativity of their language; just as code can create a simulation of reality, so words can call characters and settings into being. When faced with the challenge of a new medium, Pynchon, like Woolf and Joyce before him, asserts that code is merely a new iteration of writing itself. The association of digital code with hieroglyphs emphasises the totalising possibilities of media forms and provides a way of imagining the discord and potential unity of a globalised world.

As in so many twentieth-century works, hieroglyphs serve both as emblems of the possibility of linguistic and cultural interconnection and as metaphors for the relationship between writing and new media. They embody both the similarities and differences among various media forms and the similarities and differences among various nations or languages. Like the Rosetta Stone, with its three distinct languages that nonetheless communicate an identical message, hieroglyphs serve as the emblems of liminality itself: whether it comes to language, race or media, they are always both different and the same.

Notes

1. Lindsay, p. xxxvi.
2. This strain is particularly strong in theoretical writings by the modernists themselves, like Ezra Pound's *ABC of Reading* up through Hugh Kenner's *The Pound Era* to Michael North's *Camera Works*. As Morag Shiach writes in her '"To Purify the Dialect of the Tribe": Modernism and Language Reform', p. 21, grounding this desire in more widespread philosophical discourses, 'modernist cultural practice can be understood in relation to an aspiration towards linguistic reform, not simply in the sense of aesthetic innovation and experiment, but also in the context of educational, cultural, and political initiatives designed to transform linguistic usage and norms.'
3. Hulme and Csengeri, p. 70.
4. For more on the influence of Hulme on modernism, particularly on Pound, whose 'explanations of poetry also repeatedly turn to visual analogy', see Beasley, p. 52.
5. While my focus on hieroglyphics is indebted to John Irwin's account of the interest in hieroglyphics as symbols in mid-nineteenth-century American literature in his *American Hieroglyphics*, I argue that the late nineteenth and early twentieth-century rise of film and phonography transformed literary invocations of hieroglyphics from mystical symbols to metaphors for the visual and sonic qualities of new media.
6. Hayles and Pressman, 'Introduction', *Comparative Textual Media*. As Hayles and Pressman argue, their approach

> recognizes that print is itself a medium, an obvious fact that tends to be obscured by its long dominance within Western culture. [. . .] It is possible once again to see print in a comparative context with other textual media, including the scroll, the manuscript codex [. . .] and born-digital forms such as electronic

literature and computer games. The broad term for this approach is *comparative media studies*, which typically includes not only text but also film, installation art, and other media forms. (p. vii)

Similarly, though in reference to photography, Michael North in *Camera Works* argues for how 'the critical interrogation of the relationship between text and image' was brought about by the rise of 'mechanical recording' (p. 12).

7. As Edison writes in 'The Perfected Phonograph', p. 645, the 'Assyrians and Babylonians, 2,500 years ago, chose baked clay cylinders inscribed with cuneiform characters, as their medium for perpetuating records; while [. . .] the phonograph, uses cylinders of wax for a similar purpose.' Edison intended phonographs to supplant writing as a vehicle for dictation, and, as James Lastra explains, 'Like the phonograph, it was argued, the hieroglyph's nonarbitrary or iconic aspects rendered it a more likely candidate for the status of "universal language"' (p. 29).
8. Indeed, Garrett Stewart in *Reading Voices* has argued that this hybridity characterises 'literary textuality' itself, which consists of 'the continual confrontation, within writing, of the phonic and the graphic' (p. 24).
9. While Sara Danius claims that modern novels 'incorporate within themselves representations of other modes of cultural production, including competitors such as newspaper, cinematography, and recorded music' (p. 179), such a process takes place even on the level of how writers conceive of their own language.
10. Mitchell, p. 95.
11. Mao and Walkowitz, pp. 737–48.
12. Jay David Bolter and Richard Grusin, *Remediation: Understanding New Media*. Like Julian Murphet, I argue that 'forms perpetrated in the name of the older system [of media] will tend to "borrow" features [. . .] from that illustrious array of new media' (p. 30), but I see that pattern not only within the avant-garde and not only defined by the borrowing of 'features' but by more fundamental defining characteristics.
13. For interesting recent cross-media studies of modernism, see, for film, Andrew Shail, *The Cinema and the Origins of Literary Modernism*; Laura Marcus, *The Tenth Muse*; David Trotter, *Cinema and Modernism*; Susan McCabe, *Cinematic Modernism: Modernist Poetry and Film*; for photography, North's *Camera Works* and Paul Hansom, *Literary Modernism and Photography*; for phonography, James Lastra, *Sound Technology and the American Cinema* and Lisa Gitelman, *Scripts, Grooves, and Writing Machines*; for digital code, Lisa Gitelman, *Always Already New* and Shawn James Rosenheim, *The Cryptographic Imagination*.
14. For instance, Tom Conley in his *Film Hieroglyphs* uses the hieroglyph as a symbol to describe how film mixes text and image, but does not delve into how early film theorists made use of that same motif.
15. Herman Melville, *Moby-Dick*, p. 171; Marcel Proust, *Time Regained*, p. 342; Virginia Woolf, *The Complete Shorter Fiction of Virginia Woolf*, p. 223; James Joyce, *Finnegans Wake*, p. 122; Barnes, p. 63; Freud, p. 377.
16. Gershoni and Jankowski, *Egypt, Islam, and the Arabs*, p. 168.
17. For more on this fascination with Egypt, see Michael North, *Reading 1922*, pp. 19–30.
18. Beardsley, pp. 78, 82.
19. As Antonia Lant summarises:

    There was an association between the blackened enclosure of silent cinema and that of the Egyptian tomb, both in theoretical texts and in the use of Egyptianate architectural style for auditoriums; a perception of cinema as a necropolis, its projections mysterious and cursed, issuing a warning to spectators; an under-

> standing of cinema as a silent world that speaks through a pictorial language, as hieroglyphics revealed by light, and a consequent en-nobling of the newest visual medium through alignment with some of the oldest word-images; a noted parallel between mummification as preservation for a life beyond life and the ghostliness of cinematic images [...] an alliance between modern sexuality, particularly female screen sexuality, and myths surrounding the sphinx and its silent unreadability. (p. 90)

> For André Bazin's 'mummy-complex', see Bazin, p. 9.

20. Sharp, p. 90.
21. The same was true of the slightly earlier media of photography: 'Photography was strongly associated from its very beginnings with hieroglyphs, another form of writing that, in the popular view, bypassed sound and spoken language to reach the mind directly through the eye [...] that would also return to an ancient purity and directness, a pre-Babelic unity of word and thing' (North, *Camera Works*, p. 5). Similarly, North describes how photographs were seen as 'a sort of notation suspended between letters and pictures, a new alphabet, as it were' (p. 4).
22. For recent work on modernism and Chinese, see Christopher Bush, *Ideographic Modernism;* Eric Hayot, *Chinese Dreams*; Yuante Huang, *Transpacific Displacements,* and Rey Chow, *The Protestant Ethnic and the Spirit of Capitalism.* Daniel Albright in *Untwisting the Serpent* likewise links hieroglyphs with the mixed-media forms of the avant-garde: 'A hieroglyph dwells on the boundary among the artistic media [...] Almost every mixed-medium art-form in Europe justified itself by trying to assume the glamour of the hieroglyph' (pp. 40–1).
23. As Drucker writes:

    > The striking work of the typographically innovative French symbolist poet Stephane Mallarmé casts its influence over poetic activity of the early 1900s, inspiring the visual experiments of writers and artists [...] Ezra Pound's apocryphal (but real) fascination with art historian Ernest Fenollosa's work on the Chinese character is one of the mythic moments in the history of modern poetry's engagement with the material manifestation of language in written form. [...] And perhaps most renowned of all the revolutionary calls-to-arms is in the work of the Italian major-duomo of Futurism, Fillipo Marinetti. [...] In the 1950s and 1960s the theoretical writings of Concrete poets and Lettrists add to the log list of manifesto-like statements asserting the potential of visual poetics. (pp. 58–9)

    Similarly, Marjorie Perloff in *The Futurist Moment* sees Futurism – both Italian and Russian – as central to the new word/image relationship, again foregrounding the avant-garde and Pound.
24. See Hoptman, unpaged. This volume served also as the catalog to the MoMA exhibit.
25. Laura Marcus likewise stresses that these issues were not exclusive to the avant-garde in film either: 'The preoccupation with word and image, and with concepts of inscription, light-writing, and hieroglyphics, was not only an aspect of avant-garde discourse, but also permeated writing about cinema in a variety of contexts, including those of more mainstream film criticism' (p. 9).
26. Michel Foucault, *The Order of Things*, p. 27.
27. Balázs and Livingstone, p. 11.
28. My argument thus challenges Friedrich Kittler's claim in *Gramophone, Film, Typewriter* about how technology strips from writing its connection to embodied meaning: as Kittler argues, 'In standardized texts, paper and body, writing and soul fall apart' (p. 14).

29. Virginia Woolf, *Collected Essays*, Vol. 3, pp. 422–3.
30. Virginia Woolf, 'Modern Fiction', *The Common Reader*, p. 154.
31. These attempts themselves were partly influenced by physiognomy, a discourse that from the start used the hieroglyph as one of its central metaphors. See Graeme Tytler, *Physiognomy in the European Novel*; Christopher Rivers, *Face Value*.
32. Virginia Woolf, 'The Lady in the Looking-Glass', *Complete Shorter Fiction*, p. 223.
33. Rorty, p. 3.
34. The *Tractatus*, North claims in *Reading 1922*, 'began the famous "linguistic turn," which has made the study of language the centerpiece of contemporary philosophy' (p. 31), and Mitchell argues that 'the philosophical enactment of the pictorial turn [occurs] in the thought of Ludwig Wittgenstein' (p. 12).
35. Ludwig Wittgenstein, *Tractatus Logico-Philosophicus*, 4.016.
36. None of the critical works on Wittgenstein and literature address the connection to hieroglyphics or its implications. See Marjorie Perloff, *Wittgenstein's Ladder*; John Gibson and Wolfgang Huemar, *The Literary Wittgenstein*.
37. For a more in-depth analysis of the complexities of Wittgenstein's thought and his relation to Joyce, see Megan Quigley, *Modernist Fiction and Vagueness*.
38. Of course, Wittgenstein repudiated his earlier ideas in *Philosophical Investigations*, turning to an idea of 'language games', the fluidity of which is closer to the linguistic practice of Woolf, Joyce, etc.
39. Ferdinand de Saussure, pp. 25–6.
40. Derrida, *Of Grammatology*, p. 29. In describing this bias towards writing against phonetic speech, Derrida summarises, 'The immediate and privileged unity [. . .] is the articulated unity of sound and sense within the phonic. With regard to this unity, writing would always be derivative, accidental, particular, exterior, doubling the signifier: phonetic. "Sign of a sign," said Aristotle, Rousseau, and Hegel' (p. 9).
41. Michel Foucault and Marshall McLuhan likewise seem to subscribe to misguided notions about the differences between ideograms and hieroglyphics and alphabetical writing. As Foucault argues in *Language, Counter-Memory, Practice*, 'Alphabetical writing is already, in itself, a form of duplication, since it represents not the signified but the phonetic elements by which it is signified; the ideogram, on the other hand, directly represents the signified, independently from a phonetic system which is another mode of representation' (pp. 55–6). Again as with Pound, for Foucault the ideogram communicates 'directly', free from 'phonetics' and 'duplication'. Similarly, McLuhan in *Understanding Media* argues that 'the phonetically written word sacrifices worlds of meaning and perception that were secured by forms like the hieroglyph and the Chinese ideogram' (p. 83). Such a view, however, quickly slides into an Orientalist view of the greater integration and, even, of the greater sensuousness, of non-Western languages: 'For the ideogram is an inclusive *gestalt*, not an analytic dissociation of senses and functions like phonetic writing' (p. 84).
42. Chow, p. 62.
43. Michel Foucault, *This is Not a Pipe*, p. 21.
44. According to Metz:

> Contrary to what many of the theoreticians of the silent film declared or suggested ('*Ciné langue*,' 'visual Esperanto,' etc.), the cinema is certainly not a language system (*langue*). It can, however, be considered as a *language*, to the extent that it orders signifying elements within ordered arrangements different from those of spoken idioms – and to the extent that these elements are not traced on the perceptual configurations of reality itself (which does not tell

stories). Filmic manipulation transforms what might have been a mere visual transfer of reality into discourse. (p. 105)

45. As Wollen writes in *Signs and Meaning in the Cinema*, 'the cinema contains all three modes of the sign: indexical, iconic, and symbolic. What has always happened is that theorists of the cinema have seized on one or other of these dimensions and used it as the ground for an aesthetic firman. Metz is no exception' (p. 125). Yet Wollen is just as guilty of seizing upon one 'of these dimensions': in his case, the 'iconic'.
46. Lindsay, p. 224. Or, as Balázs writes, 'It is the cinematograph, a technology for the multiplication and dissemination of the products of the human mind, just like the printing press, and its impact on human culture will not be less momentous' (p. 9).
47. Hansen, *From Babel to Babylon*, p. 191.
48. Ogden uses the phrase 'problem of Babel' in his book *Debabelization*, and the phrase was widespread at the time. See Ogden, *Debabelization*, p. 7; Bernard Eustace Long, *Esperanto: Its Aims and Claims*, p. 5; Wyndham Lewis, p. 120. For a comprehensive transhistorical account of the influence of the myth of Babel and the problems of translation, see George Steiner, *After Babel*.
49. This era also saw some of the most famous early uses of the hieroglyph as a model of literature: the poems of George Herbert. Indeed, the English court mathematician Thomas Hariot, who voyaged to America as part of the ill-fated Roanoke colony, wrote not only an account of his encounters with Native Americans but also a new symbolic logic. See Daniel J. Cohen, p. 26.
50. Anderson, p. 14.
51. For modernism and primitivism, see, for example, Marianna Torgovnick, *Gone Primitive*.
52. As Elliott Colla writes in *Conflicted Antiquities*, in accounts of Egyptology 'modern Egyptians simply do not figure in the story. For instance, scholars of European Egyptomania, even those attuned to its postcolonial critique, have been largely unaware of the fact that a comparable cultural phenomenon occurred in Egypt during the 1920s and 1930s as Egyptian intellectuals and artists studied ancient Egypt and considered it the source of modern Egyptian identity' (p. 13).
53. Quoted in Gershoni and Jankowski, p. 172.

PART I

I

MISREADING EGYPT

The history of hieroglyphics in the West is the history of a misconception. From the very beginning up to, in many cases, the present day, most Western interpreters believed that Egyptian hieroglyphs were something they never were: a language of symbolic or motivated signs. As Liesolette Dieckmann writes, 'What delayed the actual deciphering of the Egyptian hieroglyphics for almost four hundred years was the idea [. . .] that hieroglyphics were symbols of words or ideas rather than letters of the alphabet.'[1] For despite their visual appearance and their incorporation at times of ideographic meanings, hieroglyphs, as Jean-François Champollion discovered, are primarily phonetic and thus much closer than had been thought to contemporary alphabetical languages. In general, each hieroglyph derives its sound from the first syllable of the word used to describe the object pictured in the hieroglyph: for instance, the hieroglyph of a man carrying something – transliterated 'fɔj' – stood for the sound 'f'. These phonetic meanings are by far the most common; indeed, ideographic meanings had to be signalled to the reader through the addition of diacritical marks. As Erik Iversen writes, Egyptian writing was 'undoubtedly from the very outset essentially phonetical in character and function'.[2]

All pre-Champollion interpreters of hieroglyphics, however – most with little or no knowledge of actual Egyptian writing – persisted in the belief that hieroglyphics were motivated or sacred. They were what Gerard Genette refers to, from Plato's *Cratylus*, as a Cratylic language: one in which the word or character has a non-arbitrary relation to or depicts the object it denotes.

And/or they were a mystic one, which, when deciphered, would reveal the esoteric wisdom of the Egyptian priests.[3] Indeed, despite the worldwide attention devoted to Champollion's decipherment of the Rosetta Stone, these older misconceptions refused to fade, and even 'blossomed out with undiminished vitality', particularly after the 1922 discovery of King Tutankhamen's tomb.[4]

In this chapter I argue that the conflicting ways in which hieroglyphics were interpreted in their long history in the West structured the competing ways British, European and American modernists made sense of visual languages and visual media. From antiquity up into the nineteenth century, two camps of hieroglyphic interpreters emerged: those who stressed the Adamic, mystical and visual aspects of Egyptian writing and those who emphasised its linguistic and, later, phonetic elements and its similarity to Western alphabets. The tension between what I call, following John Irwin, these 'mystical' and 'linguistic' schools shapes understandings of visual languages and theories of new media in the post-Champollion era. Placing twentieth-century understandings of visual languages into a millennium-long tradition complicates our sense of the modernist fascination with Chinese and Egyptian scripts and exposes the links between this preoccupation and the rise of new media.

Most critical accounts of visual languages in modernism, discussed in the introduction, have focused on the 'mystical' interpretations of hieroglyphs and ideograms, centred around Fenollosa's essay 'The Chinese Written Character as a Medium for Poetry'. That essay's theories of Chinese ideograms as a motivated language consisting of 'vivid shorthand pictures' of Nature[5] has exerted such a widespread influence on the development of avant-garde poetry that it has occluded the importance of Egyptian hieroglyphics alongside Chinese ideograms, as well as the similar focus on visual languages in film theory of the period.[6] For while Ezra Pound finds in Chinese ideograms a purer, more direct alternative to Western alphabets, other twentieth-century figures like Proust and Freud draw on the 'linguistic' interpretations of visual languages, seeing hieroglyphs as similar to the languages of the West. For them, hieroglyphs become emblems of the hybrid nature of all writing and media, of the combination of phonetic, pictographic and ideographic elements.[7] Hieroglyphics thus come to symbolise both the dream of the unique capacities of each individual medium, and the reality of the interrelationship, within any medium, of sound, writing and image. Indeed, those opposing notions were bound up in interpretations of hieroglyphs throughout their history.

Emphasising the 'linguistic' view of hieroglyphs and ideograms reveals not merely how visual languages were often seen as just as hybrid – both visual and oral – as written words, but also how they were linked to narrative and to the rise of new media like film. To explore these links, this chapter not only places early twentieth-century debates about the relationship between film and writing alongside the longer genealogy of Western understandings of Egyptian writing, but also juxtaposes literary texts with early film theory. Pound and Fenollosa's theories of the Chinese ideogram as a 'mystical', universal, Cratylic language anticipate the early writings on film of Vachel Lindsay and Sergei Eisenstein, and Freud's and Proust's shared emphasis on the phonetic, linguistic nature of hieroglyphics echoes the later theories of Eisenstein. These connections reveal the intertwining of discourses about writing, film and universal languages in the modernist period, exposing how film and writing are conceptualised in strikingly similar ways through the metaphor of hieroglyphics. The specific and conflicting means by which Western writers and theorists understood Egyptian writing shape the debates about new media in the early twentieth century. But more than that, these discourses establish a defining modernist link among narrative, writing and human character that the next two chapters will go on to develop. While Pound and the avant-garde for the most part de-emphasise narrative in their use of visual languages, hieroglyphics reveal the essential link among visual languages, visual media and narrative form.

A Sacred Language

In the classical period and the Renaissance, interpreters of hieroglyphs, from Plotinus in his *Enneads* to Plutarch in his *Isis and Osiris*, saw them as a language of images that guarded the mystical and indecipherable wisdom of the ancient Egyptians.[8] In the words of Erik Iversen, these theories posit hieroglyphics as 'not ordinary writing at all, but pictorial, rebus-like expressions of divine ideas and sacred knowledge' (p. 8). For instance, Horapollo's classical text *Hieroglyphica* consists of a series of interpretations of various hieroglyphs, with each supposedly deciphered and connected with a symbolic meaning: Horapollo writes, 'When they would represent the *universe*, they delineate a SERPENT bespeckled with variegated scales, devouring its own tail: by the scales intimating the stars in the universe.'[9] In this view, hieroglyphics are removed from the realm of writing and associated exclusively with the visual, communicating their mysteries directly, albeit symbolically. Hieroglyphs thus counterintuitively serve as the embodiment of a perfectly legible language that would be 'expressed by means of concrete pictures of material objects', even as, in their continued unreadability, they also function as the ultimate emblem of an indecipherable language.[10] These interpretations look forward to the dual, contradictory uses to which writers, directors and theorists put hieroglyphics in the twentieth century. From the classical period up to the modernist period, hieroglyphs function as both emblems of illegibility and hyperlegibility; they resist reading yet somehow also promise, through their visual form, to be both a purer and more symbolic form of language.

Horapollo's *Hieroglyphica* was rediscovered in the Renaissance, inspiring another burst of interest in and misinteprations of Egyptian writing that cemented the long association between hieroglyphs and mystical spiritual beliefs. Most influential of these Renaissance works was Marsilio Ficino's translation in 1460 of the *Corpus Hermeticum* – reputedly a text written by Hermes Trismegistus, a Greek version of the Egyptian God Thoth, but in fact a later forgery – and Athanasius Kircher's *Lingua aegyptiaca restituta* (1643) and *Oedipus Aegyptiacus* (1652) on hieroglyphics and his *China Illustrata* (1667) on Chinese ideograms. These texts were soon translated or quoted in English, with John Everard publishing a version of the *Corpus Hermeticum* in England in 1650.[11] Indeed, the *Corpus Hermeticum* was re-published in a new version in London in 1924 by Walter Scott amid the burst of interest in ancient Egypt inspired by the discovery of King Tut's tomb, potentially providing the British modernists with an access point to these mystical traditions. While these texts were often surprisingly accurate in their hypotheses about aspects of Egyptian culture, they still fell victim to the notion that hieroglyphics were a directly depictive or mystical language.

This notion of hieroglyphs as sacred symbols or natural signs became increasingly popular over the course of the seventeenth and eighteenth centuries, and has persisted in various forms, despite considerable evidence to the contrary, up to the present day. By the eighteenth century the ancient Egyptian language had been so thoroughly associated with mystical knowledge that references to hieroglyphs proliferate across writings associated with alchemy, astrology, physiognomy, the Freemasons and the Rosicrucians.[12] This link is expressed most famously in Swedenborg's *A Hieroglyphic Key to Natural and Spiritual Mysteries* and in Jacob Boehme's *Signatura Rerum*. Boehme, whose notion of the hieroglyphic 'signature of all things' appears in *Ulysses*, begins his mystical treatise by writing that Man is 'God's masterpiece, a living emblem and hieroglyphic of eternity and time'.[13] As Walter Benjamin writes in reference to German Baroque drama, in order to 'guarantee the sacred character' of language, 'the written word tends toward the visual', towards 'hieroglyphics'.[14] Given these sacred associations of hieroglyphs, they came to be associated with the ur-language of humanity, the perfect language of Adam before Babel. As the English writer John Webster summarises in 1654, in a discussion of hieroglyphs, this language 'was the Paradisical language of the outflown word which Adam understood while he was unfaln in Eden'.[15] Hieroglyphs became not only a more visual or motivated language, but potentially the original language of all humanity.

This perfect language collapses the distinction between words and objects, and is revealed through the hieroglyphics of the Book of Nature, encapsulated best by Thomas Carlyle: 'We speak of the Volume of Nature: and truly a Volume it is, – whose Author and Writer is God. It is a Volume written in celestial hieroglyphs, in the true Sacred-writing.'[16] This idea of the Book of Nature was of particular importance to the German Romantics – from Franz von Baader to Novalis to Schlegel – and, through them, to Carlyle and Ralph

Waldo Emerson. Because of their supposedly primal relationship with the world – as a Cratylic language, a language of Nature – hieroglyphics were envisioned as more material than alphabetical languages, particularly because they were inscribed not only on papyrus but also on walls or tablets. Stressing this corporeal aspect of Egyptian writing, Carlyle describes how the hieroglyphic emblems of the Book of Nature 'body forth' ideas. Hieroglyphics thus often became associated with gestures – another less mediated form of communication – blurring the line between writing and the human body. In many theories of linguistic evolution drawn upon by the modernists, language evolves from gestures to hieroglyphics to alphabets. If gestures were, for writers like Vico, the original form of language, then hieroglyphics served as the link between the human body and contemporary alphabets.[17] Hieroglyphics thus become not merely a more perfect language. By collapsing the sign and the signifier, they also promised the God-like power of deciphering the hidden language of the world or the body itself.

In the late seventeenth century, however, a different interpretation of the hieroglyphics – or, at least, a new viewpoint partly inspired by ideograms and picture-writing – had started to emerge, one that would likewise structure how hieroglyphs were perceived in the West in the twentieth century. Rather than focusing on mystical forms of writing, Enlightenment philosophers like Leibniz, Locke and Bacon began to acknowledge the arbitrariness of the sign in language and to leave behind the notion that they could recapture the Adamic, pre-Babelic language. For instance, Bacon in 'Of the Advancement of Learning', while still asserting that hieroglyphs have a pictorial character 'as continued impresses and emblems', is less interested in analysing their pictorial qualities than in asserting the arbitrary nature of words: 'although some have been willing by curious inquiry, or rather by apt feigning, to have derived imposition of names from reason and intendment; a speculation elegant [. . .] but sparingly mixed with truth, and of small fruit.'[18] If a language derived from 'reason and intendment' could not be discovered, then these writers embarked instead on attempts to construct wholly new universal linguistic systems. As Umberto Eco writes, 'There was no longer a question of discovering the lost language of humanity; the new language was to be a new and totally artificial language, founded upon philosophic principles, and capable of realizing, by rational means, that which the various purported holy languages [. . .] had sought but failed to find.'[19] The focus shifts from a mystic, perfect, Cratylic language to a universal one, either through the search for or creation of a universal grammar, a universal alphabet or, in the case of Leibniz, a universal logic.[20] These philosophers leave behind the mystical notions of the Book of Nature, but still long for the language of more direct, universal communication that Western readers had for so long associated with hieroglyphs. Such a desire becomes a central feature in Western culture, recurring in the late nineteenth and early twentieth centuries in the form of International Auxiliary Languages like Esperanto and Basic English, as well as in the logical systems of Bertrand Russell and Ludwig Wittgenstein.

These two views – the 'linguistic' and the 'mystic' schools – remained deeply intertwined, with misreadings of hieroglyphs partly inspiring the projects for universal languages of the Enlightenment philosophers.[21] Leibniz, John Wilkins and Sir Francis Bacon derived their notions of logical languages, at least in part, from Chinese ideograms, and these ideograms themselves they believed were partly based on Egyptian hieroglyphs. In reflecting on the Chinese *Book of Changes* that inspired his binary arithmetic, Leibniz 'did not hesitate in identifying the true author of the *I Ching* as Hermes Trismegistus'.[22] And Athanasius Kircher, the key seventeenth-century scholar of hieroglyphics and Chinese ideograms, also published *Polygraphia nova et universalis* and *Novum hoc inventum*, projects for universal languages and cryptography that were inspired, at least in part, by the hieroglyphs of Egypt.[23] (Indeed, in his *Ars magna lucis et umbrae* he also prefigured the cinema, a medium which would be consistently seen as akin to hieroglyphs.)[24] Likewise, John Webster argued in 1654 that the hieroglyphs were a universal language similar to those being proposed at the time. As he writes, bringing together the understandings of hieroglyphs outlined above, 'Was not the expressions of things by Emblems, and Hieroglyphicks, not onely antient, but in and by them what great mysteries have been preserved and holden out to the world? And who can be ignorant of the admirable, easie and compendious use of all sorts of Symbolisms.' For Webster, these hieroglyphs – simultaneously mysterious and 'easie' – anticipate the search for 'the discovery of the universal Character' that will repair 'the ruines of Babell' (pp. 24–5). Even for those who tried to turn their backs on mysticism, hieroglyphs remained associated with more direct and universal forms of expression. While Pound and other twentieth-century writers present visual languages as opposed to logical ones, mystical notions of Egyptian writing were always intertwined with the logical systems of the Enlightenment.

Finally in the late eighteenth and early nineteenth centuries, thanks to the advances of comparative linguistics and, particularly, to the discovery of the Rosetta Stone, researchers began to notice that proper names in hieroglyphics were spelled out phonetically. So deeply engrained was the notion of hieroglyphics as non-phonetic, however, that it was not until Champollion that anyone applied that insight to all of the Egyptian language. Champollion discovered that Egyptian writing was far closer to the Latin alphabet than had previously been imagined. As Haun Saussy summarises:

> Champollion established three functional classes for Egyptian characters: *caractères mimiques*, which depict or imitate the objects to which they refer; *caractères tropiques ou symboliques*, which depict an object having

a meaningful relation to the thing or idea to which the character refers; and *caractères phonétiques*, used merely to represent or cue for sounds.[25]

The 'caractères phonétiques', however, were by far the most common and widespread of the 'three functional classes'. Hieroglyphics, it turned out, were not a more visual alternative to Western languages but rather were fundamentally hybrid, predominately phonetic and only marginally more pictorial than Western alphabets.

MELVILLE AND THE NINETEENTH CENTURY

Yet millennia of misconceptions don't go away in a moment, nor even in a century. The older Cratylic beliefs persisted in the nineteenth century, with the most famous literary and philosophical references to Egyptian writing tending to fall, as John Irwin has noted, into the 'mystical' camp, with Ralph Waldo Emerson the clearest exemplar.[26] Yet there was simultaneously a new attention to visual languages as languages rather than simply as images. Emerson demonstrates the complexities of hieroglyphic thinking in this period, how the desire to remotivate or reform language seems to follow from mystical ideas about the hieroglyphic Book of Nature. After Emerson begins his essay 'Nature' by declaring that 'Every man's condition is a solution in hieroglyphic to those inquiries he would put', he starts the section on Language by stating famously:

1. Words are signs of natural facts.
2. Particular natural facts are symbols of particular spiritual facts.
3. Nature is the symbol of spirit.[27]

The Book of Nature reveals, through its characters, the language of spirit, but language itself reveals, through etymology, a connection to natural objects: 'Every word which is used to express a moral or intellectual fact, if traced to its root, is found to be borrowed from some material appearance' (p. 48). Emerson comes close to Cratylism, with words representing 'natural symbols'. Language leads to nature which leads to spirit, in a vast hieroglyphic chain, with the mystical qualities of the Book of Nature imparted to words themselves. Emerson even asserts, obliquely, how his interest in the language of Nature goes back to Egyptian writing, tracing a line 'from the era of the Egyptians and the Brahmins to that of Pythagoras, of Plato, of Bacon, of Leibnitz (*sic*), of Swedenborg' (p. 54), which, except for the addition of Eastern religions, is the exact genealogy of Western understandings of hieroglyphs. Despite his invocation of Bacon and Leibniz, however, Emerson's concern is less with language itself than with a conjectured proto-language, which, be it hieroglyphic or not, would be closer to material objects. As he says, lamenting the loss of the primal linkage between word and world, 'new imagery ceases to be created, and old words are perverted to stand for things which are not; a paper currency is employed, when there is no bullion in the vaults' (p. 51). Emerson sounds exactly like T. E. Hulme here, revealing how deeply Hulme remains in debt to the Romanticism he claims to reject, just as Ernest Fenollosa too was deeply inspired by Emerson.[28]

Emerson derived, in part, his vision of a hieroglyphic world from Emmanuel Swedenborg. In keeping with his mystical view of Egyptian writing, Emerson admires how in Swedenborg 'every sensible object' becomes a 'picture-language', but he laments how in his work 'the warm, many-weathered, passionate-peopled world' is reduced to 'a grammar of hieroglyphs'.[29] In other words, Emerson desires the open-ended spiritual associations of hieroglyphs while rejecting any hint of their linguistic basis, their 'grammar'. Of course, Baudelaire was likewise inspired by Swedenborg in the development of his theory of 'correspondences', as Lynn Wilkinson and Anna Balakian have argued.[30] Emerson's and Baudelaire's interest in Swedenborg can help to account for the popularity of American writers like Emerson and particularly Poe with the French Symbolists.[31] Indeed, the majority of Baudelaire's references to Swedenborg occur in his essays on Poe. This engagement with Swedenborg among both American and French writers of the mid-nineteenth century reflects their larger shared fascination with universal languages and mystical notions of hieroglyphs with which Swedenborg was associated. Wilkinson, for instance, asserts that 'the notion of a universal language' was 'of such importance for the development of French literature, or at least of a certain modernist literary tradition that develops through the work of Balzac, Stendhal, Baudelaire, and Mallarmé' (p. 4). As Frank Kermode argues of Symbolism, 'the whole poetic movement was to a striking degree hermetic; the occult tradition, notably as mediated by Boehme and Swedenborg, lies behind it' (p. 111). From Baudelaire's theory of correspondences to Mallarmé's visual typographical experiments in 'Un Coup de Dés', the Symbolists share with Emerson a fascination with quasi-mystical interpretations of the natural world and attempts to purify language. As Gerard Genette argues, Mallarmé's work is characterised by a 'secondary Cratylism' in which 'the poet [. . .] is to be entrusted with compensating for the mimetic inadequacy of natural language' (p. 206). Mallarmé looks to the sounds of phonemes – as Proust will do in the twentieth century – and the physical language of dance – an 'écriture corporelle'[32] – playfully to re-inscribe a natural connection between language and the world. In part because the decipherment of the hieroglyphs dealt a blow to Cratylic views of language, the nineteenth century – in both France and America – saw an increasing valorisation of the poet's role, through formal and linguistic innovation, in reviving the possibility of a motivated language. Hieroglyphs lie at the source of the confluence between mysticism and linguistic experimentation that critics like Edmund Wilson and Frank Kermode have seen as central to modern poetry, helping to explain the fascination with the occult in Yeats and others.

Modern writers and philosophers, without discarding the vision of a more perfect, Adamic language, were increasingly influenced by the 'linguistic' school of hieroglyphics as opposed to the 'mystic' one. The idea of language shifts away from Carlyle's famous definition of the symbol from *Sartor Resartus*: 'in a Symbol there is concealment and yet revelation: here, therefore, by Silence and by Speech acting together, comes a doubled significance' (p. 166). In Carlyle's mystical conception, silence and speech parallel concealment and revelation; most modernist writers, by contrast, are cognisant of the actual combination, within language, of silence and speech, of written text and audible phonemes.

Herman Melville provides the clearest bridge between the 'mystic' and 'linguistic' interpretations of hieroglyphics, between the nineteenth and the twentieth centuries, looking forward to the modernist interest in the links between hieroglyphs and alphabetical writing. Melville, like Emerson and Carlyle, sees hieroglyphs as emblems of the language of Nature – albeit inscrutable ones – but simultaneously calls attention to the hybrid nature of all writing, between 'silence', 'speech' and vision.[33] In the chapter 'The Prairie' of *Moby-Dick*, Ishmael, having vainly attempted to analyse the brow of a sperm whale by using physiognomy and phrenology, invokes the decipherer of the Rosetta Stone:

> Champollion deciphered the wrinkled granite hieroglyphics. But there is no Champollion to decipher the Egypt of every man's and every being's face. Physiognomy, like every other human science, is but a passing fable. If then, Sir William Jones, who read in thirty languages, could not read the simplest peasant's face in its profounder and more subtle meanings, how may unlettered Ishmael hope to read the awful Chaldee of the Sperm Whale's brow? (p. 275)

At the very moment when Ishmael calls attention to the legibility of the previously indecipherable Egyptian hieroglyphics, he emphasises not the ultimate readability of nature but, rather, how the pictorial language of the world – the 'Egypt' of character – remains forever obscure. For Melville, as for the modernists, hieroglyphs allow him to bridge the gap between language and the body, to imagine an 'Egypt' of 'every man's [...] face'. But Melville rejects the post-Champollion interpretation of the hieroglyphs as a readable phonetic language, positioning himself firmly in the 'mystic' or 'metaphysical' school by emphasising the sacred meanings – or lack of meaning – of hieroglyphs, at least when it comes to the human body.[34]

Yet Melville's hieroglyphs go beyond mere mystic inscrutability; like twentieth-century writers, he also stresses the visual character of writing. In the chapter 'The Doubloon', for instance, Melville takes a basic and constitutive element of a semiotic system – a coin – and seeks to substitute depictive meanings for its arbitrary association with a simple monetary value. For the simple-minded Flask, who in his commentary on the doubloon declares, 'I see nothing here, but a round thing made of gold [. . .] It is worth sixteen dollars, that's true' (*MD* 334), the coin is simply a coin, stripped of interpretive mysteries. What it depicts on its surface is irrelevant. Flask sees the doubloon as Champollion would see it, reading past its appearance to see only its arbitrary value in a system of exchange, its 'phonetic' meaning within language. But every other character takes the opposite view, seeing the material form of the coin and the images imprinted on it, which confirm their own perceptions: Ahab's monomania, Stubb's joy in cyclicality or Starbuck's religious faith. They see not what the doubloon is supposed to stand for semiotically, but its image.

The doubloon thus serves as a hieroglyph, which exists not simply as a letter with a clearly defined phonetic or ideographic meaning but also, supposedly, as a picture of what it represents. While for Melville even an image is unreliable, providing multiple associations, that multiplicity is consistently championed over Flask's view of a fixed phonetic meaning. Thus in the Etymology section of *Moby-Dick* the 'Sub-Sub' chastises those who 'leav[e] out, through ignorance, the letter H, which almost alone makes up the signification of the word' whale (p. 7). Meaning does not reside in simple associations with sound; words are far more complex and slippery for Melville. Though he is aware of Champollion's interpretation of hieroglyphics, Melville attempts to reclaim the sacredness of language by denying that a phonetic explanation can provide the entire truth. Melville points to the importance of the visual form of words; by leaving out the silent H, you leave out the whole 'signification of the word'.[35] Like the modernists, Melville demonstrates how our words possess a visual form as well as an aural meaning, and, indeed, that this visual form somehow affects their linguistic associations. In his attention to the multiple meanings of language – between image and text – Melville anticipates the concerns of the modernists, partly accounting for why Melville was rediscovered and celebrated in the twentieth century.

But Melville also reveals the persistent linkage between hieroglyphs and narrative: as we've seen in the discussion of Foucault in the introduction, hieroglyphs function again and again as catalysts for narrative. This is most apparent with Melville's doubloon, which in its hybrid semiotic/visual qualities generates a plethora of interpretations from virtually every character on the ship. By demanding decipherment, the doubloon creates multiple narratives, a process that Melville foregrounds in the 'Etymology' and 'Extracts' sections with which the novel begins. The 'Etymology' emphasises the multiple, post-Babelic languages of the world, as well as the hybrid visual/phonetic aspects of writing. But this attention to the hybridity and history of language and languages seems naturally to require narrative – the 'Etymology' section is followed by the 'Extracts' section which expands on the word 'whale' and puts that word into multiple stories and tales, from Genesis to contemporary histories. Emphasising the problematic nature of language and the necessity of translation – either from one language to another or between visual and oral meanings – produces, in Melville, the space and need for narrative.

'Natural Suggestion': Pound, Lindsay, Eisenstein

In Melville we can see the coexistence of two conceptions of hieroglyphics: the older mystical view stands alongside a new concern with the hybrid nature of all linguistic forms. And this tension becomes even more pronounced in the early twentieth century as new media increasingly come to challenge the pre-eminence of writing. The 'mystical' and 'linguistic' schools of hieroglyphic interpretation come to correspond with the conflicting ways in which new media are interpreted – as purer alternatives to writing or as the same as writing – helping to explain the constant invocation of visual languages by directors, poets and novelists.

By far the most famous Western literary conception of visual languages during the early twentieth century was that of Ezra Pound. Through Ernest Fenollosa's treatise 'The Chinese Written Character as a Medium for Poetry', first published after Pound's editing in 1918, Ezra Pound found in the Chinese ideograms a system of motivated signs – of 'vivid shorthand pictures' – that could serve as a model for a purer and more direct language of literary expression. While it may seem inexact to rope together Egyptian hieroglyphs with the Chinese ideograms that influenced Pound, the distinction between these two languages, at least in the often misguided Western theorisations of them, was from the very start profoundly blurred. Athanasius Kircher, the famous Renaissance interpreter of the hieroglyphics, even claimed that 'China was quite simply an Egyptian colony, and its culture in all essentials of Egyptian origin.'[36] In fact, the words 'ideogram' and 'ideograph' were coined by none other than Jean-François Champollion in his discussion of Egyptian hieroglyphics.[37] As a newspaper article from the 1830s states, in one of the first recorded English uses of the word ideograph: 'Hieroglyphic characters are either ideographs, that is, representations of ideas, or phonographs, that is, representations of sounds.'[38] Such confusion carried over into the twentieth century, with both Fenollosa and Sergei Eisenstein using the words hieroglyph and ideogram interchangeably: Chinese characters, for Fenollosa, are 'visible hieroglyphics' (p. 43).

Yet despite the confusion in terminology, Pound and Fenollosa were able to claim Chinese as a privileged language for poetic expression precisely by seeing Chinese ideograms as fundamentally distinct from Egyptian hieroglyphs.

For Champollion's discovery that the hieroglyphs were a hybrid language – consisting predominately of phonemes alongside ideographic and depictive meanings – diminished, at least in theory, the millennial association between hieroglyphs and a universal, perfect, Adamic language. Hieroglyphs could no longer be seen rationally as an alternative to alphabetical, phonetic scripts, even if they often still were. But because Chinese was less widely understood in the West, it still retained its Cratylic associations, despite the fact that Chinese characters likewise have phonetic meanings. For those looking for a pure language of depictive characters, the supposedly non-phonetic language of China replaced Egyptian hieroglyphs, helping to explain the turn to China and Chinese writing as a source for poetic inspiration in the twentieth century.

And it was just that kind of Adamic language, composed of motivated signs consisting of images rather than of sounds, that Pound and Fenollosa were looking for and mistakenly found in Chinese ideograms.[39] As Fenollosa writes in 'The Chinese Written Character as a Medium for Poetry', 'But Chinese notation is something much more than arbitrary symbols. It is based upon a vivid shorthand picture of the operations of nature. In the algebraic figure and in the spoken word there is no natural connection between thing and sign: all depends upon sheer convention. But the Chinese method follows natural suggestion' (p. 45). The bêtes noirs here are logic – algebra – and phonetics, putting Fenollosa at odds both with alphabetical languages and with philosophical systems like those of Wittgenstein. Instead, Fenollosa longs for a language that is natural rather than arbitrary and conventional. While Fenollosa is forced to acknowledge that Chinese characters do possess a phonetic meaning – 'It is true that the pictorial clue of many Chinese ideographs can not now be traced, and even Chinese lexicographers admit that combinations frequently contribute only a phonetic value' (p. 59) – he resists the conclusion that Chinese is just as hybrid a language as Egyptian hieroglyphs, insisting instead on its depictive qualities. Faced with the obvious evidence that Chinese is in fact not easily legible, Fenollosa claims that the 'pictorial clue' has simply been lost in the passage of centuries. This notion of 'natural suggestion', as many critics have suggested, derives from Emerson, whom Fenollosa studied in his time at Harvard, demonstrating the debt the modernists owed to the American writers of the mid-nineteenth century and to the interest in hieroglyphs that John Irwin associates with them.[40]

In his own writings, Pound is even more explicit in his embrace of Cratylism. As he writes in the preface to *ABC of Reading*, published in 1934:

> To go back to the beginning of history, you probably know that there is spoken language and written language, and that there are two kinds of written language, one based on sound and the other on sight. [. . .]
> The Egyptians finally used abbreviated pictures to represent sounds,

but the Chinese still use abbreviated pictures AS pictures, that is to say, the Chinese ideogram does not try to be the picture of a sound, or to be a written sign recalling a sound, but it is still the picture of a thing; of a thing in a given position or relation, or of a combination of things. It *means* the thing or the action or situation, or quality germane to the several things that it pictures.

Gaudier Brzeska, who was accustomed to looking at the real shape of things, could read a certain amount of Chinese writing without ANY STUDY. He said, 'Of course, you can *see* it's a horse.'[41]

As with Fenollosa, what is important in language is not sound – despite the influence on Pound of oral Anglo-Saxon and Provençal verse forms – but rather image. According to Pound, the spoken word and the written word, the alphabetical language and the pictographic language, are diametrically opposed, and the Chinese language alone preserves that fundamental 'primitive' wholeness. It has not fallen victim to the divide between the 'picture of a thing' and a thing by resorting to phoneticism, as is the case with Egyptian hieroglyphics; rather, it uses 'pictures AS pictures'. In Pound's view, the ideogram is both ideographic – evoking 'a combination of things' – and directly depictive, synthesising two of Champollion's three classes of meaning for the hieroglyph: *caractères mimiques* and *caractères symboliques*. With the definitive discovery of the phonetic significations of hieroglyphics, Egyptian writing becomes alphabetical, and only Chinese still 'means the thing or the action or situation'.

In Pound's view – a view that has become central to accounts of modernism – Western alphabetical language needs to be reinvigorated by the model of the 'primitive' Chinese language; it needs to become closer to the concrete objects that it signifies, to allow for, in Robert Kern's words, 'greater access to the being of the world'.[42] But Pound does not merely insist on Chinese writing as a series of motivated signs here, as misguided as that might be. Pound also counterintuitively claims Chinese as universally legible: 'Of course,' he claims Gaudier-Brzeska says, 'you can *see* it's a horse.' Chinese is, in Fenollosa's words, 'the ideal language of the world' (p. 59) and serves as a model for poetic expression *and* for universal communication. Such a connection recalls the use of a hieroglyph as the pre-eminent example of Wittgenstein's universal logic in his *Tractatus Logico-Philosophicus*, analysed in the introduction, where Wittgenstein is unable to extricate his argument from the centuries-long tradition that linked visual languages like hieroglyphics with projects for more perfect communication. The hieroglyph connects aesthetics and philosophy, Pound and Wittgenstein, revealing the buried connections between Pound's high aesthetic theories and the large-scale movements for universal communication in the late nineteenth and early twentieth centuries. These movements were epitomised by the International Auxiliary Languages (IALs) Esperanto, Novial and Basic English, developed by L. L. Zamenhof, Otto Jespersen and C. K. Ogden, respectively. Indeed, Ogden translated the *Tractatus* into English, and Pound claims that the ideogram will be 'the basis of a new universal language, more basic than Ogden's Basic English and more reliable'.[43] Rather than being opposed, as T. E. Hulme would have it, the 'algebra' of logic and the visual languages of ideograms and literature are united by the hieroglyph.[44] Pound and Fenollosa's theories exist as both an extension of and a reaction against IALs and logical languages, with ideograms fulfilling Wittgenstein's and Ogden's dreams of a universal language but simultaneously restoring the concreteness of words against the abstractions of logic and algebra.

Pound's linkage of the Chinese ideograms to direct reference and to universalism echoes contemporaneous theories of the new medium of film, which likewise invoked hieroglyphics and ideograms. This connection has been largely ignored, despite Fenollosa's description of a cluster of ideograms as holding 'something of the quality of a continuous moving picture' (p. 45).[45] The ideas of 'The Chinese Written Character as a Medium for Poetry' – the final draft of which was composed in 1906, when film was becoming a widespread popular medium – seem to owe much to early understandings of cinema, crystallised by Vachel Lindsay, as a hieroglyphic, universal language of images. Indeed, Lindsay himself was associated with Pound's Imagist movement, and he saw film as the next frontier for Imagism: as he writes, 'the Imagist impulse need not be confined to verse' (p. 239).

By juxtaposing Pound's theories of the ideogram with those of Sergei Eisenstein and Vachel Lindsay – who conceive of Chinese writing and Egyptian hieroglyphics in strikingly similar ways – we can see more clearly how Pound's ideas echo the ways film directors conceptualised their own medium. In turn, these links reveal just how porous the boundaries were between the media of film and writing in the modernist period.[46] These connections are especially striking in the 1910s, when Imagism was first being theorised, Pound published Fenollosa's essay and Vachel Lindsay released his *The Art of the Moving Picture*, first published in 1915 with a revised edition in 1922. Film theorists and directors at the time use invocations of ancient scripts to argue for the internationalism of film, which supposedly, like Pound's ideograms, is universally legible across the boundaries of nations and languages. Such comparisons between film and hieroglyphics were most systematically expressed by Lindsay; he claims that 'the invention of the photoplay [film] is as great a step as was the beginning of picture-writing in the stone age', and that film was 'perfecting a medium to be used as long as Chinese ideographs have been' (pp. 171, 226). For Lindsay, each concrete image in a silent film has a clear connection to a specific abstract idea: he declares, for instance, that a sieve implies 'domesticity' and a duck implies peace (pp. 174–5). Film hieroglyphics are thus immediately legible above and beyond the limits of traditional written language; they are the democratic hope for the future, the 'moving picture Esperanto' (p. 177), an association picked up by later writers like Edward Van Zile, who declares 'the coming of the wireless and the Esperanto of the Tongue and of the Eye seem to presage some new revelation to the soul of Man.'[47] By communicating exclusively through images, silent film could supposedly transcend the curse of Babel.[48]

Such views were not confined simply to the images of film, but were seen as related to the ability of movies to probe and capture human physiognomy and gestures. As Béla Balázs argues in *The Visible Man*, 'the art of film seems to hold out the promise of redemption from the curse of Babel. The screens of the entire world are now starting to project the *first international language*, the language of gestures and facial expressions' (p. 14).[49] And the early film historian Terry Ramsaye, in his *A Million and One Nights*, prefaces his discussion of cinema with an invocation of the roots of communication in universal gestures: 'The evidences gathered by the students of language among the surviving and extinct primitives indicate that expression begins with signs of pantomime.'[50] This linkage of film, hieroglyphics, and gestures, recalling the persistent millennia-long associations between Egyptian writing and the human body, was commonplace in the silent film era, as critics like Tim Armstrong and Laura Marcus have noted, and survived even into the early sound period.[51] These views that film was 'a pictorial language, like the hieroglyphs of ancient Egypt' naturally bolstered the contention that film was also a universal language like Esperanto.[52] As Alfred Hitchcock notes in his famous interview with François Truffaut, many of the background signs in F. W. Murnau's *The Last Laugh* (1924) are written in Esperanto, as seen in the words 'Etali' and 'Farina' in Figure 1.1.[53] Murnau's choice to include Esperanto in his film is particularly apt given *The Last Laugh*'s status as one of the first films without intertitles: the Holy Grail of silent cinema for many avant-garde critics of the time. Murnau's film thus does not rely on written language; the only intertitle occurs as the film shifts to a self-consciously false and sentimental happy ending. Murnau's inclusion of Esperanto represents a clear attempt to equate the now exclusively visual language of film with the universal language of Esperanto for universalist aims; as he writes, 'Already [film] is changing the habits of mankind, making people who live in different countries and speak different language, neighbours. [. . .] It may put an end to war, for men do not fight when they understand each other's heart.'[54] And the inspiration that Murnau cites for his work in the film is, as it is for Sergei Eisenstein, the work of James Joyce.[55]

D. W. Griffith was likewise fascinated by film's potential status as a universal language, going so far as to invoke Lindsay's 'hieroglyphic' ideas, as Miriam Hansen has argued. Noting that Griffith had likely read Lindsay's *The*

Figure 1.1   Image from *The Last Laugh* (dir. F.W. Murnau, 1924, Germany)

Art of the Moving Picture, Hansen describes the images of cuneiform writing in Griffith's *Intolerance,* claiming that the film 'draws an implicit line from the disappearance of the last universal written language [. . .] to the vision of film as a new universal language, as it was being advanced by Griffith in defense of his own film practice.'[56] Yet the connection to hieroglyphics is even stronger, as Hansen notes: 'The script on the Babylonian title-card, however, is not cuneiform, but a design unmistakably imitating a hieroglyphic pictograph.'[57] For Griffith, as for Lindsay, hieroglyphics through their supposed universal legibility become the precursor of film itself.[58]

But these invocations of Egyptian writing in early twentieth-century accounts of film not only stress the universality of the movies. They also, echoing Pound, emphasise the depictive qualities of film hieroglyphics. Just as Pound and Fenollosa argue about ideograms, Vachel Lindsay takes pains to claim – against centuries of evidence to the contrary – that hieroglyphics are immediately legible: 'So when I took up hieroglyphics more seriously last summer, I found them extraordinarily easy as though I were looking at a "movie" in a book. [. . .] Any child who reads one can read the other' (p. xxxv). Hieroglyphics and film are equally and interchangeably legible; film is 'photoplay hieroglyphics'

(p. 287) and hieroglyphics are a '"movie" in a book'. Lindsay even employs phrasing that anticipates Pound's famous comment about how Chinese uses 'pictures AS pictures'. In discussing the opposition between the 'hieroglyphic civilization' of America and England, Lindsay writes, 'Still today in England the average leading citizen matches word against word – using them as algebraic formulas – rather than picture against picture' (p. 123). We get a typically Poundian or T. E. Hulmian opposition of picture and algebra, with, as in Pound, the 'pictures' – associated in Lindsay with the visual language of film and with America – more deeply connected to material reality. If Pound tries to restore a more direct relationship between language and physical reality, he does so at the same time as similar claims were being made – using similar metaphors – about the new medium of film.

Similarly, in his account of the history of film, Terry Ramsaye turns to Chinese ideograms and, like Pound, stresses their 'pictorial language': 'The written language of the Chinese to-day remains not at all an alphabet but a system of just such signs, pictures, simplified and formalized on paper with a brush. The Chinese ideographs are the persistence of a pictorial language in a state of arrested development' (p. li). Expressing the Orientalist basis of these notions of Chinese writing particularly baldly, Ramsaye sees Chinese and Egyptian writing as more primitive, a kind of 'arrested development' that has not reached the next stage of linguistic evolution: 'The next step in the continuity of development is to be found in the transition of the Egyptian hieroglyphics or picture writings into the arbitrary forms of alphabet as we know alphabets in our common use of today' (p. liii). For Ramsaye, film emerges as a new form that will supplant those 'arbitrary forms of alphabet' and restore the lost 'pictorial language' of Chinese and Egyptian.

Ramsaye and Lindsay both stress the pictorial, depictive qualities of ancient scripts in order to equate them with film. Lindsay is reluctant, however, to claim that film is actually a Cratylic language, unsure of whether his 'film hieroglyphics' are motivated and natural or simply the conventional associations created by Hollywood. By contrast, Sergei Eisenstein, in his 1929 essay 'The Cinematographic Principle and the Ideogram', published in English translation in *transition* in 1930, expresses like Pound the belief that ideograms are, to use his terms, 'depictive' as opposed to 'denotative': 'scratched out with an awl on bamboo, the plastic portrait of an object still resembles its original in every respect.'[59] Unlike Lindsay, Eisenstein's concern is not simply with universality, but with direct expression; the ideograms actually physically represent what they denote. But for Eisenstein the value of the Chinese and Japanese languages – he consistently confuses the two – only emerges once they have made the move into abstraction, once, as he says, 'The naturalistic image of an object [...] becomes slightly formalised.'[60] The hieroglyph or ideogram – he again uses the terms interchangeably – weds denotation and depiction, representation and abstraction. And Eisenstein sees this process of combination that produces ideograms as akin to his own methods of dialectical montage, in which the collision and combination of two shots leads to a synthesis with more expressive power than the original:

> The point is that the copulation (perhaps we had better say, the combination) of two hieroglyphs of the simplest series is to be regarded not as their sum but as their product, i.e. as a value of another dimension, another degree; each, separately, corresponds to an *object*, to a fact, but their combination corresponds to a *concept*. From separate hieroglyphs has been fused – the ideogram. By the combination of two 'depictables' is achieved the representation of something graphically undepictable. [. . .] But this is – montage![61]

Eisenstein's views are almost identical to Pound's, with 'concept' here seeming almost to be a synonym for Pound's word 'complex' in his definition of the Image: 'An "Image" is that which presents an intellectual and emotional complex in an instant of time.'[62] As Pound famously explains in *ABC of Reading*, published after Eisenstein's essay, the ideogram for East is supposedly composed of an amalgamation of the ideograms of man, tree and sun; each ideogram consists of a combination of its constitutive parts.[63] The Image likewise is able to encapsulate or compress multiple ideas and emotions into a single moment. As Pound writes about 'In a Station of the Metro', 'the "one image poem" is a form of super-position, that is to say, it is one idea set on top of another.'[64] For both theorists, ideograms are thus an active and motivated language of images formed from the juxtaposition of different elements, with Eisenstein's separate shots colliding in the same way as Pound imagines the combination of man, tree and sun.

This connection reveals the extent to which Pound seeks to emulate film in his theories of Chinese writing and his statements on Imagism.[65] Indeed, right after descibing the 'one image poem' as a kind of palimpsest, Pound invokes cinema, if only to denigrate it: 'The logical end of impressionist art is the cinematograph' (p. 89), he writes, in contrast to his own Vorticist art. But we might doubt just how free of the 'cinematograph' his conceptions of the image really are. For Pound and Fenollosa, the ideogram incorporates into writing many of the qualities of film, possessing a dynamic, moving energy. As Haun Saussy has argued, 'By centering his theory of the ideogram on the verb, Fenollosa reintroduces syntax, long absent from discussions of Chinese that had taken as their starting point the character as picture.'[66] While Fenollosa emphasises the character as motivated picture, he focuses on the verb rather than the noun, seeing Chinese as characterised by an active movement, by a relationship between parts rather than as a series of static signs. Fenollosa's emphasis on the verb allows Pound to sidestep

Imagism and find in ideograms an inspiration for the more active Image of Vorticism.[67]

We can then see Imagism and Vorticism, at least as Pound conceives of them, as defined by this conflict between stasis and movement, between noun and verb, with the image creating a frozen 'instant of time' that nonetheless incorporates the 'quality of a continuous moving picture' rather than being a static stand-alone image. By turning his back on phonetic alphabets (at least in his poetic theories – his practice is a different story) Pound can find a kind of writing that, harnessing the power of film, seems to wed image, language and movement, transmitting meaning immediately and legibly across cultural boundaries. Crucially, the ideogram for Pound, in its unification of noun and verb, is similar to but superior to film. For Pound claims that 'the cinema is not Art' because 'Art is a stasis'; the ideogram, by contrast, through its combination of depictive images weds film and writing, movement and stasis.[68] As he writes, 'The ideograph wants the moving image, the concrete thing plus its action.'[69]

That tension between the 'concrete thing' and its 'action' is central to the relationship between film and poetry in this period. In *The Art of the Moving Picture* it is precisely stasis that Vachel Lindsay is looking for by invoking Imagism; while movies can be too chaotic, too defined by motion, Imagism will add a note of 'Doric restraint'. They will be 'Greek vase-paintings in motion', a metaphor that encapsulates this combination of stillness and movement, as if the arrested figures on Keats's Grecian Urn somehow stirred to life. This focus on sculpture and stillness looks forward to Pound's 'Hugh Selwyn Mauberley', published five years later. There, in valorising 'Attic grace' – a similar expression to 'Doric restraint' – Pound writes of 'alabaster or the sculpture of rhyme'.[70] In that same passage Pound denigrates 'prose kinema', but as we've seen through the comparison to film theory of the period, even as he disdains the cinema and calls for an art of stasis, in valorising ideograms he strives to emulate and recreate the power of 'kinema' – of the 'moving image' – within poetry.[71] Pound and the other Imagist poets thus define their movement both against and in relation to the new medium of cinema. To return to one of Imagism's central manifestoes, the preface to *Some Imagist Poets* calls for a poetry that is 'hard and clear, never blurred and indefinite'.[72] Given the association of cinema with motion and particularly with 'blur', we can see just how clearly Imagism responds to and reacts against film, and yet that motion inherent to film remains appealing to poets like Pound.

Pound thus has a particularly fraught relationship to narrative in his theoretical writings about ideograms. On one level, the ideogram seems connected, through the comparison to film, to movement, to the 'verb' and thus to narrative itself. And Pound seeks to inject that 'movement' into poetry through his turn to Vorticism. Yet Pound also seeks to keep poetry free from narrative, emphasising the 'stasis' of art, and in his aforementioned phrase 'prose kinema', allying film and movement with 'prose' as opposed to poetry. Pound thus encapsulates how so many modernists reacted to the challenge of new media, as he seeks both to emulate and escape from the qualities of the new medium of film, borrowing its kinetic aspects while emphasising how writing in general and poetry in particular exceeds and improves upon the characteristics of film. But in calling attention to the kinetic and juxtapositional aspects of the ideogram, Pound also reveals the natural connection between visual languages and narrative.

Eisenstein also emphasises the 'movement' inherent in ideograms through his emphasis on moments of conflict and combination. While Eisenstein ignores, at least initially, the narrative aspects of the ideogram, his conceptualisation of Chinese writing is strikingly active; rather than a static image, each ideogram is almost an equation, $a + b = c$. While Eisenstein will go on to focus on the narrative elements of Chinese writing in his later writings, even in his early work the Chinese ideogram remains inextricably linked with movement and narrative.

Yet Eisenstein's theories ultimately move in a different direction from Pound's. If Pound strives through the ideogram to claim for writing those qualities – motion and direct depiction – that it lacks, then Eisenstein tries to claim for film – a medium that is self-evidently dynamic and imagistic – the qualities of language. Eisenstein is able to create through his references to ideograms a proto-genealogy for his new medium; he argues for 'the fact that our cinema is not altogether without parents and without pedigree, without a past, without the traditions and rich cultural heritage of the past epochs' and he finds that 'heritage' not only in Dickens – in his essay 'Dickens, Griffith, and Film Today' – but in hieroglyphics.[73] In his essays Eisenstein repeatedly seeks to construct a 'film grammar' or a 'film-syntax' that will provide film with a way of communicating beyond and above mere image.[74] In his discussion of the ideogram, Eisenstein thus emphasises how it can communicate more abstract and intellectual meanings. Although the ideogram is 'primarily representational', over the course of time Chinese and Japanese writings have lost many of their depictive elements: while Pound stresses how Gaudier-Brzeska can 'see' that an ideogram is 'a horse', for Eisenstein, 'In the fierily cavorting hieroglyph *ma* (a horse) it is already impossible to recognize the features of the dear little horse.'[75] Pound stresses the imagistic qualities of writing, Eisenstein the abstract qualities of the images of film. Eisenstein finds this balance between depiction and abstraction particularly appealing: 'It is exactly what we do in the cinema,' he writes, 'combining shots that are *depictive*, single in meaning, neutral in content – into *intellectual* contexts and series.'[76]

Eisenstein, like Pound, attempts to have it both ways; cinema, like the ideogram, is composed of depictive, Cratylic elements that nonetheless, through juxtaposition, can form a language with a flexibility of intellectual and emotive meanings.[77] The ideogram for them is not an inscrutable language, as for

Melville, or a universally legible one, as for Lindsay, but one that is on the cusp of falling away from its depictive roots into grammatical form. Both writers are thus able to imagine their medium as combining the direct power of the image with the fluidity and adaptability of written language. In the process, however, Pound and Eisenstein's theories sacrifice the truth about hieroglyphics and ideograms: their phonetic, oral elements.

Phoneticism: Freud, Proust, Eisenstein

Yet the phonetic meaning of hieroglyphics is precisely what Freud and Proust, by contrast, find attractive. In their focus on the hybridity of hieroglyphics they represent an important alternative to Pound and early Eisenstein in twentieth-century understandings of visual languages. For if we move from poetry towards fiction, the emphasis on the purity and universality of hieroglyphics – on their supposed proximity to the material world or concrete meaning – diminishes. When both Freud and Proust allude to hieroglyphics – at central moments in *The Interpretation of Dreams* and *Time Regained*, respectively – they avoid the Cratylic fallacy that Pound, Wittgenstein and others so frequently flirt with. Rather than ignoring Champollion's discoveries, or turning to Chinese as a way of avoiding them, Freud and Proust embrace them. What Proust and Freud ultimately find in hieroglyphics is not a purer language, but rather a more heterogeneous one, incorporating depictive, ideographic and phonetic forms at one and the same time. Hieroglyphics emerge not as distinct from Western script – a lost evolutionary branching or more primitive form – but, in their essence, as the same.

In *The Interpretation of Dreams*, Freud positions himself as akin to Champollion as the first decipherer of the heretofore illegible language of dreams. He writes:

> The dream-content, on the other hand, is expressed as it were in a pictographic script, the characters of which have to be transposed individually into the language of the dream-thoughts. If we attempted to read these characters according to their pictorial value instead of according to their symbolic relation, we should clearly be led into error. Suppose I have a picture-puzzle, a rebus, in front of me [...] Now I might be misled into raising objections and declaring that the picture as a whole and its component parts are nonsensical [...] But obviously we can only form a proper judgment of the rebus [...] if instead we try to replace each separate element by a syllable or word that can be represented by that element in some way or other. [...] A dream is a picture puzzle of this sort and our predecessors in the field of dream-interpretation have made the mistake of treating the rebus as a pictorial composition.[78]

While Freud contrasts the 'pictorial value' of the dream-content with its symbolic relation, his reference to the rebus pinpoints the more specific fallacy that he claims his rivals, like the Egyptologists such as Horapollo before Champollion, have fallen victim to: rather than interpreting pictographic scripts as phonetic, they have seen them as purely depictive. Like a hieroglyph, the pictures of the rebus – the 'pictorial composition' – have to be ignored in favour of their phonetic meaning, or the 'syllable or word' for which each image stands. Derrida is thus wrong to claim, in 'Freud and the Scene of Writing', that the dream-work 'exceeds phonetic writing and puts speech back in its place. As in hieroglyphics or rebuses, voice is circumvented.'[79] While hieroglyphics combine pictographic and phonetic elements, as Derrida recognises, they do not circumvent voice, but need rather to be translated into vocal phonemes; psychoanalysis is, after all, a 'talking cure'.

This invocation of hieroglyphs is thus distinctly different from what we've seen in Pound, Lindsay and the like. Freud denies that these pictographs really are images at all, or, at least, that their visual form ultimately matters. The dream-content is already a language, defined by its 'symbolic relation' rather than its stand-alone elements. As Jacques Lacan summarises in 'The Agency of the Letter in the Unconscious', 'Freud shows us in every possible way that the image's value as a signifier has nothing to do with its signification, giving as an example Egyptian hieroglyphics in which it would be ridiculous to deduce from the frequency in a text of a vulture [. . .] that the text has anything whatsoever to do with these ornithological specimens.'[80] Just because a hieroglyph shows the image of a bird doesn't mean that it means bird; as Lacan recognises, to understand Egyptian writing and to engage in psychoanalysis one needs to translate that initial image.

Unlike Pound, for whom the ideogram was universally legible, for Freud the hieroglyphic dream text is more difficult to decipher than phonetic text. Written alphabetical language is both the same as hieroglyphic language – since both are ultimately phonetic – and necessary for an understanding of it: as Freud writes, 'If a dream is written out it may perhaps fill half a page. The analysis setting out the dream-thoughts underlying it may occupy six, eight, or a dozen times as much space' (p. 313). Hieroglyphs are so condensed that they require an additional act of writing and of narrative; the analyst must translate into alphabetical writing the buried meanings of the dream-work and record at the same time the narrative of that process of decipherment.[81] Emphasising the hybrid nature of language and writing leads inevitably to narrative.

This emphasis on the writer as translator is characteristic of much of modernist fiction and, particularly, of Proust's *À la recherche du temps perdu*. Proust alludes to hieroglyphs in almost exactly the same way as Freud, emphasising their phonetic meaning and their status as a catalyst for narrative and writing. At what is essentially the climax of the entire *Recherche* – the narrator's realisation of the power of involuntary memory in *Le Temps retrouvé* – Proust writes:

> I used to fix before my mind [*esprit*] for its attention some image which had compelled me to look at it, a cloud, a triangle, a church spire, a flower, a stone, because I had the feeling that perhaps beneath these signs there lay something of a quite different kind which I must try to discover, some thought which they translated after the fashion of those hieroglyphic characters [*caractères hiéroglyphiques*] which at first one might suppose to represent only material objects. No doubt the process of decipherment was difficult, but only by accomplishing it could one arrive at whatever truth there was to be read [*mais seul il donnait quelque vérité à lire*].[82]

Like Freud, Proust rejects the mistaken belief that objects are meaningful simply as images, as 'material objects'. Rather they need to be 'translated', as Champollion did, to access their underlying meanings, meanings which, in Proust's case, are the result of the arbitrary associations and personal metaphors of the decipherer. The process of understanding is fundamentally linguistic, allied with the act of reading and writing: 'the function and the task of a writer are those of a translator,' he says.[83] The action of Proust's novel is, like the work of psychoanalysis, the narrative of that course of linguistic decipherment.

As Gilles Deleuze argues, 'Every act of learning is an interpretation of signs or hieroglyphs. Proust's work is based not on the exposition of memory, but on the apprenticeship to signs.'[84] However, looking at the ways in which hieroglyphs were interpreted in Proust's time allows us to understand more fully that 'apprenticeship to signs'. For Proust gives a subjectivist spin to Champollion's act of decipherment: the external world of signs has been turned inside out. Recalling the hieroglyphic Book of Nature, Proust claims that the world imprints or impresses us with its hieroglyphic language, and we must read and transform that internal book of hieroglyphs into an alphabetical language in the act of writing the novel: 'This book more laborious to decipher than any other, is also the only one which has been dictated to us by reality, the only one of which the "impression" has been printed in us [*ait été faite en nous*] by reality itself.'[85] Rather than seeking to decipher the world of nature, the subject must read that world – 'a cloud [. . .] a church spire, a flower' – only within him or herself, and only for him or herself. The book of the world is ultimately legible, although each individual must discover the unique key to his or her own language. Proust is undecided, however, about whether Marcel is creating his own arbitrary pattern through fiction or is, like Champollion, revealing the underlying essence beneath the hieroglyphics of material objects. Does the world 'compel' him to 'look at' various objects so that he can discover an ultimate truth 'which they translated', or is it Marcel himself who is doing the translation? Just as Freud hesitates between translations of the dream-language based on stable meanings or on personal associations, so Proust can never be sure how much agency he ultimately has in writing his novel.[86]

Moreover, earlier in *La recherche* Proust seems to contradict himself: 'I had in the course of my life followed a progression which was the opposite of that adopted by peoples who make use of phonetic writing only after having considered the characters as a set of symbols.'[87] Rather than moving from hieroglyphics to phonetic language, Proust here makes the opposite progression. On one level, this tension bolsters Gerard Genette's claim that Proust's novel chronicles the narrator's progressive disillusionment, which takes the form of his ultimate rejection of the Cratylism with which he initially treated names: 'Belief in the truth of names is for him an ambiguous privilege of childhood, one of those "illusions to be destroyed" which the hero must shed one after another in order to attain the state of absolute disenchantment that precedes and prepares for the final revelation' (p. 258).[88] Since the above passage occurs in *The Captive*, the narrator presumably has not yet reached the point of disillusionment that he achieves in *Time Regained*, with his realisation of the need to decipher and translate reality. However, Marcel's remark is not a dead end, but rather a transitional stage: first the narrator must learn to interpret objects as a 'series of symbols' carrying a buried meaning, not merely as empty phonemes. Then, as Genette argues, he must clear away the fallacy of motivation and see them as essentially arbitrary. Only then, once Marcel has gained a true symbolic understanding of the world, does he learn that the only way to gain access to those hieroglyphic symbols he perceives is to translate them back into 'phonetic writing'. While Deleuze claims that 'Everywhere Proust contrasts the world of signs and symptoms with the world of attributes, the world of pathos with the world of logos, the world of hieroglyphs and ideograms with the world of analytic expression, phonetic writing, and rational thought' (p. 108), Proust's final understanding of hieroglyphics allows him to bridge those binaries, to translate the world of the hieroglyph into the world of phonetic writing and to write his novel.

A similar attempt to blur the line between hieroglyphic and phonetic alphabets, and a similar link between hieroglyphics and narrative, occurs in Eisenstein's later theoretical writings. Whereas in the essays discussed above from the late 1920s Eisenstein, like Pound, emphasises the purely visual aspects of hieroglyphs and their primal connection to the objects they depict, in his collection of essays *Nonindifferent Nature* from the 1940s Eisenstein begins to sound like Freud and Proust, stressing the hybrid nature – between the visual and the oral – of Chinese and Japanese writing.[89] He even uses the same metaphor as Freud: 'The "standard" rebus is built on the fact that the sound designation of the object corresponds phonetically to several meanings.

[. . .] The solution to the rebus usually is based on the pictures being read in their second sense based on sound, just as the components of Chinese hieroglyphics are read.'[90] Eisenstein is correcting his own mistake here, realising like Champollion that even pictographic writing contains phonetic elements. Such a realisation coincides with the coming of sound, since sound film shatters the supposed purity of the filmic medium, which can no longer hold fast to the idea of being free from spoken language.[91] Eisenstein thus reinterprets the ideogram as a hybrid medium, between speech and image, so as to preserve it as an inspiration for film. In so doing, film comes to sound a lot like writing: 'As we can see, the devices lying *within oral literature* and the devices *within painting* are combined by interesting features from the area lying between them, *written literature*, that diverges from spoken literature and *that applies more to the standards of plastic visual depiction.*'[92] For Eisenstein, writing, like film, exists in a liminal zone between 'oral literature' and 'visual depiction', between sound and image.[93] Film becomes a 'genuine synthetic art', in David Bordwell's words, 'the century's gesamtkunstwerk, the "total artwork" that would unify all those arts that had become separated' (p. 196).

Eisenstein is quite explicit about this shift in his perception of ideograms over the course of his career. While he still holds fast to the vestige of his earlier beliefs, claiming that 'the hieroglyph lost its tie with its representational past to a much lesser degree than the design of letters in our alphabet', he also notes that, 'Before becoming interested in Eastern art in general, the East attracted me in other ways, partially by the hieroglyphic writing that at certain initial stages helped me form concepts about the principles of montage.'[94] Eisenstein's focus on the phonetic nature of hieroglyphs and ideograms coincides with a new emphasis on landscape painting, on how Chinese artists arranged ideograms into a narrative and pictorial framework. Eisenstein discusses the scrolls or 'ribbons' of Chinese painting, comparing them to narrative film: 'reproducing the form of the early picture scroll on the screen, but this time in the form of the *real movement* of ribbon that really *runs*'.[95] Eisenstein's concern now is less with the individual shot or cut, but with 'the "flow" of writing' or film, a flow that he sees expressed most fully in 'the famous last chapter of James Joyce's *Ulysses*'.[96]

As with Freud and Proust, the movement towards seeing hieroglyphs as hybrids between pictures and phonemes involves a simultaneous movement towards narrative. In reconceiving of the ideogram as phonetic after the advent of sound, Eisenstein imagines the ideogram as an element in a larger language rather than as an isolated pictorial image. This is not to say that Eisenstein's films became more narrative from the silent era to the sound era, but that his understanding and theorization of them emphasised narrative much more fully. In his essays in *Film Form* – from the 1920s and 1930s – Eisenstein echoes Pound's view on the juxtapositional method of the ideogram, and presents each individual editing choice in his films – each moment of montage – as akin to a single Vorticist image-in-motion. On the subject of large-scale narrative structure, on how his films as a whole – as opposed to individual sequences – are composed, Eisenstein is largely silent; as David Bordwell writes, Eisenstein 'does not posit basic questions of narrative as, say, André Bazin will in his essays' (p. 190). But this is precisely what concerns him in 'Nonindifferent Nature': he devotes pages to analyses of the innovative structures – characterised by 'counterpoint', 'polyphonic writing' and 'fugue'[97] – of the novels of Conrad, Melville and Wilkie Collins, as well as the films of Orson Welles. As he says, 'In this turn towards the story lies the historical importance of the third half-decade of Soviet cinematography (1930–1935).'[98] By reimagining and reinterpreting hieroglyphics, Eisenstein increasingly emphasises 'story' and 'plot'. The addition of spoken sound to the cinema necessitates for Eisenstein a reconceptualisation of ideograms and of narrative itself. And this linkage, through hieroglyphics, between new conceptions of language and media and new models of narrative, forms the basis of the subsequent chapter on Joseph Conrad's and Orson Welles's innovative narrative forms.

Zorns Lemma: A Narrative in Hieroglyphs

Eisenstein, over the course of his career, thus comes to embody the opposing ways in which visual languages were invoked to understand new media in the twentieth century, portraying ideograms and hieroglyphs both as non-phonetic, depictive languages and as hybrid languages similar to written letters. And one of the filmmakers Eisenstein went on to influence can help reveal the fundamental link – even in one of the most famous of avant-garde, anti-narrative films – between these views of visual language and narrative itself. Hollis Frampton, the seminal 1960s experimental filmmaker, acknowledged a deep debt to Eisenstein, and his breakthrough film *Zorns Lemma* is intimately concerned with film's status as a visual, hieroglyphic language poised uneasily between writing and images. *Zorns Lemma* exposes the double logic of discourses about hieroglyphics in the twentieth century, in which Egyptian and other forms of visual language are used both to claim film's ability to supplant writing and to assert the kinship of cinema *with* writing. Fluctuating between seeing film and ideograms as providing a less mediated access to the natural world and emphasising the qualities shared between film and writing, *Zorns Lemma* puts into action all of the at times contradictory associations among hieroglyphics, film and writing that this chapter has traced. It also reveals the extent to which a fascination with visual languages and their relationship to media involves an embrace of, rather than a retreat from, narrative itself.

Zorns Lemma consists of three segments. As Frampton explains, 'The first part is five minutes long, soundtrack with no image. A woman recites in a schoolteacherly voice 24 rhymes from the Bay State Primer which was designed to teach late eighteenth century and early nineteenth century children the alphabet.'[99] The second and by far the longest section begins with successive shots of each of the letters of the Latin alphabet, from A to Z. As these letters are cycled through over the course of 45 minutes, each of the letters is successively represented by a photograph of a word beginning with that letter: a sign on an awning reading 'Peck' for P, a fire Alarm box for A, etc. But slowly and systematically, each of these letters is gradually replaced by a repeated moving image. So steam rising from a building replaces Q and an image of wheat replaces Y. Through repetition, these clips take on alphabetical associations, with the viewer linking particular objects and images with the letters that they've replaced. The section concludes once all of the letters have been replaced with film clips.

The third section shows, in long shot, two figures and a dog moving across a field of snow, while 'six women's voices read [. . .] a text of Robert Grosseteste, who was Bishop of Lincoln. The text, *On Light, or the Ingression of Forms*, is a beautiful medieval Latin treatise which is [. . .] vulgarized by me, then cut down to about 620 words.'[100] *Zorns Lemma* returns to earlier medieval, Renaissance or Enlightenment texts or traditions and applies them to the context of new media.

As in many of Frampton's films, *Zorns Lemma* foregrounds the relationship between word and image within the medium of cinema. Building on the discourses of Lindsay and Eisenstein outlined above, Frampton seems to be constructing a cinematic grammar in which images are made to take on linguistic meaning. Just as Lindsay equates an image with a concept, so in *Zorns Lemma* images come to signal letters themselves. The film seems to represent a narrative of the replacement of language by film, of the supplanting of the word. The middle section systematically substitutes images for letters of the alphabet, and whereas the voiceover in the first section relates to grammar, the spoken text in the final section deals with optics, with the importance of 'light'.

From the opening title shot, in which the words 'Zorns Lemma' are spelled out in a mechanised type, we move by the end of the film to pure white light. Issues of language are replaced with questions of visual perception, marking an autobiographical progression in Frampton's life. As he writes, the first section symbolises how 'my adolescence and early childhood were concerned primarily with words and verbal values. I fancied myself a poet: studied living and dead languages – hence my early contacts with, for instance, Ezra Pound.' But the next section represents the 'thirteen years in New York [that] saw a gradual weaning away of my consciousness from verbal to visual interests'.[101] Indeed, the very first line from the Bay State Primer – and thus the first line of the film – is 'In Adam's Fall/we sinned all', marking the loss of Eden, a loss, as we've seen, that was frequently associated with the loss of a pure and primal language, particularly given the alphabetical associations of the primer. Having lost that possibility of direct reference, the film seems to narrate a transition from verbal to visual, with cinema replacing language or at least forming a better and more visual kind of language, recalling Lindsay and Eisenstein's ideas of hieroglyphs.

Zorns Lemma's engagement with these issues is no coincidence, as Frampton was obsessed with many of the writers and theorists discussed above. By far the two most frequently cited figures in his writing are James Joyce and Ezra Pound, and as noted Frampton even visited Pound at St Elizabeth's. References to Eisenstein also abound; Frampton declares that his film 'comes not only from Pound but also from Eisenstein, who likens a film to a text, and shots to words. He speaks of reading the shots as though they were words, hence *Zorns Lemma*'s very obvious debt to Eisenstein.'[102] Indeed, critics of Frampton such as P. Adams Sitney and Federico Windhausen have stressed the importance not only of literary antecedents like Pound, but even of literary scholars like Hugh Kenner, who emphasised how Pound's concern with Chinese ideograms was central to his aesthetic project.[103]

Given these interests, Frampton naturally also invokes visual languages in his writing. While he claims that he was 'unmoved' by 'those Egyptian things in the British museum', he devotes an entire article to trying to decipher Hopi pictographs, emphasising a similarity between them and film.[104] He writes that the Hopis 'seem to have spent most of their time and energy in making and using the pictogram rolls, which were optically projected upon the walls. Sunlight, led indoors by an intricate system of mirrors, served as the illuminant.'[105] These graven pictographs, in Frampton's reading, are really a kind of proto-cinema, animated by light. In making this connection, Frampton naturally borrows from Eisenstein's and Pound's theories of Chinese ideograms: 'The connection between this visible language and speech is remote, and recalls the tenuous relationship between the ideograms of literary Chinese and their corresponding vernacular.' Like Pound, Frampton denies Hopi pictograms a verbal or phonetic content, stressing the link to the supposedly non-phonetic ancient Chinese scripts imagined by Fenollosa. Frampton goes on to claim that 'The pictograms clearly constitute a language. The semantic unit, however, is not the single glyph, but a cluster of two or more pictures which denote the *limits* of a significance.'[106] Again like Pound and Eisenstein, Frampton imagines meaning as constituted by the combination or collision of multiple pictograms, making these Hopi pictograms almost entirely parallel to motion pictures – they are 'optically projected' and attain significance through the juxtaposition of individual shots or hieroglyphs.

Frampton thus seems firmly in the Pound/Lindsay/Eisenstein tradition outlined above, denying the phoneticism of visual languages in order to use them as a metaphor for the possibilities of direct reference of the medium of film. Yet Frampton's film can just as easily be seen as stressing that language and images remain inextricably related, with cinema a hybrid of the textual and the visual. Indeed, Frampton in his essay 'Film in the House of the World' is dismissive of the desire of film to free itself from language, criticising how 'the syndrome of logophobia has been pandemic throughout recent practice in the visual arts'. Invoking Eisenstein, he argues, 'Every artistic dialogue that concludes in a decision to ostracize the word is disingenuous to the degree that it succeeds in concealing from itself its fear of the word [. . .] In this regard, Eisenstein is characteristically abrupt, claiming for film [. . .] something of the power of language.'[107] For Frampton, Eisenstein is trying to coopt and emulate the power of language rather than to escape from it; indeed, this is just what we've seen in Eisenstein's desire to construct a cinematic grammar.

If we view *Zorns Lemma* through this lens we can see the film not as a narrative of the visual replacing the verbal, but rather as a statement about the delicate balance between word and image within the medium of cinema. Frampton is particularly careful to equate the grammar of film with the grammar of language: oddly, Frampton includes only 24 letters of the 26 in the alphabet. Frampton does not simply want to return to the older Latin alphabet, with its 24 letters, but as his reference to the speed of film – 24 frames per second – in his notes on *Zorns Lemma* makes clear, Frampton desires to equate the basic building block of film – the frame – with letters themselves. Frampton therefore emphasises how the combination of images and words in his film constitute 'word-images'; the verbal and visual are inseparable.[108] His task in *Zorns Lemma* is to reveal the 'Word as a graphic element that brought one back to reading (and being conscious of looking at a mark on a surface).'[109] Rather than stressing the difference between words and images, Frampton's film, like the work of Woolf, makes the viewer aware of how words themselves are just as visual and 'graphic' as the images of film, composed of 'a mark on a surface'. And through his juxtapositions of letters and film clips, images take on the linguistic associations of words and letters. The film in fact doesn't even chronicle a shift from words to images, as all of the shots of signs in the first part of part two are in fact not still shots but rather film clips; even those moments of the film that emphasise the linguistic are themselves part of the 'motion picture'. Frampton's film thus destroys the media barriers that it seems to set up. The visual image that replaces 'A' in the film is of a man reading a book, reinforcing the symbiotic relationship between texts and films. *Zorns Lemma* thus embodies the opposing ways in which twentieth-century writers and theorists imagined, through the metaphor of hieroglyphics, the link between film and writing. Writing and film are two sides of the same coin in Frampton's film, with writing taking on the 'graphic' characteristics of film images and film revealing its necessary and unbreakable link with 'the power of language'.

As *Zorns Lemma* fluctuates between film and writing, so it is animated by a tension between the static qualities of individual film clips and how those clips are merged into a narrative. Like Pound and Eisenstein, Frampton emphasises both the depictive aspects of glyphs or images and how they take on meaning through combination. Like much of avant-garde film, *Zorns Lemma* seems aggressively anti-narrative, resisting narrative conventions by not having characters or a plot and taking on meaning simply through repetition. Yet Frampton's engagement with the hybrid nature of film seems to lead towards an increasing narrative momentum in *Zorns Lemma*. The second section of the film, with the photographs of signs being replaced by film clips, creates a great deal of suspense and narrative interest in guessing which letter will be the next to be replaced and in trying to figure out the methodology behind the order of replacements. This increasing sense of narrative is literalised in the final section, which features the seemingly thematically unrelated image of a couple and a dog walking across a snowy field. While this clip seems to have nothing to do with the larger issue of the relationship between word and image, it constitutes a basic unit of narrative: a journey. From resisting narrative in its initial segment, *Zorns Lemma* moves towards an embrace of it. As with Eisenstein's essay 'Nonindifferent Nature', Frampton's film confirms that far from resisting narrative, as we might expect from the avant-garde, the fascination with visual languages involves a fundamental engagement with narrative.

Zorns Lemma and the modernist engagement with hieroglyphics that it invokes can explain one of the central tensions in modernism: how writers, filmmakers and visual artists can both desire a language of direct reference and a language without reference; how they can simultaneously emphasise both the non-communicative material properties of language and its potential for universal communication. On one level, hieroglyphs, because of their history of competing interpretations and their cultural Otherness in the West, can express both sides of that binary, existing at one and the same time as unreadable language and as motivated sign. But more than that, the persistent emphasis on the use of visual languages in the avant-garde and the focus on making language non-referential has unnecessarily confused the issue. For so many modernist writers, invoking hieroglyphics to emphasise the material properties of their own medium of written words counterintuitively also underlines its communicative potential, how it can impart meaning not simply through phonemes but also through visual associations. Far from limiting communication or emphasising a different kind of communication, for the modernists a focus on language's materiality makes it more expressive, deepening its referential power.

Notes

1. Dieckmann, p. 31.
2. Iversen, pp. 24, 12.
3. Genette, *Mimologics*. Cratylus thinks that names 'are natural and not conventional; not a portion of the human voice which men agree to use; but that there is a truth or correctness in them.' Plato, p. 422.
4. Dieckmann, p. 228. Or, as John Irwin writes in *American Hieroglyphics*, 'Champollion's discoveries did not, however, topple the metaphysical school of interpretation. It continued, often using misreadings of Champollion's work as justification for its efforts' (p. 6).
5. Fenollosa, p. 45. For accounts of Chinese ideograms and modernism, see Bush, Hayot, Huang, Chow.
6. The Pound-centred narratives like those of Marjorie Perloff and Johanna Drucker focus on literature and painting, and emphasise the 'mystical' view of ideograms and hieroglyphics. They stress the modernist desire to create an Adamic language that would break down the gap between signifier and signified to capture, in Wallace Stevens's words, 'not ideas about the thing but the thing itself' (see Perloff, *The Futurist Moment*; Drucker). As Robert Kern writes in *Orientalism, Modernism, and the American Poem*, 'the early period of modernism [is] characterized by a further or continuing revival of an Adamicist outlook, in which linguistic progress depends [. . .] on a constant effort to invent new imagery and to circumvent what Hulme calls "the inadequacy of the usual" through a return to the primary use or re-poetizing of language' (pp. 24–5).
7. This hybridity of hieroglyphics largely applies as well to the Chinese ideograms that served as a misguided inspiration for Pound: 'Simple characters [. . .] and ideograms [. . .] comprise only about 10 percent of the total number of characters. The rest are phonetic compounds.' Géfin, p. 24.
8. Iversen, p. 45. See Plotinus, p. 417; Plutarch, p. 27.
9. Horapollo, p. 7.
10. Iversen, p. 49.
11. See Everard, trans., *The Divine Pymander of Hermes Mercurius Trismegistus*.
12. According to these interpretations, hieroglyphics, in the words of Erik Iversen, 'had nothing in common with ordinary graphic systems operating with words and letters and, although they appeared as ordinary pictures of material objects, the individual signs were in reality symbolic entities, revealing their true meaning only to the initiated readers by means of a divinely inspired process of intellectual enlightenment' (p. 64).
13. See Swedenborg, *A Hieroglyphic Key to Natural and Spiritual Mysteries*; Behmen, *Signatura Rerum*, unpaged.
14. Benjamin, *The Origin of the German Tragic Drama*, p. 176.
15. Webster, p. 27.
16. Carlyle, p. 195. Or, as Dieckmann writes, 'what we see and feel and touch in nature is not the "meaning" of nature, [but] behind the tangible "characters" there is an intangible text [. . .] in need of interpretation' (p. 66), recalling Foucault's epistemology.
17. Vico stresses the originary aspects of hieroglyphics: 'The first nations thought in poetic characters, spoke in fables, and wrote in hieroglyphs' (p. 139).
18. Bacon, p. 82. See also Locke's statement that 'There is no natural connection between particular sounds and particular ideas (if there were, there would be only one human language); but people arbitrarily chose to use such and such a word as the mark of such and such an idea' (p. 187). As Hans Aarleff summarises Locke's

views, 'Locke's argument was aimed at the most widely held seventeenth-century view of the nature of language, a doctrine that can best be called by the umbrella term the Adamic language. In the Adamic doctrine the relation between signifier and signified is not arbitrary; the linguistic sign is not double but unitary' (p. 25).
19. Eco, p. 220.
20. As Eco summarises, 'Leibniz's intention was thus to create a logical language, like algebra, which might lead to the discovery of unknown truths simply by applying syntactical rules to symbols' (p. 281), which Eco compares to Wittgenstein's 'picture theory of language', discussed in Chapter 1.
21. As Robert Kern argues about the late nineteenth century, 'if this was a period in which mythic or Adamic notions of language were being revived, it was also a period which witnessed the birth of a new science of language, comparative philology, although the mythic and the scientific were by no means impermeable' (p. 10).
22. Eco, p. 286. Likewise, 'Kircher presumed that the mysteries of hieroglyphic writing had been introduced to the Chinese by Noah's son Ham.' Indeed, Leibniz and Kircher even corresponded (pp. 159, 273).
23. As Eco writes, Kircher's universal icons 'are reminiscent of those that one might find today in airports and railway stations: some were schematically representative [...] Some were furthermore superficially derived from Egyptian hieroglyphics' (p. 204). Indeed, those 'airport and railway station' icons were often based on Otto Neurath's twentieth-century visual International Auxiliary Language called Isotype.
24. As Charles Musser writes, 'While recent research has clearly shown that Kircher did not invent the magic lantern, his *Ars magna lucis et umbrae* still occupies a privileged place at the start of the screen's history' (p. 17).
25. Saussy, p. 45.
26. For a systematic account of the American Renaissance view of hieroglyphics as mystical, inscrutable symbols, see John Irwin.
27. Emerson, *Nature and Selected Essays*, pp. 36, 48.
28. As Frank Kermode argues in *Romantic Image*, Hulme's 'thought derives, with no fundamental variation, from the historical theory of the Image' and 'Pound's ideogram is yet another variety of the Romantic Image' (pp. 120, 136). Indeed, as many critics have pointed out, Ernest Fenollosa was profoundly influenced by Emersonian thought and the hieroglyphic tradition he represents. As Hugh Kenner writes in *The Pound Era*, 'He [Fenollosa] was teaching Emerson to his best Japanese students at the time he began looking closely into ideograms, there to find confirmation of Emerson's etymologist who "finds the deadest word to have been once a brilliant picture"' (p. 230).
29. Emerson, *Emerson: Essays and Poems*, pp. 674, 687.
30. See Wilkinson; Balakian.
31. For more on Emerson and Poe's influence on Baudelaire, see Gilman, pp. 211–22; Culler, pp. 61–73; Lawler, pp. 95–110.
32. Mallarmé, p. 171.
33. Hieroglyphics are scrawled throughout Melville's 'wonder-world' of *Moby-Dick*, from the 'Chilean whale, marked like an old tortoise with mystic hieroglyphics upon the back' to the whale whose 'hieroglyphic' marks remind Ishmael of old 'Indian characters chiseled on the famous hieroglyphic palisades' (pp. 171, 246).
34. As Ishmael says, the tattoing of 'hieroglyphic marks' on Queequeg's skin that forms 'a complete theory of the heavens and the earth' is 'destined in the end to moulder away with the living parchment whereon they were inscribed and so be unsolved to the last' (p. 367). Hieroglyphs in Melville hold the promise of total

knowledge, but leave us with an autotelic script whose meaning can never fully be read.
35. The true value of language – be it written text or the Book of Nature – thus lies for Melville in what is shown or in what is not shown, but never in what is said. Indeed, the paragraph in which Melville discusses the 'genius' of the sperm whale, a genius that is expressed through its 'pyramidical silence', directly precedes the passage invoking Champollion quoted earlier.
36. Iversen, p. 107. Indeed, Chinese and Egyptian scripts have wrongly been seen as related going back at least to the Renaissance; see Hudson, *Writing and European Thought 1600–1830*; Hartman, pp. 101–18; Unger, p. 18.
37. Saussy, p. 6.
38. The same goes for the first reference to ideograms, from a newspaper article by the same author, in which the word is used interchangeably with hieroglyphic: 'Nor was Dr. Young less successful with the hieroglyphic ideograms (or symbolic characters direct and indirect), many of which he determined' (*OED*).
39. Given the overemphasis on 'The Chinese Written Character' in discussions of modernism, countless books and articles have discussed Fenollosa's theories, and I will be drawing in particularly for my summary of these arguments on Kern and Kenner, as well as works by Hayot, Huang and Bush.
40. In *The Roots of Lyric*, Andrew Welsh argues that 'Behind his [Fenollosa's] theory stands a basically Emersonian assumption that language is "natural" rather than arbitrary, that it reflects basic structures and processes in nature' (p. 118).
41. Pound, *ABC of Reading*, p. 20.
42. As Haun Saussy argues, Pound looks beyond alphabetical writing towards a different kind of writing, 'One response to the inadequacy of writing has been to exalt some other kind of writing – occasionally a language reformer's pet project, but more frequently the writing of the angels, of the citizens of some utopia, of the scholars of some faraway kingdom, or of the forces of nature' (p. 35). For Pound, Chinese is that 'other kind of writing'.
43. See Saussy, 'Fenollosa Compounded', in Fenollosa et al., p. 7. Pound also responds to Ogden's essays in his article 'Debabelization and Ogden', pp. 410–11.
44. Indeed, Andrew Thacker even traces the connections between Hulme and C. K. Ogden and Bertrand Russell, whom he knew personally at Cambridge, and claims 'That Wittgenstein's theory is visually based [. . .] can again be linked to the emphasis on visuality in language to be found in Hulme' (p. 43).
45. Hugh Kenner notes but does not explore this connection between ideogram and film: 'both exist for the sake of their blended succession, the moving picture, the sentence, the poetic line' (p. 289). Michael North in *Camera Works* has also traced the links between Pound and various avant-garde filmmakers; as he writes, 'Though he declared himself flatly against cinema in 1918, Pound found himself drawn into a Parisian literary world that was fascinated by it' (p. 27).
46. Indeed, Eisenstein's essays were reprinted in two central modernist journals of the period: *Close-Up*, associated with H.D. and Dorothy Richardson, among others; and *transition*, edited by Eugene Jolas.
47. Van Zile, p. 195. As Christian Metz observes in *Film Language*, the comparison of Esperanto to silent film is notoriously and interestingly inexact:

> The theoreticians of the silent film liked to speak of the cinema as a kind of Esperanto. Nothing is further from the truth. Certainly Esperanto does differ from ordinary languages, but that is because it accomplishes to perfection what they strive for but never attain: a system that is totally conventional, specific, and organized. Film also differs from true language but in the opposite

way. It would be more correct to say that the true languages are caught between two Esperantos: the true Esperanto [. . .] which is reached through an excess of linguisticity, and the other, the cinema, which has a dearth of linguisticity. (pp. 63–4)

48. Interestingly, Lindsay's utopian dream of a one-to-one correspondence of image and meaning in silent film is, in the theory of Theodor Adorno, profoundly dystopian. In characterising the images of the culture industry as hieroglyphs in his 'The Schema of Mass Culture', he critiques precisely this direct, simplistic form of communication: 'In the dreams of those in charge of mummifying the world mass culture represents a priestly hieroglyphic script which addresses its images to those who have been subjugated not in order that they might be enjoyed but only that they be read. The authentic images of the film screen as well as the inauthentic ones encountered in hit melodies and the well-worn written phrase appear so rigidly and so frequently that they are no longer perceived in their own right but only as repetitions whose perpetual sameness always expresses an identical meaning' (p. 93). This emphasis on 'sameness' and 'identical meaning' – and the Egyptological references – sound similar to Lindsay, even if Adorno associates these clichés of ideology more with the sound cinema than the silent period.
49. Similarly, German director Fritz Lang claims that 'The first important gift for which we have film to thank was in a certain sense *the rediscovery of the human face*' (p. 623).
50. Ramsaye, p. xi.
51. Armstrong, pp. 220–47. As Laura Marcus writes, 'Conceptions of film hieroglyphics [. . .] were, however, connected not only to representations of speech and of writing, but also [. . .] to a language of the body' (p. 10). Or, as Rachel Moore summarises, 'By regaining access to gesture, the cinema could reveal the secrets of things and souls inexpressible in the impoverished language of mere words. The cinema opened its subjects anew to physiognomic inspection' (p. 20).
52. Jean Epstein, 'On Certain Characteristics of Photogenie', in *French Film Theory*, ed. by Richard Abel, p. 315.
53. *The Last Laugh (Der letzte Mann)*, dir. by F. W. Murnau (UFA, 1924).
54. Murnau, 'Films of the Future', p. 90. Similarly, Fritz Lang echoes the desire for film to transcend linguistic boundaries: 'The internationalism of filmic language will become the strongest instrument available for the mutual understanding of peoples, who otherwise have such difficulty understanding each other in all too many languages' (p. 623).
55. Murnau, 'The Ideal Picture Needs No Titles', p. 72.
56. Hansen, *From Babel to Babylon*, pp. 193, 184. See *Intolerance*, dir. by D. W. Griffith (Triangle Film Corporation, 1916).
57. Hansen, *From Babel to Babylon*, p. 192.
58. Like much of the discourses about hieroglyphics at the time, Griffith's film and his aesthetics are thus caught between using the hieroglyphic analogy to claim film's superiority to writing and its similarity to writing. As Hansen argues in *From Babel to Babylon*, 'if *Intolerance* is proposing to recover a unity of popular and high art, it does so not by replacing writing with a superior language of visual presence, but by retrieving the common roots of both film and literature in the hieroglyphic tradition', and yet the film works 'to demonstrate at once the analogy and superiority of film in relation to verbal language' (pp. 195, 186).
59. Sergei Eisenstein, 'The Cinematographic Principle and the Ideogram', in Eisenstein and Leyda, *Film Form*, pp. 29–30.

60. Eisenstein and Leyda, *Film Form*, pp. 91–2.
61. Eisenstein and Leyda, *Film Form*, pp. 29–30.
62. Ezra Pound, 'A Few Don'ts by an *Imagiste*', p. 200.
63. Pound, p. 21.
64. Pound, *Gaudier-Brzeska*, p. 89.
65. Julian Murphet likewise juxtaposes Griffith and Pound, but ignores their shared interest in visual and universal languages. See Murphet, pp. 93–122.
66. Saussy, p. 40. See also Beasley, p. 129.
67. As Haun Saussy writes, 'But if the cherry tree is to be understood as a wave or "bundle of energies" inseparable from all the other particulars [. . .] the Image properly denotes a Vortex.' Saussy, 'Fenollosa Compounded', in Fenollosa et al., p. 23.
68. Quoted in *Ezra Pound and the Visual Arts*, ed. by Harriet Zinnes, p. 78.
69. Ezra Pound, 'How to Write', in *Machine Art and Other Writings*, p. 88.
70. Ezra Pound, 'Hugh Selwyn Mauberley', in *Poems and Translations*, p. 550.
71. For more on Pound's engagement with but contempt for cinema see Beasley, p. 188.
72. H.D. and Richard Aldington, *Some Imagist Poets: An Anthology*, p. vii.
73. Eisenstein and Leyda, *Film Form*, p. 232.
74. Eisenstein and Leyda, *Film Form*, pp. 52, 55. As David Bordwell writes in *The Cinema of Eisenstein*, 'Some theorists of the era were tempted to draw analogies to verbal language. It was commonplace to talk of a "film language," as in Eikhenbaum's conception of "cine-phrases" and "cine-periods"' (p. 126).
75. Eisenstein and Leyda, *Film Form*, pp. 28, 29.
76. Eisenstein and Leyda, *Film Form*, p. 30.
77. As Vjaceslav Ivanov argues, Eisenstein is interested in the 'evolution of iconic signs into symbolic ones' and the 'transformation of drawn pictographs into stylized ideographic symbols' (p. 223).
78. Freud, p. 312. Likewise, Freud states later that 'the productions of the dream-work [. . .] present no greater difficulties to their translators than do the ancient hieroglyphic scripts to those who seek to read them' (p. 377).
79. Derrida, 'Freud and the Scene of Writing', p. 101.
80. Lacan, p. 151.
81. Freud's treatment of the dream-work as hieroglyphic even went on to influence film, especially through the link H.D. forged between the hieroglyphic language of dreams and the hieroglyphic cinematic language. As Laura Marcus argues, 'The promise of the film as "universal language" [. . .] becomes increasingly inseparable from a model of the "universal language" of the dream, and both were closely connected for H.D. with the "hieroglyph"' (p. 364).
82. Proust, *Time Regained*, p. 273; *Le Temps retrouvé*, p. 185.
83. Proust, *Time Regained*, p. 291.
84. Deleuze and Howard, p. 4.
85. Proust: *Time Regained*, p. 275; *Le Temps retrouvé*, p.186. Or, 'The book whose hieroglyphs [*caractères figurés*] are patterns not traced by us is the only book that really belongs to us' (p. 275; p. 186).
86. As Maria Torok writes, this tension about how to decipher the dream-content was consistent throughout Freud's career: 'Freud rejected, accepted, and nuanced by turns the use of symbolism in dream interpretation. He eschewed its arbitrariness, and yet he would have liked to translate dreams into a stable, authentic and indisputably universal code' (p. 578).
87. Proust, *The Captive and the Fugitive*, p. 109.
88. As Genette argues more fully:

> Marcel's poetic reveries display, therefore, that same tendency to motivate language that also inspires the solecisms of Françoise [...] The motivation operates, more subtly, both on the form of that word (the way its 'substance,' phonic or otherwise, is perceived, concretized, and interpreted) and on the form of its meaning (the 'image' of the place) in order of make them compatible, harmonious, mutually suggestive. (p. 254)

But these 'reveries' are undermined and proved incorrect:

> Against all this, and therefore against the instinctive Cratylism of the young hero, who is convinced that an immediate relationship exists between the *present* form of the name and the timeless essence of the thing, Brichot, symbol of the new linguistics, reinstates the deceptive truth of historical filiation, phonetic erosion – in short, the diachronic dimension of language. (p. 257)

89. Miriam Hansen is one of the few critics to note this shift: as she writes:

    > In most commentaries during the silent era, the comparison between cinema and hieroglyphics is celebratory [...] The underlying concept of hieroglyphics is one of a language of mystical correspondence and visual self-evidence, reincarnated in the new universal language of film. [...] During the 1930s [Eisenstein] abandoned this [...] model in favor of a more complex notion of film as ideographic writing based on the psycholinguistic concept of 'inner speech [...]' [This] analogy [...] entailed an emphasis on the composite character of the cinematic sign, its mixing of figural, graphic, and phonic matters of expression. If the filmic hieroglyph is thus conceived as fundamentally heterogeneous, however, its mode of signification is anything but self evident, self-identical and universal. (Hansen, 'Mass Culture as Hieroglyphic Writing: Adorno, Derrida, Kracauer', p. 59)

90. Eisenstein, *Nonindifferent Nature*, p. 223.
91. As Laura Marcus notes, 'For exponents of the silent cinema, sound was a technology too far, a mechanical intrusion into a perfected art which had made its appeal to the eye alone' (p. 37).
92. Eisenstein and Marshall, *Nonindifferent Nature*, p. 222.
93. Eisenstein and Leyda, *Film Form*, pp. 193–4.
94. Eisenstein and Marshall, *Nonindifferent Nature*, pp. 224, 252.
95. Eisenstein and Marshall, *Nonindifferent Nature*, p. 248.
96. Eisenstein and Marshall, *Nonindifferent Nature*, p. 249. Of course, some of the changes in Eisenstein's aesthetic over this period are no doubt due to the Stalinist crackdown on modernist aesthetic innovation and the embrace of Socialist Realism. However, I don't think that Eisenstein's thinking can be reduced entirely to political pressures; while the form of his films does change radically, his theorisation of them remains, aside from the shift I am discussing, rather similar.
97. Eisenstein and Marshall, *Nonindifferent Nature*, p. 265.
98. Eisenstein and Leyda, *Film Form*, p. 17.
99. Gidal, p. 94. See *Zorns Lemma*, dir. by Hollis Frampton (1970).
100. Gidal, pp. 97–8.
101. Frampton, '*Zorns Lemma*: Scripts and Notations', in *On the Camera Arts*, p. 197.
102. Dusinberre and Christie, p. 111.
103. Sitney, p. 67; Windhausen, p. 79.
104. Gidal, p. 99.
105. Frampton, 'A Stipulation of Terms from Maternal Hopi', in *On the Camera Arts*, p. 304.

106. Frampton, *On The Camera Arts*, p. 304.
107. Frampton, 'Film in the House of the Word', in *On the Camera Arts*, p. 167.
108. Frampton, *On the Camera Arts*, pp. 196, 9.
109. Gidal, p. 93.

2

THE HIEROGLYPHICS OF CHARACTER

In Virginia Woolf's 1926 essay about the characteristics and possibilities of the medium of film, entitled 'The Cinema', Woolf asks, 'Is there [. . .] some secret language which we feel and see, but never speak, and, if so, could this be made visible to the eye? Is there any characteristic which thought possesses that can be rendered visible without the help of words?'[1] Can film, as a relatively new visual medium, Woolf wonders, surpass writing itself, capturing the previously inexpressible flux of our inmost thoughts? Woolf's engagement with these questions and with the new medium of film helped to define her treatment of language and of literary character. Through her many references to hieroglyphs, Woolf re-imagines the relationship among human identity, written words and visual images, with Egyptian writing emerging as a metaphor for this 'secret language' in her novels and essays. For Woolf, if writing changes, then 'human character' must change as well, and vice versa. The modernist interpretation of hieroglyphs as hybrid, traced through Freud, Proust and Eisenstein in Chapter 1, thus in Woolf goes hand in hand with new techniques for representing literary character.

Particularly in the mid-1920s – when she was writing *To the Lighthouse* and *Mrs. Dalloway*, as well as 'The Cinema' and her story 'The Lady in the Looking-Glass' – Woolf, spurred by her encounter with film, increasingly emphasises the hybrid qualities of written words, between image and sound. This period saw an outpouring of writing about film in modernist journals and in mainstream magazines like *Vogue*, with writers like Iris Barry attempting to define, to use the title of one of her articles, 'The Future of the Cinema'. Woolf's essay 'The Cinema' emerged from this ferment and served as a means for Woolf to define the possibilities of her own medium of written words. Responding to and resisting Vachel Lindsay's ideas of film hieroglyphs, analysed in Chapter 1, Woolf ultimately sees in the cinema a more conventional form of expression and communication rather than a utopian 'secret language'. In delimiting the proper scope and subjects for film and for literature, she subsumes film within writing. She argues, like Proust and Freud, that writing as a hybrid form encompassing image, sound and text can uniquely incorporate the visual qualities of film. Even if film finally fulfilled its ultimate function and confined itself to abstraction, as Woolf argues in her essay, cinema would remain only a lesser form of writing. While film and its images may promise, for Ezra Pound and Vachel Lindsay, a 'secret language', the true language of identity for Woolf can only be expressed with 'the help of words'.

But Woolf's engagement with hieroglyphic theories of film goes beyond simply re-affirming the primacy of writing, with hieroglyphs serving also as a way for her to imagine the embodied language of character. Woolf repeatedly represents the essential identity of her characters as engraved upon hieroglyphic 'sacred tablets', with hieroglyphs becoming almost the language of our minds. Woolf often invokes Egyptian writing in her work, mentioning 'spindly and hieroglyphic' furniture in her story 'The Lady in the Looking-Glass', discussing the 'hieroglyphs written on other people's faces' in *The Waves*, and referring to the 'hieroglyphics of misery' in her essay *On Being Ill*.[2] And in a key moment in *To the Lighthouse*, Lily Briscoe wonders how she can uncover and read the internal 'tablets bearing sacred inscriptions [. . .] that would teach one everything' about Mrs Ramsay's character.[3] The invocation of these 'tablets' points to how, for Woolf, human character is defined by language and, more specifically, by a graven and embodied form of writing that finds its ultimate expression in Egyptian hieroglyphs. By invoking hieroglyphs and these 'sacred tablets' of her characters' minds and hearts, Woolf in her fiction searches for a written form of the 'secret language' she alludes to in 'The Cinema', composed at the same time as *To the Lighthouse*. Playing off the double meanings of 'impression' and 'character', with their associations with the process of printing or engraving, Woolf imagines the basis of perception and of identity itself not as visual, but as linguistic.[4] By blurring the gap between writing and images in 'The Cinema', Woolf succeeds in imagining the inmost selves of her characters as a visual language which the writer, like Champollion, must translate.

Indeed, such views were not uncommon in the 1920s, with the novelist Dorothy Richardson conceptualising the relationship between film, writing and human bodies in strikingly similar ways in her novels and film criticism. If we examine Woolf through the lens of Richardson, we can see the stakes of this interest in hieroglyphs; in both Richardson and Woolf, hieroglyphs are persistently linked with women, with Egyptian writing serving not only as the language of identity, but also as a more embodied and intimate alternative to the alphabetical writing associated with men. Whether it comes to deciphering the truths of identity or searching for better, more feminine, forms of language, Woolf strives, as in 'The Cinema', to make the visual linguistic, turning the world into writing.

Yet that process of translating the hieroglyphic 'sacred tablets' of identity is always deeply fraught in Woolf's novels. Woolf's epistemology of literary character, in fact, comes to mirror the central tension in discourses about hieroglyphs and the new media they came to symbolise in the modernist period, with hieroglyphs, as we've seen, either a mystical, pure and universal language or an everyday, alphabetical language. Woolf similarly fluctuates between treating identity as transcendentally legible or as possessing only a pedestrian level of meaning. Character in Woolf is either totally meaningful or not meaningful at all, almost banal, quite similar to the conflicting interpretations of hieroglyphs at the time. Woolf in her fiction longs for a pure and unmediated glimpse of the hieroglyphic 'tablets' that seem to embody the truth of character, but that truth remains fundamentally unknowable, only partially to be deduced through physical facts or the writerly imagination. Woolf flirts with the possibility of a hieroglyphic 'secret language', associated with film and recalling Pound's Cratylic ideograms, but acknowledges that the closest thing to such a language is the hybrid form of writing itself. Woolf thus makes a double argument about media. She claims that written text already incorporates image and sound and thus subsumes other new media like film and sound recording. Yet simultaneously she argues that the hieroglyphic language of the world and the truths of identity it embodies are not immediately legible, but need to be translated by the writer into alphabetical words.

VOGUE AND LONDON FILM CULTURE

Woolf's concerns with the nature of writing come to the fore because of a confrontation with the new medium of film. The period of 1925 to 1927 saw a blossoming of interest in film among London intellectuals, witnessing the founding by H.D., Bryher and Kenneth Macpherson of the journal *Close-Up*, which featured translations of Eisenstein's essays, and the creation of the Film Society of London. It was there in 1926 that Woolf most likely saw the film *The Cabinet of Dr. Caligari* that she discusses in her essay 'The Cinema'.[5] But interest in film was not confined to specialised screenings or journals; more-literary focused modernist magazines, and even mainstream periodicals, devoted increasing space to articles theorising cinema in the two years prior to the publication of Woolf's 'The Cinema'. Indeed, even a writer like Woolf, with no in-depth knowledge of film aesthetics or film history, could have an essay on film published in this period. That essay was intended not for one of the 'little magazines', but for *Vogue*, which in the period of autumn 1925 to spring 1926 leading up to Woolf's composition of 'The Cinema' was a veritable clearing house of contributions from members of the Bloomsbury Group, featuring two book reviews by Woolf, countless essays on art by regular contributor Clive Bell, a feature on Vanessa Bell by Duncan Grant and a profile of John Maynard Keynes. Indeed, *Vogue* provides a perfect example of how the periodicals of the time provided a forum for transnational, transmedia debates about the nature of film, debates that went on to influence Woolf's essay. These magazines consistently bridged national boundaries; in particular, *transition*, discussed in more depth in Chapter 5, featured contributions from Americans like H.D., Elliott Paul and William Carlos Williams and published translated essays by Sergei Eisenstein and others. Likewise, Woolf's 'The Cinema', originally intended for London *Vogue*, was first published in New York in *The Arts* before being re-published in revised form both in *The Nation and Athenaeum*, based in London, and *The New Republic*, based in New York.

These journals did not merely cross national boundaries; they also transgressed the divisions among media. The early March 1926 issue of *Vogue*, for instance, featured an essay on film by Iris Barry, but also a book review by Woolf – 'The Life of John Mytton' – and an article about the paintings of Georges Braque.[6] An edition of *Vogue* from early December 1925 even featured an ad for the Victoria Cinema College and Studios encouraging subscribers to 'Develop your latent film talent!'[7] Such conjunctions between film and literature were common, and the fact that Woolf's essays were frequently featured in the same issues as articles about film show just how deeply her work was linked with discussions of the cinema in the period.

This is particularly the case in the months before her April 1926 composition of 'The Cinema'. In the January 1926 issue of *The New Criterion*, Woolf's essay 'On Being Ill' – which mentions hieroglyphs – is featured along with Walter Hanks Shaw's article 'Cinema and Ballet in Paris', which discusses the abstract film *A Quoi Revent les Jeunes Films*. Shaw writes:

> This film is the first attempt that has been made to produce an entirely abstract film; one in which there is no story of any kind nor even any 'human interest'; a film which would be, in reality, 'moving pictures.' Every possible use was made of the medium [...] in an attempt to keep entirely within the field of the cinema and to keep it pure cinema.[8]

Such a view is quite similar to the ideas that Woolf goes on to propose in her own essay about 'The Cinema': the desire to keep the cinema 'pure' from the influence of other media, the valorisation of 'entirely abstract' film, and the notion that cinema must confine itself to being only 'moving pictures'. Woolf's theories of film thus emerge directly from larger discourses circulating in the London magazines of the time about the proper place and goals for the new medium of the cinema.

These articles about film – and the other content of the journals that surround them – also frequently invoke hieroglyphs, just as Woolf does in her essay 'On Being Ill'. In the Winter 1926 edition of *The Little Review*, for instance, Comte de Beaumont, who starred in *A Quoi Revent les Jeunes Films*, published an article about the film. De Beaumont writes:

> In 1900 a Swede found a block of magnetic steel which retained the invisible vibrations of sound and retranslated them for the human ear. The steel, when demagnetized, became deaf and dumb. [. . .] If matter hears and speaks, do not objects see? [. . .] Similarly, do not the vibrations of the cinema have speech, thought, will? Scientific investigators may track down the evidences of this life; Egyptian hieroglyphists may interpret its system of logic.[9]

De Beaumont seems to hint at the idea that film can somehow directly translate the phenomena of nature into recorded form, just as the 'magnetic steel' records and translates sound. And again, these grandiose and potentially mystical claims for what film or other new technologies might be able to accomplish are associated with 'Egyptian hieroglyphists', who are somehow attuned to the 'vibrations of the cinema'. While de Beaumont's argument remains rather fuzzy, his invocation of hieroglyphs reveals just how customary the conjunction of Egyptian writing and film was in writings about cinema after Vachel Lindsay, particularly when writers sought to invoke the possibility of film making 'matter' hear and speak. Indeed, readers would not have had to look far to find other references to ancient Egypt in journals at this time. The same issue of *The Adelphi* that featured Iris Barry's essay 'Three Films' included on one of its back pages the ad shown in Figure 2.1.[10] (In fact, James Baikie, author of the volume advertised, also wrote *Peeps at Other Lands: Ancient Egypt*, which was translated into Arabic by Naguib Mafouz, as discussed in Chapter 4, showing the complex interplay between Egypt and England.) Ads like these were common at the time; the previous issue of *The Adelphi* featured the ad in Figure 2.2.[11] While these ads do not make a connection between hieroglyphs and film, they demonstrate just how widespread the fascination with ancient Egypt was in the early 1920s after the discovery of King Tut's tomb. And as Laura Marcus points out, Arthur Weigall, the film critic in the early 1920s for the *Daily Mail*, was a former Egyptologist himself who went on to cover the opening of King Tut's tomb for the paper.[12] Likewise, two of the important British journals of Egyptian archaeology, the *Journal of Ancient Egypt* and the *Journal of Egyptian Archaeology*, started in this period: in 1914 and 1915, respectively. Hieroglyphs were thus naturally a metaphor upon which film theorists and novelists like Woolf could draw almost without

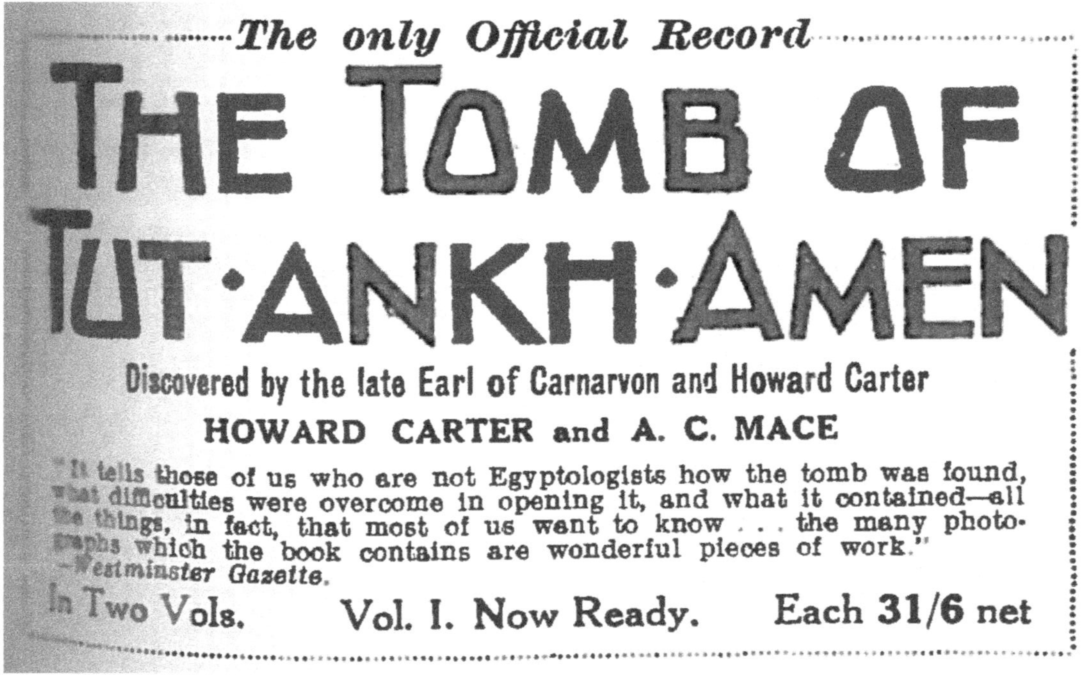

Figure 2.1 Advertisement from *The Adelphi* I (March 1924), p. 949

Figure 2.2   Advertisement from *The Adelphi* I (February 1924), p. 857

thinking: hieroglyphs harkened back to Lindsay's work and the widespread invocations of Egyptian writing in film theory of the time that it spawned but also gestured outward towards popular culture more broadly.

Woolf's interest in hieroglyphic theories of film in her essay 'The Cinema' is even more overdetermined, however. For in the months leading up to her composition of that essay, Woolf was corresponding with Vita Sackville-West while she was away in Egypt, providing yet another reason why Woolf would have had hieroglyphs on the brain. Even Woolf's geographical location in London in this period would have led to an interest in ancient Egypt. For Woolf's Tavistock Square home in Bloomsbury in the 1920s was not only in close proximity to the British Museum – where the Rosetta Stone was and is on display – but also right around the corner from the headquarters of the Egypt Exploration Society, publishers of the *Journal of Egyptian Archaeology*. Woolf only had to walk a few steps from her house to be reminded of Egypt and its ancient past.

The film which Woolf invokes in 'The Cinema' – *The Cabinet of Dr. Caligari* – was itself by far the most discussed film in journals and magazines of the 1920s. Thus while I find persuasive Leslie Kathleen Hankins's and David

Trotter's arguments that Woolf attended the London Film Society screening of *Caligari* directly before she wrote 'The Cinema', that fact seems almost beside the point, as Woolf would undoubtedly have already been intimately aware of the film from her reading.[13] Clive Bell credited *Caligari* as the most promising new direction in film in an article in *Vanity Fair* from 1922, and Iris Barry discusses *Caligari* in her 1924 essay 'Three Films' from *The Adelphi*; sounding like Woolf, she writes:

> Is life like that to a madman, I ask, looking outwards. And, what then is life like to me? I add, looking inward. Perhaps it is only in degree less like reality than the madman's story is like fact. I suddenly doubt the evidence of my senses, which I had thoughtlessly accepted as testimony on the appearance of the world.[14]

Barry's essay not only invokes *Caligari*, but also foregrounds the question of perception, which is at the heart of Woolf's engagement with film in 'The Cinema' and elsewhere. References to *Caligari* likewise recur in *Vogue* in the months leading up to the composition of 'The Cinema', with a 'Seen on the Stage' article in late January discussing a later film by Robert Weine, the director of *Caligari*.

The Secret Language of 'The Cinema'

Woolf would have been exposed to discourses about film and, particularly, to the overarching question which so often recurred in debates about cinema in the 1920s – what were the fundamental capacities and capabilities of this new medium, and were they or could they be somehow distinct from literature? It is this question that Woolf, as noted earlier, asks in her essay 'The Cinema', 'Is there [. . .] some secret language which we feel and see, but never speak, and, if so, could this be made visible to the eye? Is there any characteristic which thought possesses that can be rendered visible without the help of words?' As a writer of fiction, a lot is at stake for Woolf in this question, given writers like Vachel Lindsay's contention, outlined in Chapter 1, that film might potentially be a better communicative medium than writing. Or, as Béla Balázs claims, using almost the same words as Woolf, 'Every evening many millions of people sit and experience human destinies, characters, feelings, and moods of every kind with their eyes, and without the need for words.'[15] Could the non-phonetic language of film – a language that for Woolf, crucially, 'we feel and see, but never *speak*' [emphasis mine] – replace written language?

Woolf answers this question quite simply: no. Or, at least, not yet. Woolf in 'The Cinema' carves out distinct zones for film and for literature; she argues that filmmakers should stop adapting novels like *Anna Karenina*, for instance, and focus instead on more abstract forms of representation. However, the very qualities that Woolf sees as essential to film – its ability to depict the 'passage of time and the suggestiveness of reality' – sound like descriptions of the novels – *Mrs. Dalloway* and *To the Lighthouse* – that she was in the midst of writing at the time.[16] The aspects of reality that supposedly are best captured in film have been abandoned by filmmakers and picked up by novelists like Woolf. Nothing, it appears, stands outside the 'help of words', or, at least, only the smallest possible space: 'Some residue of visual emotion which is of no use either to painter or to poet may still await the cinema' (p. 271). Film must content itself with a 'residue'.[17]

Yet if Woolf implies the primacy of writing over film here, she still flirts with a desire to find that 'secret language' mentioned above, but to do so within writing itself. For Woolf in her essay alludes, implicitly, to Vachel Lindsay's characterisation of film as composed of hieroglyphs, which efface the gap between images and writing. In criticising mainstream films, Woolf writes: 'So we spell them out in words of one syllable, written, too, in the scrawl of an illiterate schoolboy. A kiss is love. A broken cup is jealousy. A grin is happiness. Death is a hearse' (p. 270). This seems like a direct reference to Lindsay, who as noted traces the correspondences between specific images or 'hieroglyphs' in silent film and the associations they give rise to. Just as Lindsay links a sieve with 'domesticity', or a lion with 'terror', so Woolf describes how films create a language in which each image clearly but simplistically communicates an idea without the help of words: as she says, 'A kiss is love.' But Woolf even directly quotes from Lindsay without acknowledging it; she talks about how 'we spell them out in words of one syllable', and Lindsay writes that 'the Hieroglyphic chapter is in words of one syllable' (p. xxxv).

This echo indicates that Woolf had likely read Lindsay, but even if she had not, she would have been aware – from the little magazines mentioned above and her attendance at the London Film Society – about the association between cinema and hieroglyphs. Lindsay's book – as the first book-length study of film – was quite prominent, with the initial 1915 publication supplemented with a new edition in 1922, and film theory of the period was awash in hieroglyphs. But Woolf seems to critique Lindsay's conception of the new language of film – it's not some mystical Adamic language, it's just simplistic and purely conventional. Indeed, in her 1937 radio essay 'Craftsmanship' Woolf has a similar attitude towards visual languages, placing them outside of the realm of creative expression occupied by words. She says:

> We are beginning to invent another language – a language perfectly and beautifully adapted to express useful statements, a language of signs. There is one great living master of this language to whom we are all indebted, that anonymous writer – whether man, woman or disembodied spirit nobody knows – who describes hotels in the Michelin Guide. He wants to

tell us that one hotel is moderate, another good, and a third the best in the place. How does he do it? Not with words; words would at once bring into being shrubberies and billiard tables, men and women, the moon rising and the long splash of the summer sea – all good things, but all here beside the point. He sticks to signs; one gable; two gables; three gables.[18]

As in 'The Cinema', Woolf links images – 'a language of signs' – to the simplistic, one-to-one correspondence between object and idea that Lindsay describes in *The Art of the Moving Picture*, and again hieroglyphs emerge as a buried source for Woolf's understanding of this language. For in the above passage Woolf directly paraphrases a chapter about hieroglyphic and ideographic writing in H. G. Wells's *The Outline of History*. Wells writes, 'Quite kindred to such picture writing is the pictograph that one finds still in use to-day in international railway time-tables upon the continent of Europe. [. . .] Similar signs are used in the well-known Michelin guides [. . .] The quality of hotels is shown by an inn with one, two, three, or four gables.'[19] Woolf was certainly familiar with Wells's text, since Mrs Swithin reads it in *Between the Acts*, composed at the same time. Woolf, like Wells, positions the Michelin language as a new form of ancient hieroglyphs, one that, like film, is wholly successful as simple and universal communication but wholly lacking in the associative qualities that Woolf sees as essential to literature, which are the province solely of words.[20] Moreover, the medium of Woolf's lecture – a radio broadcast – itself undermines even the supposed universality of this new Michelin language. For because they lack any oral or phonetic qualities, images would of course be incapable of transmission over the radio, a medium which itself was often imagined as a vehicle for international communication. When it comes to the radio, words are not merely more expressive, but also more universal.

Visual languages for Woolf, unlike for Pound, seem not to provide an inspiration for literary expression; rather, they exclude 'the imagination, the memory'. But in 'The Cinema' she substitutes for this false visual language simply a different, more abstract one. After discussing how a random and accidental blot – a 'shadow shaped like a tadpole' – on the screen during a showing of *The Cabinet of Dr. Caligari* created in her more fear and terror than the actual film, Woolf writes, 'The monstrous quivering tadpole seemed to be fear itself, and not the statement "I am afraid"' (p. 270). Woolf here seems to subscribe to the idea of images as a potentially motivated and universal language – the blot on the screen actually is 'fear itself', without the need for words. Thus, Woolf argues, we don't need to dispense with the idea of a visual language when it comes to film, we just need a better one: 'Anger is not merely rant and rhetoric, red faces and clenched fists. It is perhaps a black line wriggling upon a white sheet' (p. 270). For Woolf, film could be the 'secret language' if we discover its abstract signs, but, essentially, that abstract language already is writing, as a 'black line wriggling upon a white sheet' seems almost to describe a letter of the alphabet. What cinema adds simply is motion – it sets the letter 'wriggling' – but, intentionally or not, the pure cinema of the future for Woolf would be more like writing, rather than less.[21] This emphasis is confirmed by the initial draft of the above line in the version of the essay published in *The Arts*: 'Anger might writhe like an infuriated worm in black zigzags across a white sheet.'[22] Again Woolf emphasises the motion of film – its 'writh[ing]' – but describes the abstract language of film as resembling the 'black zigzags' of letters. In rewriting this sentence, however, Woolf makes that connection more explicit by adding the word 'line', with its association with the lines of written text.

While Woolf rejects the visual language of film, she does so by imagining words themselves as active and alive – as 'wriggling' – qualities which are more naturally associated with film. Words, for Woolf in 'Craftsmanship', live 'much as human beings live, by ranging hither and thither, by falling in love, and mating together' (p. 205). Words are not static and dead, as T. E. Hulme would have it, but rather are more vibrant and more changeable than fixed and lifeless images. In both 'The Cinema' and 'Craftsmanship', Woolf imagines words as capable of an active embodiment that images can never attain.

Tablets Graven with Eternal Truth

This link between words and bodies – which is key to the representation of character in Woolf's fiction – achieves its clearest expression in Woolf's short story of 1929, 'The Lady in the Looking-Glass: A Reflection', in which she directly mentions hieroglyphs and presents them both as a lifeless system of rigid correspondences and as an unattainable dream of living, embodied expression.[23] Woolf's story reveals the connection between new media and human character, between words and bodies, which is implicit in discourses about film as a new medium in the 1920s. As Béla Balázs, the foremost theorist of 'physiognomic' ideas of film at the time, argues, 'But the new language of gestures [captured by film] [. . .] arises from our yearning for the *embodied human* being who has fallen silent, who has been forgotten and has become invisible' (p. 11).[24] Juxtaposing Woolf's 'The Cinema' with 'The Lady in the Looking-Glass' and *To the Lighthouse* can expose the extent to which Woolf likewise searches for a way of better representing the 'embodied human', seeking a form of language that might itself be more material.

Especially in the film journal *Close-Up*, ideas about human character – and particularly psychology and psychological development – were routinely associated with film and hieroglyphs in the years during and directly after Woolf was writing 'The Cinema' and 'The Lady in the Looking-Glass'. Indeed, as we'll see, Dorothy Richardson's novels and her columns in *Close-Up*, which include references to hieroglyphs, directly echo Woolf's understandings of the relationship between language and character. *Close-Up* included contributions from psychologists like Barbara Low and Hanns Sachs, commenting both on how films portrayed psychological states and on how spectatorship might affect childhood development. As Laura Marcus has argued, the link between hieroglyphs, film and Freudian psychoanalysis was central to H.D., one of the founders of *Close-Up*.[25] Indeed, she had been analysed by Freud himself. As H.D. writes in *Tribute to Freud*:

> The picture-writing, the hieroglyph of the dream, was the common property of the whole race; in the dream, man, as at the beginning of time, spoke a universal language, and man, meeting in the universal understanding of the unconscious or the subconscious, would forgo barriers of time and space, and man, understanding man, would save mankind.[26]

Picking up on Freud's own linkage of dreams and hieroglyphs and narrative, discussed in Chapter 1, H.D. makes hieroglyphs the 'universal language' not just of film, but of our psyches.[27] Woolf's own interest in hieroglyphs as a metaphor for human character in 'The Lady in the Looking-Glass' responds to and anticipates the widespread connection between Egyptian writing and human psychology in this period.

Woolf's 'The Lady in the Looking-Glass' begins by detailing the nameless narrator's attempts to describe Isabella Tyson, first by looking at her surroundings: the furnishings of her house, her clothing, etc. Despairing of truly understanding her, the narrator tries to make sense of her through metaphors, but rejects the inherent falsity of those comparisons. The speaker then goes on to imagine the contents of Isabella's letters in an effort to uncover the 'profounder state of her being' but, after the momentary possibility of capturing her interiority, Isabella is revealed before her mirror, stripped of the embellishments of the imagination, as 'perfectly empty', with no thoughts and no friends.[28] Framed by the image of the looking-glass – a classic metaphor for mimesis itself – Woolf's short story investigates how a writer can truly know or represent anyone else.

Yet to connect this story to 'The Cinema', that knowledge of another person in 'The Lady in the Looking-Glass' is always portrayed as fundamentally linguistic; knowledge of character derives from 'characters' or letters, and Woolf constantly harps on Isabella's letters, her correspondences. But these letters reveal only facts; we need more to reach her essence. So in analysing the contents of Isabella's room for traces of her, Woolf turns to the 'legs of chairs and tables' that are 'spindly and hieroglyphic' (p. 223). This passage looks back again to Lindsay's *The Art of the Moving Picture*, in which he describes how silent films – particularly those using stop-motion effects – express a 'yearning for personality in furniture' (p. 33). This odd linkage between film and material objects became rather commonplace in film theory, with Béla Balázs predicting that 'the magnifying glass of the film [. . .] will show you the adventures and the ultimate fate of the cigar in your unsuspecting hand and the secret – because unheeded – life of all the things that accompany you on your way and that taken together make up the events of your life' (p. 38). In Woolf's story these articles of furniture – these 'things that accompany you' – likewise promise a deeper understanding of Isabella's 'personality', one the narrator finds inaccessible. This scene thus complicates Woolf's famous critical remarks about the Edwardian novelists in 'Modern Fiction', who she argues are obsessed with the material details of their characters' lives to the point of losing sight of their interior, spiritual presences. Woolf in 'The Lady in the Looking-Glass' provides a catalogue of Isabella's material possessions, which seem to have a greater understanding of Isabella, albeit a knowledge that is incommunicable.

The reference to 'spindly and hieroglyphic' furniture ushers in the essential transformative moment of Woolf's sketch. The next paragraph after the word 'hieroglyphic' describes the intrusion into the scene of a 'large black form' that recalls the 'shadow shaped like a tadpole' in 'The Cinema'. Indeed, the first sentence describes how 'these reflections were ended violently and yet without a sound' (p. 223), recalling the soundlessness of cinema itself at the time. References to film proliferate in this paragraph, with the narrator commenting on how the world has been rendered 'entirely out of focus' (p. 223).[29] Likewise, the speaker describes how 'the looking glass began to pour over her a light that seemed to fix her; that seemed like some acid to bite off the unessential and superficial and to leave only the truth' (p. 225), rendering the decipherment of Isabella's character into a process of photographic development. Given this cinematic/photographic context, the phrase 'the picture was entirely altered' in this paragraph may serve to refer not to a static image or painting but to the new medium of the 'pictures', the movies; indeed, Woolf employs the term 'pictures' repeatedly in 'The Cinema'.

These parallels to 'The Cinema' are not surprising, since the sudden presence in 'The Lady in the Looking-Glass' of the 'unrecognizable', 'irrational' and abstract black form – which turns out to be the mailman – functions in the same way as the blot in 'The Cinema', as a spur to the formation of a new and better form of language. Just as in 'The Cinema' that blot evokes the possibility of a more direct form of communication, so in 'The Lady in the Looking-Glass' Isabella's letters are

> Invested with a new reality and significance and with a greater heaviness, too, as if it would have needed a chisel to dislodge them from the table. And whether it was fancy or not, they seemed to have become not merely a handful of casual letters but to be tablets graven with eternal truth – if one could read them, one could know everything there was to be known about Isabella, yes, and about life, too. The pages inside

those marble-looking envelopes must be cut deep and scored thick with meaning. (p. 223)

In other words, this move towards abstraction and defamiliarisation, provoked by a chance event, renders language more material. It makes these 'letters' like hieroglyphs, chiseled or graven, just as physical as the actual furniture. From just a handful of random notes, we have been given the ultimate clue to Isabella's character. Character here is not unstable or incoherent, composed merely of a bundle of impressions. It is fixed and permanent, a literal impression engraved in rock, albeit, of course, unreadable. These 'tablets graven with eternal truth' approach the 'secret language' that film promises access to – a hieroglyphic language more material and more visual than mere words – and come close to capturing the 'profounder state of being that one wanted to catch and turn to words' (p. 224). Hieroglyphs become the language of our minds; just as in *The Waves*, drawing on centuries of discourses about physiognomy, Woolf describes how 'Thus, in a few seconds, deftly, adroitly, we decipher the hieroglyphs written on other people's faces.'[30] In each case the hieroglyph is connected to the truth of character; the only difference is whether the marks are inscribed on the inside or on the surface. Like Champollion, the narrator must 'turn' the hieroglyphic marks of character into phonetic 'words', and it is this task that, for Woolf, remains always unfulfilled.

Woolf concludes her story by deconstructing the idea that there is any sacred language of character or any privileged knowledge of Isabella's essence. The moment of meaning and stability gives way to emptiness. The 'hard wall beneath' exposes that Isabella is 'perfectly empty', with no thoughts, and the letters are in fact only bills. But this seeming revelation does not undo what comes before – even if Isabella is empty, the sympathetic imagination fills those depths, as the preceding story has proven. Moreover, even this absence of meaning is imagined as linguistic and, indeed, almost as hieroglyphic. For the truth revealed at the end of the story is described as a 'hard wall', a blank space like a sheet of paper, or the movie screen in 'The Cinema', onto which meanings – characters – might be, but have not been, inscribed. We end the story with the 'tablets' mentioned earlier, but with their sacred inscriptions having been effaced. 'The Lady in the Looking-Glass' thus should not be seen as a progression towards an understanding that the work of the imagination is fundamentally false, but rather as a fluctuation between three distinct epistemologies. Firstly, that Isabella's everyday activities – her letters and her furniture – can encapsulate her character; secondly, that imagination – and, particularly, the writing imagination – can reveal the hieroglyphic 'sacred tablets' that contain the secret of Isabella's essence; and thirdly, that there is no depth to be revealed, that Isabella's life and character are empty and meaningless. Such a fluctuation, albeit a slightly simpler one, also occurs in

'The Cinema', in the opposition between the more perfect abstract language and the current debased and quotidian cinematic language.

Of course, these multiple possibilities for interpretation are the very same as the varying ways in which hieroglyphs themselves were interpreted at the time. Hieroglyphs and ideograms, as we've seen, can be a motivated language that provides a universal and essential relationship to the truth of things; they can be a sacred, unreadable and autotelic language that holds its true meanings secret; and they can be a phonetic language that is ultimately similar to contemporary alphabetical languages. We get the same possibilities as in Woolf's treatment of Isabella Tyson – total meaning, no meaning or a kind of everyday meaning. Woolf's references to hieroglyphs thus are no coincidence, since she conceives of literary character according to the same logics with which hieroglyphs had been read and misread for centuries in the West.

Woolf's association here between hieroglyphs and the truth of character – with the human essence inscribed on 'tablets' or 'walls' – transforms our understanding of Woolf's 'impressionist' technique and her conception of human perception more generally. For Woolf, who famously wrote that 'the mind receives a myriad impressions – trivial, fantastic, evanescent, or engraved with the sharpness of steel', not only is our inmost script composed of a graven language, but our perceptions are always inscriptions.[31] The world writes itself upon the tablets of our minds in a language akin to hieroglyphs. Indeed, Woolf's references to the word 'impression' in her works often link the process of vision to that of writing, as the meaning of impression itself implies. James Ramsay describes 'the infinite series of impressions which time had laid down, leaf upon leaf, fold upon fold softly, incessantly upon his brain', with the words 'leaf' and 'fold' here tying those visual impressions to the pages of a book.[32] Likewise, in *Night and Day*, Woolf writes: 'She hastily recalled her first view of him, in the little room where the relics were kept, and ran a bar through half her impressions, as one cancels a badly written sentence, having found the right one.'[33] The impression of some outer reality or some other person is compared, implicitly or explicitly, to the action of a pen on paper. The mind for Woolf seems to be imagined as a text – a blank page, an undeveloped negative – upon which the language of the world is written.

As Bernard says in *The Waves*:

> This bare visual impression is unattached to any line of reason, it springs up as one might see the fin of a porpoise on the horizon. Visual impressions often communicate thus briefly statements that we shall in time to come uncover and coax into words. I note under F., therefore, 'Fin in a waste of waters.' I, who am perpetually making notes in the margin of my mind for some final statement, make this mark, waiting for some winter's evening. (p. 189)

On first glance this passage seems a contradiction; the visual impression comes before language, and only in retrospect can it be translated into words, just as in Proust the trace left in the past can only be 'uncovered' and made sense of with the passage of time.[34] Such a view corresponds with the comment that Woolf makes in a letter to Vita Sackville-West in the month leading up to her composition of 'The Cinema':

> Now this is very profound, what rhythm is, and goes far deeper than words. A sight, an emotion, creates this wave in the mind, long before it makes words to fit it; and in writing (such is my present belief) one has to recapture this, and set this working (which has nothing apparently to do with words) and then, as it breaks and tumbles in the mind, it makes words to fit it.[35]

As in 'The Cinema', Woolf invokes the idea of rhythm, but also seems to believe in something beyond words, or at least before words. Woolf, however, far more frequently refuses to see anything as prior to language. In the passage from *The Waves* above, for instance, the 'bare visual impression', while seemingly 'unattached to any line of reason', still communicates itself as a 'statement' in the form of language. And, indeed, the impression seems indistinguishable from the written line 'Fin in a waste of waters', since it is that line, described as 'this mark', which is the source for the 'final statement' that, in the fullness of time, Bernard hopes to make. While the impression is subject to chance and cannot be anticipated – much like involuntary memory in Proust – it exists from the very beginning as language, but as a visual language that the writer, like Champollion, must coax into alphabetical words. Even if there is something prior to language, as in Woolf's letter, the only access to that 'wave' is to find 'words' to 'fit' it.

Woolf's interest in hieroglyphs and visual language thus complicates Jesse Matz's argument about literary Impressionism:

> Our deep inner experiences and perceptions are impressions printed obscurely by reality; it takes enormous inner scrutiny to decipher them; and our best books are those that decipher and transmit these impressions in art. 'Impression' appears here in quotes because of a pun on printing: the best books are those that reality itself prints, as if there were no interference between that printing and what we see on the page. This of course is the dream of the literary Impressionist – this production of a book which bypasses all the interference that our perceptual categories place between reality and writing. (p. 10)

The key to this blurring of the line 'between reality and writing' is the hieroglyph, for it allows visual impressions to be conceived of as writing already, albeit a different form of writing. While Matz describes impressions as printing 'in a foreign language', that language for the modernists is always specifically a hieroglyphic one (p. 11). Reality thus truly can write itself upon the minds of its perceivers, and that writing, rendered legible by the author, can become the text of a novel. This is not to say that modernist writers like Woolf truly believed that they were writing in the language of the world, but that hieroglyphs allowed a way of imagining the breakdown of the gap between nature and language. By imagining hieroglyphs as hybrid – combining vision, language and sound – rather than as motivated signs, Woolf was able to imagine the world, or our perceptions of it, as already linguistic, and our written alphabetical language as akin to the hieroglyphic language of the world. The 'interference [. . .] between reality and writing' is a problem only of translation.

Woolf thus imagines the relationship between language and visual perception according to the same logic as she imagines the interaction between writing and film. She encloses vision, encloses film, within writing. Just as visual impressions can only be made sense of when translated into alphabetical writing, so, for Woolf, film images require writing to inspire or explain them. The abstract film of the future resembles writing, consisting of black lines 'wriggling on a white sheet', and, in fact, it incorporates words: film requires 'the very slightest help from words or music to make itself intelligible'.[36] Film is not pure or independent, as Lindsay seeks to argue; it needs words.

To the Lighthouse's Black Line Wriggling

By bridging the gap between images and phonemes, hieroglyphs for Woolf become symbols for writing itself and models for the more visual and more embodied form of language that she strives for in her novels. Yet why, ultimately, would Woolf consistently invoke this dream of a better, more embodied 'secret' language? We can answer this question by noting the connections between 'The Cinema' and *To the Lighthouse*; indeed, Woolf was working on the 'Time Passes' section of the novel when she wrote her essay about film. The very title of that section recalls Woolf's notion that film can capture 'the passage of time', and the focus on the sea and 'the wave falling' in *To the Lighthouse* is echoed by the attention to waves that 'break' or 'will not wet our feet' in 'The Cinema'. As David Trotter and Laura Marcus have argued, even Woolf's more general attempt to imagine the passage of time absent human perception or presence may be partly inspired by her encounter with the 'eyeless' medium of cinema; as she describes in 'The Cinema', 'We behold them as they are when we are not there. We see life as it is when we have no part in it' (p. 268).[37] But more directly, Woolf's attempt to mark the impact of world historical events – and, in particular, the First World War – on the fluidity of time seems related to her comment in 'The Cinema' about watching old newsreels: 'Brides are emerging from the abbey – they are now mothers; ushers are ardent – they are now silent; mothers are tearful; guests are joyful; this has been won and that has been lost, and it is over and done with. The war sprung its chasm at the feet of all this innocence and ignorance' (p. 268). Like these newsreels, Woolf in *To the Lighthouse* tries to capture both the 'innocence and ignorance' of the pre-war period and the way the 'chasm' of the war – evoked specifically in 'Time Passes' – disrupts that innocence.[38]

The links between 'Time Passes' and 'The Cinema' proliferate if we read *To the Lighthouse* alongside not only Woolf's essay on film but also 'The Lady in the Looking-Glass'. For Woolf's descriptions in the 'Time Passes' section look forward to her descriptions of Isabella Tyson's rooms in that later story. In *To the Lighthouse*, Woolf writes of 'the torn letters in the waste-paper basket, the flowers, the books, all of which were now open to them' (p. 126), anticipating the focus on correspondences in 'Looking-Glass'. Just as in her later story Woolf singles out the 'legs and chairs of tables that are spindly and hieroglyphic', so in 'Time Passes' she describes

> the bare legs of tables, saucepans and china already furred, tarnished, cracked. What people had shed and left – a pair of shoes, a shooting cap, some faded skirts and coats in wardrobes – those alone kept the human shape and in the emptiness indicated how once they were filled and animated; how once hands were busy with hooks and buttons; how once the looking-glass had held a face. (p. 129)

As in 'The Lady in the Looking-Glass', Woolf is looking for a human presence in inanimate objects, 'yearning for personality in furniture', as Lindsay would say, and the thematic link between story and novel is confirmed by the invocation of the looking-glass here as well. By acknowledging the invocation of hieroglyphs and the link to 'The Cinema' in Woolf's later story, we can see how *To the Lighthouse* likewise strives for a better, more tangible and more visual form of knowledge or communication.

In Woolf's novel, the act of trying to decipher physical objects is, as in 'The Lady in the Looking-Glass', linked to language itself. Woolf describes 'the gloom of cathedral caves where gold letters on marble pages describe death in battle and how bones bleach and burn far away in Indian sands' (p. 127), invoking again a more physicalised form of language which, while not linked to hieroglyphs per se, likewise evokes an Orientalist exoticism. These notions of a more tangible, physical language are amplified in an earlier passage from *To the Lighthouse* that Woolf directly re-writes into the description of the 'tablets graven with eternal truth' in 'The Lady in the Looking-Glass'. Attempting to describe Mrs Ramsay, Lily

> imagined how in the chambers of the mind and heart of the woman who was, physically, touching her, were stood, like the treasures in the

tombs of kings, tablets bearing sacred inscriptions, which if one could spell them out, would teach one everything, but they would never be offered openly, never made public. What art was there, known to love or cunning, by which one pressed through into those secret chambers? What device for becoming, like waters poured into one jar, inextricably the same, one with the object one adored? Could the body achieve, or the mind, subtly mingling in the intricate passages of the brain? or the heart? Could loving, as people called it, make her and Mrs. Ramsay one? for it was not knowledge but unity that she desired, not inscriptions on tablets, nothing that could be written in any language known to men, but intimacy itself, which is knowledge, she had thought, leaning her head on Mrs. Ramsay's knee. (p. 51)

This description recalls the Mosaic tablets, particularly given the later reference to 'James the lawgiver, with the tablets of eternal wisdom laid open on his knee' (p. 168). Yet the invocation of the 'tombs of kings' makes the connection to Egypt even more explicit here than in 'The Lady in the Looking-Glass', with the locus of character again imagined as an interior 'chamber' or room containing sacred tablets. Furthermore, the word 'spell' links this passage to the multiple meanings of hieroglyphs outlined there. For 'spell', in the form of a magical spell, evokes the mystic, sacred, non-'public' meanings of hieroglyphs expressed in Melville, Carlyle and Emerson, while simultaneously expressing an awareness of the physical form of text – 'To read (a book, etc.) letter by letter' – and the vocal utterances that usually accompany it: 'to discourse or preach' or 'to enunciate or write letter by letter'. 'Spell' encompasses mystical, visual and phonetic meanings.

Woolf here though seems to reject these 'sacred tablets', which, as 'a language known to men' – and later specifically to James – are inadequate compared to the knowledge found through 'intimacy itself'. Yet in this passage Woolf is still looking for a specifically aesthetic form of communion – an 'art' or 'device' – that will allow her access to the interiority of another character. This, of course, is the central question of so much of Woolf's fiction, 'The Lady in the Looking-Glass' most notably: with what language or with what form of knowledge can the writer 'mingle' and become 'one with the object'? Woolf does not merely acknowledge the fundamental inscrutability of human character, embodied by Mrs Ramsay's 'wedge-shaped core of darkness, something invisible to others' (pp. 62–3). Rather in *To the Lighthouse* she systemically engages in a quest for different forms of language – for a 'secret language' as in 'The Cinema' – that would better express the inner complexities of her characters.[39] Just as Lily Briscoe searches for an abstracted means of expression in her painting – which transforms Mrs Ramsay to a purple triangle – so Woolf searches for a language that will be more physical and more embodied and thus could capture the 'sacred tablets' of Mrs Ramsay's identity.

Woolf specifically casts alphabetical languages – the very form of language that hieroglyphs were seen as different from – as the potentially oppressive language of men. It is no coincidence that Mr Ramsay's knowledge is expressed alphabetically, as the attempt to move from Q to R. Like Wittgenstein, he imagines the world according to a precise, abstracted, logical system. For Mr Ramsay there is a profound disconnect between the world of objects – the world of vision – and the world of words:

> He stopped to light his pipe, looked once at his wife and son in the window, and as one raises one's eyes from a page in an express train and sees a farm, a tree, a cluster of cottages as an illustration, a confirmation of something on the printed page, to which one returns, fortified, and satisfied. (p. 33)

The material world is only 'illustration' or 'confirmation' of the 'printed page', but Woolf longs for a way of incorporating the former into the later. Rather than the universal abstractions of Mr Ramsay, Woolf, as in 'The Lady in the Looking-Glass', imagines how language and knowledge could be conceived of as more material than a disembodied table: as imparted through physical intimacy or through hieroglyphs graven in rocks and tablets. Woolf strives not to be like the Mr Ramsays of the world, 'the steady goers of superhuman strength who, plodding and persevering, repeat the whole alphabet in order, twenty-six letters in all, from start to finish', but, in aspiring towards a better language, to be 'the gifted, the inspired who, miraculously, lump all the letters together in one flash – the way of genius' (p. 34).[40] These new languages might answer Lily's question: 'How could one express in words these emotions of the body?' (p. 178). They might come close to the new 'more primitive, more sensual' language that the ill aspire towards in Woolf's contemporaneous essay 'On Being Ill'. That language again is connected to the hieroglyph, with Woolf lamenting how habit prevents us from 'turning the old beggar's hieroglyphic of misery into volumes of sordid suffering'.[41] Like Djuna Barnes's 'hieroglyphics of sleep and pain', the hieroglyph is associated with the body and with narrative; it needs to be turned into 'volumes' of suffering, and, as with Lily, it is only women who are capable of that act of translation: 'Sympathy nowadays is dispensed chiefly by the laggards and failures, women for the most part.'[42] The hieroglyph serves as a more embodied, feminine alternative to the alphabetical languages 'known to men'.

Dorothy Richardson, a novelist even more deeply engaged with film than was Woolf, echoes this connection between hieroglyphs, the female body and the new medium of film. While Richardson is less engaged with theorising the representation of character than Woolf, the juxtaposition of the two reveals just how commonly the metaphor of hieroglyphs was invoked to imagine a more embodied form of writing, one figured, for both writers, as an alternative to masculine modes of communication. In her 1933 essay 'The Film Gone Male', part of the 'Continuous Performance' columns that she wrote in *Close-Up* from 1927 to 1933, Richardson seeks to align silent film with the 'essentially feminine'.[43] For Richardson, while men are associated with speech – and thus with the new sound film that she dislikes – women 'are humanity's silent half, without much faith in speech as a medium of communication' (p. 206). Indeed, such a view was not uncommon, with Tim Armstrong describing the coming of sound as implying 'a "masculinization" in the commentaries which surround it; a regulation of the image and of desire and a return of voice and discursive power to a dominant ideology'.[44]

Moreover, while Richardson characterises the memory of men as a 'straight-line thinkers memory, as a mere glance over the shoulder along a past seen as a progression from the near end of which mankind goes forward', the truer memory of women, in Richardson's essay, is 'distinct from a mere backward glance' and has 'neither speech nor language' (pp. 205, 206). Richardson thus seems to be setting out an opposition similar to the kind expressed by Woolf in the passage about 'tablets bearing sacred inscriptions' quoted above. There, the language known to men, associated with Mr Ramsay's linear and alphabetical forms of knowledge, is in opposition to a more feminine, more embodied kind of knowledge, linked with ancient written inscriptions. Likewise, in 'The Film Gone Male', Richardson imagines male knowledge as linear – 'a straight-line thinker' – and as associated with speech as opposed to silence, unlike the female form of expression embodied by silent film with a power 'to evoke, suggest, reflect, express [. . .] something of the changeless being at the heart of all becoming' (p. 206). As in Woolf, Richardson contrasts the evocative silence of female expression with linear masculine writing.

In Richardson's novel *Dawn's Left Hand* – the tenth volume of *Pilgrimage* – published in 1931 and written during the period of her writings for *Close-Up*, Richardson aligns these ideas about masculine and feminine expression directly with the metaphor of hieroglyphics. She shows how her 'essentially feminine' form of knowledge, rather than being 'neither speech nor language', is an embodied, hybrid form between speech and writing quite similar to the 'tablets bearing sacred inscriptions' of Woolf's *To the Lighthouse*. At a key moment in *Dawn's Left Hand*, Miriam receives a letter from her new friend Amabel, with whom she's become briefly infatuated. Miriam reads the message, describing the letters as a 'strange pattern of curves and straight strokes rapidly set down. Each separately. Gaps not only between each letter but also between the straight and curved part of a single letter'.[45] Describing each character according to its visual appearance rather than its semantic meaning, Miriam notes how 'each was expressive, before its meaning appeared. Each letter carelessly dashed down, under pressure of feeling, was a picture, framed in the surrounding space' (p. 215). Rather than stress the alphabetical nature of each letter, Miriam looks past its grammatical meaning and calls attention to its visual form, its appearance as 'picture'. Yet Miriam, and Richardson, do not quite fall victim to the Cratylic fallacy; rather, like Woolf, they stress the hybrid nature of these alphabetical letters. While they have a visual form, they also possess a phonetic meaning: 'When meanings were discovered they sounded; as if spoken' (p. 215). Amabel's letters are simultaneously visual and oral, and it is this hybrid quality – exactly what Woolf points to in her treatment of film and of writing – that Miriam finds so entrancing: 'It was this strange, direct, as if spoken communication, punctuated only by dashes sloped at various angles like the sharp, forcible uprights of the script, and seeming to be the pauses of a voice in speech, that was making the reading of this letter so new an experience' (p. 215). Indeed, in her film writing Richardson likewise stresses the interdependence of the visual and textual; in discussing intertitles in silent film, she writes

> the artist can no more eliminate the caption than he can eliminate himself. Art and literature, Siamese twins making their first curtsey to the public in a script that was a series of pictures, have never yet been separated. In its uppermost abstraction art is still a word about life and literature never ceases to be pictorial.[46]

Rather than seeking to privilege the image over text, Richardson like Woolf expresses their inseparability.

The embodiment of these letters is what is so new and enlivening for Miriam: 'These written words were alive in a way no others she had met had been alive' (p. 215). And just as in Woolf the invocation of a more graven or pictorial form of expression opens the possibility of a more material and feminine form of communication, Miriam proceeds to explain how:

> Instead of calling her attention to the way the pen was held, to the many expressivenesses of a given handwriting, apart from what it was being used to express, instead of bringing as did the majority of letters, especially those written by men, a picture of the writer seated and thoughtfully using a medium of communication, recognizing its limitations and remaining docile with them [. . .] it called her directly to the girl herself, making her, and not the letter, the medium of expression. Each word, each letter, was Amabel, was one of the many poses of her body. (p. 215)

This passage could almost function as a direct gloss on the excerpt from *To the Lighthouse* about the 'tablets bearing sacred inscriptions'. Richardson carefully distinguishes this letter from those 'written by men', in which the letter is merely a 'medium of communication'. In opposition to that 'medium of communication' – and recall Richardson's note that women reject 'speech as a medium of communication' in 'The Film Gone Male' – Richardson's ideal written language would not merely communicate, but would bring the female bodies of writer and recipient together. The letter thus fulfils Lily's desire for a 'device for becoming [. . .] one with the object one adored', a moment which looks forward to Richardson's invocation of the 'changeless being at the heart of all becoming' in her later film essay. Like Lily longing for Mrs Ramsay rather than a language known to men, so Miriam gets, through this more embodied, pictorial form of language, 'the girl herself'. The passage at first resembles Cratylism, but Richardson stresses not direct meaning, but rather a gesturally embodied language, with the letters analogous to the curves of Amabel's body, rendering her the medium itself. As for Woolf, for Miriam it is 'not knowledge but unity that she desired', and this hybrid form of writing provides that united connection.

As in Woolf's writing, with its connection between Egyptian writing and a feminine language, the hieroglyph in *Dawn's Left Hand* serves as the metaphor to encapsulate this relationship between the female body and a hybrid visual/oral form of language. The one line that Miriam actually reads from the letter is, 'Isn't – E-g-y-p-t – a beautiful word?' and, after parsing the meaning of that sentence, Miriam concludes:

> Returning, from scribbling in various styles of handwriting the difficult combination, she gazed once more at the word on the page and saw that as written by the girl it was not a word at all. It was a picture, a hieroglyph, each letter lovely in itself. Beautiful, yet, and suggesting all its associations more powerfully than did the sight of the word written closely. (p. 216)

Here Richardson denies the linguistic aspects of the letter, rendering them 'pictures' whose 'beautiful' and suggestive visual aspects surpass mere semantic meanings. Yet as the previous descriptions of the letters indicate, that suggestiveness is precisely the product of a hieroglyph's hybridity – its status as picture and as word, as silence and as sound. It seems for both writers to make possible the dream of a more embodied language like the 'tablets graven with sacred inscriptions' that will make Lily and Mrs Ramsay one and the 'picture', the 'hieroglyph', that will, in Richardson's novel, provide through writing 'the girl itself'. For Richardson and for Woolf, the hieroglyph embodies the possibility of a new form of language that can better represent the female body. And for both that hieroglyphic language arises from an engagement with the new medium of film.

To return to *To the Lighthouse*, we can now see how that novel as a whole is framed by a search for this new kind of language: a hybrid mode of expression between the visual, the bodily and the written. In the first few pages Woolf juxtaposes the 'pictures from the illustrated catalogue of the Army and Navy stores' (p. 3), part of the visual language of advertising, with the more abstract images of Lily Briscoe's painting, and contrasts James's 'private code, his secret language' (p. 4) with Mr Ramsay's public and audible pronouncements of Tennyson's poetry. Language is imagined according to all of the possibilities outlined above – as communicative image, as abstract pattern, as private mystery or as spoken utterance. And by the end of the novel, Lily Briscoe's painting has come to symbolise and synthesise all of these conflicted ideas about the relationship among writing, sound and image. Like a hieroglyph, like the sacred tablets of Mrs Ramsay's character, it stands at a midpoint between image and text and provides a potentially more embodied alternative to the 'language[s] known to men'. As critics have noted, Lily's painting is described in linguistic as well as pictorial terms; in attempting to paint it, she thinks, 'Phrases came. Visions came. Beautiful pictures. Beautiful phrases' (p. 193). The painting, like a hieroglyph, is a hybrid of language and image, with the double musical meaning of 'phrases' linking the painting not only with language but with sound itself. Lily's art recalls Mrs Ramsay's synaesthetic linkage of words, sounds, vision and movement, when she thinks, in remembering a poem, of 'words, like little shaded lights, one red, one blue, one yellow, lit up in the dark of her mind [. . .] leaving their perches up there to fly across and across, or to cry out and be echoed' (p. 119).

Lily's artwork seems to fulfil Woolf's demand in 'The Cinema' for a language consisting of 'a black line wriggling on a white sheet': as Woolf famously ends her novel, 'With a sudden intensity, as if she saw it clear for a second, she drew a line there, in the centre' (p. 209). The line of Lily's painting, on some level, is the same as the 'black line' of 'The Cinema'. It is an emblem of an ultimate language that will bridge writing and image, especially given the association of the word line with the 'lines' of Carmichael's poetry. But Woolf also calls attention to the dynamism – the 'wriggling' – in Lily's painting: 'And so pausing and so flickering, she attained a dancing rhythmical movement, as if the pauses were one part of the rhythm and the strokes another, and all were related; and so, lightly and swiftly pausing, striking, she scored her canvas with brown running nervous lines' (p. 158). Like the abstract language of film, like Mrs Ramsay's words that fly like birds, Lily's art achieves a kind of movement and rhythm.[47] At the conclusion of the novel, Woolf has succeeded in finding a modern manifestation of the 'tablets graven with sacred inscriptions' in the section 'The Window'. Lily's work of art consists of linguistic 'lines', but those lines have taken on pictorial and rhythmic form. As Lily says, 'The words became symbols, wrote themselves all over the grey-green walls. If only she could put them together, she felt, write them out in some sentence, then she would have got at the truth of things' (p. 147). By transforming words to symbols, by imagining them as hieroglyphs graven on walls, Lily completes her painting, a painting that is still always imagined as hybrid, as a linguistic 'sentence' or 'scrawl' (p. 179).

If Woolf reimagines writing as akin to painting, she does so to emphasise the predominance of written text. For Lily's artwork is not only characterised as textual, it is also inspired by writing, specifically by Mrs Ramsay's letters. Exactly as in 'The Lady in the Looking-Glass', when the intrusion of the postman transforms Isabella's correspondences into hieroglyphs, letters – a linguistic form that is intimate and communicative, unlike the abstractions of Mr Ramsay's alphabet – provide the catalyst in *To the Lighthouse* for the creation of a hybrid language. Of course, letters are also more personal, connecting this new language, as in 'The Lady in the Looking-Glass', with the ability to represent the truths of character and identity.

Lily's final 'vision' that allows her to complete her painting derives from her memory of Mrs Ramsay that affects her 'almost like a work of art':

> When she thought of herself and Charles throwing ducks and drakes and of the whole scene on the beach, it seemed to depend somehow upon Mrs. Ramsay sitting under the rock, with a pad on her knee, writing letters. (She wrote innumerable letters, and sometimes the wind took them and she and Charles just saved a page from the sea.) But what a power was in the human soul! she thought. That woman sitting there writing under the rock resolved everything into simplicity. (p. 160)

Writing itself, at least in the form of letters, achieves nearly the same effect – the creation of a moment of being, a moment of vision – that Lily strives for in her painting and that Woolf strives for in her novel. In opposition to the 'language known to men' of Mr Ramsay's letters – Q, R, etc. – Woolf posits Mrs Ramsay's more feminine letters: language that unites abstraction and intimacy and communicates directly and personally. As such, it is no coincidence that the vision of a hieroglyph-like language in *Dawn's Left Hand* is also provided through Amabel's letter. Unlike Charles Tansley and Mr Ramsay, who read books and rarely write letters – and Charles is carrying a book in the scene described above – Mrs Ramsay's letters provide for Lily a model for a more embodied and unitary form of language. And just as in 'The Cinema' and 'The Lady in the Looking-Glass', this new language is also inspired by the intrusion of a shadow; while painting towards the end of the novel, Lily notes 'an odd-shaped triangular shadow over the step' (p. 201), a chance encounter that Lily finds 'interesting' and 'useful' and which spurs the 'mood' that will lead to the completion of her artwork. Woolf thus both imagines painting as akin to writing in the final descriptions of Lily's artwork and also portrays that artwork as ultimately 'depend'ing on Mrs Ramsay's writing for inspiration, just as Lily's final act of creation is overseen by the poet Carmichael. For Woolf, images require writing, but writing already consists of images.

Given the importance of Woolf's understandings of film and its hieroglyphs to her novel, we can thus speculate on the meaning of its central image: the lighthouse. For as it returns again and again throughout the novel, playing across the interior and exterior landscapes, it begins more and more to resemble the cinematic apparatus itself, casting its intermittent beam of light across surfaces. As Woolf describes, 'In the evening one looked up and saw the eye opening and shutting and the light seemed to reach them' (p. 186), recalling the constant alternation of light and shadow in the act of projection. And the focus on the 'eye' of the lighthouse emphasises again the links between the world and the body, and between film and perception, that Woolf builds into her novel. While we should not diminish the multiple symbolic significances of the radically overdetermined lighthouse, on some level it acknowledges just how deeply Woolf's novel is haunted by her concerns with the relationship between film and writing in the period.

Coda: *Mrs. Dalloway*'s Skywriting

Tracing these connections among film, hieroglyphs and the search for a new form of language in Woolf's fiction can lead to a new understanding of the famous episode with the skywriting airplane in *Mrs. Dalloway*. The letters traced by the airplane in the sky recall the tradition, familiar from Emerson and Carlyle, of looking for the celestial hieroglyphs of God's creation. This cosmic language, now reduced to the realm of advertising, points to the absence of religion in the modern world but the persistence of religious epistemologies, as characters search for meaningful clues in the fabric of nature. From Mrs Coates to Mrs Bletchley, they attempt to find the 'K-E-Y' to meaning in the illegible and fading letters.[48] Like Melville before her, Woolf makes use of these traditions to demonstrate the fundamental indecipherability of the world, which yet seems to require a futile task of interpretation on the part of its inhabitants. Woolf estranges the words of the advertisement – a seemingly interpretatively simple medium, one which, like film, was seen as potentially universal – and renders them just as difficult to decipher as Melville's faces and hieroglyphs. This ambiguity is fundamentally generative, giving rise to the myriad viewpoints and narratives created by the observers throughout London, which range from the mundane to the highly symbolic. Again, Woolf imagines a more embodied and visual form of language – still consisting of alphabetical letters, but now written in smoke and inscribed onto the natural world – while simultaneously demonstrating how even this language requires a process of translation through narrative.

Yet Woolf's characterisation of the letters produced by the airplane goes further, for she insistently points to the hybrid nature of these letters, how they exist simultaneously as images, sounds and elements in language. Woolf writes:

The aeroplane turned and raced and swooped exactly where it liked, swiftly, freely, like a skater –

'That's an E,' said Mrs. Bletchley –

or a dancer –

'It's toffee,' murmured Mr. Bowley. (p. 21)

By interspersing the comments about the letters with the description of the airplane, Woolf transforms the 'E' into a physical object: 'That's an E' [. . .] or a dancer.' Woolf gives to letters an active rhythm and a physical form, simultaneously evoking the history of associations between hieroglyphs and dance and gesture. This episode is not merely a commentary on the human need for interpretation or revelation, but also a statement about the visual and physical nature of language itself. It further links Woolf's concern with the hybridity of language with the question of how best to represent character, as the equation of an 'E' with a dancer literalises the connection between letters and the human body.

The comment 'It's toffee' at the end of this exchange adds another element to Woolf's hybrid conception of language, since the last syllable of toffee echoes the sound of the letter 'E', just as later Woolf writes, '"K . . . R . . ." said the nursemaid, and Septimus heard her say "Kay Arr' close to his ear' (p. 22). By translating 'K . . . R . . .' into 'Kay Arr', Woolf turns each letter into its associated sound, pointing to the phonetic meaning inherent in each character. Rather than passing invisibly over the signs of language, Woolf's novel forces the reader to take notice of the auditory qualities of letters. At the same moment, Woolf emphasises the visual aspects of words, since the only way in which Woolf can mimic the sound of the letters is through written text, by spelling out 'K' and 'R' and making them into new words: 'Kay Arr'. By pronouncing the sound of each letter, the reader must also notice its visual form. Woolf thus demonstrates how words and letters are both written and spoken, and how this hybrid language – visual, aural, grammatical – gives rise to myriad associations. As the visual form of 'E' may summon up a 'dancer' while its vocal sound evokes 'Toffee', so the phoneme 'K' can recall the woman's name 'Kay'. Again, language becomes embodied – K becomes Kay – revealing the profound link between Woolf's ideas about written words and her desire to represent human character and bodily forms (and the choice of a female name again connects this embodiment with women). What Dr Bradshaw says of Septimus is true of all the readers of Woolf's fiction: 'He was attaching meanings to words of a symbolical kind' (p. 96).

Woolf thus seeks to imagine a new hybrid form of language and representation. As she goes on to do in 'The Cinema', with its linkage between the movement of film and the visual form of text, she insists on the pictorial and embodied nature of written words. The cinema was so fascinating and disturbing to Woolf precisely because it seemed to represent this possibility of a more embodied form of language that she was already seeking to imagine in her fiction. And hieroglyphs, in 'The Cinema', in 'The Lady in the Looking-Glass' and elsewhere, serve to symbolise the visual and oral characteristics of written words as they are, and to encapsulate the possibility of a better form of expression, perhaps even an alternative to the 'language[s] known to men'. They come to embody in Woolf's fiction the unknowable language of our perceptions and our characters, which the writer must try to translate into alphabetical words, like Champollion deciphering the Rosetta Stone. If written words can be imagined as more embodied, as more like hieroglyphs, then they can serve to represent the hidden graven writing of our hearts. These everyday words are capable of subsuming the qualities of film and phonography. New media do not supplant writing in Woolf's work; they *are* writing. While every image requires a caption, while every film requires an intertitle to reveal its full meaning, only writing itself – by its hybrid nature – stands as the ultimate means, in Woolf's post-Babelic world, of communication and expression.

NOTES

1. Woolf, 'The Cinema', *Collected Essays, Vol. 2*, pp. 270–2.
2. Woolf, 'The Lady in the Looking-Glass', *Complete Shorter Fiction*, p. 223; *The Waves*, p. 175; *On Being Ill*, p. 9.
3. Woolf, *To the Lighthouse*, p. 51.
4. These meanings would have been particularly apparent to Woolf, given her work at typesetting for the Hogarth Press.
5. For more discussion of *Close-Up* and of Woolf's interest in film, see *Close Up, 1927–33: Cinema and Modernism*, ed. by James Donald, Anne Friedberg and Laura Marcus; Leslie Kathleen Hankins, '"Across the Screen of My Brain": Virginia Woolf's "the Cinema" and Film Forums of the Twenties', in *The Multiple Muses of Virginia Woolf*, ed. by Diane F. Gillespie, pp. 148–79; Maggie Humm, *Modernist Women and Visual Cultures*; Paul Tiessen, pp. 75–83.
6. As Leslie Kathleen Hankins writes about *Vogue* and 'The Cinema': 'Though Woolf's essay was not finally published there, Vogue remains a fascinating companion piece for her essay; its cinema articles from 1924–1926 shaped her discussion of film.' Hankins, 'Virginia Woolf and Film,' in *The Edinburgh Companion to Virginia Woolf and the Arts*, p. 356.
7. *Vogue* 66: 11 (December 1925), p. 146.
8. Shaw, pp. 178–9.
9. de Beaumont, p. 73.
10. *The Adelphi* 1 (March 1924), p. 949.
11. *The Adelphi* 1 (February 1924), p. 857.
12. Laura Marcus, '"Hieroglyphics in motion": representing ancient Egypt and the Middle East in film theory and criticism of the silent period', in *The Ancient World in Silent Cinema*, ed. by Pantelis Michelakis and Maria Wyke, pp. 74–90.
13. Hankins, 'Across the Screen of my Brain'; Trotter, 'Virginia Woolf and Cinema', pp. 13–26.
14. Clive Bell, pp. 39–40; Barry, p. 928.
15. Balázs, p. 10.
16. Woolf, *Collected Essays*, p. 269.

17. In the first published version of 'The Cinema', published in *The Arts* in June 1926, Woolf is a bit more definitive: 'But if so much of our thinking and feeling is connected with seeing there must be some residue of visual emotion not seized by artist or painter-poet which may await the cinema.' In revising this line, however, Woolf turns from 'must' to 'may', diminishing the possibilities for cinema. However, at the same time, Woolf adds the central line, 'Is there, we ask, some secret language which we feel and see, but never speak, and, if so, could this be made visible to the eye?' which is not present in the initial version. Even as she seems to question whether there is a 'residue of visual emotion', she continues to ponder the existence of a 'secret language' for film. Virginia Woolf, 'The Cinema', *The Arts*, p. 316.
18. Virginia Woolf, *The Death of the Moth*, p. 200.
19. Wells, p. 169.
20. The same goes for the universal language of logic, which, as Megan Quigley points out, Woolf would have been familiar with because of her acquaintance with Bertrand Russell and G. E. Moore. As Quigley writes, contrasting Woolf's view in 'Craftsmanship' with Russell's logic, 'The vagueness of language is its strength; it refuses to fix concepts the way Russell's ideal language seeks to do.' Quigley even conjectures that the reference to 'Passing Russell Square' in 'Craftsmanship' may be a buried allusion to Bertrand Russell (pp. 66, 75).
21. My argument thus differs from that of Laura Marcus, who notes in passing that 'the demand here is for a new mode of symbolization, one not dependent on literature but capable of conveying the emotions in visual terms, and in the form, it is implied, of hieroglyphics: that mode of representation [. . .] which had become [. . .] the most appropriate way of conceiving of the new "language" of film' (p. 117). Woolf, I contend, always sees film as 'dependent' on literature.
22. Woolf, 'The Cinema', *The Arts*, p. 315.
23. The few articles on this story, while considering the question of how the 'self can be inscribed and known', focus largely on Woolf's treatment of time, boredom, or mirrors. See Crangle, p. 227; Howard, pp. 44–54; Chapman, pp. 331–7; Seeley, pp. 89–116.
24. For more on the links between early film and physiognomy, see Gunning, pp. 1–29.
25. 'The broader context for H.D.'s conceptualizations of film, is, undoubtedly, the concept and dream of a "universal language" which began to flourish in the seventeenth century, was revived in the latter part of the nineteenth century, and subsequently became closely linked with the image of (silent) film as a form of hieroglyphics, a thinking in pictures rather than words.' Laura Marcus, 'The Contribution of H.D.: Introduction', in Donald, Friedberg and Marcus, p. 102.
26. H.D. [Hilda Doolittle], *Tribute to Freud*, p. 108.
27. For more on H.D.'s deep engagement with Egyptology, see Bryant and Eaverly, pp. 435–54.
28. Woolf, *Complete Shorter Fiction*, pp. 224, 225.
29. In the manuscript draft, the speaker laments that she cannot 'get them [the letters] in to focus'. Woolf, 'The lady in the looking-glass. Typescript with the author's ms. corrections. 1929 May 28'.
30. Woolf, *The Waves*, p. 175.
31. Woolf, 'Modern Fiction', *The Common Reader*, p. 154.
32. Woolf, *Lighthouse*, p. 169.
33. Woolf, *Night and Day*, p. 96. Or, also from *Night and Day*, 'Katharine waited as though for him to receive a full impression, and then she said: "This is his writing-table. He used this pen," and she lifted a quill pen and laid it down again' (p. 15).
34. As Jesse Matz has written in *Literary Impressionism and Modernist Aesthetics*, 'The conflicting demands of receptivity and judgment become functions of experi-

ence and retrospection: a former self first receives an impression, and a later self receives its later counterpart and does the work of retrospective analysis' (pp. 8–9).
35. Woolf, *Letters of Virginia Woolf, Vol. 3: 1923–1928*, p. 247.
36. Woolf, *Collected Essays*, p. 271.
37. See Trotter, *Cinema and Modernism*, pp.168–75; Marcus, *The Tenth Muse*, pp. 1–17.
38. Woolf's manuscripts of 'The Cinema' reveal even more connections to 'Time Passes'. Woolf in her early drafts focuses on time-lapse films that she likely saw at the London Film Society, describing how 'The chrysalis split and let forth a death-head moth with crumbled wings', and we can see 'Time Passes' itself as a kind of time-lapse film, speeding past daily incident to focus on the larger scale of growth and decay. See Woolf, 'Class Distinctions. Holograph fragment'.
39. As Gayatri Spivak argues, 'The project to catch the essence of Mrs. Ramsay is articulated in terms of finding an adequate language', and the language of 'Lily's desired "discourse"' is 'a script, half design, half word, combining words and picturing' (pp. 310, 321).
40. Woolf thus links Mr Ramsay to the alphabet not simply, as Makiko Minow-Pinkey argues in *Virginia Woolf and the Problem of the Subject*, to show 'the linearity of Ramsay's thought' or to contrast 'the rigorous propositional discourse of the philosopher [. . .] with the symbolic language of art' (pp. 93, 85).
41. Woolf, *On Being Ill*, pp. 7, 9.
42. Barnes, p. 63; Woolf, *On Being Ill*, p. 10. Like Lily, in 'On Being Ill' Woolf laments that 'Of all this daily drama of the body there is no record', and declares 'Let a sufferer try to describe a pain in his head to a doctor and language at once runs dry [. . .] He is forced to coin words himself [. . .] (as perhaps the people of Babel did in the beginning)' (p. 5).
43. Richardson, 'Continuous Performance: The Film Gone Male', in Donald, Friedberg and Marcus, p. 206.
44. Armstrong, p. 247.
45. Richardson, *Pilgrimage 4*, p. 214.
46. Richardson, 'Continuous Performance III: Captions', in Donald, Friedberg and Marcus, p. 165.
47. As Patricia Laurence argues, this 'line' may also be influenced by Woolf's contact with Chinese calligraphy, which Roger Fry stressed was also characterised by its 'rhythm': for him, Chinese painting 'never loses the evidence of the linear rhythm as the main method of expression. [. . .] A painting was always conceived as the visible record of a rhythmic gesture.' The line between writing and painting is thus blurred: 'Painting is an extension, philosophically and pragmatically, of calligraphy or writing' (p. 370).
48. Woolf, *Mrs. Dalloway*, p. 20.

3

SOUND ENCLOSURES

When Orson Welles went to Hollywood after being given a contract by RKO Pictures in 1939, he wanted his first project to be an adaptation of *Heart of Darkness*. Welles would have played Kurtz, but the camera itself would have served as the film's Marlow, with the movie consisting entirely of point-of-view shots. Welles eventually abandoned the project, turning to *Citizen Kane*, but despite his protestations to the contrary he never wholly gave up on his attempt to adapt Conrad's novella.[1] *Citizen Kane* can be seen, if not as a straight adaptation of *Heart of Darkness*, then as a grafting of its thematic and formal concerns onto the story of Charles Foster Kane.[2] Kane emerges as the double of Kurtz, falling from idealism to corruption, with the ultimate clue to his identity remaining forever inaccessible.[3]

On a larger level, however, the link between Welles and Conrad reveals how Welles takes from Conrad's works not only the structuring use of frame narratives and multiple perspectives, but also Conrad's concern with the relationship among speech, writing and image, a relationship being transformed in the late nineteenth and early twentieth centuries by Welles's own new medium of cinema and new technologies of sound recording. The increasingly common understandings of these new media as hieroglyphic forms of inscription that blurred the line among the oral, the visual and the lexical shaped the ways in which Welles, influenced by Conrad, conceived of language and of cinema. As we have seen in the discussion of Vachel Lindsay's and Sergei Eisenstein's film theories in Chapter 1, these technologies threatened to supplant the medium of writing, turning the natural phenomena of sound and images into grooves inscribed in wax or shadows on a screen, forms of 'natural' or motivated writing that were frequently seen as akin to Egyptian hieroglyphics.[4] And yet phonography and cinema demonstrated simultaneously the fundamental hybridity of all media, with sounds rendered into pictorial or written form through the process of recording and with the images of film combined with spoken words or written intertitles.

Conrad was aware of phonographic technologies, as his unnerved reaction to his first exposure to the 'waves' of a phonograph in an 1898 letter, discussed later, makes clear.[5] Given that awareness of and the larger concern with the relationship between oral and written discourse in his work, we can see how Conrad's novels and Welles's films after them emerge out of the widespread debates about the connection between writing and speech spurred by the rise of new media. This chapter departs slightly from the focus of the book so far to take a more expansive view of the relationship between media in the modernist period. Having demonstrated how allusions to Egyptian hieroglyphs are used to establish the hybrid nature of film and of writing, this chapter explores how those views of media shape narrative structure. As we've seen in Woolf, an emphasis on the hybridity of writing and film leads to a focus on the processes of decipherment and translation, on how the hieroglyphs of the world might be rendered readable. Woolf strives to incorporate visual media within writing by stressing the linguistic nature of visual perception and of human identity. Welles and Conrad similarly attempt in their works to incorporate the qualities of other media, but they do so through their adoption of innovative narrative forms. Conrad and Welles use frame narratives, detective plots and metaphorical inquests to show how their own medium of written words or film can uniquely 'enclose' and transmit the many phonetic or pictorial elements of language and the world. For Conrad and Welles, their respective media are already inherently hybrid, and their plot structures consistently work to emphasise that hybridity.

References to hieroglyphs recur frequently in early descriptions of sound recording technologies. But rather than starting from specific allusions to Egyptian writing in their works, this chapter traces more broadly Conrad's and Welles's engagement with these discourses about the hieroglyphic interrelation of images and oral and written discourse in all media forms. The challenge of new media contributes not just, as in Woolf, to the development of new epistemologies of literary character, but also to the deployment of new narrative methods. In contrast to the dominant reading of Conrad by Edward Said, Fredric Jameson and others, I argue that Conrad's novels do not privilege oral storytelling over the written word. Rather than simply emulating spoken words, Conrad repeatedly calls attention to how those spoken words are enclosed within a written text, enclosed within the pages of a printed book.

Thus the opening narrator of *Heart of Darkness* or the third person narration that begins *Lord Jim* do not represent old-fashioned alternatives to the more modernist experimentation of the rest of the novels, but rather are precisely what makes these novels experimental, foregrounding the 'power of the written word', as Conrad puts it in his 'Preface' to *The Nigger of the 'Narcissus'*.[6] For Conrad, new technologies of sound recording reveal how writing needs to be conceived of as a medium among others, as an older but still powerful form of technology with its own unique ability to represent both sound and image.

While Conrad privileges writing for its ability to incorporate speech, in *Citizen Kane* Orson Welles, building on the legacy of *Heart of Darkness*, simultaneously asserts and questions film's power to enclose and represent text. Welles's view of cinema is thus symbolised by the hieroglyphic equation that he wanted to present to the viewer at the opening of his planned adaptation of *Heart of Darkness* as a way of explaining its point-of-view form: 👁 = i.[7] For the rest of the film, Welles's equation sought to convey, the camera would serve as Marlow's eyes. Through the medium of cinema, Welles flirts with the possibility of collapsing the distinction between language and vision, between 👁 and i, but that equation in his films is always deeply problematic. Just as Conrad in his novels suggests that the written word can 'enclose' the spoken, so Welles in his proposed adaptation of *Heart of Darkness*, as in *Citizen Kane*, demonstrates how through its hybrid language the medium of cinema can uniquely incorporate sound, vision and text. Like Woolf, who argues that film is only a limited form of writing, Conrad and Welles seek to reveal through the narrative strategies of their works how their own medium can enclose its medial rivals.

But enclosure is not the same as equivalence. Welles and Conrad do not assert that their own medium provides, like phonography promised, a purer, more direct form of inscription. While Conrad and Welles obsessively seek to represent visual and auditory signs – 'Rosebud' in *Citizen Kane* or 'The horror! The horror!' in *Heart of Darkness* – they reject the idea that words can be translated perfectly from sound or image into writing, or, more deeply, from signs into fixed meanings. The medium of cinema can never fully capture Kane's character, just as in *Heart of Darkness* Conrad can render Marlow's and Kurtz's speech into writing but never fully access Kurtz's hollow core.[8] Like Virginia Woolf, both Conrad and Welles emphasise the hybrid nature of their own medium while simultaneously casting doubt on whether any medium can fully translate the hidden language of human character. Even in the hieroglyphic medium of cinema, the perfect phonographic or photographic mapping of the aural and the visual onto the lexical is, for Welles, impossible. In *Citizen Kane* we are left with the emblem 'Rosebud' perpetually divided among pictorial, lexical and auditory meanings. Both Welles and Conrad turn to narrative forms that emphasise the hybrid communicative potential of their own medium, but simultaneously leave their audience and readers to interpret and decipher for themselves the hieroglyphic sights and sounds of the world and human character.

Edison and Sound Writing

Writers, inventors and film theorists in the early twentieth century – Woolf, Lindsay and Eisenstein among them – were obsessed, as we have seen, with the relationship between writing and the new medium of film. Did cinema, they wondered, promise a better mode of communication than written language, or was it simply a new iteration of writing itself? Yet these questions – and the metaphor of the hieroglyph so often used to encapsulate them – were centred not merely on film and photography, but on phonography as well. Welles's and Conrad's understanding of cinema and of writing – and their ability or inability to incorporate or transcend other media – emerged out of these ongoing debates about the relationship between writing and speech not only in film, but also in new technologies of audio recording like, most famously, Thomas Edison's phonograph.

Edison's machines for the first time made possible the preservation of sounds and, particularly, of spoken words; indeed, Edison saw his technologies more as dictation machines than as devices for recording and transmitting music.[9] Given its method of inscription with a 'stylus', the phonograph was seen as akin to hieroglyphics; as a commentator at the time wrote, 'the Assyrian hieroglyphic, was made by an instrumentality very similar to the phonographic needle of to-day impressing itself upon plastic material.'[10] Like cinema, phonography promised the mystical possibility of a motivated connection between signifier and signified, so long associated with hieroglyphics, with sound recording turning the very substance of the world – its sounds and speech – perfectly and accurately into writing, into grooves or images. As in Woolf's treatment of film, sound waves were capable of producing graphic 'impressions': as Edison says, 'How easily the particles of solid matter may receive an imparted motion, or take an impression, from delicate liquid waves, air waves, or waves of sound.'[11] For, as their names imply, the grooves of the phonograph and gramophone were for Edison literally a form of writing, one which the stylus or needle read.

In the realm of print technology, the nineteenth century also saw the invention of new techniques to capture sounds in writing: stenographic shorthand and the International Phonetic Alphabet. Both promised, like phonography – indeed, they were referred to as phonography – to be universal forms of writing that would create a one-to-one correspondence between vocal and written speech, accurately rendering the sounds of all of the world's spoken languages.[12] For Alexander Melville Bell, father of the more famous Alexander Graham Bell, his own phonetic alphabet 'Visible Language' would not only be universal, but perfect: its new 'symbols for pure phonetic qualities' would be motivated and natural.[13] As James Lastra writes, he 'claimed that what he had really invented was a universal alphabet [...] and that his letters, instead of being arbitrary characters, were symbolic representations of the organs of speech'.[14]

These phonographic technologies both mimic and challenge the practice of writing, since they emulate the process of inscription but assert themselves as better, more accurate forms of recording. As Edison writes, 'We are now able to register all sorts of sound and all articulate utterance [...] in lines or dots which are an absolute equivalent for the emission of sound by the lips' (p. 642).[15] These 'lines or dots' are an 'absolute equivalent' of the phenomena of nature, not merely a representation like writing, and threaten to render writing irrelevant. Indeed, Edison saw the phonograph precisely as an alternative to forms of writing: to printed dictation, personal notes or, even, novels themselves. As he says, writers now will be able to 'publish their novels or essays exclusively in phonogram form' (p. 647), dispensing with written words entirely. And just as photography challenged the realist novel in its extraordinary precision of detail, so phonography promised to do the same with sound: 'The most skillful observers, listeners, and realistic novelists, or even stenographers, cannot reproduce a conversation exactly as it occurred [...] But the phonograph receives, and then transmits to our ears again, every least thing that was said – exactly as it was said – with the faultless fidelity of an instantaneous photograph' (p. 648).

Edison thus promoted phonography as a new form of inscription that, like hieroglyphs, might be purer or more direct than alphabetical writing, providing privileged access to the natural world. But just as hieroglyphs were used at the same time to point to the essential heterogeneity of all media, so discourses about phonography frequently seek to dissolve the boundaries between sound recording and writing. Phonography revealed that, as a series of vibrations, sound potentially was already and inextricably constituted *as* writing, rendered into material grooves – seen as akin to Egyptian writing – through the act of recording. Phonography was both an alternative to writing and the same as writing. This sense of the hybrid nature of sound was also inspired by Ernst Chladni's earlier experiments, first published in 1787, in which he found that different pitches of sound waves produced different patterns, or 'Chladni figures', on a dust-covered glass plate. The figures transformed the workings of sound waves into images, what Adorno calls 'script-like Ur-figures of sound'.[16] Edison's phonograph was not only a method of recording; it also demonstrated how sound was not purely aural, but somehow simultaneously possessed an inherent visual and written form in grooves or Chladni figures. Adorno claims that the phonograph 'reestablishes [...] an age-old, submerged, and yet warranted relationship: that between music and *writing*'.[17]

As Jonathan Sterne reminds us, all 'modern technologies of sound reproduction use devices called transducers, which turn sound into something else and that something else back into sound' (p. 22). Phonography is not a pure mapping of sound onto writing, since that writing is illegible; rather, writing – in the forms of grooves or Chladni figures – acts as the essential intermediary between natural sound and its reproduction. While sound recordings promise unmediated access to natural phenomena, they simply reinforce the necessity of translation, with the needle re-tracing the grooves it has previously inscribed. Indeed, the writer Robert Herring made this exact lament in the film journal *Close-Up* in 1929: 'This is very thrilling of course, that the noise made by a person some time ago can be let out again later [. . .] But it remains reproduction. You can't get voice pure, but reproduced voice.'[18] Sound is not 'pure' transcription; sound requires writing for its preservation. The oral cannot be privileged over the written; writing is necessary for the recording and transmission of sound.

Theories of phonography in this period therefore exist in a liminal space between a belief in each medium as pure and essential and an awareness of the hybrid nature of phonographic inscriptions, with hieroglyphs serving as the emblem of both sides of this binary. Building off these discourses on new media, Welles and Conrad do not insist on the purity of their own medium because of its supposed primal connection to the natural world. Rather, cinema or writing is for them superior precisely because of its hybridity, its ability to incorporate the properties of images, of sound and of writing.

'THREE DISTINCT ENCLOSURES': SPEECH AND WRITING IN LORD JIM

This sense of the fraught relationship between speech and writing travelled between fiction and cinema, animating Conrad's fiction and, through his influence, Orson Welles's conceptions of the hybrid nature of the cinematic medium. Recent scholarship by John Picker and Ivan Kreilkamp has worked to establish how Conrad was influenced by phonographic discourses of the time, with Kreilkamp emphasising how phonography 'opened the way to a new conception of voice not as the sign of presence but as the fragmentary material phonemes of a circulating, authorless language'.[19] I argue, however, that for Conrad the phonograph – and the hieroglyphs frequently associated with it – was more important for how it blurred the line among sound, speech and written words. Indeed, this is partly how Conrad reacted to a phonograph when he was first exposed to one. In an 1898 letter recounting how he listened to one of the earliest commercial phonographs, Conrad writes:

> It was so – said the Doctor – and there is no space, time, matter, mind as vulgarly understood, there is only the eternal something that waves and an eternal force that causes the waves – it's not much – and by virtue of

these two eternities exists that Corot and that Whistler [. . .] and Munro's here writings and your Nigger and Graham's politics and Paderewski's playing (in the phonograph) and what more do you want? (p. 95)

The phonograph reveals a universe in which everything – from art to literature to music – is constituted by waves, and that possibility seems potentially disturbing here for Conrad, as evidenced by the 'it's not much' and the 'what more do you want?' But the phonograph as Conrad conceives of it also winds up equating writing – Conrad's novel *The Nigger of the 'Narcissus'* – with other art forms and media: paintings and sound. While phonography threatens to collapse the distance between different media, as we've seen, that collapse has the potential of validating the importance of writing – and of Conrad's own novel – which emerges as not separate or worse but fundamentally the same as art, politics and new technologies of recording.

However, most critics of Conrad, from Edward Said to Fredric Jameson, have argued that, as Said claims, 'Conrad's writing tries in fact overtly to negate itself *as writing*.'[20] Instead, critics argue that Conrad validates speech; in the words of Michael Greaney, 'Conrad's fiction endeavours to negate its own writtenness, usually by ventriloquizing a raconteur – Marlow or one of his many counterparts – behind whose garrulous personal presence the text silently effaces itself' for, in Fredric Jameson's words, nostalgic and conservative aims: 'The representational fiction of a storytelling situation organized around Marlow marks the vain attempt to conjure back the older unity of the literary institution.'[21] For Greaney and Jameson, Conrad turns away from writing towards oral storytelling.

Such an interpretation emphasises the communicative efficacy of speech as opposed to writing, with Kurtz's final spoken words in *Heart of Darkness* – 'The horror! The horror!' – providing a privileged glimpse into the core of his character.[22] But by looking at Conrad through the lens of discourses about the relationship between spoken and written words in new media at the time – one revealed by the juxtaposition with Welles – we can see how Conrad just as frequently calls attention to the power and efficacy of written words as spoken ones. While Said, Jameson and others emphasise the difference between oral and written modes, discourses about phonography at the time consistently muddle that distinction, emphasising the sound-writing of phonographic grooves or phonography's potential to mimic and replace writing. Likewise, Conrad does not seek to privilege sound over writing, but to emphasise their interconnection. For Conrad, the form of the novel and the medium of printed words allow both voice and writing to share a place within the covers of his book.

Throughout his novelistic career, Conrad persistently undermines the communicative utility of oral speech and the possibility of clearly translating vocal, written or semiotic meanings. After lamenting that Kurtz is 'just a word for me' and berating his listeners for their failure to 'see' his story, Marlow in *Heart of Darkness* concludes that 'it is impossible to convey the life-sensation of any given epoch of one's existence.'[23] Similarly, in *Lord Jim*, Marlow declares, 'I can't with mere words convey to you the impression of his total and utter isolation.'[24] Language seems inadequate for Marlow, and thus in *Heart of Darkness* the novel seems to enact a search for a better, purer form of expression. As Peter Brooks and others have argued, the voyage down the river involves a journey to the 'primitive' roots of language, with written discourse and eloquent words devolving into 'a burst of yells, a whirl of black limbs, a mass of hands clapping, of feet stamping, of bodies swaying, of eyes rolling' (p. 64).[25] Oral speech becomes 'amazing words that resembled no sounds of human language' (p. 126) and written text becomes 'cipher', emptied of meaning, although that writing is ultimately revealed to be Russian. According to this reading of the text, Conrad's novel seeks to restore a hieroglyphic connection not between image and text, but between speech and body, culminating in Kurtz's final deathbed cry 'that was no more than a breath' (p. 130). Human speech becomes physiological, inextricably linked to the most basic of human processes: breath.

Heart of Darkness would thus seem to privilege oral discourse as somehow closer to the essence of things, with Conrad falling victim to the phonocentrism that Derrida sees as characteristic of the West. The ultimate insight to Kurtz's character can only be delivered through his voice – he 'presented himself as a voice' (p. 86) – or through his gestures, while his writing, as an overlay of civilisation, is inherently obscuring. But, as we've seen with Woolf, a fascination with supposedly more primitive and direct forms of language does not necessarily involve a turning away from written text; indeed, it can even affirm what is essential and important about written words as opposed to spoken ones. For Conrad does not truly acclaim oral speech over written discourse. Conversely, the novel suggests that the problem of communication lies not in writing, or even in language, but specifically in the oral forms of storytelling that Marlow employs. When Marlow says that Kurtz's 'feelings were too much for speech' (p. 109), Conrad exploits the double meaning of 'speech', sliding between a more narrowly focused rejection of the communicative power of oral discourse and a more far-reaching questioning of the efficacy of human language more generally. Similarly, in *Lord Jim* Marlow declares, 'There are no words for the sort of things I wanted to say. If I had opened my lips just then I would have simply howled like an animal' (p. 134). He then recounts Jim's broken-off utterance '"You don't [. . .]" words seemed to fail him' (p. 137). Words and communication consistently fail, but those words are almost always vocal words. Are they simply inadequate when compared to more primitive howling, or is the problem that they are vocal rather than written?

Lord Jim provides the most sustained engagement in Conrad's *oeuvre* with the relationship between writing and speech, with Conrad seeking to mimic the stuttering and hesitations of oral discourse while simultaneously calling attention to the status of his novel as a printed work. As in contemporaneous discourses of phonography, Conrad seeks to treat oral discourse as another form of writing – in this case, by turning spoken words into printed words enclosed in a novel. Throughout, Conrad insists that the voices of his characters can only be communicated to the reader through 'written words' and consistently calls attention to the written-ness of the narrative. From the very beginning of *Lord Jim*, Jim is self-consciously portrayed as a character in a novel, 'unflinching as a hero in a book'; his later story is even characterised as 'like something you read of in books' (pp. 47, 215). But Jim is not simply a Bovary-figure, caught up in the adventure romances he grew up reading; rather, Conrad reminds the reader that Jim remains merely a product of Conrad's written words. Conrad thus insistently links the visual action of the novel to his process of writing: in describing the chart of the *Patna*, he writes:

> The sheet of paper portraying the depths of the sea presented a shiny surface under the light of a bull's-eye lamp lashed to a stanchion, a surface as level and smooth as the glimmering surface of the waters. Parallel rulers with a pair of dividers reposed on it; the ship's position at last noon was marked with a small black cross, and the straight pencil-line drawn firmly as far as Perim figured the course of the ship. (p. 57)

Here the map of the sea that Conrad is describing becomes the 'sheet of paper' on which he is describing it, as Conrad dramatises his own scene of writing, complete with lamp, desk, pencil and paper with 'parallel rulers'. Conrad as writer marks on the paper the position of the ship and its future course, with his language calling attention to how writing can 'figure' or 'portray' the visual world it represents. And that writing, like all writing, is always graphic, rendered as a 'small black cross', just as later in the novel Marlow explains that Jim 'described graphically' (p. 133).

Far from seeking to efface its written-ness and emulate speech, *Lord Jim* consistently emphasises its status as a written text. On the next page Conrad further tips his hand, describing how when Jim 'happened to glance back he saw the white streak of the wake drawn as straight by the ship's keel upon the sea as the black line drawn by the pencil upon the chart' (p. 58). The action of a pencil not only records the action of the ship, but the ship becomes that pencil, becomes Conrad's pencil, moving across the paper of the sea and leaving the black mark of writing. The ship is simultaneously a real ship – at least in the reader's mind – and a series of figures on a white page, just as later a river is compared to 'an immense letter S' (p. 234). Likewise, Conrad describes how on 'on each side of the Patna two deep folds of water, permanent and sombre on the unwrinkled shimmer, enclosed within their straight and diverging ridges a few white swirls of foam bursting in a low hiss, a few wavelets, a few ripples' (p. 55). The *Patna* is 'enclosed', to use a word I will return to, by two deep 'folds', with the linkage between folds and the pages of a book rendering the line of the ship into the very spine of the book we read. The ship becomes a pencil mark on the 'unwrinkled shimmer' of a page, surrounded by 'straight and diverging ridges' and 'swirls' and 'ripples' that recall the material appearance of handwriting or the grooves inscribed by a phonograph needle. In these early scenes, Conrad foregrounds the materiality of the story he is telling, blurring the gap between 'the written word' and the visual descriptions that it 'make[s] you see'. While contemporary discourses about the hieroglyphs of film and phonography often emphasised how those media efface the gap between the world and its representations, Conrad insists on the power of the older medium of alphabetical writing to create the sounds and images it describes.

Conrad in *Lord Jim* goes even further, seeming to question the power of the spoken word by demonstrating its profound unreliability when compared to the medium of written or printed words. This conflict between the oral and the written is best encapsulated in a scene mid-way through the novel, when Marlow waits to listen to Jim recount the story of his past. As soon as he guides Jim into his room, Marlow bends 'over [the] writing-desk like a medieval scribe, and, but for the movement of the hand holding the pen, remained anxiously quiet' (p. 168). Throughout the duration of the scene as he waits and hopes for Jim to speak, Marlow writes 'letters', obsessively, endlessly: 'I wrote and wrote; I liquidated all the arrears of my correspondence, and then went on writing to people who had no reason whatever to expect from me a gossipy letter about nothing at all' (p. 169). This passage seems to re-inscribe the notion of the primacy of speech; while Marlow's letters are mere gossip, Jim's possible vocal utterances hold the promise, for Marlow, of revelation. As Marlow says, 'There is a weird power in a spoken word' (p. 170). As noted earlier, critics have taken Marlow's view as synonymous with Conrad's, but such an equation is far from exact. For this section also asserts the creative power of writing, with Marlow seeing 'all at once, on the blank page, under the very point of the pen, the two figures of Chester and his antique partner, very distinct and complete' (p. 170). Writing is capable of evoking, to the mind's eye, the visual objects it describes, of seemingly calling characters into being.

Indeed, in this passage Conrad takes care to undermine Marlow's statement about the 'weird power in a spoken word'. It is not the spoken word that matters here, but the written; Jim cannot get over the 'empty formality, a piece of parchment' (p. 170) of the inquiry. The written word chains him to the past, and there is even the suggestion that written words will provide him an opportunity for future redemption. For Marlow here seems to be writing the narrative of Jim's life, of Jim's possible future stories that will take up the rest of the novel. As he says, 'Perhaps he [Jim] did take it too much to heart. And if so then – Chester's offer [. . .] At this point I took up a fresh sheet and began to write resolutely' (p. 170). Maybe Marlow is writing to Chester here, offering Jim for Chester's earlier plan to employ Jim as an overseer on his guano island, but he almost seems to be creating a possible future for Jim in the act of writing, to be narrating a new end to his aborted *Bildungsroman*. This suggestion is heightened when Conrad ends this passage, after the vision of Chester appearing on his page, with Marlow declaring, 'No. They were too phantasmal and extravagant to enter into anyone's fate' (p. 171). Marlow rejects that narrative, that fate for Jim, and instead embarks on a new act of writing: a letter to Stein, which leads to the Patusan plot that takes up the rest of the novel. In his act of writing, Marlow seems to take over the role of plotter or author. Even as he asserts the primacy of the spoken word, he demonstrates the power of the written. Even as he waits for Jim's supposedly privileged spoken word, the real authority rests in his own writing. In his novels, Conrad thus recreates the logic of discourses about phonography, which likewise privilege speech but, by turning speech into a form of hieroglyphic writing, end up potentially re-emphasising the power of writing.

Marlow's choice to write 'letters' is also revealing because they call attention to the written character – the letters – from which any word is composed. Letters, or correspondences, likewise recur in Conrad's fiction, especially in reference to envelopes, as we shall see in *The Secret Agent*. Indeed, the idea of the envelope – the encloser of language – helps to define Conrad's peculiar narrative structures. Returning briefly to *Heart of Darkness*, we can see how the use of the frame narrator does not simply extend Marlow's 'storytelling situation', as Jameson and others would have it, but situates Marlow's vocal performance within the realm of writing. The frame narrative is fundamentally different in terms of style from Marlow's account. As Kreilkamp writes:

> *Heart of Darkness* begins in the voice of an unnamed frame narrator whose words acknowledge no distinction between voice and writing, a storyteller/scribe in whom those two identities do not seem to be in conflict. He is the kind of narrator that nineteenth-century fiction since Jane Austen had consistently produced, a seamless author/speaker in whose 'voice' the novel passes itself off as a sort of storytelling in print. Yet when this narrator introduces Marlow, *Heart of Darkness* veers off in a new direction, seeming precisely to mimic a pre-modern oral storytelling situation. (p. 234)

Yet I want to resist the conclusion that what is new in Conrad is this 'pre-modern oral storytelling situation', which represents a departure from nineteenth-century modes of discourse. What is radical in Conrad's technique is not the inclusion of Marlow's storytelling but the inclusion of both kinds of voices in the same story and, specifically, the bracketing of one within another. Conrad's narrative techniques represent a strategy of containment. Just as in *Heart of Darkness* the kernel of Marlow's tale is 'enveloped' by its halo, so Conrad seeks consistently to incorporate oral speech into his narratives and to 'enclose' that orality within plot structures that call attention to the status of the novel as a written text. Like Edison, Conrad is concerned with rendering voice into writing, but rather than phonographic inscription, Conrad's medium is the novel.

Thus the beginning of *Lord Jim* does not merely enact the fall from omniscience into perspectivalism, the fall, to put it metaphorically, from the nineteenth century into modernism. Rather, Conrad's inclusion of the third-person opening also insists on the novel as an act of writing; it encloses Marlow's spoken narrative and the testimonies of his various interlocutors within the space of the printed text. The structure of the court inquest that Conrad employs in the first half of the novel is thus particularly appropriate, since, as Tony Jackson has argued, court testimony represents a case of oral speech placed into its most 'written' context.[26] The oral testimony of the witnesses is translated into writing by stenography, a technology which, as noted, prized itself on the direct transcription of spoken sound into writing, of words into phonemes. Edison thus proposed the phonograph as a new tool for lawyers, who should 'compel witnesses in court to speak directly into the phonograph, in order to thus obtain an unimpeachable record of their testimony'.[27] Just as an inquest translates a plethora of spoken facts into a clear written narrative or 'record', so Conrad's novel renders Marlow's speech into printed words.

And it is at the very moment of the inquest, when Conrad calls attention to the relationship between speech and writing – to the ability of writing fully to capture and preserve oral discourse – that the narrative can make its switch from third person to first, from text to voice, embarking on Marlow's more psychological inquest of Jim's motivations. Conrad has already established the power of writing to enclose speech and thus can transition into oral storytelling. Indeed, this scene of the inquest includes the second reference in the novel to the act of enclosing: Jim's mind, Conrad writes,

> positively flew round and round the serried circle of facts that had surged up all about him to cut him off from the rest of his kind: it was like a creature that, finding itself imprisoned within an enclosure of high stakes, dashes round and round, distracted in the night, trying to find a weak spot, a crevice, a place to scale, some opening through which it may squeeze itself and escape. (p. 65)

At the very moment in which verbal testimony is converted into written records, with Conrad lingering on the 'blotting paper' held by the magistrates,

Conrad turns to the metaphor of enclosure which is already associated, in the passage quoted earlier, with the linkage between written language and material reality.[28] Jim is 'enclosed' by written words just as much as he is enclosed within the 'serried circle of facts' of the inquest, from which no aspect of his identity can 'escape'.

These metaphors of enclosure crop up frequently in the Patusan section of the novel, with Jim imprisoned in a 'stinking enclosure', 'a vast enclosure with palms and fruit trees', and Doramin, using a word even more explicitly linked to paper, 'enfolded in a red-and-gold headkerchief' (pp. 226, 231, 234). Such metaphors not only call attention to how Jim is enclosed within a book, but also symbolise Stein's, Marlow's and the reader's attempts to come to know and understand Jim's motivations, to pin down and 'enclose' him as if he were one of Stein's captured butterflies, marked by 'oblong slips of paper blackened with minute handwriting' (p. 193). Looking forward to Woolf, Conrad allies, through the metaphor of enclosure, the epistemology of literary character with the hybrid nature of language. Just as Marlow attempts to enclose and reveal Jim's identity, so Conrad strives to enclose spoken words and visual descriptions within the act of writing. Conrad thus anticipates Woolf's 'impressionism' in his insistence on the connection between language and identity.

Far more than in Woolf, however, this linkage shapes the way in which the narrative of *Lord Jim* is structured, as Marlow's later letter to the 'privileged man' makes clear. By far the most frequent references to 'enclosure' occur in that scene, when the last words of Marlow's spoken narrative have faded away and the final revelations are revealed, instead, in print: 'contained in a thick packet addressed in Marlow's upright and angular handwriting' (p. 292). From the oral we have moved back to the written, albeit a more personal form of writing: Marlow's characteristic 'handwriting'. Again Conrad calls attention to how words and stories are 'contained', looking back to the frame narrative with which *Lord Jim*, like *Heart of Darkness*, began. The novel reveals its own materiality, as the stories with which the narrative will conclude are exposed as written texts: 'At first he saw three distinct enclosures. A good many pages closely blackened and pinned together; a loose square sheet of greyish paper with a few words traced in a handwriting he had never seen before, and an explanatory letter from Marlow. From this last fell another letter, yellowed by time and frayed on the folds' (p. 292). Even more explicitly, Marlow states, 'The story of the last events you will find in the few pages enclosed here' (p. 295). The story becomes the 'greyish paper' and the 'explanatory letter', and it is the task of the novel to deliver to its reader in his or her private setting the printed 'envelope' that will contain the narrative.

The rest of the novel, while still resembling Marlow's earlier oral storytelling, is thus revealed as communicated solely through written words. Retroactively, the earlier sections of the novel are exposed as similarly mediated, with

Marlow's dialogues rendered into Conrad's printed text. *Lord Jim* thus seems to celebrate Conrad's ability to turn the oral into the written, the same capacity that phonography promised, but one which in Conrad's case calls attention to the primacy of his own medium of writing. Yet by including voice and text side by side, by calling attention to the material process of writing, Conrad opens a gap between the oral and the written; the two cannot be made precisely equivalent in his novels, and the best Conrad can do is to enclose – through his use of frame narrators and juxtapositions of oral and written sources – the former within the latter. *Lord Jim* thus seems animated by the same ambivalence as in contemporaneous discourses about phonography and film, poised between asserting the primacy of one medium – be it sound or written words – and acknowledging the fundamental interrelation between speech and writing.

'Voice Won't Do': Newspapers and *The Secret Agent*

Yet Conrad's insistence on the power of the written word for good and for evil is not confined to his novels with frame narrators. In *The Secret Agent*, Conrad similarly calls attention to the materials of writing and, particularly, to printed text as a medium: one disseminated, with uncanny power, through the newspapers. In *The Secret Agent*, writing is always a vehicle for personal or mass communication, and unlike Conrad's treatment of oral discourse, these printed words tend to reach their intended recipients. While Michael Greaney has argued that Conrad in *The Secret Agent* is disgusted by print, fearful that his own novel will be contaminated by its connection to supposedly debased written forms like newspapers and pornographic writings, Conrad throughout *The Secret Agent* insists rather on the peculiarly appealing power of writing.[29] When faced with new media like photography and phonography that promise a more direct access to reality, Conrad emphasises instead the greater communicative utility of print.

As in the references to 'letters' discussed earlier, the first two pages of *The Secret Agent* repeatedly mention 'envelopes', with an 'envelope', like a passkey, allowing Mr Verloc free passage into the Embassy.[30] The tools of writing from the very beginning of the novel exert an almost talismanic power. As in *Lord Jim*, printed words start to penetrate the world of the characters, with Conrad referring repeatedly to Mr Verloc's 'mortal envelope', as if he too were constituted by print. Conrad even includes a fervent denunciation of oral discourse; as Mr Vladimir says, 'Voice won't do. We have no use for your voice. We don't want a voice. We want facts – startling facts – damn you' (p. 61). While Vladimir's statements cannot entirely be trusted, Conrad confirms his distrust of speech by continually associating the powerful in his novel – Vladimir, the Assistant Commissioner, Sir Ethelred – with the written word, as all three are portrayed as sitting at their 'writing-tables'. As shadowy, behind-the-scenes figures, their voices are silent, but their written words have a national impact.

Indeed, the public in the novel seem mere puppets of the printed word in the form of newspapers. As the narrator notes, 'It was impossible to say yet whether it [the public] would roar or not. That in the last instance depended, of course, on the newspaper press' (p. 126).

The repetition of words, their permanence – exactly what print allows – fundamentally shapes the consciousness of Conrad's characters and his aesthetic technique. Conrad routinely repeats verbal phrases in his novels, hollowing out their meanings and opening them to multiple interpretive possibilities. Through repetition, a phrase like 'The horror! The horror' loses its status as transparent language, and takes on significance as a verbal sign, a hieroglyph which must be deciphered. Nowhere is this process more apparent than in *The Secret Agent*. While Conrad's use of the epithet 'the ticket-of-leave apostle' for Michaelis is reminiscent of the oral form of epic, the vast majority of Conrad's repeated phrases are associated with the newspapers. For Mrs Verloc, who reminds herself repeatedly that the world 'did not stand looking into very much', is haunted by the phrase 'the drop given was fourteen feet' in a crime article that she reads, and Ossipon's overblown faith in himself is obliterated by the sheer repetition in his mind of the sentence from the account of Mrs Verloc's suicide: 'An impenetrable mystery seems destined to hang for ever over this act of madness or despair' (pp. 172, 238, 266). Conrad in *The Secret Agent* literalises the cliché; he demonstrates how his characters' banal patterns of thought are shaped by the decisions of writers, printers and typesetters. But Conrad is not entirely negative in his attitude towards these clichés, despite Greaney's argument. As the narrator writes, 'in the lament of poor humanity rich in suffering but indigent in words, the truth – the very cry of truth – was found in a worn and artificial shape picked up somewhere among the phrases of sham sentiment' (p. 260). This statement represents somewhat of an aesthetic credo for Conrad, who, in his 'Preface' to the *Nigger of the 'Narcissus'*, similarly asserts that the artist's task is to reinvest meaning to the 'worn' surface of words. While his characters do not possess the ability of the artist, words – and even the debased words picked up from magazines 'among the phrases of sham sentiment' – still hold the only possibility of capturing 'the very cry of truth'. At a time when phonographic inscriptions promised a new, more natural form of 'writing', Conrad returns to the power of an older form of inscription: printed and written text.

For Conrad, unlike for the Professor, 'the social order' does indeed seem to be 'built up on paper and ink' (p. 95), and thus the figure of the Professor crystallises Conrad's anxieties about the printed medium. The Professor, like Vladimir, believes that words aren't enough: only action can move the public, and he condemns those who 'talk, print, plot, and do nothing' (p. 96). This statement represents an attack against Conrad the author, who also prints, plots and does nothing in writing his novels. And yet the Professor is himself a figure for the artist, trying to move humanity, by bombs if not by words. He asks, 'What if nothing could move them? Such moments come to all men whose ambition aims at a direct grasp upon humanity – to artists, politicians, thinkers, reformers, or saints' (p. 103). The Professor expresses Conrad's central concern: do printed words, despite their power, have any ultimate ability to affect or 'move' the public, especially when compared to the Professor's terroristic violence, which is explicitly associated with the new medium of photography? As the Professor explains, 'The pressing of this ball actuates a detonator inside the flask I carry in my pocket. It's the principle of the pneumatic shutter for a camera lens' (p. 91).

The Professor's bombs thus seem an analogue to photography, as a new medium that will render writing ineffectual. Yet despite the Professor's terroristic force, and the promises of photographic technologies, the novel uses the power of print to undermine the Professor's grandiose dreams. For directly after his harangue, the Professor is discouraged precisely by the printed medium of newspapers:

> In front of the great doorway a dismal row of newspaper sellers standing clear of the pavement dealt with their wares from the gutter [. . .] The grimy sky, the mud of the street, the rags of the dirty men harmonized excellently with the eruption of the damp, rubbishy sheets of paper soiled with printers' ink. The posters, maculated with filth, garnished like tapestry the sweep of the kerbstone. The trade in afternoon papers was brisk, yet, in comparison with the swift, constant march of foot traffic, the effect was of indifference, of a disregarded distribution. (p. 101)

Newspapers may be seemingly ignored by the public, they may embody, as Michael Greaney argues, the sordidness of the world, but they also shape opinion and move the masses in a way even the Professor cannot contend with. The newspapers may represent a 'disregarded distribution', but that distribution of the printed word is the best means, in Conrad's novels, of any kind of expression or communication. Even the Professor's violence, even the Greenwich bomb explosion, is ultimately mediated through the newspapers; printed words are the medium through which the message of terror must be broadcast if it is to have its chilling effect. By experimenting with narrative forms that recall the court inquest – which itself was included in newspaper accounts of the Greenwich Bomb plot of 1894 – Conrad emphasises the ability of his own medium to incorporate not only spoken words, but also images and events.[31] Through his plot structures, Conrad demonstrates the ultimate power of the printed word, be it in a newspaper or a novel.

Given Conrad's insistence on the power of written words, we need to reconsider that typical Conradian adjective, 'unspeakable'. Certainly in *Lord Jim* and *Heart of Darkness* Marlow constantly, overinsistently, claims that his listeners will not be able to understand him, with the true meaning of his tale remaining 'unspeakable', but that word does not necessarily mean the same thing as incommunicable. It also means, simply, 'unsayable'. Behind Marlow's back, as it were, Conrad demonstrates that what cannot be said can, indeed, be written or, at least, that the best possible way of communicating is through words and 'letters'. If Conrad is conservative, he nevertheless does not desire to return to a 'pre-modern oral community'; rather, he seeks simply to preserve and demonstrate the enduring power of printed and written text. While phonography and photography create new and supposedly better forms of writing, Conrad insists on the lasting ability of plain old written words – 'the old, old words, worn thin, defaced by ages of careless usage' – to mimic and incorporate voice and vision.[32]

WELLES'S *HEART OF DARKNESS*

Returning to Orson Welles's *Citizen Kane*, we can see much more clearly the new relationship among technology, perception and identity – and among voice, writing and image – in Conrad's novel and Welles's film. For *Citizen Kane* is just as concerned with the hybridity of media as are *Heart of Darkness* and *Lord Jim*; as Conrad encloses oral storytelling within writing, so Welles encloses writing and speech within film. In calling attention to the heterogeneous nature of his cinematic medium, Welles both claims for cinema the power to reveal a deeper level of meaning beyond mere words – even the essence of character itself – and self-consciously undermines that claim. By looking at Welles's film, we can see how both Conrad and Welles cast doubt on whether there can truly be an unambivalent translation between speech, writing and image like the kind embodied by hieroglyphic theories of cinema and phonography. Together, Conrad and Welles forge a new paradigm of narrative – definitively different from the detective plots that they seem to resemble – in which signs and clues ultimately resist clear decipherment, splintering into multiple interpretive possibilities.

While the factual details of Charles Foster Kane's life are taken from the biography of William Randolph Hearst, the overarching structure of his history seems to derive, at least in part, from Conrad's anti-hero Kurtz.[33] Kane begins in high idealism, or at least a kind of narcissistic idealism, running for Governor on an anti-corruption ticket. He thus mirrors the progressive, albeit misguided, aspirations that Kurtz propounds in his essay on colonialism for the 'International Society for the Suppression of Savage Customs'. But both characters end in degradation and isolation, linked, in both cases, to authoritarianism and extreme politics: in Kane's case through his meeting with Hitler in the 'News on the March' segment, in Kurtz's case through his cousin's remark that 'He would have been a splendid leader of an extreme party.' In an interview with Peter Bogdanovich, Welles even explicitly states that his version of 'Heart of Darkness was a kind of parable of fascism.'[34] Kane's 'methods' are just as 'unsound' as those of Kurtz; as Kane's guardian Walter Thatcher laments about Kane, in a clear nod to Conrad, 'Yes, yes, but your methods.'[35]

Kane's Xanadu, the isolated heart of darkness to which he retreats at the film's end, even seems partly inspired by the Africa that Kurtz inhabits. The opening shots of the film and the 'News on the March' section include images of the giraffes and other 'beasts of the jungle' that surround Xanadu. Like Kurtz sending back his ivory to colonial Belgium, Kane surrounds himself with 'the loot of the world'. Kane figuratively fulfils Jeb Leland's prophecy that he will 'sail away to a desert island, probably, and lord it over the monkeys'. Indeed, in the picnic scene near the end of the film, Welles uses rear projection footage of a jungle from the adventure movie *The Son of Kong*.

Not only is Kane inspired by Kurtz, but the narrative structures in which both characters are revealed or concealed are also similar. Sergei Eisenstein suggested such a connection in 'Nonindifferent Nature', his essay on Chinese ideograms and hieroglyphs discussed in Chapter 1. In characterising what he calls the 'fugue', 'counterpoint' or 'polyphonic writing', he turns to the 'beautiful film of Orson Welles, *Citizen Kane*, where whole fragments of the biography of the hero are expounded by different characters who had known him in his lifetime'.[36] Such a structure, Eisenstein claims, derives from Conrad, 'which alongside of Wilkie Collins makes him one of the direct precursors of *Citizen Kane*' (p. 273). One of Welles's comments on *Heart of Darkness* stresses this narrative connection; he says of Conrad's novel, 'The story is marvelously interesting, and it does have one thing which is in *Kane* and which is a thing I like very much in pictures: the search for the key to something.'[37]

That 'something', in *Citizen Kane,* is Kane's central deathbed utterance: 'Rosebud.' The only equivalently famous last words in the twentieth century are Kurtz's: 'The horror! The horror!' In both cases, the narratives locate meaning in the gnomic words of their central characters, with these short verbal phrases seeming to encapsulate Kane's and Kurtz's experiences but ultimately providing little definitive explanatory power. Rather, they necessitate a vain search for the true meaning behind these words. In *Citizen Kane*, the reporter Thompson serves as Welles's equivalent of Marlow, although, unlike Marlow, Thompson is not allowed to become a full-fledged character. He serves merely as a screen through which to view the central figure of the narrative, as a detective attempting to track down the clues to the identity of Kane. Thompson represents a more successful means of translating the modernist narrator into visual terms than Welles employed in his initial attempt to adapt *Heart of Darkness*. Rather than awkwardly resorting exclusively to point-of-view shots, as Robert Montgomery would go on to do in *Lady in the Lake*, Welles turns that observing presence into an actual character but never lets us see his face.[38] As critics have noted, *Citizen Kane* has a proliferation of narrators: not only Thompson and those he interviews, but the camera itself, particularly at the beginning and the end of the film, to which I will return.[39] In this way, Welles more fully replicates the multiple framing devices that Conrad utilises in *Heart of Darkness*.

More parallels emerge in *Lord Jim*.[40] In many ways, *Citizen Kane* adopts the narrative form of that novel; just as *Lord Jim* begins with an omniscient third-person narrative and then collapses, at the moment of Jim's failure of courage on the deck of the *Patna* and the subsequent inquest, into a first-person, perspectivilist, modernist novel, so *Citizen Kane* starts, after the scene of Kane's death, with the omniscient voice and clear, unambivalent narrative of the 'News on the March' segment. This portion proves inadequate for the newsreel editor, and so the narrative transforms itself into one in which truth is not clearly and completely known but must be reconstructed through interviews with other characters. Just as Marlow goes around interviewing the engineer, Brierly, and Stein, so Thompson must make the rounds from Bernstein to Susan Alexander to Jed Leland, and so on. Eschewing a linear chronology, the narrative doubles back on itself, returning to the same event – Susan Alexander's opera performance – from different perspectives.[41] In each case the epistemological certainty of the opening of each text dissolves into a new epistemology, one in which the core of meaning or the 'kernel' of the tale, to use Marlow's terminology, is absent or unreadable. That meaning must be re-constructed or deduced from varying perspectives or from linguistic signs or symbols.

The parallels between *Heart of Darkness* and *Citizen Kane* thus provide another model of adaptation in which the thematic concerns and structural form of one work influence another even as the outward content remains radically different. But *Citizen Kane* also demonstrates that Hollywood film, at least in its more experimental forms, was deeply influenced by modernism in literature and the arts. While we can see in the film noirs of the 1940s an increasing concern with subjectivity and the regression to primitive psychological impulses, as well as a tendency, typical of modernism, to depart from linear and chronological plots through flashbacks, these trends need not be based on the zeitgeist of the times but can be traced, at least partly, to the specific influence of literary modernism in general and *Heart of Darkness* in particular. The long shadow that *Citizen Kane* cast over 1940s Hollywood film can be seen as part of an extended genealogy of modernism – a dialogue between the literary and the cinematic – with the editing techniques of early silent film influencing the development of modern fiction, which in turn influenced the aforementioned tendencies in Hollywood sound film post-*Citizen Kane*. Through its parallels to *Heart of Darkness*, *Kane* provides the crucial direct link between literary modernism and the Hollywood film culture of the 1940s.

More deeply, however, Welles derives from *Heart of Darkness* his concern, implicit in *Citizen Kane*, with the interrelation of sound, image and writing within the cinematic medium. As befits a director switching media – from radio and plays to film – Welles is from the very beginning of *Citizen Kane* highly aware of the qualities unique to cinema and of the characteristics shared with other media, especially writing and radio. As Tony Jackson has argued, *Citizen Kane* is saturated with written texts: newspapers, most obviously, but also the letters sent by Kane, the legal document signed by Kane's mother, the affidavit read by Thatcher and countless others.[42] As Welles proclaims, 'I haven't got anything at all against a lot of words in movies.'[43] The opening shots of the film consistently juxtapose written texts, sounds and filmic techniques: from the self-consciously literary pre-title card 'A Mercury Theater Production by Orson Welles' to the jarringly silent title; from the 'No Trespassing' sign to the succession of dissolves that move us closer to Xanadu; from the whispered 'Rosebud' to the unexpected shot from within the broken shards of the snow globe.

The same near-simultaneous use of sounds, written texts, images and camera movements recurs when Welles introduces subsequent characters, from Susan Alexander to Walter Thatcher. The viewer has already become accustomed to this juxtaposition from the 'News on the March' section, which, as Jackson argues, 'is an almost encyclopedic mixture of the technological means of telling a man's story at this time in history: picture magazine, photography, painting, newspaper, radio news, and film'.[44] But Welles is even more ambitious in his goals for the 'News on the March' section, as he implies by his inclusion of the intertitle '1895–1941. All of these years he covered, many of these he was.' While 1895 is an odd start date to choose, as it is not Kane's birthdate, nor does it match the 1887 or 1896 beginnings of William Randolph Hearst's newspapers, the years 1895–1941 do match, perfectly, with the history of cinema. The 'News on the March' newsreel is thus not merely a Brechtian alienation effect or an omniscient third-person narration in need of complication. The newsreel also serves to establish *Citizen Kane* as an exploration of the evolution of cinema, blurring the line between silent film and the sound film that supplanted it. For unlike silent cinema, which combines intertitles with images, or sound film, which for the most part eschews onscreen text for a combination of images and spoken words, the 'News on the March' section utilises all three. For Welles, cinema is made up of and can incorporate the medium that he is adapting – the novel – and the medium with which he began his career: radio.

Rather than emphasising film's purity – its hieroglyphic status as a more direct means of visual communication – Welles invokes the alternate interpretation of hieroglyphs seen in Proust, Woolf and others, representing film as a hybrid of image, sound and written text. But when we do discover what Rosebud means, the vehicle for that knowledge, crucially, is the camera itself.

A disembodied crane shot, not tied to the viewpoint of any one character, sweeps over the detritus of Kane's accumulations to glimpse the sled being destroyed in the fire.⁴⁵ Welles at the end of the movie seems to be privileging the medium of cinema over the medium of written words. Conrad's novel, tied as it is to language itself, can give us only the signifier – the verbal phrase 'The horror! The horror!' – with the signified remaining irretrievably lost, only partially to be reconstructed by Marlow. Welles, however, can substitute the actual physical signified – the sled itself – for the verbal signifier 'Rosebud', and so can solve the mystery of the movie.⁴⁶ Cinema as a medium can move beyond Kane's spoken words, communicating to the audience the meaning of 'Rosebud' by revealing the image and word inscribed on the sled.

Cinema seems to fulfil Kane's goal, stated early in the movie, of finding the 'something I've got to get into this paper beside pictures and print'. By exceeding purely visual, auditory or written meanings, cinema – or, at least, Welles's film – provides what newspapers and, despite their cinematic nature, what newsreels miss. Through the mechanics and motion of cinema itself Welles can impart a greater access to Kane's character and psychology than through written text, revealing the ultimate clue to his identity. *Citizen Kane* thus looks forward to the ending of Welles's *Touch of Evil*, which similarly seems to call attention to the inadequacy of words. As Marlene Dietrich's character Tana says when asked to provide a final word on Orson Welles's dying Hank Quinlan, 'He was some kind of a man. What does it matter what you say about people?' Welles here specifically casts doubt on language as the vehicle for meaning; what we 'say' about people does not matter compared to their actions, and cinema can actually show a character's actions, not to the mind's eye but to the eye itself. In *Citizen Kane*, as in *Touch of Evil*, cinema, rather than language, has the last word or, rather, the last image.

Yet Welles ultimately is not entirely sanguine about cinema's potential to reveal the truths of character. For on another level Welles in *Touch of Evil* is simply reiterating Thompson's speech from *Citizen Kane*: as Thompson says, rejecting the notion that 'Rosebud' would have explained everything:

> No, I don't think so; no. Mr. Kane was a man who got everything he wanted and then lost it. Maybe Rosebud was something he couldn't get, or something he lost. Anyway, it wouldn't have explained anything ... I don't think any word can explain a man's life. No, I guess Rosebud is just a piece in a jigsaw puzzle ... a missing piece.

Welles is far too deeply in debt to Conrad to believe that a life – be it Quinlan's or Kane's – can be totally or definitively summed up, even by the medium of cinema. Even when we learn the final clue to Kane's character, he remains – like Kurtz, like Jim – perpetually 'under a cloud'.

As befits a film which consistently invokes Freudian psychoanalytic explanations for Kane's behaviour, the ending of *Citizen Kane* disproves the idea that every aspect of an individual's motivations can be truly known. The camera pulls back and we return to the first shot of the film – a 'No Trespassing' sign – underlining cinematically the idea that Kane retains some core of meaning to which we are not allowed access.[47] One visual/lexical emblem, one hieroglyph – the sled with the word 'rosebud' – is replaced by another, the 'No Trespassing' sign. Yet, for Welles, the medium of cinema itself, unlike speech or writing, seems to provide a privileged, albeit not total, glimpse beyond that forbidding sign. It allows us access to writing, image and object – the word 'Rosebud', the picture of a rosebud and the sled itself – rather than merely the words 'No Trespassing'. As in the motif of lingering on shut doors in the film – to Thatcher's library, to Susan's room at Xanadu – Welles wants to capture the barriers to knowledge even as he tries to move beyond them. The final shot of the film thus expresses the balance between language and image that cinema is able to provide. In the foreground we see the letter K on the gate of Xanadu, while in the background appears Xanadu itself; as he has done throughout the film, Welles in the final shot of *Citizen Kane* again juxtaposes the visual with the linguistic.

👁 = I

The relationship among writing, sound and image in *Citizen Kane* is, however, even more complex, particularly in its final scenes. While the revelation of the sled by the camera provides the viewer with more information, that information is oddly excessive: we get both word and image, both 'Rosebud' and the picture of a rosebud. This may not seem particularly unconventional, except for the fact that Welles consistently doubles image and writing, and writing and voice, throughout *Citizen Kane*. Characters repeatedly speak out loud words that the viewers can read on the screen: the newspaper headlines read by Thatcher in an early montage, the inscription on the 'Welcome Home Mr. Kane' trophy or the words 'News on the March' in the newsreel. And, in the memorable shot in the political rally, Kane in the flesh is doubled by a visual representation of himself on the banner behind him.

On one level, Welles, as in the 'News on the March' section, is insisting like Conrad that language exists as the visual marks of writing and as the phonetic sounds of speech, both of which can be captured by the technologies of photographic and phonographic inscription inherent to sound film. But truly to understand what Welles is doing here, we need to return to *Heart of Darkness* or, at least, to Welles's proposed adaptation of it. Before the film began, Welles was to have provided an extended introduction, which would have featured scenes of the point-of-view camera being electrocuted, shot and fed as if it were a canary. This opening was intended to demonstrate to the audience that, for the course of the film, the camera would represent not an

Figure 3.1 Publicity photo for Orson Welles's planned adaptation of *Heart of Darkness* (1939), Welles Mss., Box 30, Courtesy of the Lilly Library, Indiana University, Bloomington. Likeness of Orson Welles appears courtesy of The Estate of Orson Welles, represented exclusively by Reeder Brand Management.

omniscient perspective but rather the sightlines of the viewer, who would figuratively play the part of Marlow. This sequence was to have culminated with a card showing the equation pictured in Figure 3.1: 👁 = i. Through Welles's radical aesthetic innovations (which would have required new technologies for 'feather wipes' and gyroscopic camera rigs, like today's Steadicams), the viewer would gain a new, less mediated relationship to the story. The audience's eyes would become Marlow's. The audience would be immersed, as in recent 3-D technologies, in the action of the film.[48] Yet recalling Woolf's comments in 'The Cinema', Welles's claim for the immediacy of his cinematic technique can be expressed only in terms of language, as a sentence or, at least, as a homophonic equation between a pictogram and an alphabetic letter: 👁 = i. Welles asserts the primacy of cinema but in doing so shows how cinema is inseparable from a combination of written text, sound and vision. The visual emblem of an eye becomes not only the letter 'i', but also the phoneme 'i', particularly because this scene would have been accompanied by Welles's voiceover narration. His equation would be a rebus, with the eye standing both for its visual meaning – the spectator's eye – and the shared phoneme for 'eye' and 'i'. The 👁 would become a hybrid hieroglyph, fluctuating among its visual, ideographic and phonetic meanings.

Immediately after providing the viewer with this equation, Welles would have shown an auditorium with its seats filled with movie cameras, literalising the almost cyborg-like connection between spectator and medium, with the viewer turning into a 'camera-eye' like the kind called for by Dziga Vertov. Welles's equation thus encapsulates the new relation between technology and language for which I am arguing in this project. The medium and technology of cinema, embodied by those cameras in the audience, helps to reveal the hieroglyphic interdependence of sound, vision and written text in all language and media. Just as writing for Conrad is able to incorporate speech and vision, so cinema for Welles is able to enclose and capture all of the functions of language, be they aural or visual.

Welles's equation in *Heart of Darkness* is not simply linguistic, of course; it also connects language and character, since 'i' is not only the letter 'i' but also the 'First Person Singular', as Welles titled the series of radio programmes in which he first adapted, in 1938, Conrad's *Heart of Darkness*. 'I' becomes '👁', with perception being transformed into identity in much the same way as Woolf blurs the gap between our 'impressions' and the linguistic 'sacred tablets' of our character, or how Conrad calls attention to how Jim's identity is constructed out of the visual marks of print.

If we return to *Citizen Kane*, we can now more fully understand Welles's conflicted attitude towards the revelation of Rosebud at the end of the film. The camera in the final sequence promises to reveal Kane's fundamental 'I' to the spectator's eye, echoing Welles's linkage of technology, identity and perception in the introduction to *Heart of Darkness*. Through the medium of cinema, language becomes vision becomes sound, just as the sound of Kane's dying words, the picture of a rosebud and the written word Rosebud blur into one another. Welles thus seems to echo earlier understandings of cinematic and recording technologies as purer or more direct. Just as phonographs promised to transfer sounds into writing, so Welles's film takes the spoken word 'Rosebud' – pronounced by Kane before we know who he is – and turns it into the word Rosebud, painted onto a sled. Sound is able to be perfectly mapped into written text, just as the eye, through the hybrid medium of the cinema, can capture perfectly the 'I' of the onscreen character. Indeed, as we've seen in Chapter 2's discussion of film and character, this is just the sort of equation that Béla Balázs saw in the 'microphysiognomy' of cinema: 'whatever is expressed in his face and his movements arises from a stratum of the soul that can never be brought to the light of day by words' (p. 9). Through cinema, the face and the soul render up their secrets to the viewer.[49]

While Welles seems to forge a new unmediated unity between sound and writing, between perception and identity, he ultimately deconstructs that unity. Again, we need to return to the doubling of image and words on the sled, in which we are given almost a Saussurean diagram of signifier and signified: the word Rosebud and a drawing of a rosebud. Yet by doubling the lexical and the pictorial, Welles simultaneously asserts and undermines his own claims for the unique power of cinema. The viewer does not need the juxtaposition of both Rosebud the word and rosebud the image for the meaning of Kane's last words to be revealed. The word 'Rosebud' itself would have been sufficient; the image is oddly redundant. What the viewer, like Thompson and Rawlston, is looking for is not the linguistic meaning of Rosebud, but its personal meaning for Kane himself. For Kane the word Rosebud does not signify a flower but rather a sled. Cinema is able to provide to the eye of the spectator the actual physical signified, to attach Kane's dying word to the sled to which it refers. But that knowledge still relies on the written word Rosebud. And the idea that this ultimate revelation provides a privileged insight into Kane's character, rather than just being 'another piece in the puzzle', is undermined not only by Thompson's ultimate speech, but by the sled itself. If the word Rosebud does not always refer to the bud of a rose, then why should Kane's final utterance have a similarly fixed and unambiguous meaning? If Rosebud doesn't equal Rosebud, then why should Rosebud equal a sled, or the core of Kane's character?

The redundancies that Welles builds into his film, his doubling of spoken words and written text, thus point to the dual nature of all language, which exists as both spoken and written. Welles claims for cinema the ability to capture, at one and the same time, the visual and the aural. But Welles simultaneously calls attention to the gap between these different kinds of language, which the revelation of the sled at the end of the film makes clear. Welles is able both to assert the power of cinema to enclose and incorporate other media and to resist the idea that cinema – and, in particular, its images – allows a mystic, gnomic access to human character or material reality. Cinema is not, for Welles, a universal, Cratylic language that provides clear, unmediated communication. Building on the influence of Conrad, Welles is able to preserve the essential 'heart of darkness' in human character, that interior zone that remains forever impenetrable, regardless of the possibilities of his new medium. Like Conrad, Welles turns away from the perfect mapping of sound or image onto written text promised by cinema and phonography and instead invokes the idea of 'incorporating' and 'enclosure'. While images or sounds may not equal written words, cinema, by its hybrid nature, can incorporate all three.

Technology and Narrative Form

In this vacillation between knowledge and inscrutability, between writing and speech, Welles and Conrad express an epistemology similar to that described by Carlo Ginzburg in his 'Clues: Roots of an Evidential Paradigm'.[50] For Ginzburg, the dominant epistemology of the late nineteenth century – in detective fiction, art history, physiognomy, fingerprinting and psychoanalysis – was what he calls 'medical semiotics': 'that discipline which permits the diagnosis of diseases inaccessible to direct observation based on superficial symptoms [...] It was an attitude oriented towards the analysis of specific cases which could be reconstructed only through traces, symptoms, and clues' (pp. 102, 104). Recalling Foucault's episteme outlined in the Introduction, Ginzburg emphasises the pictorial sign or hieroglyph – the mark or clue – which serves as the symbol to be read and deciphered. Total knowledge of the 'thing in itself' of disease or of character, however, can only be conjectured rather than truly known. The investigator is left with interpretation, commentary and narrative. Indeed, Ginzburg sees all of narrative as going back to the 'primal scene' of this epistemological model, the pre-historic reading of animal tracks: 'the hunter would have been the first "to tell a story" because he alone was able to read, in the silent, nearly imperceptible tracks left by his prey, a coherent sequence of events' (p. 103). Pictographs lead, through a process of reconstruction, to narrative.

In this episteme, as it is in Welles's rebus of the eye, vision is what is valued: the ability, through Foucault's 'medical gaze' or Sherlock Holmes's uncanny observational abilities, to scrutinise the seemingly insignificant sign or symptom and turn it into the disease or the identity of the criminal, to turn it into 'I'. As in Welles's formulation, the 'I' of the perceiver is conflated with the 'eye', and through that gaze the spectator is able to approach as close as possible to true knowledge. Welles's equation, with its blurring of the line between technology in the form of the motion picture camera and the human eye, thus acknowledges what Friedrich Kittler argues that Ginzburg neglects: how 'medical semiotics' is itself dependent on new technologies of inscription, like phonography and photography, which allow for recording of the seemingly insignificant visual or aural phenomena that provide the initial 'trace' or 'clue'.[51]

'Medical semiotics' provides the basis of knowledge for both Welles and Conrad, with their similar attempts to read meaning into the clues of Kurtz's or Kane's last words. *Heart of Darkness* even foregrounds medicine when Marlow has his head measured by the Company doctor, who attempts from the minute surface details of physiognomy to acquire general laws about psychology and madness, even as he acknowledges that 'the changes take place inside, you know' (p. 17). While 'medical semiotics' emphasises the possibility of deciphering those objects that seem most beyond the purview of science – seemingly insignificant aspects of the human face, or verbal tics or slips, as in Freud – that decipherment, in Welles and Conrad, is always incomplete, conjectured rather than definitely known. This same fluctuation between complete knowledge and inscrutability animates the narrative technique of Conrad's novel, encapsulated by the narrator's famous remark about the 'kernel' of Marlow's tale and the 'halo' that surrounds it. Marlow attempts from the signs of Kurtz's life and words to generate 'enveloping' narratives that force access to his depths, but that kernel remains ultimately inaccessible. 'Rosebud' in *Citizen Kane* works similarly, seemingly providing through a chance utterance the ultimate clue to Kane's identity, but a clue that even after the revelation of the sled leaves the viewer only with his or her own conjectures about its meaning.

Welles and Conrad reveal how this epistemology is both bolstered and threatened by new technologies of inscription. Welles's equation ☻ = i in the prologue to *Heart of Darkness* seems to promise more than mere conjecture; language and vision will fuse and perception, through the medium of cinema, will provide a complete knowledge of identity. Through technological innovations that allow them to be rendered one into another, the visual and the auditory and the linguistic become not merely decipherable and readable, but equivalent, blurring the gap between signs and language. They break down the paradigm of medical semiotics, which has at its foundation language, writing and narrative. For Sherlock Holmes, for the medical examiner, language itself was the stable and proper vehicle for recording and transmitting knowledge. It was the telos of investigation, in which the narrative of the successful deciphering of visual signs could be told and recorded. But the new understanding of language as hybrid – as made up of sound and vision – renders writing radically unstable, since it obliterates its foundational position as the endpoint of knowledge. Writing is just as much in need of deciphering or translating among oral, visual and lexical meanings as any visual sign. Indeed, this is exactly how Conrad treats language in his novels. For Conrad, spoken or written words – 'The horror! The horror!' or 'this act of madness and despair' – are broken down into distinct and repeated verbal phrases, into signs which must be deciphered. For Conrad, as for Welles with his focus on the spoken word 'Rosebud', language itself is just as subject to decipherment as the physical marks of the world.

Thus we see a new paradigm of narrative emerging in the early twentieth century. As Peter Brooks has argued, one of the dominant models for nineteenth-century fiction (perhaps even the model for all of narrative) was the detective tale, with its story of the decipherment of a crime. In that paradigm, the detective starts from an inciting event – the discovery of a crime or the narrating of a dream – and then deciphers, through interrogations and observations of concealed clues, the true, buried narrative of the crime or the trauma. In other words, the story represents the narrative of the reconstructive decoding of a narrative, concluding with its telling, and fits Ginzburg's semiotic model perfectly.

But in Welles and Conrad something has changed. *Heart of Darkness*, *Lord Jim* and *Citizen Kane* all seem to represent narratives of decipherment, with their detective figures Thompson and Marlow retrospectively seeking access to the true narrative or the motivations of another. But structurally these narratives are dramatically different, as Brooks acknowledges. Given their use of frame narrators – the unnamed narrator of *Heart of Darkness*, the third-person voice of *Lord Jim*, the camera in *Citizen Kane* – these plots involve the narrative of the narrative of the failed decoding of a narrative. In other words, a frame narrator tells the story of another character telling his narrative about his inability, ultimately, to decipher. Of course, many late nineteenth-century novels that heavily influenced Conrad, from *The Moonstone* to *Dracula* to *The Island of Dr. Moreau*, incorporate frame narratives and sections written from the perspective of different characters. Yet these novels wind up at least largely resolving the epistemological uncertainties that they open up. *Heart of Darkness* and *Citizen Kane*, by contrast, conclude not with a complete and satisfying story, but with an indeterminate sign, a linguistic or visual and auditory hieroglyph: 'The horror! The horror!' or the sled.

Even *Lord Jim*, while resolving more definitively, still circles around the ultimately impenetrable act of Jim's abandonment of the *Patna*, and the second half of the book represents a narrative of decipherment, but simply a turn, through Marlow's acts of writing mentioned earlier, to a new and different kind of plot. While the technique of 'delayed decoding' in Conrad seems to parallel the detective plot, on a larger structural level we never achieve any kind of ultimate decoding. Even in a novel like *The Secret Agent*, which seems to follow a more traditional narrative of decipherment, with the various detective figures eventually figuring out the events that led to the failed bombing of the Greenwich Observatory, the ending of the novel again underlines the ultimate lack of knowledge. While Inspector Heat initially laments that 'The first term of the problem was unreadable' (p. 108), rendering, like Welles, the narrative into an algebraic formula, he eventually stumbles upon the 'plot' that forms the plot of the novel. But what we're left with is the 'impenetrable mystery' of Mrs Verloc's death, with the final details of her life extrapolated from witness accounts and never entirely represented for the reader. And interestingly, this 'impenetrable mystery' – embodied in the printed form of a newspaper – destroys Ossipon's belief in a legible world. Ossipon, as a doctor, is a full adherent to the episteme of 'medical semiotics'; a worshipper of the criminologist Lombroso, he believes that character is graven physionogmically on the face and can be easily and clearly deciphered, that Mrs Verloc is 'a degenerate herself – of a murdering type' (p. 259). He is thus reminiscent of Stein, whose meetings with Marlow are characterised as like a 'medical consultation', but who similarly ends the novel in despair at his failure properly to diagnose the specimen of Jim. In *The Secret Agent*, language – the disembodied words from the newspaper – reminds us and Ossipon that there is always some 'mystery' left over, some element to the plot that resists complete decipherment. Definitive narrative and knowledge are impossible and thus, like *Heart of Darkness*, *The Secret Agent* ends only with the repetition of a linguistic phrase: 'this act of madness and despair'.[52]

If detective fiction renders signs and clues into writing and story, then in Conrad and Welles, by contrast, the stable narratives at the opening of their works break down into signs and conflicting perspectives, with the 'News on the March' segment and *Lord Jim*'s third-person narrator dissolving into multiple narratives. They move from narrative into signs, rather than from signs into narrative. This shift goes hand in hand with the new understandings of language and media as hybrids of sound and image. Conrad and Welles's works leave the viewer or reader with indeterminate visual and aural signs that can never be wholly synthesised, leading to a multitude of potential narratives and interpretations. In *Heart of Darkness* Kurtz's ungrounded cry 'The horror! The horror!', while capable of being captured in writing, cannot be successfully translated into a definitive meaning. Similarly in *Citizen Kane*, the film concludes with the shattering of the bond between signifier and signified, with Rosebud fracturing into image, object, word and sound: all of which cinema can capture, but which never can be fully integrated into a complete narrative of Kane's character.

While new technologies like cinema and phonography challenge the preeminence of writing, promising a pure translation between inscription and the natural world, Welles and Conrad point to the impossibility, in any medium, of fully translating among visual, oral and lexical meanings. Conrad and Welles both turn away from a faith in language, which is revealed as ultimately heterogeneous and never entirely reliable or clear, and towards the medium itself, insisting on the power of their own medium to 'enclose' through narrative rather than to translate. While there no longer exists a simple connection among sound, image and writing, written words – for Conrad – or cinema – for Welles – still are capable of incorporating the aural, pictorial and written elements of the signs that the reader or viewer must interpret. Through the hybridity of its signs, film, like writing, becomes fundamentally generative, spawning a proliferation of narratives and meanings unique to each interpreter. While 'i' can no longer equal '👁', while vision can no longer make complete sense of the signs of character, the word Rosebud and its image can still be enclosed within the medium of cinema and transmitted to the viewer. Cinema for Welles, like the written word for Conrad, can incorporate the 'i' and the '👁' – the visual, the sonic and the linguistic – even if the equals sign between them has been smudged or effaced.

NOTES

1. When asked by Peter Bogdanovich if there are similarities between *Kane* and *Heart of Darkness*, Welles responds, 'Not at all' (Welles and Bogdanovich, p. 32).
2. I am bracketing the issue of who was responsible for the screenplay for *Kane*, which has been debated inconclusively for decades. But I'm assuming, for the purposes of this chapter, that Welles was largely responsible, through his role as director as well as screenwriter, for the content of *Kane*. Indeed, I think that the connections with *Heart of Darkness* provide another reason to side with those who see Welles as primarily, if not exclusively, the so-called author of his film.
3. Hubert Cohen first noted this similarity in 'The "Heart of Darkness" in "Citizen Kane"', though he oversells certain connections between subsidiary characters and does not reflect on the significance of the larger links. Likewise, Guerric DeBona, in a discussion of Welles's script for *Heart of Darkness*, notes in passing the connections between Kane and Kurtz and the narrative structure of *Citizen Kane*. See DeBona, pp. 16–34.
4. For background on the invention of phonography and the metaphor of hieroglyphs, see Gitelman, *Scripts*; Lastra, *Sound Technology*; and Sterne, *The Audible Past*.
5. Conrad, *The Collected Letters of Joseph Conrad*, Vol. 2, p. 95.
6. Conrad, 'Preface', *The Nigger of the 'Narcissus'*, p. 147.
7. For a fuller description of this sequence, see Rippy, *Orson Welles and the Unfinished RKO Projects*; Rosenbaum, *Discovering Orson Welles*; and the original script, Welles Mss. Box 14, Folders 15–17, Lilly Library, Indiana University, Bloomington.
8. While Laura Mulvey comments on '*Citizen Kane*'s narrational strategy and its exploitation of the cinema's hieroglyphic potential to create a space for a deciphering spectator' (p. 219), the hieroglyphic status of cinema, as well as its connection to *Kane*'s narrative, is left unexplored.
9. See Edison, 'The Perfected Phonograph', p. 646. As Ivan Kreilkamp writes, 'in the years following [the phonograph's] invention nearly all uses suggested for it involved not music but language' (p. 216). Indeed, only two of Edison's twelve functions for the phonograph were related to music.
10. Quoted in Gitelman, *Scripts*, p. 139. As Walter L. Welch and Leah Brodbeck Stenzel Burt note in *From Tinfoil to Stereo*, 'The stylus [the needle for engraving sound inscriptions] had its origin, in name at least, in the engraving or embossing tool used for making pictographs and hieroglyphics by the ancient Assyrians and Egyptians' (pp. 4–5).
11. Edison, 'The Perfected Phonograph', p. 642.
12. As Gitelman writes, the International Phonetic Alphabet 'and its antecedents all sought to broker similar transactions [. . .] between the visibility and stability of texts and the multifarious sounds of speech. Each shorthand alphabet, spelling

reform, or international phonetic alphabet presupposed that signs could represent sounds' (*Scripts*, pp. 56–7).
13. See Alexander Melville Bell, p. 25.
14. Lastra, *Sound Technology*, p. 28. According to Robert Brain, phonography even led to the development of the concept of the phoneme in twentieth-century linguistics and, indirectly, to the validation of spoken discourse over writing in the works of Saussure:

> Graphic studies of vocalization played an indispensable role in the formation of modern linguistics, especially the system developed by Breal's protégé Ferdinand de Saussure. They rendered fleeting and unseen phenomenon of speech as a materialized and visible object [and] served to codify the concept of the elementary linguistic signal, or phoneme, the key notion for the constitution of the modern science of linguistics. (p. 168)

15. As Kreilkamp describes, 'The phonograph was, then, a new technology of inscription which threatened to render pen-to-paper writing obsolete [...] In Edison's first prototypes strips of paper were used, so that the phonograph made good on its name: it was a machine that reproduced sound by literally inscribing the page' (p. 218).
16. Adorno, 'The Form of the Phonograph Record', p. 60. Similarly, Jonathan Sterne describes how the 'ear phonautograph produced tracings of sound on a sheet of smoked glass when sound entered the mouthpiece' (p. 42).
17. Adorno, 'Phonograph Record', p. 59.
18. Herring, 'A New Cinema, Magic, and the Avant Garde', in Donald, Freiberg and Marcus, pp. 55–6.
19. Kreilkamp, p. 214; John Picker, *Victorian Soundscapes*.
20. Said, 'Conrad: The Presentation of Narrative', p. 130.
21. Greaney, p. 3; Jameson, *The Political Unconscious*, p. 219.
22. One exception to these views is John Picker, who, in discussing the influence of phonography on *Heart of Darkness*, claims that 'The disembodied voices of Kurtz and Marlow, the acts of retelling and replaying by Marlow and the unnamed narrator, are not enough to clarify or resuscitate the past, the silent, or the dead, but only conjure them in mysterious, incomplete, and distant ways' (p. 141). Picker does not discuss, however, how phonographic technologies translate these voices into writing.
23. Conrad, *Heart of Darkness*, pp. 47–8.
24. Conrad, *Lord Jim*, p. 243.
25. '"The Horror!" appears as minimal language, language on the verge of reversion to savagery, on the verge of a fall from language' (Brooks, p. 250).
26. Jackson, *The Technology of the Novel*.
27. Edison, 'The Phonograph and Its Future', p. 533.
28. Indeed, 'enclose' even has an appropriate, though obscure, legal meaning: 'To put (a jury) in the "box"' (*OED*).
29. 'One suspects however that the disgust lavished on newsprint by *The Secret Agent* is a form of deflected self-loathing: the novel heaps odium on a narrative mode that it all too clearly resembles' (Greaney, p. 143).
30. Conrad, *The Secret Agent*, pp. 45, 46.
31. 'The Greenwich Explosion', *Times of London*, 20 February 1894, p. 5.
32. Conrad, '*Narcissus*', p. 147.
33. *Citizen Kane*, dir. by Orson Welles (RKO, 1941).
34. Welles and Bogdanovich, p. 32.
35. There even seem to be parallels – or prophetic parallels – between Kurtz and

Welles, with Kurtz's exasperation with the interference of the petty Company bureaucrats for his grand plans anticipating Welles's similar problems with studio executives throughout his career.
36. Eisenstein, *Nonindifferent Nature*, p. 265.
37. Welles and Bogdanovich, p. 33.
38. Appropriately, the protagonist of *Lady in the Lake*, the first film to use the POV technique that Welles invented for *Heart of Darkness*, is Raymond Chandler's aptly named detective Philip Marlowe.
39. 'In effect, there is a second framing narrative – the prologue and the epilogue to the film – which is narrated by the filmmaker(s), the implicit or inscribed author' (Wollen, 'Citizen Kane', p. 256).
40. Welles had read *Lord Jim*. As Welles says in discussing film adaptations of Conrad, 'Think what *Lord Jim* could have been, if some attention had been paid to the original book' (Welles and Bogdanovich, p. 32).
41. As Welles says, 'I'd been nursing an old notion – the idea of telling the same thing several times – and showing exactly the same scene from wholly different points of view' (Welles and Bogdanovich, p. 53).
42. Jackson, 'Writing, Orality, Cinema', pp. 29–45.
43. Welles and Bogdanovich, p. 31.
44. Tony Jackson, 'Writing, Orality, Cinema', p. 35.
45. The medium thus returns to its nature as fundamentally authorless – just what continues to be claimed by critics like David Trotter as distinctive about film and photography – or, at least, calls attention to the real author of the film, Welles himself. (And as such Welles includes the pre-title card 'A Mercury Theater Production by Orson Welles'.)
46. As Tony Jackson writes, 'no one in the film learns what the dying word "rosebud" means. With our privileged look at the name written on the burning sled we have the final proof of what only film can do' ('Writing, Orality, Cinema', p. 43).
47. As Robert Carringer argues:

    Since the camera imparts information in these sequences that is not known to any of the characters, it has been a common practice to assume that the point of view in them is omniscient, like something in an eighteenth-century novel (one critic has even described these sequences as being the 'God's-eye-view') and that they reveal the kind of definitive information about Kane that is missing in the narrative testimonies. Such an interpretation directly violates the underlying rationale of multiple testimony narratives. Welles himself has cautioned that Kane is 'never judged with the objectivity of an author.' (p. 186)

48. As with all technological innovations that promise greater realism, however, the very newness of his technology would have been offputting to the audience, calling attention to his filmic techniques and thus requiring an extended introduction.
49. As Tom Gunning argues, this physiognomic idea was essential to cinema: 'The ambition of nineteenth century science to discover not only the characteristic lineaments of the face as interpreted by physiognomy, but the laws of motion and the temporal processes of the body and the face led directly to the technical invention of the cinema' (p. 16).
50. See Ginzburg, 'Clues: Roots of an Evidential Paradigm', in *Clues, Myths, and the Historical Method*.
51. 'Ginzburg fails to see that the shift in technologies of power simply follows the switch from writing to media. But unconsciously treacherous signs like fingerprints, pitch, and foot tracks fall into the purview of media without which they could neither be stored nor evaluated' (Kittler, p. 83). Indeed, the 'medical gaze'

that Foucault discusses was not constituted entirely by vision but also, through the invention of the stethoscope, through sound. As Jonathan Sterne argues, echoed later by John Picker, 'The use of the stethoscope marked medicine for over a century, and, through its use, hearing surpassed sight as a diagnostic tool. The specificities of listening were themselves able to be applied to the body of the patient; medical listening rendered the interior motions of the human body to medical thought in a new clarity' (p. 98).
52. For Conrad's distrust of science and medicine, see John Peters, *Conrad and Impressionism*, pp. 11–13.

PART II

4

THE 'ESSENCE' OF EGYPT

So far the fascination with hieroglyphs has been a British, American and European story, with Western writers co-opting Egyptian writing as a metaphor for their concerns with the relationship between writing and new media, just as Champollion and others literally and figuratively co-opted the cultural and linguistic legacy of Pharaonic Egypt. The Western interest in hieroglyphs is proto-typically Orientalist: Western linguists and anthropologists make the unreadable East readable. But while the year 1922 is more famous in Europe and America for Howard Carter's discovery of King Tutankhamen's tomb, it also saw the winning of Egypt's nominal independence from England after the 1919 revolution. The renewal of interest in ancient Egyptian civilisation was thus naturally not confined to Europeans and Americans, but became widespread among Egyptians themselves from 1922 onward. Aside from the invocation of hieroglyphs in British and American discourses about cinema, the decade of the 1920s also saw the rise of what critics have called the 'Pharaonicist' movement in Egypt. The Pharaonicists, most notably Salama Musa and Muhammad Husayn Haykal, sought to reclaim the heritage of ancient Egypt, pointing to the continuities between the Pharaonic and modern eras.[1] If Egypt once possessed a glorious civilisation, so might the newly independent nation of Egypt regain its worldwide importance. For Haykal and Musa, forging a link to the Pharaonic past allowed them to create a unified nation of Egypt in the present. Later Pharaonicist-influenced novelists like Tawfiq al-Hakim take up the Orientalist discourses of the West but co-opt them to assert both Egypt's link to Europe and its own ineffaceable national 'essence'. Forever linking ancient past with revolutionary present, al-Hakim in his novel *The Return of the Spirit* (written in 1927 and published in 1933) posits an unchanging Egyptian identity that, having given birth to Pharaonic civilisation, will lead to a 'return of the spirit' in the future.

By focusing on the historical context of Egypt in the 1920s and the literature being produced there, this chapter seeks not only to expand the diversity of texts available to modernist scholars but also to forge new approaches to even the most canonical of modern British novels. The last ten years have seen numerous calls for more transnational approaches and methodologies, from Susan Stanford Friedman's notion of planetary modernism to, in American Studies, Wai Chee Dimock's theory of 'deep time'.[2] Yet juxtapositions of different literary traditions, especially when reliant on translation, tend to be greeted with trepidation. Emily Apter in *Against World Literature* has argued that the concept of world literature is based on a 'translatability assumption' that denies 'incommensurability and what has been called the Untranslatable' and Ástráður Eysteinsson describes how 'the notion of the problem and the problematic tends to tune in with translation's difficult and trouble-ridden situation [. . .] how it sits uncomfortably with other kinds of text-production'.[3] Certainly the concept of world literature is at risk of effacing the cultural context of individual texts and portraying certain national literatures as solely existing in the service of the literatures of more powerful nations. But the discomfort with translation has the danger of in practice reinforcing the marginalisation or silencing of traditions outside of Europe and America. More importantly, these concerns close off potentially fertile dialogues about the aesthetics of modernism and the relationship between nationalist and Orientalist discourses instead of broadening the kinds of questions that are asked and the variety of texts included in modernist studies. In fact, Tawfiq al-Hakim's foundational novel *The Return of the Spirit* was begun not only in France, but in French, and by a writer exposed to the works of Pirandello, Ibsen, Shakespeare and Goethe.[4] Juxtaposing and translating between Western and Arabic notions of modernity and modernism can lead us to re-think both the periodisation of modernism and the status of al-Hakim's novel *The Return of the Spirit* as a modernist text. The idea of translation seems particularly relevant given that the example par excellence of translation is, of course, the Rosetta Stone, with Susan Stanford Friedman returning again and again to both the Rosetta Stone and the Tower of Babel in making an argument for a more inclusive planetary modernism. Indeed, as I argue in Chapter 5, the idea of translation is central to James Joyce's aesthetics.

Like the work of translation itself – and those three languages presented on the Rosetta Stone – the juxtaposition of Egyptian and British writers can be mutually illuminating, exposing a common desire for a linguistic or cultural origin point found in ancient Egypt. Examining the ways Egyptian writers Tawfiq al-Hakim and Naguib Mahfouz use the legacy of ancient Egypt for contemporary nationalist aims reveals how James Joyce and Thomas Pynchon likewise employ the metaphor of hieroglyphs not only to make sense of the hybridity of media but also to imagine the possibility of linguistic, cultural and national unity and interconnection. The debates about the relationship between writing and media traced in the first half of the book, from Pound to Woolf to Conrad, open out into larger political questions about the potential universality or divisions among races and ethnic groups. The following chapters thus explore how understandings of hieroglyphs break down the distinctions not only among film, phonography and written words, but also among linguistic groups, among racial categories and between humans and machines. If by their engagement with new media, writers increasingly focus on the material, oral and visual qualities of all written words, emphasising the links among language, media and perception, then that focus also stresses the connections between different languages and, by extension, different nations and cultures. When it comes both to the relationship between cultures and the relationship between media, all of these writers, to varying degrees, embrace hybridity, establishing the primacy of their own medium or nation by blurring the lines among them. Given the claims that new media like film could abolish cultural boundaries, medial and national hybridity go hand in hand.

In their invocations of and fantasies about the ancient Egyptian past, both British and Egyptian writers in the 1920s and 1930s strike a precarious balance between nationalism and universalism. I resist the idea of Egyptian writers like al-Hakim and Mahfouz 'writing back' to the modernists, what Susan Stanford Friedman calls 'The old mold of modernist studies [that] narrates just such a tale of informal developmentalism – "we" did it first in the West [...] and then "they" did it elsewhere: derivative and belated' (p. 55). Instead, Egyptians were examining their history at exactly the same time and in similar ways as the modernist writers who invoke hieroglyphs. Al-Hakim and Mahfouz find in ancient Egypt a means of stressing the commonalities between Europe and Egypt while also emphasising the supposed essence of Egypt. In that tension between affirming their own nation and forging links with others they parallel Joyce's own engagement with Irish nationhood and the ancient linguistic past. Rather than rejecting the Orientalist discourses through which they were subjugated, al-Hakim and Mahfouz negotiate the essentialising gaze of the West in order to craft a new narrative of national identity. Al-Hakim and Mahfouz's relationship to the West goes beyond a binary of resistance versus replication, with them both affirming and validating many of the values the West has projected onto Egypt while also projecting the exoticism or timelessness once associated with Egypt onto a different racial or cultural Other: the Sudanese, the Bedouins or the peasantry. Egyptian novelists and critics of the period thus engage in what Homi Bhabha calls 'colonial mimicry', yet that mimicry is less subversive than creatively appropriative.[5] For Pharaonic writers like Salama Musa, the prospect of independence from Britain leads counterintuitively to a desire to stress Egypt's *connections* to Europe and Britain, partly by denying Egypt's African-ness. While in the late nineteenth and early twentieth centuries African-American writers like Frederick Douglass and W. E. B. Dubois were invoking the African origins of Egypt, Egyptian writers of the 1920s turn to ancient Egypt to exclude Africa from the newfound Egyptian nation.[6]

In their attempt to navigate the connections among different nations, al-Hakim and Mahfouz naturally also turn at moments in their careers to the old and new media that were likewise threatening or promising to bridge the gap between cultures and languages. The engagement with media becomes more implicit and diffuse in modern Egyptian texts, with the urgent problems of postcolonial independence rather than the mode of communicating these problems taking precedence. But questions about media still lurk in the background. Indeed, film and the legacy of ancient Egypt were always profoundly connected, and not simply through the metaphor of hieroglyphs. Egypt was also one of the prime subjects of early motion pictures, with Antonia Lant having traced the myriad films of the silent period, both travelogues and fictional narratives, that use Egypt – and, particularly, its mummies or relics – as their subject matter.[7] The British occupation of Egypt was thus not merely an imperial endeavour, but also an imaginative one forged through the medium of cinema, with British and American films effacing Egypt's present political reality and substituting for it a fantastical, exotic past. In fact, the year after the discovery of King Tut's tomb and Egypt's independence also saw the production and release of what is often considered the first Egyptian film, entitled, naturally enough, *In the Land of Tutankhamen*, directed by Victor Rossitto and photographed by the important Egyptian filmmaker Mohamed Bayoumi. Egypt's independence coincides with an act of media independence, with the new nation of Egypt taking up the media that had been used to exoticise it and re-claiming its Egyptian past through a new form. Indeed, the first two newsreels put out by Mohamed Bayoumi's Amon Newsreel company – the name of which invokes ancient Egypt – were footage of the 1919 Revolution hero Saad Zaghloul (in 1923) and an account of the opening of King Tut's tomb (in 1924).[8] March 1924 witnessed the unveiling of King Tut's tomb, the opening of Egypt's Parliament, and the filming of one of the first documentary films made by an Egyptian. This conjunction points to the persistent intertwining of the modern Egyptian nation, the Egyptian film industry and the Pharaonic past.

While Egyptian writers of the 1920s seem hesitant to invoke the new media of film, Naguib Mahfouz in his Pharaonicist novel *Khufu's Wisdom*, published in 1939, emphasises the commonalities between Egyptian hieroglyphs and contemporary languages, particularly the more calligraphic language of Arabic. Like the European modernists, most of whom he had read, Mahfouz brings together hieroglyphs and the alphabet. If the writing systems of past and present don't fundamentally differ, Mahfouz implies, then why should the larger Egyptian essence? For Mahfouz, the medium of writing itself becomes the necessary vehicle for linking the Pharaonic and the national eras.

The Pharaonicist engagement with media – and film specifically – becomes more apparent over the course of the century. Not only does Mahfouz, who already alludes to text as a media form in *Khufu's Wisdom*, play a central role in the Egyptian film industry in the 1950s, but one of the greatest of all Egyptian films, Shadi Abd al-Salam's *al-Mummia*, from 1969, revives the tradition of early twentieth-century Pharaonicism by linking the desire to reclaim the past with the capabilities of the medium of film. Like the Egyptologist Ahmad Kamal in the film who seeks to preserve the relics of ancient Egypt, so the director Abd al-Salam can through the medium of film preserve, enclose and transmit the hieroglyphs and mummies of the Pharaohs for the audience of the Egyptian nation.

For al-Hakim, Mahfouz and Abd al-Salam, as for Vachel Lindsay, ancient Egypt and its hieroglyphs become the focal point for questions about national or international unity. The Egyptian hieroglyphs reach back towards the myth of Babel – used to anchor conflicting theories of racial or linguistic origin – and ahead to the relationship between writing and new media, the so-called problem of Babel, discussed in Chapter 5. Hieroglyphs and the ancient Egyptian culture associated with them simultaneously embody the differences between new media and writing and the similarities among film, phonography and written words. And at one and the same time they are used as proof of the ultimate unity of all races, languages and cultures, and of the primacy or difference of one or more races, languages or cultures, with al-Hakim and Mahfouz, Haykal and Musa, linking Egypt to the West and policing its difference from the rest of Africa. Just as a nation might be the same as but better than other nations, so any medium might be the same as but better than other media. Given these similar logics, ideas about politics and about media are inherently interrelated in the early twentieth century, with ancient Egypt emerging as the point of commonality between theories of media and speculations about national or international unity. Egypt emerges as a locus of modernism, both in terms of the texts produced by Egyptian writers of the period and in the widespread imaginative interest in Egypt on the part of modernists in Europe and America.

Egypt White or Black

The discovery of King Tut's tomb wasn't just a sensation for Europeans and Americans; it also proved to be a key event in Egyptian nationalism, coming as it did right as Egypt threw off the yoke of British control. While still nominally under the authority of the Ottoman Empire, Egypt had been under British occupation since 1882. Political decisions were made by the British Consul-General (Lord Cromer between 1882 and 1907), with power ostensibly residing in the Egyptian Khedive, or viceroy for the Ottoman Empire. With the outbreak of the First World War, Britain established a Protectorate over Egypt and placed it under martial law, in the process deposing the pro-Turkish Khedive Abbas II and appointing his uncle in the position of Sultan. The hardships of the war years under direct British occupation fuelled nationalist sentiment, which crystallised in 1918–19 under Saad Zaghloul and his Wafd party. In March 1919, Zaghloul was arrested and exiled to Malta, unleashing a wave of unrest across Egypt: the revolution of 1919, recounted in *The Return of the Spirit*. There were mass strikes and demonstrations across the country among all social classes, as well as violent attacks on British soldiers. Over the course of the next three years, Britain gradually acceded to the demands for Egyptian independence, finally granting it on 28 February 1922.[9] However, Britain still retained a strong measure of control, including authority over 'the security of the communications of the British Empire' and 'the protection of foreign interests in Egypt'.[10] Egypt's history in the period thus in some ways parallels that of Ireland: the subject of Chapter 5. Both involve uprisings against British rule – the 1916 Easter Rising in Ireland and the Revolution of 1919 in Egypt – followed by the winning of a measure of independence or Home Rule: in 1921 for Ireland, and in 1922 for Egypt.

A constitutional monarchy was finally established in Egypt in April 1923, with Parliament opening with Zaghloul as its Prime Minister in March 1924, timed to coincide with the ceremonial unveiling of King Tut's tomb. That conjunction cut both ways; while the discovery of the tomb by Howard Carter provided further evidence of Europe's continued cultural imperialism, it also served as proof of the former glory of Egyptian civilisation. These archaeological discoveries were for Egyptian writers of the time a fortuitous reminder that the nation of Egypt might yet regain the wonders and power of its ancient civilisation. Suddenly magazines and journals were touting their connection to the pyramids and hieroglyphs of the Egyptian past.[11] As Benedict Anderson argues, this sense of a limitless timescale is essential to the construction of a nation: 'If nation-states are widely conceded to be "new" and "historical," the nations to which they give political expression always loom out of an immemorial past, and, still more important, glide into a limitless future' (p. 11). By excavating the 'immemorial past', Egyptian writers of the time hoped to construct a new nation-state with a 'limitless future'. The turn to ancient Egypt served as a way of celebrating Egyptian identity as part of a larger anti-imperial nationalist struggle against continued British military and economic domination leading up to the Revolution of 1952.

Israel Gershoni and James Jankowski have defined this resurgence of interest in ancient history in Egypt in the 1920s as Pharaonicism. For them:

> Pharaonicism may be defined as that body of opinion which postulated the existence of a unique and durable Egyptian national essence persisting from the Pharaonic era to the present. According to advocates of the theory, the people of contemporary Egypt were the direct descendants of the people of ancient Egypt and as such possessed the same essential characteristics, qualities, and potential.[12]

Just as European modernists were invoking ancient Egyptian hieroglyphs in their attempt to understand new media, so Egyptians themselves were rediscovering their own cultural heritage. A focus on the cultural ferment of Egypt in the 1920s can clarify how the legacy of ancient Egypt was used to forge a distinctly Egyptian national identity, either through identification with or opposition to Europe, and through opposition to the rest of Africa. In so doing, Egyptian writers of the 1920s adopted the Orientalist discourses by which they were surrounded. The Pharaonicists seem to embody a 'mimetic' form of nationalism: as Neil Lazarus summarises, 'Many contemporary poscolonial scholars [. . .] view anti-colonial nationalism [. . .] as not only an elitist and authoritarian but also a *mimetic* discourse – that is, as a metapractice, one modeled – in certain key aspects, at least – on diverse metropolitan nation-projects.'[13] As Partha Chatterjee, one of the key proponents of this theory, writes, 'There is, consequently, an inherent contradictoriness in nationalist thinking, because it reasons within a framework of knowledge whose representational structure corresponds to the very structure of power nationalist thought seeks to repudiate.'[14] An analysis of Pharaonicist thought, however, reveals that while Egyptian writers repeat Western Orientalist and nationalist discourses rather than oppose them, they warp and deflect them to serve their own ends, asserting a positive Egyptian essence through which they could forge a coherent nation.

Literature was the key vehicle for Pharaonicism, a way for nationalist ideas to be disseminated across society.[15] The most prominent spreaders of Pharaonicist ideas were the writers Muhammad Husayn Haykal and Salama Musa, who edited, encouraged and inspired the work of later writers, and, through their editorship of prominent journals, published and disseminated Pharaonicist works. Though it predates the Pharaonicist period, Haykal himself published what is considered the first modern Egyptian novel – *Zainab* – and Musa and Haykal were strong influences on the two writers I focus on in this chapter – indeed, arguably two of the most prominent writers of the twentieth century: Tawfiq al-Hakim and Naguib Mahfouz.

One of the hallmarks of the Pharaonicism of the 1920s was a kind of universalism: a turn to the ancient Egyptian past as a way to establish connections between Egypt and other nations. But as we'll see with Joyce, for Musa, Haykal and others universalism and nationalism go hand in hand; as Edward Said has argued, nationalist writers frequently invoke anti-nationalist or cosmopolitan views, with the Egyptian writer Taha Hussein, discussed later, serving as one of his main examples.[16] Thus Egypt was both connected to and made the source of all of civilisation; the Pharaonicist writers

> emphasized that the Egyptian contribution to human development had been an absolutely unique and unparalleled one. No other civilization or society remotely approached Egypt in its contribution to world history. On the other, the articles stressed the scope of the Egyptian contribution – that Pharaonic elements and influences could be identified in every 'high culture' that emerged in Asia, Africa, Europe, and the Americas. [...] Egypt's temporal precedence was denoted by such phrases as 'Egypt, cradle of world civilization; Egypt, source of civilization; Egypt, mother of the world; Egypt, mother of civilization; and Egypt, mother of humanity.'[17]

Egypt becomes the first civilisation, the cause of the splendours of ancient Greece and Rome. Musa and Haykal thus assert Egypt's prominence, but do so by pointing to the connections between Egypt and other cultures. Egypt becomes the cultural and even the linguistic origin point: as one Pharaonicist, Nashid Sayfin, writes, 'Egypt is the cradle of civilization [...] It is Egypt which invented the art of writing.'[18] Indeed, Egyptian syllabi in primary and secondary schools during the 1920s and 1930s insisted on Pharaonic Egypt as the birthplace of writing, a medium that Egypt spread throughout the world; all of culture, all of writing, becomes a legacy of Egypt.[19]

Salama Musa even invokes the possibility of the direct linguistic influence of ancient Egypt upon modern England. He writes, 'it is true that the English have occupied our country, but history confirms that we occupied their country two thousand five hundred years ago, and that our Egyptian names live on in their cities, rivers, and gulfs.'[20] Written at a moment when Egypt was beginning to re-emerge from the shadow of colonial conquest, Musa's articles assert that the current subaltern position of Egypt is decidedly unnatural. Not only did Egypt influence England, it actually occupied it, and the tables might be turned again. Musa thus encapsulates the logic of Pharaonicist thought. If Egypt held sway in the past, then it might once again occupy a prime place on the world's stage in the future. But this passage also displays the importance of language to Pharaonicist ideas. It's not enough to recount the glories of ancient Egypt – the Great Pyramid, etc. – there must also be a linguistic influence, in which Egypt inhabits even the words and place-names of the country of its colonial occupier. Given how Britain had mined Egypt's cultural legacy – taking its ancient hieroglyphs, in the form of the Rosetta Stone, to the British Museum – Musa naturally wants to claim an ownership of the English language in the same way that England more literally owns ancient Egyptian writing.

But while Musa uses the links between Egypt and Europe to establish Egypt's prominence, there are limits to his embrace of the connections among cultures. If universalism is one Pharaonicist strategy, exclusion is another. Given the racialised discourses of the time, it was far easier to establish the importance of Egypt by turning away from a link with Africa. Indeed, African-American writers of the late nineteenth and early twentieth centuries routinely sought to counteract racist ethnographers by focusing precisely on Egypt and pointing to the links between Egypt and Ethiopia. In his address 'The Claims of the Negro Ethnologically Considered', for instance, Frederick Douglass turns to ancient Egypt as he sets out to prove a point that he finds ridiculous that he has to prove: 'that what are technically called the Negro race, are a part of the human family, and are descended from a common ancestry, with the rest of mankind' (p. 230).[21] Yet this is just what Josiah Nott and George Gliddon in their *Types of Mankind* sought to deny, rejecting the 'unity of races' and arguing that all races were fundamentally separate and unequal. This argument was made, in part, through invocations of ancient Egypt. Nott contemptuously remembers how 'For many centuries prior to the present [...] the Egyptian were reputed to be Negroes, and Egyptian civilization was believed to have descended the Nile from Ethiopia!'[22] By contrast, he sets out to argue, quoting Samuel Morton's *Crania Aegyptiaca*, that 'The Valley of the Nile, both in Egypt and Nubia, was originally peopled by a branch of the Caucasian race.'[23]

So in opposing Nott and Glidden, Douglass observes:

> The fact that Egypt was one of the earliest abodes of learning and civilization is as firmly established as are the everlasting hills [...] Greece and Rome – and through them Europe and America have received their civilization from the ancient Egyptians. This fact is not denied by anybody. But Egypt is in Africa. Pity that it had not been in Europe, or in Asia, or better still in America! Another unhappy circumstance is, that the ancient Egyptians were not white people; but were, undoubtedly, just about as dark in complexion as many in this country who are considered genuine Negroes. (p. 233)

By arguing that this 'abode of learning and civilization' was black, Douglass not only establishes the importance and influence of African civilisation on the West, but counters Morton's and Nott and Glidden's claims for the 'polygenesis' of races. If Egypt is black, as Douglass argues, and if its culture gave rise to the glories of European and American civilisation, then how can blacks be seen as inferior or as fundamentally distinct?[24]

If Douglass uses Egypt's status as African to establish the links between races and the importance of African civilisation, Musa and Haykal disassociate their national heritage from their African neighbours. The reasons for doing so are twofold. Firstly, the desire to establish a self-governing Egyptian nation involves a process of policing what is and is not Egyptian, of imaginatively creating an Egyptian heritage or essence that only some members of the state can be a part of. And secondly, the claim that ancient Egypt is the 'mother of civilization' becomes more palatable to European audiences if that mother is white. Of course, these varying efforts by African-American and Egyptian writers to grapple with the legacy of ancient Egypt are two sides of same coin, with two differing groups of oppressed subjects attempting in opposing ways to assert their value in the West.

Much of the Pharaonicist discourse is thus explicitly racialised. For Musa and others, there was a frequent emphasis on 'blood' – on a biological Egyptian essence. As he writes, 'we have never ceased to be, first and foremost, Egyptians with respect to our racial composition. The same blood flows in our veins which flowed in the veins of our ancestors five thousand years ago.'[25] Or, as his fellow Pharaonicist Hasan Subhi claims, 'It is true that my language is Arabic and Turkish. But if you speak of my blood – there you will find no other influence but that of Egyptianism.'[26] In trying to establish what is, at heart, a fairly dubious claim of Egyptian commonality across millennia – particularly because of the influence and migrations of the Arabs and Turks into Egypt – the Pharaonicists turn to the discourse of race and blood.[27] Thus Musa claims that 'Rather than being swamped by groups of foreign origin, the racial stock native to Egypt had been able to maintain its purity.'[28] As Subhi's quote indicates, however, language is particularly problematic for this claim, given the clear differences between hieroglyphs and Arabic, accounting for Naguib Mahfouz's attempt to assert the commonalities of those languages in his novel *Khufu's Wisdom*.

The 'purity' of Egypt that Musa invokes involves not just denying links to Turkey or the rest of the Arab world, but also to Africa. Musa was fascinated by the work of the anatomist Grafton Elliot Smith: work not all that far removed from the pseudo-scientific racism of Nott and Glidden. Many of Musa's articles, included in his *Misr asl al-Hadara*, serve as summaries of Smith's theories, which centre on the assertion of an eternal Egyptian essence and of Egypt's place as the fount of European culture. As Smith says, 'the essential elements of civilization did really originate in Egypt', which 'affected at their source the very springs of European civilization'.[29] But Smith argues not only for Egypt's influence, but also for the continuity of its racial characteristics, ideas that are essential to Pharaonicist thought and which play a dominant role in *The Return of the Spirit* and *Khufu's Wisdom*. While, unlike Nott or Gliddon, Smith stresses racial admixture rather than polygenesis, he nonetheless finds in Egypt a pure racial stock unsullied by outside influences. Egypt demonstrates 'a gradual and apparently undisturbed development of the distinctive Egyptian culture. Its growth was too vigorous and sturdy to be warped or deflected by even a considerable foreign element. [...] There may be profound changes in language, religion, customs, and crafts, with little or no alteration in the racial characteristics of a population' (p. 44). Even as Smith acknowledges the cosmopolitanism of Egyptian history, he persists in finding an enduring racial essence in the Egyptian people, the exact essence that the Pharaonicists sought to reclaim.

Asserting Egyptian influence involves a denial of Egyptian links with the rest of Africa, and even a denigration of the African 'race' itself. As Omnia El Shakry writes, 'most Africans, according to Musa, were savages' and 'Pharaonicism also functioned as an exclusionary discourse, situating Egypt within a heritage highly prized by the West and disembedding it from its African context' (pp. 60, 83). Such ideas again derive in part from Grafton Elliott Smith's works; he concedes that 'Within recent years many scholars have advocated the view that there is a large element of Negro in the composition of the Proto-Egyptian population', but concludes by asserting the 'profound gap that separates the Negro from the rest of mankind, including the Egyptian' (pp. 79, 80). As we will see again in *The Return of the Spirit*, Musa co-opts the racist and exclusionary discourses of Western pseudo-science and anthropology – discourses used previously to exoticise Egypt – and displaces those ideas of difference onto Africa or the East in order to assert a commonality between Egypt and Europe.

This balance of exclusion and inclusion when it comes to the formation of modern Egyptian culture finds its most famous expression in Taha Hussein's influential *The Future of Culture in Egypt*, published in 1938. In it, he advocates for educational methods that will increase Egypt's learning and standing in the world. While writing after the height of Pharaonicism in Egypt, he nonetheless builds upon the ideas of Musa and Haykal. On the opening pages of his essay he states, 'I therefore believe that the new Egypt will not come into being except from the ancient, eternal Egypt', linking modern Egypt to its Pharaonic heritage.[30] Such a statement was controversial at the time, since forging connections with the past – and insisting on the 'eternal' nature of Egypt – seems to minimise any pan-Arabic aspirations. The 'ancient, eternal Egypt' was not an Islamic nation, and thus Islamist critics were uncomfortable with the discourse of Pharaonicism.[31] For them, an Islamic pan-Arabic unity was more important than constructing a national consciousness.

But Hussein was not interested in aligning Egypt with the rest of the Arab world. Instead, like Haykal and Musa, he sought to emphasise connections with Europe. As he states, 'we shall not find any evidence to justify the thesis that there is a fundamental difference between the European and Egyptian minds' (p. 10). We can see the hallmarks of Pharaonicist thought here in the emphasis on the influence – or at least the parallels – between Egypt and

Europe, one that Hussein further calls attention to by linking ancient Egypt and ancient Greece. He writes: 'The Egyptian mind had no serious contact with the Far Eastern mind; nor did it live harmoniously with the Persian mind. The Egyptian mind has had regular, peaceful, and mutually beneficial relations only with the Near East and Greece' (p. 4). Egypt again becomes the potential source for – or an equal partner in – classical civilisation.

Yet Hussein, like Salama Musa, can only make the connection to Greece and Rome by severing Egypt's connection with another part of the world – in this case, Persia. Indeed, Hussein's insistence on Egypt's affiliation with the West involves him repeatedly setting up other nations – like Persia – as emblems of difference. As he writes, 'No, the spiritual East by which some Europeans are fascinated is clearly not the Near East but the Far East. It is the East of India, China, and Hapan with religions and philosophies that scarcely resemble our own' (p. 22). If Egypt is like Europe, then it cannot be like Persia or the Far East. Such a statement is particularly interesting given the famous modernist interest in Chinese ideograms in the twentieth century, traced in Chapter 1. By denying any link between Egypt and the East, Hussein is seeking to displace Western Orientalism (which so often was focused on Egypt) onto a different object. Egypt is not exotic and never was, he claims, emphasising the links among the ancient civilisations of Egypt, Greece and Rome. Instead, the objectifying gaze of the West can find another object – the East – and in so doing Egypt can become part of that gaze, as opposed to being the subject of it. Indeed, this project has emphasised that same shift from Egypt to the East: in the twentieth century, Chinese ideograms increasingly become the object of Western fascination as a model for a purer, better form of language. This 'exotic', 'authentic' writing of Chinese begins to replace the earlier focus on Egyptian hieroglyphics, which are now seen as not predominately different from the languages of the West, but, in their phonetic basis, as similar to them. If Western focus does turn from Egypt to the East, then Egyptian writers like Hussein seem conscious of that shift and seek to exploit it to emphasise their own connections to the West.[32]

Hussein shows how Egyptian writers of the post-1919 era did not reject the Orientalist discourses that had so long been placed upon them. Rather, they sought to make use of them for their own creative ends by displacing or co-opting them. While Partha Chatterjee sees anti-imperial nationalist discourse as reinforcing the 'superiority of the West', the culture of which must be combined with the 'spiritual' aspect of the East, Hussein interestingly both embraces that supposed spiritualism and deflects it.[33] Hussein does not object to the Western interest in the 'spiritual' side of the East; rather, he seeks to exclude his own nation from that spiritual interest and position Egypt and its beliefs as Western. Only by exclusion can Egypt become part of Europe. As we shall see, Tawfiq al-Hakim likewise makes use of classic Orientalist beliefs, making them the foundation for the possibility of a future Egyptian nation that might take its proper place alongside the Western powers. And for al-Hakim that validation of Egyptian possibility likewise involves a separation of Egypt and its heritage from other cultures: in his case from the Turks, the Bedouins and the Sudanese.

Return of the Pharaonic Spirit

From its title to its epigraph to its abrupt invocation of the Egyptian Revolution of 1919 in its final chapter, Tawfiq al-Hakim's *The Return of the Spirit*, like the articles of Musa and Haykal that helped inspire it, seeks to draw connections between the ancient Egyptian past and its nationalist present. Its second section begins with the quote, 'Arise! Arise, Osiris. I am your son Horus. / I have come to restore life to you', taken from the Egyptian Book of the Dead, thus invoking not only the Pharaonic past but also the processes of resurrection and reincarnation narrated in the Book of the Dead.[34] But the more important link is between the former glory of Pharaonic Egypt and the possible future glory of an independent Egyptian state, with al-Hakim throughout the novel seeing the nationalist ferment of the late 1910s and 1920s as 'the return of the spirit' of ancient Egypt. Published in 1933 but written in 1927, during the heyday of the Pharaonic movement in Egypt, *The Return of the Spirit* represents the ultimate literary example of the spirit of Pharaonicism embodied by Muhammed Husayn Haykal and Salama Musa.

Al-Hakim's work is also key to understanding the status and the periodisation of modernist literature in Egypt. As Anna Bernard writes:

> In Arabic literature, two recent periods foreground the idea of the modern: the *nahda* ('awakening' or 'renaissance'), most closely associated with literary production in Egypt and the Levant in the late nineteenth and early twentieth centuries; and the 1950s–1980s, marked by [...] new forms of experimentation and innovation. In this second period, the notion of modernism (*hadātha*) becomes most crucial to Arab writers' sense of their practice [...] However, these specific post-colonial developments are also part of a longer engagement with the idea of literary modernity (again, *hadātha*), which has seemed especially urgent at particular historical junctures: during the late nineteenth century; after the First and Second World Wars [...][35]

Arabic literature – and al-Hakim's work above all – thus adds to questions about the temporality of modernism and the relationship between modernism and modernity that Susan Stanford Friedman raises. In histories of Britain and Europe there's usually a temporal gap between the rise of modernity – dating as far back as the Enlightenment but often associated with the industrialisation of the mid-nineteenth century – and the aesthetic innovations – modernism

– that supposedly respond to the changes of modernity. While *nahda* is not exactly parallel with modernity – with *nahda* more associated with the literary or aesthetic – in Egypt similarly the *nahda* pre-dates the literary experimentalism of *hadātha*, which is usually seen as beginning in the 1940s in Egypt with the avowedly anti-nationalist Surrealist-influenced poets of the Art and Liberty movement.[36] But as the above quote suggests, we should perhaps see modernism as a recurring strategy in response to periodic moments of historical or representational crisis, rather than as an uninterrupted and clearly bounded stretch. We might then move the moment (or one moment) of modernism in Egypt earlier, to the Pharaonic movement in the aftermath of the Revolution of 1919. For if we juxtapose al-Hakim's *The Return of the Spirit* with the other novels in this study, it can emerge as similarly modernist in style, employing a number of odd narrative devices, from seemingly unrelated excurses to tonal shifts to the jagged incursion of the Revolution of 1919 into the plot at its end. Indeed, al-Hakim's plays – for which he is more famous – are often characterised as modernist.[37] Just as the innovations of modernism in Europe, England and America are rooted in part in new opportunities for cross-cultural dialogue, whether among these regions or between them and Africa and Asia, so the *nahda* in Egypt is likewise transnational; as Bernard writes, 'Rather than seeing the *nahda* as an embrace of European "modernity" at the expense of Arab "tradition", then, we might see it as a "fruitful meeting" between indigenous and Western forms' (p. 465). In its use of connections between Europe and Egypt to forge a distinctly Egyptian 'essence', *The Return of the Spirit* – like the Pharaonic movement that inspired it – captures that sense of a 'fruitful meeting'.

Similarly Walter Armbrust, writing about later twentieth-century Egyptian mass media, asks, 'What is modernity in Egypt? In the West modernity emphasized discontinuity as a means of clearing the ground for more rational forms of society [. . .] Egyptian modernity is also avowedly rationalist, but puts a greater emphasis on maintaining continuity with the past.'[38] Yet as this book has traced, that balance between discontinuity and 'maintaining continuity with the past' is central to modernism both in Egypt and in England; modernists like Woolf and Joyce link new mass media technologies to ancient forms of inscription, and al-Hakim ties together the nationalist upheaval of the 1920s with the glories of the Pharaonic period. Modernism is defined by that attempt to connect the present and the past, and to bridge the gaps between one nation or one language or one media and another, in Egypt as in Britain.

The Return of the Spirit tells the story of Muhsin, an adolescent boy living with his uncles in Cairo and going to school there. Part comic *Bildungsroman*, the novel focuses on the unfulfilled lust of Muhsin and two of his uncles for the girl next door, Saniya, but as the novel progresses it becomes increasingly less conventional, shifting its focus to different characters and locations and then abruptly turning to the Revolution.³⁹ From beginning to end, al-Hakim, like Musa and Haykal, emphasises the continuity of Egyptian culture through the millennia, despite the changes wrought by Turkish and British occupation and the transition to Islam. As Muhsin hears from a fellow train traveller, 'the people of Egypt are a deeply rooted nation. Why, we've been in the Nile valley for seven thousand years. We knew how to plant and cultivate, had villages, farms, and farmers at a time when Europe hadn't even achieved barbarism,' to which another passenger replies, 'You're right: it all depends on one's lineage, Mr. Effendi' (p. 158).⁴⁰ Al-Hakim sounds the dominant strains of Pharaonic thought – the emphasis on a fully developed Egyptian civilisation that predated that of Europe, and a nationalist attention to the roots and shared identity of Egyptians across time.

Such a view is given its fullest expression in a chapter late in the novel that features a conversation between two characters who appear only in that one episode – a visiting British Inspector of Irrigation and a French archaeologist. Over the course of the section, the Frenchman – attuned through his job to the ancient past – extolls the possibilities for future Egyptian glory, tying it to the past civilisation of the Pharaohs. Again, that link is made through 'blood' and through the Egyptian peasants. When the British Inspector objects, 'I didn't think you were serious when you claimed there's a link between Egypt today and Egypt yesterday', the archaeologist replies, 'And what a link! I said and say again that the essence [الجوهر] is eternal. These fellahin who are singing from a single heart are many different individuals joined into a single person by emotion and belief' (p. 186).⁴¹

The archaeologist's rejoinder serves to encompass the main ideas in his chapter-long discourse: a validation of the peasants, a link between the 'eternal essence' of ancient and modern Egyptians, an invocation of the 'heart' of Egyptians and a championing of the unity of the people that represents 'many different individuals joined into a single person'. That link between past and present is 'in their blood [دمه] without their knowing it' since 'this is an ancient people' who possess knowledge 'by the heart [بقلبه], not the intellect [بعقله]' (pp. 182–3; p. 54). For the archaeologist, the aspect of ancient Egypt to emphasise is thus not the hieroglyphs, but the pyramids, which embody the shared endeavour of the Egyptian people and particularly the Egyptian peasants. Thus while the archaeologist invokes Champollion, he refers not to his decipherment of Egyptian writing, but rather to his commentary on the wonder of the pyramids. These pyramids, according to his fellow Frenchman, were made through a happy collective effort: 'We cannot conceptualize the emotions that transform this people into a single individual able to bear on his shoulders tremendous stone slabs for twenty years, with a smiling face and a happy heart. [...] Yes, their bodies suffered, but even that gave them a secret pleasure, the pleasure in sharing pain for a common cause' (p. 185;

pp. 59–60). The common objective in building the pyramids thus expresses the 'spirit' of the Egyptian people, a spirit that may be recaptured: 'The present-day Egyptian people still preserves that spirit [الروح]. [. . .] Don't be surprised if these people, who stand together as one [. . .] bring forth another miracle besides the pyramids' (pp. 186–7; p. 63). For the Frenchman, Egyptian unity is most important – the ability of the Egyptian peasants happily to give up their own well-being for the sake of the larger good.

Of course, the Frenchman's speech smacks of the most obvious kind of textbook Orientalism.[42] He emphasises the more embodied Egyptian spirit – its heart – as opposed to the intellect, and he proudly proclaims a unique and unchanging Egyptian essence. Egypt thus seems to exist eternally, outside of time, what Johannes Fabian terms the 'denial of coevalness'.[43] Al-Hakim's choice to put these words into a colloquy between an Englishman and a Frenchman opens up these speeches to clear ironisation: after all, the English and the French are most associated with co-opting and stealing the very ancient Egyptian heritage that they are celebrating.[44] The context of this chapter also provides fodder for an ironic reading. While the Englishman and Frenchman are conversing, the servants and their aristocratic hosts are desperately trying to fulfil their desire for a post-prandial bit of cheese, one that can only be fulfilled by digging up a mould-ridden rind of 'Greek' cheese used to bait mousetraps which the unsuspecting visitors barely notice and consume happily. The novel thus emphasises the more basic and material needs that underlie the high-blown speechifying about Egypt's past and future; indeed, this is a common pattern in the novel, which returns to eating and preparing foods as one of its constant motifs.

We could then consider this chapter as an example of Homi Bhabha's 'colonial mimicry', defined as 'at once a mode of appropriation and of resistance, from the disciplined to the desiring', as a 'more ambivalent, third choice: camouflage, mimicry, black skins/white masks' (p. 162). Indeed, al-Hakim's appropriation of the words and discourses of Egypt's colonial authorities seems a clear example of 'camouflage', opening up a space for critique. Yet the mode of 'resistance', so central to this kind of mimicry, is largely absent here. For despite the possibility for an ironic reading of the Frenchman's words, we can't dismiss his viewpoint, since the novel ultimately explicitly confirms his prophecy. The penultimate chapter of the book, which concerns the Revolution of 1919, begins: 'Events bore out the French archaeologist's prediction: "a nation that at the dawn of humanity brought forth the miracle of the pyramids will be able to bring forth another miracle . . . or many." [. . .] Perhaps this archaeologist who lived in the past saw the future of Egypt more clearly than anyone else' (p. 280; p. 240). Again and again the novel seems to subscribe to the Frenchman's views of an unchanging essence in Egyptian culture. The peasants are constantly validated and seen as an inspiration and precisely for the same reasons cited by the Frenchman: their uncomplaining unity, their ability to work together towards a common goal. Al-Hakim even underlines that the inspiration for the 1919 Revolution, Saad Zaghloul, himself began as a peasant. And this validation of the peasants fits with the views of Pharaonicism, with Salama Musa claiming that 'Ancient Egypt or the Egypt of the Pharaohs is still alive among our fellahin'.[45]

The seeming approval of the French archaeologist's speech demonstrates again the affinity between Orientalist and nationalist discourses. For the idea of a unique Egyptian essence, a link between ancient and modern, is precisely what is required for those Egyptian intellectuals seeking to forge a nation and an identity for that nation. In a country with both Christians and Muslims, in a country occupied by the Turkish and the English and the French, the ancient past becomes a way of insisting on the unity of the people and thus the inevitability of its future as an independent nation-state. The nationalist background thus explains al-Hakim's emphasis on the 'heart' or the 'spirit' as opposed to the intellect. After all, ancient Egypt had very little in common with the Egypt of the 1920s, and the religious differences between ancient Egypt and Islam made Pharaonicism inherently controversial among Islamist leaders. Thus al-Hakim naturally does not dwell on hieroglyphs as a form of inscription, since these likewise emphasise the fact that the present-day language of Egypt – Arabic – derived from elsewhere and was associated with Islam. By bypassing the intellect and lodging the Egyptian essence somewhere deeper, al-Hakim is able to unite the nation for his nationalist aims while skirting the obvious linguistic and religious differences between past and present. Thus the pyramid becomes the central symbol of Egyptian nationalism, confirming the glories of the ancient past and serving as a model for how a people can unite for a national project: in this case, the project of revolution.

As it was for Musa and Haykal, al-Hakim's nationalism also involves drawing a line between what is purely Egyptian and what is not. As the archaeologist says, 'Rest assured [. . .] that any corruption of their manners is not native to Egypt but introduced here by other peoples like the Bedouins or the Turks, for example' (p. 184; p. 57). Defining an Egyptian essence, imagining an Egyptian nation united in common endeavour, involves excluding that which is not Egyptian, which in the novel is frequently figured as Bedouins or, in the case of Muhsin's negatively characterised mother, as Turkish.[46] Or, interestingly, given the desire by African-American writers to claim Egypt as black, as African. In the most bizarre moment of the novel, an episode that critics seems to have largely ignored or treated as an embarrassing aberration, a side character, Dr Hilmi – the father of Saniya – tells the story of his past journey to the Sudan.[47] Unmotivated by any reason of the plot, or by any need to know this character further (he appears on only one other brief occasion, as a blocking agent for Saniya's marriage), Dr Hilmi's story serves to crystallise how Africa serves as both inspiration for and foil against which to define the prospect of Egyptian national unity.

Al-Hakim recounts how Dr Hilmi sits in the café outside his house and talks to the other patrons, and suddenly from the midst of a gently comic romantic *Bildungsroman* we're in *Heart of Darkness*. He tells of his journey with a group of soldiers into the Sudan:

> Then they carried their kit, tents, and waterskins and went deep into the dense and far-reaching forests and thickets. A black guide, one of the local inhabitants, preceded them. Whenever they had completed a stage and night overcame them, they stopped and lit fires to keep the beasts of the jungle away. [. . .] Those nights were hot and at times magnificently moonlit and profoundly still. The only sound was the roaring of a lion prowling around in search of a portion of the meat. (p. 142)[48]

The jungle world seems to take on the threatening, primitive aspects of the Congo in Conrad's novella, complete with the references to stillness and distant, menacing sounds. Going ahead of his companions, the doctor encounters and shoots a monkey at a well. Al-Hakim recounts how

> The doctor went forward at once towards the well and leaned over to look at the monkey in it and to see how much water it contained. What he saw there astonished him. He found more than a hundred monkeys had also fallen down it. [. . .] [He] came to an amazing realization: these monkeys had actually come to drink from the well and their method of reaching the distant water was for that large monkey to stand and grasp a second monkey who let himself down. This second monkey grabbed hold of a third who let himself down below him in the same way, and the third a fourth. Thus some of the monkeys made a ladder of their bodies down the well so others could climb down and then back up [. . .] He was amazed and commented to himself on the solidarity [تضامن] of these monkeys and on the great sacrifice that large monkey had made on behalf of the group. (p. 143; pp. 262–3)

The monkeys eventually return to attack the group and avenge the death of their fellow monkey, but the episode ultimately becomes not one of horror but of inspiration. The 'solidarity' of the monkeys becomes a kind of thematic model for the rest of the novel, looking backward to the solidarity of the Egyptian peasants who built the pyramid and forward to the prospect of Egyptian national unity. Indeed, the rest of the novel is filled with examples of the unity of Egyptians in a collective effort, and, indeed, the unity of man and beast: particularly in Muhsin's encounter with a cow nursing a peasant boy and in the scene bookending the novel of Muhsin and his uncles happily sharing a room with each other and their animals. The encounter with the monkeys, however potentially horrifying, thus seems to foreshadow the communal spirit that al-Hakim sees as essential to the Egyptian people and their nationalist revolution.

While the encounter with ancient Egypt and other non-Western cultures on the part of Western novelists and filmmakers is always at least partly defined by primitivist and Orientalist discourses, *The Return of the Spirit* demonstrates how that primitivism is at least partially shared by the Egyptians themselves. Egypt is not merely the object of a Western primitivist imagination; rather, Egyptian writers impose that same kind of primitivism onto their own neighbours to the South – the Sudanese. As with Western Orientalist discourses, the so-called primitivism of Africa serves to define Egypt as separate and distinct from its neighbours but also to provide a vision of a more authentic and fulfilling form of life. Thus, as in *Heart of Darkness*, the Egyptian expedition into Africa seems to proceed into an earlier and potentially threatening stage of development, out of the confines of civilisation, where people are almost replaced by the racialised image of the monkeys. Yet if that new world is hazardous, it is also somehow purer, with the monkeys reflecting a communal ideal that the 'civilised' Egyptians may strive for but have not yet succeeded in fulfilling. Indeed, the trip to Sudan functions in the same way as the other trip back in time in the novel: the invocation of Egypt's own ancient Pharaonic past, where the same collectivist ideals held sway (the fact that these ideas were less collectivist than authoritarian is elided in al-Hakim's vision). Or rather, the encounter with the 'primitive' Sudan seems to pave the way for and make possible the subsequent invocation of an authentically Egyptian sense of community a few chapters later in the novel. For soon after this moment in the text, Muhsin leaves Cairo for his parents' home, and there the novel becomes far more explicit in its validation of the peasants and their 'eternal' spirit. This section also contains the conversation between the British inspector and the French archaeologist. The narrative of the journey to Sudan thus crystallises and calls into being the themes of Egyptian essence and national solidarity that lead to the outbreak of revolution at the end of the novel. Indeed, this scene seems almost to literalise Homi Bhabha's declaration that 'it is in between the edict of Englishness and the assault of the dark unruly spaces of the earth, through an act of repetition, that the colonial text emerges uncertainly' (p. 149). *Return of the Spirit*'s transformation into a nationalist text seems to 'emerge' uncertainly in this moment through the act of repeating or potentially re-writing *Heart of Darkness*, with Egyptian identity defined as between England and Sudan, as aspiring to an essence distinct from the rest of Africa and free from but connected to Europe.

For the journey South serves also as a way to sever Egypt from southern Africa, to define the territorial and communal boundaries of the nation. For in Dr Hilmi's narrative, al-Hakim stresses the separation between Egypt and

Sudan as representative of the rest of Africa. As we've seen, Sudan is described as wild and untamed, potentially even at an earlier stage of development than Egypt. But Egyptians are also defined as not black; al-Hakim stresses that 'A black guide, one of the local inhabitants, preceded them [يتقدمهم دليل زنجي من أهل البلاد]'. Indeed, al-Hakim's use of the Arabic word زنجي is more derogatory and offensive than simply describing the guide as black. Black people are at home in this 'uncivilised' locale, where the foreign Egyptians find themselves out of place. This stressing of the difference between Africa and Egypt naturally goes along with the impulses of so much of Pharaonicism. Not only does Egypt need to be defined as a territorially and culturally bounded unit in order to succeed as a nation-state, but also, given the racialised discourses of the time, Egypt's claims to be linked with Europe, made by Musa, Haykal and Taha Hussein, are more easily made if Egypt is seen as its own entity distinct from Africa and the African race. The creation of an Egyptian/African division thus works both to establish a uniquely Egyptian state and to make a claim for the commonalities of Egypt and Europe.

THE WISDOM OF THE PAST

The desire to use the legacy of ancient Egypt to assert Egypt's newfound nationhood recurs in the first novel by the most famous figure in Egypt's twentieth-century literature: Nobel Prize winner Naguib Mahfouz. But in his novel *Khufu's Wisdom*, from 1939, Mahfouz not only uses the pyramid to stress Egypt's potential for collective action; he also turns to the Egyptian language of hieroglyphs. Mahfouz calls attention to writing itself, attempting to link hieroglyphs with modern alphabetical languages in order to forge a connection between Egyptian past and present. Perhaps anticipating his own later interest in film, Mahfouz in his novel treats written text – words and characters, be they hieroglyphs or Arabic letters – as another form of media.

Mahfouz came of age during the period of Pharaonicism and Egyptian nationalism described above. Mahfouz recounts how 'From a small room on the roof' he 'used to see the demonstrations of the 1919 revolution' including 'English soldiers firing at the demonstrators', concluding that 'the one thing which most shook the security of my childhood was the 1919 revolution'.[49] But Mahfouz was influenced not just by the revolution, but by the Pharaonic movement it inspired, with Salama Musa one of his earliest mentors. Elliott Colla describes, 'Mahfouz's association with Musa during the first years of his life as an emerging public intellectual and literary artist is crucial, since it places Mahfouz directly at the center of one of the most prominent institutions of cultural and political Pharaonism.'[50] Indeed, Mahfouz claims, 'I had studied the Pharaonic history of Egypt completely, almost to the point of specialization', and his first published work was a translation of the English children's book *Peeps at Many Lands: Ancient Egypt* by James Baikie (whose later book was featured in the advertisement shown in Figure 2.1).[51] Indeed, Salama Musa helped arrange for publication of both *Khufu's Wisdom* – suggesting its Arabic title *'Abath al-aqdar* – and his translation of *Peeps at Many Lands*.[52] Thus when Mahfouz turned to writing his first novel, he chose as his subject matter ancient Egypt and a similar period to the one referred to by al-Hakim: the Pharaohship of Khufu, builder of the Great Pyramid. The novel takes as its starting point a variant on the Oedipus myth, in which Khufu sets out to kill the child prophesised to displace him and be his heir. While the child is believed killed, he survives to be adopted and raised as Djedef, who becomes a celebrated soldier who rises in the Pharaoh's army, eventually falling in love with Khufu's daughter. When Djedef successfully foils Khufu's son's plot against the Pharaoh, Khufu, now aware that Djedef was the child prophesised to be his heir, decides to anoint him as Pharaoh over the rest of his sons.

For Elliott Colla, *Khufu's Wisdom* is 'an allegory of racial purity and territorial nationalism', and in those aspects the novel shares much with al-Hakim's *The Return of the Spirit*.[53] Like al-Hakim, Mahfouz emphasises the communal spirit of the Egyptian people and specifically the peasantry, who unite to form a collective identity under the Pharaoh. But again like al-Hakim, that shared spirit presupposes an exclusion of those who are not considered Egyptian. As Mahfouz writes:

> As for those workers who are in fact Egyptians, most of them are from the southern part of the country. These are people with self-respect, pride, steadfastness, and faith. They are able to bear terrific torment, and to patiently tolerate overwhelming tragedies. Unlike those aliens [prisoners of war and foreign settlers], they are aware of what they are doing. They believe in their hearts that the hard labor to which they devote their lives is a splendid religious obligation, a duty to the deity to whom they pray, and a form of obedience owed to the title of him who sits upon the throne.[54]

Like al-Hakim, Mahfouz celebrates the peasants (those from the 'southern part of the country') for their ability blindly to obey and work happily towards the collective good. Despite the socialist politics of many of the Pharaonicists, they champion an almost authoritarian aesthetic, one which proves useful for them as they seek to fashion a united Egyptian nation. While al-Hakim casts out the Sudanese and the Bedouins, here it is prisoners of war, foreign settlers and, again, Bedouins who are denied that Egyptian essence. Despite the fact that large portions of the Egyptian population consist of descendants of foreign settlers, the novel creates an image of Egypt as a nation protecting itself from those who are without a nation: the Bedouin tribes, against whom Djedef wins a decisive battle at the climax of the novel.

Again this essence of Egyptian glory is embodied by the Great Pyramid which Khufu is constructing in the novel. As its architect describes it:

> It will remain standing throughout the continuous generations to come [. . .] We celebrate today [. . .] Egypt's eternal emblem, and its truthful epithet, born of the strength that binds her North with her South. It is the offspring of the patience that overflows in all her children, from the tiller of the earth with his hoe, to the scribe with her sheet of papyrus. [. . .] It is the exemplar of the genius that has made our homeland sovereign over the earth' (p. 81; p. 94)

The passage expresses all of the themes of the Pharaonicist movement of the 1920s – the use of the pyramid as a symbol of Egyptian glory, the emphasis on the primacy of the Egyptian homeland (which is 'sovereign over the earth'), the focus on the unity of Egypt despite regional and class differences, and the notion that Egypt's past greatness emblematises its possible renewed future. As in *The Return of the Spirit*, if Egypt was once great and united, then it can be so again.

But Mahfouz departs from al-Hakim in also emphasising the Egyptian language. Just as Mahfouz seeks to minimise all of the differences in religion and culture between ancient and modern Egypt in an effort to assert its eternal essence, so he focuses on the links between hieroglyphs and contemporary Arabic writing. Like the modernists – and Joyce specifically, who likewise strives to link Arabic and hieroglyphs in *Finnegans Wake* – Mahfouz refuses to see hieroglyphs as a pictorial language; instead, he represents the ancient Egyptian language as a virtually identical form to the modern alphabetical language of Arabic. Indeed, Mahfouz was deeply influenced by European modernism, having read and appreciated Proust, Kafka and Melville, and saying that he admired 'the all-encompassing outlook in Conrad's *Heart of Darkness*'. Mahfouz also studied in depth Henri Bergson's philosophy during his time at university, with that influence reinforced by his interest in the Bergson-influenced works of Proust. And while he claims that 'As for Joyce [. . .] he was just a writer that you had to read [. . .] *Ulysses* was a terrible novel, but it created a trend', he also acknowledges that 'I sometimes encounter a Joycean moment in my hero's life, so I render it in Joyce's manner with some modification'.[55]

Throughout *Khufu's Wisdom*, Mahfouz like other modernists insists on a strict separation between pictures and the language of hieroglyphs. While hieroglyphs are linked with practitioners of visual art – particularly Djedef's brother Nafa – Mahfouz never implies, like Ezra Pound or others, that they are depictive. As part of his training, Djedef 'avidly applies himself to the beautiful language of the hieroglyphs [الهيروغليفية]', but that description is juxtaposed on the following page with an account of him leafing 'through books adorned with pictures' including the 'image of Apis, the sacred bull'

THE 'ESSENCE' OF EGYPT

(pp. 62–3; pp. 74, 76). While Mahfouz calls attention to the visual form of the hieroglyphs, he insists on their status as a language, one distinct from the actual images that Djedef admires in the book. Similarly, when Nafa opens his art studio, Mahfouz describes how he 'made and displayed his artistic creations, and composed a sign in immaculate hieroglyphs that he hung outside, which read: "Nafa, son of Bisharu, Graduate of the Khufu School of Fine Arts"' (p. 67; p. 79). Again, hieroglyphs are juxtaposed with 'artistic creations', but they communicate just like contemporary Western languages, spelling out the name of Nafa.

This desire to call attention to the artistic qualities of hieroglyphs even as he insists on their difference from images thus aligns Mahfouz with modernists like Woolf. Mahfouz seems to view ancient Egyptian writing as a strictly linguistic form that nonetheless, in its visual appearance, has its own aesthetic qualities. Indeed, that's exactly how hieroglyphs are portrayed in the English children's book that Mahfouz translated into Arabic; there, Baikie writes of hieroglyphs:

> It is nothing but little pictures from beginning to end. The Egyptians began by putting down a picture of the thing which was represented by the word they wanted to use, and, though by-and-by they formed a sort of alphabet to spell words with, and had, besides, signs that represented the different syllables of a word, still, these signs were all little pictures.'[56]

Unlike so many of the commentators that this project has looked at, Baikie is accurate about the phonetic nature of hieroglyphs; while he consistently stresses how beautiful the individual glyphs are, he never denies their primarily phonetic nature. In that way, hieroglyphs come to seem similar to Arabic: a phonetic language that places more of an emphasis on its calligraphic, visual form than many other alphabetical scripts. If the ancient language of Egypt was phonetic and visual, then, in Mahfouz's imaginative representation, it was not so far removed from the contemporary language of Egypt.

Mahfouz consistently emphasises the phonetic nature of hieroglyphs. He describes how a character enters a scribe's office, where 'the walls were filled with shelves stacked with papyrus scrolls', and how 'the scribe went to search in the record books, pulling out one and unrolling its pages, looking up the sign [حرف] "k" and the name "Karda"' (pp. 50, 52; pp. 61, 63). This language is signalled as hieroglyphs by the historical setting and the focus on papyrus, but Mahfouz uses these hieroglyphs to emphasise the phoneme 'k', rather than a word or object it pictures. Indeed, the Arabic حرف is closer to 'letter' than 'sign'. The scene thus has a strikingly modern, almost bureaucratic feel, with no sense of the distance between past and present. The hieroglyphs are portrayed as just as phonetic as contemporary Arabic. Just as there is no difference in essence between the modern and ancient Egyptian, so in Mahfouz's novel there is no essential difference between the linguistic systems of the Pharaonic past and the Islamic present.

While Mahfouz does not directly invoke new media, he nonetheless focuses on the importance of the old medium of writing, putting writing and its history in a privileged place in his novel. As we'll see in Joyce as well, the history of writing is inseparable from the history of cultures, and these issues seem particularly central in the postcolonial context of both Egypt and Ireland. The Pharaonicist focus on ancient Egypt, like Joyce's interest in ancient linguistic forms traced in the next chapter, thus fits with Edward Said's claim that 'along with these nationalistic adumbrations of the decolonized identity, there always goes an almost magically inspired, quasi-alchemical redevelopment of the native language.'[57] Thus while both al-Hakim's and Mahfouz's novels seem to turn away from hieroglyphs as a central metaphor, finding in the Great Pyramid a model of Egyptian glory and collective national endeavour, Mahfouz in particular returns again and again to writing itself. His novel suggests that the sources of Egyptian heritage are captured not only in the built environment, but also in the hieroglyphs. While the Great Pyramid is a form of transmission that 'will remain standing throughout the continuous generations to come', the 'book of wisdom' that Khufu sets out to write – and the language in which that book is written – also seem to share in that memorialisation of ancient Egyptian power and influence. Indeed, Khufu decides to write his book in the central chamber of the pyramid being built for him. Pyramid and written text are linked with each other, with each embodying the persistent glory of Egyptian civilisation.

This focus on the primacy and influence of words and writings is likewise present in *Peeps at Many Lands: Ancient Egypt*. There, Baikie writes:

> When we talk of the Bible, which just means 'the Book,' we are using one of the words which the Greeks used to describe the plant out of which the Egyptians made the material on which they wrote; and when we talk of paper, we are using another name, the commoner name, of the same plant. For the Egyptians were the first people to make paper. (p. 66)

The ancient Egyptians not only supposedly invented writing, they invented the words for writing, words which were passed down into English. Language itself expresses Egyptian influence. The Pharaonic novelists of the 1920s and 1930s thus do not turn away from an engagement with writing and media, finding inspiration only in the pyramids of ancient Egypt. Rather they combine the two, uniting the hieroglyph and the pyramid, making writing itself into a monument. Even in *The Return of the Spirit*, in which al-Hakim seems uninterested in the ancient Egyptian writing system, he remains invested in championing the power of writing. For the novel is not only an exploration of the ancient past and its effect on the present of Egypt, but also a *Kunstlerroman*: the story of the main character Muhsin's evolution into a writer who can express the newfound glories of Egypt. If ancient Egypt inspires or foreshadows revolution, it also inspires writing, with Muhsin proclaiming to his friend, 'tomorrow we're going to be the eloquent tongue of the nation' (p. 79; p. 124). For writers like al-Hakim and Mahfouz, ancient Egyptian hieroglyphics come to stand for the power of the written word itself, even as these writers seek to move beyond writing towards revolution or an imaginative forging of Egyptian national identity.

Film as Resurrection

While Mahfouz connects hieroglyphs and his own literary language, Shadi Abd al-Salam's 1969 film *al-Mummia* (*The Mummy*, or *The Night of Counting the Years*) further seeks to express the continuities of Egyptian history through an engagement with the relationship between film and writing.[58] In so doing, *al-Mummia* reflects both the enduring power of Pharaonicist thought in the later twentieth century and how the legacy of ancient Egypt remains inextricably linked to early twentieth-century understandings of the characteristics and potentials of film.

Egypt and its antiquities were not only the subject matter of Western films in the early twentieth century, but Egypt itself also had the most robust film culture in the Middle East during this period. Films by the Lumière Brothers were shown in Alexandria and Cairo as early as 1896, and a Lumière film was shot in Egypt in 1897. In that same year the Cinèmatographe Lumière in Alexandria began periodic screenings, and in 1906 Pathé started the first devoted movie theatre in Cairo, followed soon by a handful of others. The number of films made in Egypt steadily increased over the next decade, with 146 released between 1907 and 1930, though made almost exclusively by foreigners or recent immigrants.[59] In 1923, *In the Land of Tutankhamen*, the first full-length Egyptian film, was released, with its cinematographer Mohamed Bayoumi going on to direct a series of newsreels during that year as well as the short film *Master Barsum Looking for a Job*. While Bayoumi's own career eventually sputtered out, funding opportunities, and thus the number of films released, accelerated between 1923 and 1934. This growth culminated in the establishment of Studio Misr in 1935, which ushered in the Golden Age of Egyptian cinema over the following thirty years.[60]

Film thus occupied an important place in Egyptian society during the 1920s, with Egyptian filmmakers like Bayoumi using their medium to reclaim the legacy of ancient Egypt from its appropriation and exoticisation by Western films. Much as the actual relics of Egypt had been taken to Paris, Berlin and London, so the worldwide representation of Egypt had been co-opted, through the movies, by London, New York and Hollywood.[61] At the same time as Western directors were fascinated with ancient Egypt and cranked out film after film about mummies and Egyptian princesses, Egyptians were establishing their own filmmaking industry. Bayoumi's films thus insist on Egypt's present reality – either through actuality footage of its historical monuments and its nationalist heroes or through fictional representations of contemporary life – against Western films that insist on exoticising Egypt and its past. We might thus see Mahfouz's first three novels – all set in Pharaonic Egypt – as attempting the same project as the films of the period: seeking to reassert Egyptian imaginative control over ancient Egypt. While over the course of his career Mahfouz turns more towards realist representations of contemporary Egypt, he begins by first engaging with Egypt's past. In his early novels, Mahfouz needs to claim that past as Egyptian and as related to writing, as opposed to Western and mediated through film.

The juxtaposition of Mahfouz and early Egyptian cinema reveals the larger connection between film and the Pharaonicist and nationalist ferment of the 1920s and 1930s. Just as Egyptian writers tried to reclaim the ancient past as a vehicle for nationalist aims, so filmmakers at the time increasingly shook off the shackles of Western domination and likewise turned to Pharaonic and nationalist subjects. By re-examining this period through the lens of the later film *al-Mummia*, we can thus see how the rise of film as a new medium accompanied the flowering of nationalism in Egypt in the 1920s; as Benedict Anderson argues, new media like print helped create the 'imagined community' of a nation, and the same goes for film when it comes to Egypt.

Indeed, Mahfouz and al-Hakim specifically respond to cinema in their later works. Mahfouz's engagement with writing as a form of media in *Khufu's Wisdom* thus perhaps anticipates his later sustained contribution to another media: film. As Nathaniel Greenberg discusses, Mahfouz was a key part of the Egyptian film industry between 1947 and 1959, co-writing 'some twenty odd scripts, many of them among the most successful in Egyptian history'.[62] Mahfouz was thus by far the most directly involved in film of all of the figures in this book. And Mahfouz saw in film a way of expressing Egypt's importance; as he writes, 'I want Egyptian films to find their way onto the world market first and foremost by way of their self-worth; for the technique to reach the highest levels of esteem.'[63] While it's difficult to say for sure whether Mahfouz's Pharaonicism helped to inspire his interest in film, or whether that engagement with film led to his turn towards contemporary realism in his famous novels of the 1950s and 1960s, Mahfouz himself embodies the connection between a fascination with the ancient Egyptian past and with the new medium of film.

But both Mahfouz and al-Hakim share a profound ambivalence about film as a medium. While Mahfouz was part of the film industry, he nonetheless affirms the greater value of literature: 'It is certainly true that the cinema is the most modern medium, but we must distinguish between "most modern" and "most important." In my opinion, no other medium of expression surpasses the written word.'[64] Likewise, in his 1960 memoir *The Prison of Life*, al-Hakim describes his youthful fascination with the cinema in Alexandria, but portrays that interest as antithetical with his literary career. He writes:

> As soon I was out in the streets of this great city and saw the throngs outside the 'cinematograph,' I lost my head. That particular picture-house was called 'The American Cosmograph.' [. . .] Colored posters dazzled one's eyes [. . .]. Satan the accursed tempted me to go in and see.[65]

After that first encounter, al-Hakim frequently skips his schoolwork to see the French serials *Zigomar* and *Fantomas*. And while the condemnation of the cinematograph in the above passage is ironically excessive, he ultimately needs to give up on his fascination with the cinema to achieve a literary career. After being caught at a film, he promises 'not to set foot in any cinematograph until after I had got my baccalaureate certificate at the end of secondary schooling' (p. 89), a vow that is juxtaposed in the memoir with the arrival in his school of a new teacher who instills in him a 'conscious interest in Arabic literature' (p. 90). We thus might see the description of 'Satan the accursed' tempting al-Hakim to the cinema as not wholly ironic; film, with its associations with the colonial power of France, does seem to dazzle him for a moment away from his future writing Egyptian literature. Indeed, his later interest in drama, the memoir implies, can be seen as a kind of fusion of cinema and literature. Al-Hakim describes the 'five piasters' in his pocket with which he pays for film admission, which later is echoed by the 'five piasters' with which he attends the theatre (pp. 88, 97). Much as Woolf is both attracted to and ambivalent about film, and much as she seeks to fold film into writing, so al-Hakim in his dramas seeks to bring the sensory attractions of film into the domain of print.

Al-Hakim and Mahfouz thus both seem to treat film as a fascinating but ultimately limited or even dangerous rival to literature. If we turn to *al-Mummia*, however, we can see a much more specific link between an engagement with the relationship of film and writing and an interest in the Pharaonic past, one that perhaps exposes how that same conjunction of film and Pharaonicism lurks in the background even in the 1920s and 1930s.

Despite its persistent lack of popular success, its much delayed release in 1975 and its years of VHS and DVD neglect in Europe and America, *al-Mummia* has come to be considered by critics as one of the greatest of all Egyptian films. Based on the actual 1881 discovery of a huge cache of mummies in the Valley of the Kings, the film opens with a shot of ancient Egyptian inscriptions, followed by a scene in which the French director of excavations and antiquities in Egypt at the time, Gaston Maspero, after reading from the Egyptian Book of the Dead, reveals that priceless Pharaonic antiquities are being sold on the black market. His Egyptian assistant, Ahmad Kamal, is tasked with discovering how and from where these relics have been stolen. The film then tells the story of Wahid, the son of one of the chieftains of the Hobarat tribe in Upper Egypt. After the death of his father, the other chiefs reveal to him and his brother that the tribe has been supporting itself by raiding a cache of mummies they have discovered; Wahid and his brother are appalled, and the tribe responds by murdering Wahid's brother. Not yet aware of the murder, Wahid agonises over how to respond, tempted to reveal to Ahmad Kamal and the other Cairean archaeologists and soldiers the secret of his tribe. After much indecision, Wahid tells Kamal, and the mummies are taken from their trove by boat back to Cairo for safekeeping as a priceless cultural heritage.

On first glance, *al-Mummia* seems merely to repeat the dominant tropes of Pharaonicism that *The Return of the Spirit* and *Khufu's Wisdom* have set out. The Egyptian people, as emblematised by the Hobarat tribe, have cut themselves off from the wellspring of Egyptian culture, denying their connection to the past. As the chieftains say, when Wahid's brother objects to their grave-robbing, 'Those whom you call "the dead" are but ashes or wood thousands of years old. Nobody can recall their parents or their children.'[66] The Pharaonic past is seen as Other, divorced from the Egyptian present. The task of the film, like the task of Ahmad Kamal, is to reclaim that Pharaonic heritage and preserve it as an inspiration for the present. The film thus ends with the intertitle: 'Arise [...] thou shalt not perish. Thou hast been called by name. Thou hast been resurrected', linking the rediscovery of the past with the promise of a bright future.[67] Such a reading of the film as Pharaonicist text gibes with Abd al-Salam's comments:

> Sometimes we say, 'We're seven thousand years old and don't even know it.' This phrase has very large implications. For if, of these seven thousand years, I only know forty, then I'm like the person who is thirty years old but only remembers the last five. The state of profound personal confusion from which he would be suffering can be compared to the [Nation-] State that is afflicted by the sickness of this memory loss. I believe that we have generations suffering from cultural and historical amnesia.[68]

Abd al-Salam's film thus seeks both to represent and to make up for that 'cultural and historical amnesia' by calling attention to the 'seven thousand' year heritage of the Pharaonic past.

The general critical consensus about the film is as 'a straightforward story about the eternal spirit of Egypt, an ancient spirit that was reawakened and nurtured by the modern nation-state'.[69] However, looking back to Mahfouz, the establishment of that link between ancient and modern Egypt involves a specific awareness of ancient Egyptian writing: the heritage of the past is carried not simply in the mummies of the film's title, but in the hieroglyphic inscriptions used to identify those mummies. Indeed, two of the climactic

Figure 4.1   Image from *al-Mummia* (dir. Shadi abd al-Salam, 1969, Egypt)

scenes in the film involve a close attention to the details of Egyptian writing. Ahmad Kamal, capable of reading the hieroglyphs, slowly reads off the names of all of the Pharaohs whose bodies are stored in the tombs, knowledge that is not accessible to the Hobarat tribe. This awareness of the readability of the ancient inscriptions is crucially important to Wahid's agonised decision to reveal his tribe's secret. In a long conversation with a 'Stranger', set against a backdrop of walls engraved with hieroglyphic inscriptions, Wahid is told, 'They say they seek people upon whose ruins we live today. They call them ancestors, and can read their writings and their names on the stone. They care for them.'[70] Shocked, Wahid protests, echoing his chieftains, that 'They are dead! Dead! No one can recall their parents or their children' before crying in despair, 'Tell me no more! You make the stone images seem alive to me.'[71] The scene concludes with Wahid staring up at the seemingly endlessly tall wall of hieroglyphs shown in Figure 4.1, with the camera lingering on them as if seeking to read them. Wahid's ultimate awareness of the living presence of the Pharaonic past – and of the need to preserve it – is thus brought about through the encounter with writing itself.

But while *al-Mummia*, and Abd al-Salam's comments about it, may seem to present an unambiguous Pharaonicist view, the context of the film – which is made after and set before the British colonial occupation – stresses not Western colonialism but rather the divisions within Egypt itself: as Iman Haman writes, the film captures 'a vision of an Egypt fragmented by geography and class', an Egypt torn between Upper and Lower Egypt.[72] The film thus provides an interesting contrast with *The Return of the Spirit*. While both texts share Pharaonicist concerns, the treatment of the Egyptian peasants is starkly different. For Muhsin in al-Hakim's novel, the trip away from Cairo involves a re-acquaintance with the roots of Egyptian culture, with the peasants attached to the wellsprings of an ancient Egyptian past that can provide a model for a nationalist and united future. *Al-Mummia* presents a radically different vision: the Hobarat, structurally similar to the peasants of *The Return of the Spirit* – rural, uncultured, Southern – are not the inspiration for a renewed connection to the Egyptian past, but rather are alienated from that past and distanced from and distrustful of the cultural and governmental leaders in Cairo. The film thus seems to reject the Orientalist celebration of an authentic timeless peasantry that al-Hakim invokes. Instead of the South teaching the North the lessons of nationalism and Pharaonicism, the North must teach the South. Of course, the treatment of the peasants by al-Hakim and Abd al-Salam represent two sides of the same coin – whether seeking to condemn the Hobarat for their amnesia or celebrate them for their 'spirit', both figures seek, in Elliott Colla's words, to 'subordinate the South to the needs of the North', to bring the south of the country under the imaginative and discursive control of Cairo.[73]

Al-Salam's film thus echoes another strain of Orientalist discourse: the Cairean leaders are the benevolent civilisers who must appropriate and remove the legacy of the Pharaonic past so that it will not be despoiled and sold, so that it may be preserved for posterity. In other words, the Caireans function in the same position as the English or French in the colonial era (indeed, the movie begins with Maspero, an actual European). The film displaces the metropole-colony binary of Orientalist discourse: instead of Paris or London as metropole to Cairo's colony, now Cairo has become the metropole to Upper Egypt's colony.

The film is actually far more ambiguous about the removal of the mummies from the Hobarat tribe, however, than Abd al-Salam's comments about the film would have us believe. The final procession of the mummies out of their hiding place echoes the funeral scene early in the film and is attended by hundreds of Hobarat tribespeople in a kind of mourning. The film then ends with a freeze-frame of the ship carrying the antiquities back to Cairo disappearing from view; these relics are not, in the film, enshrined for posterity, but simply taken away. As Elliot Colla argues, 'Abd al-Salam is also conflicted: at times he admits to a real ambivalence about the desirability of the "progress" associated with statist enlightenment and discusses the project in terms of tragedy and loss.'⁷⁴ The removal of the mummies is simultaneously an act of preservation and despoliation.

The film ultimately seems less interested in imaginatively forging national unity – as in al-Hakim and Mahfouz – than in pointing to the persistent divisions within Egyptian culture and the Egyptian nation, the 'huge difference between [the] respective cultures' of Upper and Lower Egypt, in Abd al-Salam's words.⁷⁵ In other words, *al-Mummia* embeds within the Egyptian nation the challenge of cultural Otherness that al-Hakim and Mahfouz had earlier located in the Sudanese and the Bedouin. In *The Return of the Spirit* and *Khufu's Wisdom*, al-Hakim and Mahfouz define a unified Egypt by excluding those who racially or culturally supposedly do not descend from the Pharaohs. In *al-Mummia*, however, the Hobarat – itself a separate tribe, not fused into a potential future Egyptian nation – becomes the Other that must be subordinated or excluded for the sake of the nation. Of course, the fact that this tribe is likewise in the shadow of their 'ancestors' of the Pharaonic era calls into question the entire project of national unity upon which Pharaonicism is founded. While the Pharaonicist discourse remains virtually unchanged from the 1920s and the 1930s, the nationalist hope has been stripped away; while modern Egypt remains inextricably linked to the glories of its past, those glories are lost, and its present remains irredeemably divided.

If *al-Mummia* expresses despair about the divisions in Egypt, it finds solace in media itself. The film not only looks to the past to grapple with the possibility of an enduring Egyptian nation but also examines hieroglyphs and their association with the medium of film. As in Mahfouz, the focus on the ancient history of Egypt for nationalist aims involves an attention to writing, as if the connection of past and present can only be totally convincing if that connection is a medial one: in his case, the link of hieroglyphs and the alphabet. But in *al-Mummia*, that media subtext in accounts of the ancient Egyptian past becomes far more explicit, as the film seems to ally Maspero and Ahmed Kamal's act of appropriating and protecting the mummies with Abd al-Salam's ability, through film, to capture the experience of the Egyptian past and, particularly, the hieroglyphs that preserve it.

Like *Khufu's Wisdom*, *al-Mummia* concentrates throughout on the medium of language, and not just when it comes to its focus on recording the hieroglyphs. Egypt, like the rest of the Arab world, has a unique relationship between spoken and written language, given the differences between classical written Arabic – the language of the literary world and of high culture – and vernacular spoken Arabic, the oral dialect of the people and of new media like film. *Al-Mummia*, however, departs in an unprecedented way from the traditions of film in Egypt by presenting all dialogue – even that spoken by the Hobarat tribe – in formal Arabic. We can better understand Abd al-Salam's focus on hieroglyphics in the film in the context of this tension between written and vernacular linguistic forms. As Abd al-Salam states, he 'preferred that they all spoke in the same style so as not to reconfirm unnecessarily the social differences between them.'[76] Much like al-Hakim bridging class differences by using the peasants as an inspiration for the Cairo middle classes, the language choice of *al-Mummia* seeks to gloss over the gulfs in class, culture and geography within Egypt. The interest in ancient Egyptian writing works in a similar way. Despite the lack of connection between Arabic and the hieroglyphs, the turn to hieroglyphs allows Abd al-Salam to create a common linguistic heritage for all Egypt that might blur the contemporary divide between the classical and the vernacular, between writing and speech, and between the various regional and class differences of Egypt. While imposing his own 'universal language' of classical Arabic on the peasants in his film, Abd al-Salam, as Joyce does, still looks to hieroglyphs as a way of finding a more natural linguistic connection among the divided Egyptian people, at least in the distant past. And because of the associations between hieroglyphs and film, and, in modern Egypt, between the oral vernacular and film, the turn to ancient Egyptian text also seems to abolish the media distinctions between writing and the cinema.

For *al-Mummia* not only examines the media of writing, but also of film. The connection to new visual media is most apparent in the opening scene of the movie; Maspero shows the other Egyptologists a photographic slide which provides proof that Egyptian antiquities have been stolen and placed on the market. Rather than a simple verbal account or the evidence of documents, Maspero holds up and passes around the actual visual image. The film thus seems to equate the power of these Cairo Egyptologists with the new media that they command. Not only do they have the ability – lacked by the Hobarat tribe – of reading the hieroglyphs, but they have the ability to preserve those hieroglyphs and other relics of the ancient Egyptian past within new media forms. Even though the relic itself has been stolen, new visual media allow them to capture the proof of its existence. Of course, the same can be said for the film itself: much as Maspero's photographic slide reproduces ancient Egyptian artefacts, so *al-Mummia*, like the early Egyptian newsreels of the 1920s, preserves the linguistic legacy of ancient Egypt through its obsessive focus on the hieroglyphs engraved on the walls of Pharaonic ruins. Film becomes the tool of preservation, the natural vehicle to bring the vestiges of the Pharaonic period into the contested present. As in *Citizen Kane*, the medium of film is able to capture and transmit writing as well as images.

Of course, such associations with film were apparent from the very inception of the medium, not only in the metaphor of hieroglyphs that this project traces but also in André Bazin's mummy-complex, which emphasised precisely film's status as a recorder and preserver of the past: 'Now, for the first time, the image of things is likewise the image of their duration, change mummified as it were.'[77] *Al-Mummia* thus strips from hieroglyphs and mummies their veil of metaphor; the Western fascination with media has abstracted Egyptian relics, turning them into free-floating signifiers of the relation between writing and new media, akin to the portable photographic slide that, one presumes, has been sold to Westerners like Maspero at the beginning of *al-Mummia*. Abd al-Salam returns, through the medium of film, to the actual objects that serve as the basis for those metaphors. While making use of the filmic medium of the West, a medium routinely used to exoticise and estrange Egypt from Europe, Abd al-Salam can yet restore hieroglyphs and mummies to their historical and cultural context. In so doing, the film not only re-claims the legacy of ancient Egypt, but simultaneously affirms the power of Abd al-Salam's own medium of film to capture and enclose text. Even as Abd al-Salam seeks to counteract the Western equation of Egyptology and early cinema, he invokes the same logic that was used in early twentieth-century conceptions of hieroglyphs to understand the relation between film and writing.

Abd al-Salam may indeed have been aware of these larger discourses of early film theory, given his association with Roberto Rossellini, for whom he served as assistant director and who became a mentor for him and producer of *al-Mummia*. And, of course, Rossellini was one of the favourite directors and served as the pre-eminent example for André Bazin's realist film theory. Indeed, we might see Maspero in the film as a stand-in for Rossellini: the largely supportive European figure who masters the photographic medium and empowers the Egyptian Ahmad Kamal, like Abd al-Salam, to preserve the ancient past. In his film, Abd al-Salam thus serves as Egypt's own media archaeologist, preserving the story of the mummies through film for an Egyptian, rather than a European, audience (though the film, ironically, has tended to be more popular in Europe than in Egypt).

But even if Abd al-Salam was not aware of the persistent Egyptological associations of early film theory, he certainly would have been aware of the Egyptian content. Abd al-Salam's choice to title his film *al-Mummia* further emphasises his act of re-appropriation of Western media understandings of Egypt. The title invokes, of course, the famous mummy films of the silent and early sound era, most notably Karl Freund's *The Mummy* from 1932, but also four other films with the same title between 1911 and 1923. By removing 'the mummy' from its associations with spectacle, menace and exoticism, and inserting it into an historically grounded political reality, Abd al-Salam reclaims the mummies for Egypt – not as monsters but as specifically Egyptian relics. Like Ahmad Kamal taking the mummies off the market and preserving them, making them – at least potentially – a reminder of Egyptian glory, so Abd al-Salam takes *The Mummy* and turns it into *al-Mummia*, re-claiming as Egyptian the Pharaonic past so often co-opted by Europe and America in both film and in life.

Abd al-Salam in *al-Mummia* thus persistently aligns the power of new media like film to preserve and enclose text to the power of the Cairo authorities – including himself as well as his character Ahmad Kamal – to preserve the legacy of ancient Egypt for nationalist aims. Abd al-Salam's equation of media and preservation is of course a natural one, encoded into early understandings of film as a hieroglyphic medium that functions with the preserving power of a mummy. And in invoking a photographic slide in its opening scene, the film, like Welles's *Citizen Kane* before it, asserts the power of the cinematic medium to enclose and transmit text; in this case the literal, as opposed to metaphorical, hieroglyphs of the Valley of the Kings. Yet Abd al-Salam's self-conscious attention to the power of film as a medium is particularly appropriate, given how Western film was used to exoticise and estrange Egypt, to transform it into an Orientalist wonderland of spectacle and fantasy as opposed to a contemporary community of people with aspirations for nationhood. Much like Egypt's first film, *In the Land of Tutankhamen*, *al-Mummia* seeks to reclaim the set of content used to exoticise Egypt, telling the story of the ancient past not to emphasise its Otherness, but to link it with the present reality and political struggles of the Egyptian nation. Like Mahfouz who calls attention to linguistic as well as cultural continuities between past and present, Abd al-Salam invokes the medium of film in articulating the links between ancient and modern. When it comes to Egypt, to tell a story about the past is to tell a story about media, since understandings of the relationship between Europe and Egypt, Egypt and Africa, the present and the past, one race and another, are inextricably intertwined not only with the media representations of Egypt in early cinema, but with the ways in which these media came to be theorised through the metaphor of hieroglyphs.

The history of ancient Egypt thus intervenes both in attempts to come to terms with the relationship between a nation or race and the larger world and between writing and new media. For al-Hakim, Mahfouz and Abd al-Salam, ancient Egypt provides a way to imagine the future glory and coherent national identity of a newly independent Egypt, while basing that identity in part on the connections between Egypt and the West. Likewise, as the subsequent chapter explores, for James Joyce the language of hieroglyphs allows him to point to the links between film and writing and among the cultures and nations of the world while at the same time asserting Ireland's equal place on the world stage. In each case, Egypt serves as a means of claiming a unique national or racial essence through forging commonalities with other races and cultures. That tension between similarity and difference – that desire simultaneously to link with and to surpass – also animates contemporary understandings of the relationship between writing and new media with which, through references to Egypt, these political goals are so often linked. In their long twentieth-century history of appropriation and re-appropriation, hieroglyphics serve as the emblem of liminality itself: bridging or seeking to enforce the gap between present and past, between new media and writing, between Europe and America, Africa and Egypt.

NOTES

1. For Romanisation of Arabic names, I have employed throughout the most commonly used forms for English-language readers, regardless of whether they utilise different styles. Where there is not a dominant English-language form, I've defaulted to ALA-LC style.
2. See Friedman, *Planetary Modernisms*; Dimock, *Through Other Continents*.
3. Apter, *Against World Literature*, p. 3; Eysteinsson, p. 12. Susan Stanford Friedman is more positive and pragmatic about the use of translation: 'Multilingual scholars are the avant-garde of such recoveries, locating buried and forgotten texts in the global archive of languages, but scholars working in translation are also essential to bring knowledge of these modernisms into the *lingua franca* of the field' (p. 77).
4. Brugman, pp. 279, 281.
5. Bhabha, pp. 144–65.
6. Douglass, pp. 226–44.
7. See Lant, pp. 102–3 for a full list of these films; as an example, 'Five versions of Cleopatra were filmed between 1908 and 1918 alone, in 1908, 1909, 1913, 1917, and 1918' and 'there were two of The Egyptian Mummy (1913 and 1914); two of just The Mummy (1911 and 1914); The Egyptian Mystery (1909); An Egyptian Princess (1914); The Mummy and the Cowpunchers (1912); The Mummy and the Hummingbird (1915); and so on.' For background on the early Lumière films made in Egypt, see Farid, p. 4.
8. 'Mohamed Bayoumi', Alex Cinema http://www.bibalex.org/alexcinema/cinematographers/Mohamed_Bayoumi.html (accessed 18 January 2017).
9. For more on Egyptian history, see Vatikiokis, *The History of Modern Egypt*, 4th edn.
10. 'Declaration to Egypt by His Britannic Majesty's Government', 28 February 1922.
11. 'Following the discovery of King Tutankhamen's tomb in 1922 [. . .] Pharaonic themes exploded across the mainstream culture of Egypt's press iconography' (Colla, *Conflicted Antiquities*, p. 211).
12. Gershoni and Jankowski, *Egypt, Islam*, p. 164.
13. Lazarus, p. 121.
14. Chatterjee, p. 38.
15. As Jeff Shalan has argued, the modern Arabic novel and Egyptian nationalism grew up together: 'The modern Arabic novel developed in conjunction with a specifically nationalist mode of thought, and [. . .] it was instrumental not only in the dissemination of that thought, but in its very formation as well' (p. 213).
16. Said, 'Nationalism, Human Rights, and Interpretation', pp. 41–2.
17. Gershoni and Jankowski, p. 179.
18. Quoted in Gershoni and Jankowski, p. 179.
19. Barak A. Salmoni, 'Historical Consciousness for Modern Citizenship: Egyptian Schooling and the Lessons of History During the Constitutional Monarchy', in *Re-Envisioning Egypt 1919–1952*, ed. by Arthur Goldschmidt, Amy J. Johnson, Barak A. Salmoni, p. 174.
20. Quoted in Gershoni and Jankowski, p. 179.
21. Douglass, p. 230.
22. Nott and Gliddon, p. 212.
23. Quoted in Nott and Gliddon, p. 214; originally in Morton, p. 65.
24. Such claims for the Ethiopian origin of Egyptian civilisation – and through Egypt,

all of Western culture – recur widely throughout later texts of African-American anthropology. Indeed, attempts to align Africa and Egypt have been central to contemporary Pan-Africanism, particularly in Cheikh Anta Diop's *The African Origin of Civilization* and Martin Bernal's *Black Athena*. As Paul Gilroy has argued, 'the appeal of Egypt as evidence of the greatness of pre-slave African cultures, like the enduring symbol that Egypt supplies for black creativity and civilization, has had a special significance within black Atlantic responses to modernity' (Gilroy, *The Black Atlantic*, p. 60). For more on Pan-Africanism and Egypt, see Stephen Howe, *Afrocentrism: Mythical Pasts and Imagined Homes*.
25. Quoted in Gershoni and Jankowski, p. 165.
26. Quoted in Gershoni and Jankowski, p. 166.
27. As Omnia El Shakry writes, 'thinkers such as Salama Musa, Marcus Simaika, Muhammad Husayn Haykal, and Ahmad Husayn went so far as to claim a biological or racial link between the ancient pharaohs and the modern Egyptians' (p. 62).
28. Quoted in Gershoni and Jankowski, p. 166.
29. Smith, pp. xi, 177.
30. Husayn, *The Future of Culture in Egypt*, p. 2; see also Ḥusayn, *Mustaqbal al-thaqāfah fī Miṣr*.
31. For more on the Pharaonicist views on the separation of religion and society, see Gershoni and Jankowski, p. 140. For the eventual eclipse of Pharaonicist ideas by Islam, see Gershoni and Jankowski, *Redefining the Egyptian Nation, 1930–1945*.
32. For more on the conflict between 'East' and 'West' in twentieth-century Egypt, see Badawi, pp. 83–97.
33. 'Nationalist thought at its moment of departure formulates the following characteristic answer: it asserts that the superiority of the West lies in the materiality of its culture, exemplified by its science, technology and love of progress. But the East is superior in the spiritual aspect of culture. True modernity for the non-European nations would lie in combining the superior material qualities of Western cultures with the spiritual greatness of the East' (Chatterjee, p. 51).
34. Tawfīq al-Hakim, *Return of the Spirit*, p. 153; Tawfīq Ḥakīm, *'Awdat al-rūḥ*, Vol. 2.
35. Anna Barnard, 'The Crisis of the Present: Literature in the Middle East and North Africa', in *The Modernist World*, ed. by Allana Lindgren and Stephen Ross, p. 464.
36. See Bardaouil, *Surrealism in Egypt: Modernism and the Art and Liberty Group*.
37. Dina Amin, 'Arab Theatre Between Tradition and Modernity', in *The Modernist World*, ed. by Allana Lindgren and Stephen Ross, p. 484.
38. Armbrust, p. 7.
39. Indeed, most critics see this shift from domestic novel to the Revolution as a narrative flaw: Matti Moosa claims that the characters' 'participation in the revolt of 1919 is presented not as the consequence of the gradual development of their political views but as a sudden and impetuous action', creating a 'tenuous connection between the realistic and symbolic aspects of the novel' (p. 179). Jeff Shalan argues, by contrast, for the continuity of the two halves of the novel: the first romantic section about Saniya and the later, more political and symbolic section. As he says, 'just as Isis is displaced by Horus, who usurped her (re)generative power in myth, so too is Saniya's disruptive power displaced by the change in setting and by what Muhsin will discover upon his return to the country: the real heart of Egypt in the solidarity of peasant life' (p. 238).
40. Ḥakīm, *'Awdat al-rūḥ*, Vol. 1, pp. 8–9.
41. Ḥakīm, *'Awdat al-rūḥ*, Vol. 2, p. 62.
42. As the Egyptian critic Anouar Abdel-Malek puts it in a classic formulation:

> According to the traditional orientalists, an essence should exist – sometimes even clearly described in metaphysical terms which constitutes the inalienable and common basis of all the beings considered; this essence is both 'historical,' since it goes back to the dawn of history, and fundamentally a-historical, since it transfixes the being, 'the object' of study, within its inalienable and non-evolutive specificity, instead of defining it as all other beings, states, nations, peoples and cultures – as a product, a resultant of the vection of the forces operating in the field of historical evolution. (p. 108)

43. As Fabian defines the 'denial of coevalness', 'by that I mean a persistent and systematic tendency to place the referent(s) of anthropology in a Time other than the present of the producer of anthropological discourse' (p. 31).
44. Indeed, Jeff Shalan argues that, at least initially, the novel suggests that Muhsin's ideas of national revival are only a ventriloquism of a colonialist worldview: 'And, at least for a moment, the purported source of the nation is displaced by the derivative source of the nationalist discourse itself: the self's (Egypt's) reading of the other's (Europe's) reading of the self' (p. 243). Yet the novel ultimately endorses those discourses.
45. Milson, p. 71. For more on the validation of the peasants during the nationalist period, see Samia Kholoussi, '*Fallahin*: The "Mud Bearers" of Egypt's "Liberal Age"', in *Re-Envisioning Egypt*, ed. by Goldschmidt, Johnson and Salmoni, pp. 277–315.
46. As Paul Starkey notes in *From the Ivory Tower: A Critical Study of Tawfiq al-Hakim*, 'the fact that his [Muhsin's] mother is not of pure Egyptian descent is important, for it introduces a new element of symbolism into the novel: she is a direct representative of foreign values' (p. 90).
47. For instance, Hamdi Sakkut claims that 'Hakim does however occasionally insert passages dealing with subjects which are irrelevant to the action, such as the description of the Sudan' (p. 88), and Paul Starkey argues that the Sudan flashback 'is misused, since the recollections do nothing to illuminate the surrounding text' (p. 222).
48. Ḥakīm, '*Awdat al-rūḥ*, Vol. 1, p. 260.
49. El-Enany, pp. 3–4.
50. Colla, *Conflicted Antiquities*, p. 243.
51. Colla, *Conflicted Antiquities*, p. 242.
52. Milson, p. 70.
53. Colla, *Conflicted Antiquities*, p. 251.
54. Mahfouz, *Khufu's Wisdom*, p. 8; Maḥfūẓ, '*Abath al-aqdār [ta'līf]*, p. 11.
55. El-Enany, pp. 17, 15, 20.
56. Baikie, p. 67.
57. Said, 'Yeats and Decolonization', p. 79.
58. *The Mummy, or The Night of Counting the Years (Al-Mummia)*, dir. by Shadi Abd al-Salam (General Egyptian Cinema Organization, 1969).
59. Farid, p. 4.
60. For the history of Egyptian cinema in this period, see Shafik, *Arab Cinema: History and Cultural Identity*, pp. 9–18; Shafik, 'Egyptian Cinema', pp. 23–5; Darwish, *Dream Makers on the Nile*.
61. For more on continuing controversies about American films in Egypt see Vitalis, pp. 269–91.
62. Greenberg, p. xvi.
63. Greenberg, p. xvii.
64. Milson, p. 47.

65. Al-Hakim, *The Prison of Life*, p. 84.
66. Al-Salam and Toufic, p. 98.
67. Al-Salam and Toufic, p. 126.
68. Quoted in Colla, 'Counting the Years: Shadi 'Abd al-Salam's Words', p. 136.
69. Colla, 'Shadi Abd al-Salam's al-Mumiya: Ambivalence and the Egyptian Nation-State', p. 112.
70. Al-Salam and Toufic, p. 118.
71. Al-Salam and Toufic, p. 119.
72. Haman, p. 33.
73. Colla, 'Shadi Abd al-Salam's al-Mumiya', p. 118.
74. Colla, 'Shadi Abd al-Salam's al-Mumiya', p. 133.
75. Quoted in Colla, 'Shadi Abd al-Salam's Al-Mumiya', p. 115.
76. Al-Salam and Toufic, p. 129.
77. Bazin, p. 15. As Haman notes, 'At the turn of the nineteenth century, photography and the presence of mummies (particularly in early cinema) coincided with Egyptomania' (p. 37).

5

SOLVING THE PROBLEM OF BABEL

The March 1932 issue of Eugene Jolas's modernist periodical *transition* featured a side-by-side comparison of two versions of the 'Anna Livia Plurabelle' section of *Finnegans Wake*: Joyce's text, which had been serialised in *transition* five years earlier, and a translation into Basic English, a universal language created and promoted by the philosopher C. K. Ogden in the early 1930s. As Ogden wrote in his introduction, here 'the simplest and most complex languages of man are placed side by side'.[1] Despite the obvious differences between the language of *Finnegans Wake* and the radically simplified vocabulary of Basic English, Joyce had an extended association with Ogden at this time, with Ogden writing an introduction to a published version of 'Anna Livia Plurabelle' and arranging for Joyce's audio recording of it.[2] Joyce even went so far as to imply, however humorously, a link between his own work and Ogden's, describing the contents of ALP's letter in *Finnegans Wake* as 'basically English'.[3]

This unexpected relationship between Ogden and Joyce demonstrates just how deeply Joyce was influenced by one of the most important cultural obsessions of his time: the problem of Babel, or of how individuals speaking different languages could effectively communicate with each other. This period saw the invention of numerous 'universal languages' like Basic English: Esperanto, Novial, Volapük, Ido and Isotype. These 'International Auxiliary Languages' (IALs) were promoted by the philosophers of language C. K. Ogden, Richard Paget and Otto Jespersen in their treatises *Debabelization*, *Babel* and *An*

International Language, all of which Joyce had read.⁴ Indeed, the word Babel is referred to at least twenty-one times in *Finnegans Wake*, particularly in its very first pages, when Finnegan's fall represents, on one of its myriad levels, the fall of the Tower of Babel, the 'baubeltop' (p. 5). The resultant cacophony creates the form of the text, with its incorporation of seventy or so different languages. Joyce's aesthetics, however highflown and elitist they may seem, thus emerge, at least in part, from his deep and extended engagement with attempts to solve the problem of Babel: attempts not confined to literature and the avant-garde but pervasive also in popular culture in the newly created IALs of the time.

Joyce was exposed to debates about universal languages through the pages of *transition*, the periodical founded by his friend Eugene Jolas. Besides serialising the *Wake* and featuring Ogden's translation of it, the magazine provided a forum for extended discussion of both high aesthetic and more practical projects to forge a worldwide linguistic unity. Given the universalism underlying *transition* and the IALs, Joyce's continued interest in them sheds light on his political beliefs. While attracted by the siren's call of a universal language, in *Ulysses* and *Finnegans Wake* Joyce rejects the hegemonic imposition of a new IAL called for by Ogden. For Joyce, the only possible universal language is not to be found in the present or future, but in the past – and, particularly, in visual languages like Egyptian hieroglyphics. Like Naguib Mahfouz, who invokes hieroglyphs and ancient Egypt as a way of linking Egypt with the rest of the world and demonstrating its importance, so Joyce likewise turns to Egyptian writing for universalist aims.

Against the rise of Aryan racial theories, Joyce in his novels imagines hieroglyphs as the common source for all of the world's languages and nations, revealing the way every alphabet, Western or non-Western, possesses a visual and a material form. Visual languages allow Joyce to establish a linguistic unity in the past that preserves the variety of contemporary languages and cultures. Joyce does not only, like Woolf, Conrad and Orson Welles, call attention to the hybrid nature – between sound, image and text – of writing and contemporary media forms. Through his references to hieroglyphs, film, advertisements and illuminated manuscripts, he uses that insight to make a larger argument for the underlying transhistorical links among all cultures. Again recalling al-Hakim and Mahfouz, Joyce finds in ancient Egypt and its hieroglyphs a way of expressing both the underlying links among races, cultures and languages, and, subtly, the significance of his own nation of Ireland. And as in those Egyptian novelists, that turn to the Egyptian past also involves a grappling with the relationship between writing and new media.

Joyce is consistently fascinated by visual languages like hieroglyphs. In his novels, he refers to advertisements, to 'highpriest's hieroglyph of kettletom', to 'rubrics' and to 'moving pictures', alongside his allusions to the IALs 'esperanto', 'auxiliary neutral idiom' and 'universal'.[5] While critics have discussed Joyce's interest in IALs, they have largely ignored how at the time pictorial and gestural languages – film, photography, dance, comic books, advertisements, hieroglyphs, illuminated manuscripts – were also considered universal languages.[6] Precisely because of their visuality, critics and writers, including many in *transition,* believed that these media could transcend the barriers of traditional written languages and become a better universal language than Esperanto and its like.[7] Visual and gestural languages, as we've seen, were linked to the dream of recovering an entirely pure language, one which was lost either with the expulsion from Eden or the fall of the tower of Babel.[8] Giambattista Vico, one of Joyce's great influences, argued that gesture and hieroglyphs were languages that came as close as possible to uniting the sign and its referent. Such a pure language would, in theory, be understood by everyone; it would be the true, and not simply auxiliary, universal language.

Considering Joyce's references to film, advertisements and hieroglyphs alongside his engagement with Basic English reveals how Joyce's interest in visual languages goes beyond the forging of transcultural links that Ogden and others saw as the purpose of their projects for international communication.[9] By invoking myriad linguistic forms that bridge the divide between the visual and the textual, Joyce unites the new media of modernity with ancient forms like hieroglyphs and illuminated manuscripts. Rather than seeing pictographic languages as fundamentally different and more primitive than the Latin alphabet, Joyce demonstrates how even our daily words and letters have, like a hieroglyph, a visual appearance as well as a semantic content.[10]

In *Ulysses* and *Finnegans Wake,* Joyce seeks to illustrate language's 'verbivocovisual' roots, but, like Mahfouz, he does so for a political purpose. He turns to gestures and hieroglyphs in an effort playfully to question the Indo-European hypothesis: that Western languages descended from one ur-language unrelated to ancient Chinese or Egyptian traditions.[11] Instead, Joyce constructs an alternative genealogy of language that finds its origins in the gestures and pictograms he sees as common to all humanity.[12] He seeks to discount the belief, prevalent both in Irish nationalism and in Nazism, that 'Aryan' languages – Irish or German in particular – were somehow purer than others, a view inspired by the misuse of theories of Indo-European language and culture.[13] All languages in Joyce, even the language of images, are impure and subject to ambiguity and opposing interpretations.

Joyce links the insights of structural linguistics concerning the arbitrariness of language – derived in part from Ogden's and I. A. Richards's *The Meaning of Meaning,* alluded to in the *Wake* (p. 267) – with the objectives of historical linguistics.[14] By substituting images and gestures for proto-Indo-European and by repeatedly invoking hybrid visual-textual media, Joyce preserves the possibility of the monogenesis of language: the idea that, instead of deriving from unrelated groups like Indo-European, Sino-Tibetan, Finno-Ugric and the like, all languages began in universal signs and signals.[15] Joyce does not merely, as Derek Attridge contends, deconstruct language and linguistic origins, demonstrating how words are by their 'very nature [. . .] unstable and ambiguous'.[16] Rather, he conceives of a new, more inclusive source for the world's languages, one based in images and the movements of the human body. Joyce shares the desire for world understanding of Ogden and the other creators of IALs, but instead of seeking to impose a new language, he strives through references to visual languages to rediscover the supposedly lost genealogical connections between cultures.[17] Joyce intertwines the aesthetic and the political even at the level of his language.

TRANSITION'S NEW HIEROGLYPHICS

Joyce's most obvious cluster of references to universal languages – to 'basically English', 'universal' and 'auxiliary neutral idiom' – occurs in book I, chapter 5 of *Finnegans Wake*. These passages, however, were not included in the original 1927 publication in Eugene Jolas's *transition* but were added later in the 1930s when Joyce extensively revised the manuscript. Although he had an abiding interest in Esperanto and in linguistic history, Joyce's increasing engagement with universal languages while composing *Finnegans Wake* demonstrates the complex interplay between his work and *transition*. Joyce's experimentation with new forms of language in *Finnegans Wake* helped to inspire the goals of Eugene Jolas's periodical, which was self-consciously set up to justify the linguistic techniques of the *Wake*.[18] In his desire for a 'revolution of the word' – the aesthetic catchphrase of *transition* – Jolas was influenced both by *Finnegans Wake* and by the larger problem of Babel; Jolas even titled his autobiography *Man from Babel*.[19] But both the general aesthetic aims of *transition* and many of the issues that were written about in it – including film and universal languages, as Ogden's translation indicates – went on in turn to influence Joyce as he revised the *Wake* from its initial versions. A closer attention to *transition* thus elucidates Joyce's own political aesthetic, since the connections forged in *transition* between IALs, political universalism and the visual languages of the present and the past – film and hieroglyphs – recur in the *Wake*'s attempt to imagine the common roots of language in gestures and pictograms.[20]

In *transition*, Jolas and the other contributors presented their attempts to create a new 'word' as akin to, yet competing with, those of philologists and philosophers who developed universal languages like Esperanto or Volapük. Jolas had a copy of *Esperanto Internacia*, a magazine of the Esperanto movement, in his archives, and many times in the pages of *transition* writers describe Joyce's *Wake*-ese as a new and better universal language: 'He does not intend to create a new literary esperanto, but he wishes to originate a flexible language that might be an esperanto of the subconscious.'[21] In issue after issue, Jolas, inspired by *Finnegans Wake*, called for other writers to emulate Joyce and create new and better languages – if not for communication, then, fitting Jolas's neo-Romantic tendencies, for expression. As Jolas writes, in a typical pronouncement, 'The language of night I have in mind will make the intercontinental synthesis of the inner and outer language. It may thus become the truly universal language [. . .] a language that will dance and sing.'[22] Jolas sees his own aims as similar to but distinct from those who favour 'auxiliary languages': 'Neither Esperanto nor Novial will ever bring about the dream of international brotherhood. The international languages will, I believe, remain forever mere technical, auxiliary equipments for specialists.' His own longed-for language, made complex rather than simple, would, he believes, create that 'dream' of 'an inter-racial language [. . .] to express the collective inner vision of mankind'.[23]

There is thus an implicit universalism in *transition*'s mission, a Jungian sense – Jung was even a contributor – that all nations and cultures possess the same or similar 'collective inner vision[s]' and that cultural differences are not essential but rather the product of language. By forging a new language for literature, Jolas believed, the artist could destroy racial boundaries and create world peace, the same grandiose goals that inspired Ogden to create Basic English. As Jolas and his fellow editors write, 'Was not the greatest period of human history the Renaissance, the Humanistic Age, when the idea of nationality [. . .] was unknown [. . .] We don't want to be good Europeans, but good universalists.'[24] The pages of *transition* thus function as a kind of IAL, a Basic English that through Jolas's remarkable output of translations allowed English-language readers access to the works of writers from all cultures. As Jolas writes in the first issue, 'To the writers of all other countries, *transition* extends an invitation to appear, side by side, in a language Americans can read and understand.'[25]

Alongside the high aesthetic manifestoes about 'the revolution of the word', Jolas also gave space to more popular and pragmatic efforts to expand communication, namely Basic English, which, although no longer referred to as such, has had probably the largest influence of any of the IALs under discussion.[26] *transition* published Ogden's aforementioned translation of the *Wake*, as well his response to Jolas's call for a 'revolution of the word'. Joyce's association with *transition* thus exposed him to the problem of Babel and to ideas about how a new universalism might be forged, both through Jolas's theories and Ogden's projects.

The writings about international languages included in *transition* did not, of course, exclusively spark Joyce's interest in IALs, if, indeed, he even read all the articles in the journal. He was already intrigued by Esperanto, as his inclusion of it in drafts of *Finnegans Wake* attests.[27] As early as 1925, when

Joyce revised the page proofs of 'Anna Livia Plurabelle' for its publication in *Le Navire d'argent*, he added in the margins allusions to the history of language in all its forms, from 'franca langua' and 'cunniform letters' (cuneiform), to 'eure sanscreed into oure eryan' (Sanskrit and Aryan), to the 'turrace of Babbel' (pp. 198, 215, 199).[28] The pace of these changes and additions, however, increased in the late 1930s, after Joyce's association with *transition* and after the publication of works on IALs by Ogden, Paget and Jespersen. Against the backdrop of the rise of the Nazis and their cooptation of 'Aryan' linguistic theories, Joyce in his revisions of the *Wake* from its initial versions in *transition* engaged much more fully with past and present universal languages. But while Jolas strived for a 'language of night' that will 'bind the races in a fabulous unity', Joyce attempted to achieve that unity not simply by creating a 'night language' in *Finnegans Wake* but by going beyond language to gestures and hieroglyphs.[29]

The central passages alluding to IALs occur in book I, chapter 5 of the *Wake*:

> For if the lingo gasped between kicksheets, however basically English, were to be preached from the mouths of wickerchurchwardens and metaphysicians in the row and advokaatoes, allvoyous, demivoyelles, languoaths, lesbiels, dentelles, gutterhowls and furtz [. . .] however apically Volapucky grunted and fromwelled, ichabod, habakuk, opanoff, uggamyg, hapaxle, gomenon, ppppfff, over country stiles. (p. 116)

This passage, absent from the version published in *transition*, not only proves the extent to which Joyce expanded his engagement with universal languages in his revisions of the *Wake* but also helps us understand his ambivalent attitude towards them. Partially a parody of bombast and long-windedness, this passage invokes linguistic analysis – demivowels, labials and dentals – as well as Basic English and Volapük. Joyce makes fun of these IALs, dismissing them as pedantic, but the references also reflect a deep curiosity about linguistics in general and IALs in particular. Joyce goes on to mention even more forms of universal language: 'It is told in sounds in utter that, in signs so adds to, in universal, in polygluttural, in each auxiliary neutral idiom, sordomutics, florilingua, sheltafocal, flayflutter, a con's cubane, a pro's tutute, strassareb, ereperse and anythongue athall' (p. 117). Joyce alludes here to Esperanto, Ido and Idiom Neutral, as well as the gestural language of deaf-mutes ('sordomutics') and the language of flowers familiar to us from Martha Clifford's letter in *Ulysses*. Similarly, the 'shelta' of 'sheltafocal' refers to '[a] cryptic jargon used by tinkers, composed partly of Irish or Gaelic words' (*OED*) and the focal may refer to photography, which was also considered a universal language at the time. The reference to 'strassareb' also evokes Arabic, a language that is both connected to hieroglyphs through its use in Egypt and, given its more calligraphic nature, a form of writing that calls attention to its visuality, as

Mahfouz emphasises in *Khufu's Wisdom*.[30] Since this passage describes ALP's letter, which serves at least in part as a microcosm for *Finnegans Wake*, Joyce here seems to be comparing his own novel to a universal language, one which, incorporating seventy languages, can be 'anythongue athall'. These sections, however, are largely comic, contained as they are in a parody of Sir Edward Sullivan's commentary on the Book of Kells. While this passage confirms Joyce's interest in IALs and represents an attempt to incorporate all linguistic forms into his own text, his attitude towards these languages remains unsure.

The tone of gentle parody when it comes to IALs also occurs in *Ulysses*, which expresses in preliminary form many of the ideas about universal languages that Joyce would develop in the *Wake*. Bloom in 'Circe' lists numerous progressive reforms to foster world peace, including the adoption of 'esperanto the universal language with universal brotherhood'.[31] Esperanto seems admirable but absurd, further ironized by its juxtaposition with Bloom's proposal for 'Saloon motor hearses. Compulsory manual labor for all'. Particularly because the inventor of Esperanto, L. L. Zamenhof, was Jewish, the language naturally becomes associated with Bloom's messianism. While Joyce seems sympathetic to the aims of IALs, he here portrays universal languages as merely the idealistic dream of naïve reformers.[32]

Like Jolas, Joyce mentions not only Esperanto but also gestural and visual forms of universal language: most notably, hieroglyphs, advertising and film. At the beginning of 'Circe', Stephen proclaims, 'So that gesture, not music, not odours, would be a universal language, the gift of tongues rendering visible not the lay sense but the first entelechy, the structural rhythm' (p. 353). Invoking the idea of a 'universal language', Stephen calls not for an IAL but rather a language that would be gestural and visible (the fact that this language is available only through the 'gift of tongues' brings in the oral as well, forming a 'verbivocovisual' language like the kind Joyce will create in *Finnegans Wake*). Stephen's use of the word 'rhythm' here anticipates the theories of Marcel Jousse, another theorist of gestural languages whose lectures Joyce later attended, who declared, 'In the beginning was the rhythmic gesture', a declaration Joyce echoes in *Finnegans Wake* as 'in the beginning was the gest he jousstly says' (p. 486).[33]

Like Jolas, Joyce is just as steeped in non-linguistic visual or gestural languages as he is in the IALs of Ogden and Zamenhof. As Jolas writes in his autobiography, Joyce 'was interested in the experiments of the French Jesuit Jousse and the English philologist Sir Paget, and *Finnegans Wake* is full of applications of their gesture theory. He spoke however with a certain derision of such auxiliary languages as Esperanto and Ido.'[34] The ideas of Jousse and Paget that so interested Joyce were based, in many cases, on Vico's theories of language, particularly his claim that language evolved from gestures to hieroglyphs to alphabets, with an increasing distance between the signifier and the signified.³⁵ As Vico says, 'The first language in the first mute times of the nations must have begun with signs, whether gestures or physical objects, which had natural relations to the ideas' (p. 127). Later he declares that 'The first nations thought in poetic characters, spoke in fables, and wrote in hieroglyphs' (p. 139). A language of gestures would be purely embodied, but if Joyce, using the medium of writing, cannot reach a purely gestural language, as Stephen Dedalus desires, then he must strive for a visual one. Indeed, despite the seemingly unbridgeable gap between gestures and hieroglyphs, Vico, Jousse and Paget consistently portray them as fundamentally related to each other: as Jousse writes, 'Here too, we must "take from the life" the evolution of semiological gesture and, instead of studying exclusively Chaldeo-Elamite, Egyptian, Chinese and Indian hieroglyphs, those graphic but dead images of animated ancient semiological gestures, one must [. . .] study living "gestural" speech' (p. 45). Hieroglyphs are simply 'dead' versions of living gestures, evolving slowly towards alphabetical text. This evolutionary pattern is also expressed by the film writer Terry Ramsaye, who links gestures and hieroglyphs to film, as Joyce goes on to do; Ramsaye writes, 'Picture making went on and grew in association with sound, just as pantomime did. Ideas in word-sounds had companions in idea-pictures. [. . .] When pictures were divorced from their pure pictorial meaning and wedded to the sound they, by that step, became an alphabet' (pp. xlix–l). Through the addition of images and sounds, communication evolves from pantomime to 'idea-pictures' to the alphabet. Hieroglyphs – as more material, embodied forms of inscription – thus have the potential to be almost as powerful as gestures, and certainly far more universal than the exclusively linguistic IALs.

Stephen is therefore not making a great leap by claiming that the visual and the gestural could be universal languages, since as we've seen film and photography were often compared to Esperanto in this period by writers like Edward Van Zile. Hieroglyphics, as a visual and supposedly universal language, provided for theorists like Vachel Lindsay and Sergei Eisenstein one of the most common ways of conceiving of these new visual media, and Jolas and the other editors of *transition* were some of the most important sources of this cult of hieroglyphics in modernism. Allusions to hieroglyphs appear frequently in issues of *transition* at the time, particularly in the work of Jolas, who treats them as a primitive antecedent of the new forms of language he is seeking to create. Jolas refers to the 'hieroglyphic of homelessness' in his poem 'Landscape', describes how 'hieroglyphics emerge' in 'Flight into Geography', and details 'The hieroglyphic of the moon' and 'Tut-Ankh-Amen's Dreambook' in 'Walk through Cosmopolis'.³⁶ As he writes in one of his most famous aesthetic manifestos in *transition*, 'We need new words, new abstractions, new hieroglyphics, new symbols, new myths.'³⁷ Jolas even chose, as the epigraph of the central volume of *transition* on 'The Revolution of the

Word', Léon-Paul Fargue's quotation, 'À nous les signes idéographiques, les écritures figuratives' ('For us the ideographic signs, the figurative writing').[38] For Jolas, the hieroglyph, because of its visuality and what he calls its 'abstraction', is able to restore a sense of wonder that has been lost from traditional language and literature. As he writes of the artist, 'He is in search of new symbols and sigils, and weds them, in a voluntary arrangement, with ancient words inherited from an ancestral past. He seeks hieroglyphs to express what to many seems the inexpressible.'[39]

Yet hieroglyphs, and by extension film and photography, promised more than a universal language. Esperanto and Basic English may be universal, but visual languages and hieroglyphs, as the passages from *transition* imply, have the potential to be universal and perfect, bringing together signifier and signified.[40] They could recapture a pre-Adamic tongue, a unity between name and thing. Discussions of hieroglyphs and visual media, as we've seen, thus often fell victim to Genette's 'Cratylic fallacy' – the idea that there was or could be a necessary and motivated linkage between a word and what it described. Vico is explicit about his embrace of the Cratylic origins of hieroglyphs and alphabetical languages, rejecting those critics who 'have given peace to their ignorance by setting up the universal maxim that articulate human words have arbitrary significations' (p. 148).[41] Similarly, Richard Paget, whose *Babel* Joyce had read, alludes favourably to the *Cratylus*, arguing that tongue gestures relate naturally to the words they express.[42]

This link between hieroglyphs and the Cratylic fallacy persisted well into the twentieth century, and Joyce participated. From the very beginning of his composition of the *Wake*, he was fascinated by hieroglyphs and their role in the origins of writing. In his notes to Edward Clodd's *Story of the Alphabet* there are references to 'Rossetta [*sic*]', 'Champollion', 'pictograph', 'phonogram', 'rebus', 'stele' and Chinese ideograms.[43] In an early entry for *Finnegans Wake* he writes, 'phonetic theory is unsound', seemingly rejecting the discoveries of Champollion and returning to earlier mystical beliefs about the hieroglyphs (and, this being Joyce, doing it through a sonic pun on the word 'sound').[44] Hieroglyphs thus look back, through Vico, to the so-called primitive origins of language before the 'phonetic theory', to a mode of communication free of the gap between signifier and signified. But through their phonetic qualities, they also bridge the divide between images and the alphabet, symbolising for Joyce the hybrid nature of all writing and prefiguring the modern visual-textual media of film and photography and their potential as new universal languages. Hieroglyphics allow Joyce to imagine a universal language that will not replace or prune away modern languages – which he incorporates so obsessively into the *Wake* – but rather gave rise to them, and that will not efface linguistic history and diversity but return us to a past when the gaps between languages and the gaps between images and texts were, supposedly, far less profound.

'Ad Literature': *Ulysses* and Embodiment

Joyce's first sustained engagement with a new hybrid medium, with a synthesis between visual and textual forms, occurs in his treatment of advertisements in *Ulysses*. Through ads, Joyce begins to develop his ideas about the interrelation among bodies, words and images that will lead him to formulate an alternative genealogy of linguistic and cultural origins in *Finnegans Wake*. Joyce in *Ulysses* is captivated by the universal potential and power of the hybrid form of advertisements, and in *Finnegans Wake* he goes on to claim for all languages and systems of signs the same pictorial properties, the same embodied presence. Words in *Ulysses* are always enmeshed with images and with bodies, requiring a process of translation between their visual, vocal and semantic meanings.

If film was the most important of the potentially universal languages of modernity, then advertising, with its combination of image and caption, was its chief competitor.[45] As Jennifer Wicke has argued, 'advertising was the most powerful discursive rival of modernist literature and [...] this rivalry (or dialectic) was mutually engendering – [...] modernist literature, especially via Joyce, incorporated advertising's liminality and material hieroglyphs as its own procedures.'[46] The rise of advertisement is of course central to *Ulysses*, with Bloom as ad canvasser commenting on and thinking up countless ads over the course of the novel. Franco Moretti has argued that ads in *Ulysses* serve as a debased form of modern communication, a language empty of meaning that refuses to make distinctions between objects and thus renders them meaningless.[47] Yet such a view ignores the ways in which advertising serves as an inspiration for Joyce and even as a model for his own use of symbolism in the novel. Indeed, in *Finnegans Wake* Joyce writes, 'No, assuredly, they are not justified, those gloompourers who grouse that letters have never been quite their old selves again since that weird weekday in bleak Janiveer [...] when to the shock of both, Biddy Doran looked ad literature' (p. 112). The pun 'ad literature' at the conclusion is key here, and should cause us to take sides against the 'gloompourers' and re-examine the importance of ads in *Ulysses*. Over the course of the novel, ads come to represent a new form of hybrid language between the visual and the textual, one akin to the films, illuminated manuscripts and hieroglyphs that Joyce goes on to invoke in *Finnegans Wake*. For if 80 per cent or so of the world can recognise the logo for Coke, then ads truly have become a universal language of capitalism.[48]

Unlike in Moretti's view, ads in *Ulysses* are not emblems of insignificance; rather, they are multiply significant, webs in which various meanings can be caught. The House of Keyes ad in the novel is effective precisely because of its multiple associations, because it is meant to evoke, as Bloom points out, 'the Manx parliament. Innuendo of home rule. Tourists, you know, from the isle of Man' (p. 99). The very meaning of advertisement – 'A public notice or announcement [. . .] usually, in writing or print, by placards, or in a journal', or, in older definitions, 'The turning of the mind to anything; attention, observation, heed' (*OED*), points to its status as a privileged site of attention. Rather than scraps of meaningless detritus, ads are nodes of meaning in *Ulysses*; they focus our gaze above the stream of daily events and call for our active role of interpretation. This is the nature of advertising that Bloom describes: its 'magnetising efficacy to arrest involuntary attention, to interest, to convince, to decide' (p. 559). Or, as he says of the House of Keyes ad, 'Catches the eye, you see' and 'You can do that and just a little per calling attention' (p. 100). The emphasis on visual perception in the novel is thus not merely confined to Stephen's comments on 'The ineluctable modality of the visible' (p. 31); it is also explicit in ads themselves.[49]

Advertisement in Joyce, however, is more than merely a visual medium; it also represents a form of embodied language. In one of the most extended treatments of an ad in *Ulysses*, Bloom in Ithaca imagines his ideal advertisement: 'the modern art of advertisement if condensed in triliteral monoideal symbols, vertically of maximum visibility (divined), horizontally of maximum legibility (deciphered)' (p. 559). By calling the letters 'triliteral monoideal symbols', Joyce renders them visual images rather than transparent conveyors of linguistic meaning. This passage foreshadows the moment in *Finnegans Wake* when Joyce describes one of his sigla as the 'baffling chrismon trilithon sign' (p. 119), again turning a letter into a more physical and visual object. Not only do ads efface the boundary between text and image – with Bloom's House of Keyes ad juxtaposing a picture of crossed keys with a written caption – they also seem to expose how text is already pictorial and embodied.[50]

As we will see in *Finnegans Wake*, Joyce consistently strives towards more tangible and physical forms of language: words engraved in clay, words turned into archetypes and characters like HCE or ALP. But already in *Ulysses*, ads do not merely juxtapose the visual and the textual; they also seem capable of a life of their own. The ad for Kino's Trousers is mounted on a boat – 'saw a rowboat rock at anchor on the treacly swells lazily its plastered board' (p. 126) – and therefore is capable of movement around the city. Likewise, as Bloom and others walk through the streets in 'Lestrygonians', they encounter the moving letters of the H.E.L.Y.S. ad. Humans literally become ads, with the letters H.E.L.Y.S. taking on bodily form. Bloom's ultimate idea for an ad, directly after the reference to H.E.L.Y.S., takes this idea of embodiment in advertising to its extreme: 'I suggested to him about a transparent showcart with two smart girls sitting inside writing letters, copybooks, envelopes, blottingpaper' (p. 127). Here again not only do advertisements acquire the ability to move – as the 'showcart' would be carried around Dublin – but the human form and human gestures are transformed into ads. Yet even in this embodied and visual form, Joyce suggests that advertising remains a linguistic, textual activity; the women in the showcart are still engaged in the act of writing. Again, Joyce folds new visual media back into writing; ads seem not to preclude or replace writing, but rather to require it.

Such a desire for embodied language returns us to Stephen's proclamation about the universal language of gesture and helps to explain Joyce's fascination with gestural languages, as explored by Vico, Jousse and Paget. Like Jousse, who saw hieroglyphs as inextricably linked with gestures, forming a necessary step in the transition from purely embodied movement to alphabetical writing, Joyce insists on the materiality of visual impressions and of language. As Stephen famously says in the Proteus episode, 'Ineluctable modality of the visible: at least that if no more, thought through my eyes. Signatures of all things I am here to read, seaspawn and seawrack, the nearing tide, that rusty boot. Snotgreen, bluesilver, rust: coloured signs. Limits of the diaphane. But he adds: in bodies' (p. 31). Thought and perception enter through the visual organs, and, looking forward to Woolf's theories of the linguistic nature of sense impressions, the texture of the world is imagined as linguistic, as a series of signatures or 'coloured signs'. Like Woolf, Stephen transforms perceptions into language; the written words that Stephen later scrawls on a blank sheet of paper are elided with the language of the world, which becomes just as much 'signs on a white field' as literal writing. This view recalls Emerson's and Melville's notions of the Book of Nature, but here the source is the German mystic Jacob Boehme, with his discussions of the signatures of God.[51] The world is reduced to marks on a background, to a page of text.

But Stephen quickly moves from visual language to an emphasis on embodied language: 'But he adds: in bodies.' As the novel progresses, and we move from Stephen to the more physical Bloom, language becomes even more clearly instantiated 'in bodies' and associated with identity itself. Walking on the same beach in the 'Nausicaa' episode, Bloom thinks

> I. [. . .]
> All these rocks with lines and scars and letters. O, those transparent! Besides they don't know. What is the meaning of that other world. I called you naughty boy because I do not like.
> AM. A.
> No room. Let it go.
> Mr Bloom effaced the letters with his slow boot. (p. 312)

Bloom does not merely textualise the physical world, turning marks on rocks into 'lines and scars and letters'. Joyce also demonstrates how our identity always involves a conjunction between our bodily self and our acts of thought and writing. For Bloom here linguistically defines himself, writing 'I am a'. Recalling God's self-definition 'I am that I am' and 'I am Alpha and Omega', this passage returns to a Cratylic language in which there is no barrier between words and identity. Looking forward to Welles's equation of 'I' and eye, here Joyce turns Bloom's identity – his 'I' – into a letter of the alphabet: A. Like the signboard holders of the H.E.L.Y.S. ad, Bloom becomes part of language itself. The confirmation of this blurring of the gap between word and world is the reference to Martha Clifford's letter, with its confusion of those two words. For Joyce, language cannot be separated from the humans who employ it, and thus he naturally turns to theories of gestural languages and to the hieroglyphic forms of writing that were associated with them.

Joyce is not alone in making a connection between language and bodies; the link is present not only in Jousse and Vico, but looks back to Mallarmé's comment about the 'écriture corporelle' of ballet and forward to the theories of Béla Balázs and Antonin Artaud. As we've seen, this desire for 'embodiment' – and the link between gestures and the possibility of universal languages – was essential to Balázs and other theorists of silent film. For Artaud in particular, the bodies of performers in the theatre could create a new hieroglyphic language of gesture: 'As for ordinary objects, or even the human body, raised to the dignity of signs, it is evident that one can draw one's inspiration from hieroglyphic characters.'[52] Artaud comments that 'on the stage [. . .] the language of words may have to give way before a language of signs', before 'the visual language of objects, movements, attitudes, and gestures' (p. 107). Artaud turns the emphasis on the gestural origins of language in Jousse and others into a complete aesthetic system.[53]

Joyce similarly blurs the line between words and gestures, and not only through the H.E.L.Y.S. ad or the cart advertising stationery. The association between theatre and hieroglyphs helps to explain why Stephen's statement about the universal language of gesture leads off the 'Circe' chapter, as this episode, with its dramatic form, comes the closest that literature can to creating an embodied language. Not only do the characters take on an active life of their own, speaking without the filter of narration, but many of the important motifs of the novel return to assume a physical presence. Just as Artaud describes 'the visual language of objects', so in 'Circe' from mere words on the page, physical items – the soap, the hollybush, the buckles, the cap, the bracelets – become participants in the narrative, on a par with the human characters. The Word becomes Flesh. This tendency looks forward to *Finnegans Wake*, and particularly to Beckett's famous description of the form of the *Wake*: 'When the sense is sleep, the words go to sleep. [. . .] When the sense is dancing, the words dance. [. . .] The language is drunk. The very words are tilted and effervescent.'[54] Language becomes not so much akin to the content, although that is what Beckett is arguing here; rather, language becomes akin to the human, taking on human agency and human motion. Words, like the objects in 'Circe', become the protagonists of the narrative.

Joyce in 'Circe' thus anticipates theories of gestural language – Artaud's sense that a language of signs could replace words – but simultaneously validates the importance of words. In lending his words physical form, he implies, like Woolf, that words need not be replaced by gestures, since they always and already possess an active force in the world. Indeed, the last pages of 'Circe' consistently juxtapose words and gestures, reminding the reader that even those actions that seem only communicable through physical movements are imparted, in the pages of Joyce's novel, through mere words. While the chapter reaches its climax in an extended 'dance of death' between Stephen and the whores – and dance for Mallarmé and Artaud alike was the ultimate gestural hieroglyphic form – that dance is interrupted by the linguistic intrusion of Stephen's dead mother 'uttering a silent word' (pp. 472, 473). Stephen responds by famously declaring, 'tell me the word, mother, if you know now. The word known to all men' (p. 474). Language and gesture collide with each other, in a pattern repeated at the very end of the episode. Joyce describes with wearying precision the non-verbal communications between Bloom and Corny Kelleher: 'Corny Kelleher on the sideseat sways his head to and fro in sign of mirth at Bloom's plight. The jarvey joins in the mute pantomimic merriment nodding from the farther seat. Bloom shakes his head in mute mirthful reply. [. . .] With a slow nod Bloom conveys his gratitude [. . .] Corny Kelleher again reassuralooms with his hand' (p. 496). Yet the chapter ends not with this acknowledgement of all that can be conveyed through gestures, but with a text, with Rudy 'holding a book in his hand' and reading (p. 497). What Lynch says of Stephen in 'Circe' is true of Joyce, 'he likes dialectic, the universal language' (p. 490). But what Joyce in *Ulysses* likes is not so much the universal language of dialectic, but rather a dialectic of universal languages, a ceaseless play with juxtapositions and combinations of the potentially universal languages of words, hieroglyphs, gestures and ads.

Finnegans Wake's Verbivocovisual Language

This sense of the interrelation between gestures, images and words takes on its most complex and developed expression in *Finnegans Wake*, in which Joyce develops an extended genealogy of language, visual and otherwise. Joyce is concerned not merely with the combination of texts and bodies in ads or theatre, but also in the buried linkages – historical and transcultural – between languages and visual or gestural signs. In a far more systematic way than *Ulysses*, *Finnegans Wake* demonstrates how not only advertising or film, but language in and of itself inherently possesses not only a phonetic sound and a linguistic meaning, but a visual form. Joyce shows how writing is inextricably connected to the images and physical objects from which, he suggests, it originally derived. Thus, in the *Wake*, Joyce's letters come to embody the characters in the narrative. To the extent that the *Wake* has characters, their presence is signalled by the anagrams HCE or ALP, who represent the father figure and his mother/wife, and by various puns on the names of their children, Shaun, Shem and Izzy. These characters exist in the visual form of letters on the page, not simply as abstractions. Joyce makes his readers notice the material and visual properties and the physical processes inherent in writing. It is these qualities that provide the essential connection between seemingly disparate cultures and forms of writing, between hieroglyphs and the alphabet.

Given the link between hieroglyphs and universal languages in the discourses of Joyce's time – and the common view of hieroglyphics as a hybrid form between the visual and the textual – references to Egyptian language appear repeatedly in *Finnegans Wake*. Joyce writes of the 'highpriest's hieroglyph of kettletom' and 'strangewrote anaglyptics of those shemletters patent for His Cristian's Em' and asks 'was I not rosetted on two stellas of little egypt? had not I rockcut readers, hieros' (pp. 122, 419, 551), alluding to the Rosetta Stone as well as to the hieroglyphs graven on it. There are also occasional allusions to cuneiform and to papyrus.

Hieroglyphs, as we've seen, served as an important metaphor in the culture at large for film, phonography and other new media forms. Their importance for Joyce, however, has been ignored, despite the fact that John Bishop, Mark Troy and others have offered extended analyses of the Egyptian Book of the Dead's importance to the *Wake*. They neglect the hieroglyphic language in which it was written, despite the fact that Bishop even describes *Finnegans Wake* as written in 'comparable hieroglyphics' as the 'Bugs of the Deaf'.[55] This omission is doubly odd given Samuel Beckett's remark in his famous essay from *transition* on *Finnegans Wake:* 'Here is the savage economy of hieroglyphics.'[56]

The hieroglyph or ideogram seems to be, like advertising in *Ulysses*, a more embodied or tangible form of language, if not gestural then, by being visual, closer to the material world. Hieroglyphs fit with Joyce's desire to remind the reader of language's material nature – how it is printed, written and transmitted – a desire going back at least as far as the 'Aeolus' section of *Ulysses*. So Joyce writes, 'in the otherworld of the passing of the key of Two-tongue Common, with Nush, the carrier of the word, and with Mesh, the cutter of the reed' (p. 385). This passage illustrates the impulse, essential to universal languages, to bring together two tongues or more, something Joyce does on a far more ambitious level in *Finnegans Wake*. But through the allusion to King Tut that links back to hieroglyphics, Joyce portrays language not as print, but in an older, more physical form, as a reed pressed into a clay tablet. The word, the letter, is not a disembodied concept, but becomes tangible, capable of being moved from place to place. Nush and Mesh, or Shaun and Shem, are thus associated with language and its dissemination, with Shaun the Post, as he's called – the mailman – carrying the words, and Shem the Penman – a stand-in for Joyce – creating the words. As he does throughout the text, Joyce emphasises the various ways in which language is written and made to be 'Two Tongue Common' by translation and transmission through the mail, radio, television or film.

Throughout the *Wake*, Joyce remains fascinated by the materiality of ancient linguistic forms. Immediately after the discussion between Mutt and Jute, already linked to the pictographic drawings of cavemen, Joyce writes, '(Stoop) if you are abcedminded, to the claybook, what curios of signs (please stoop), in this allaphbed! Can you rede (since We and Thou had it out already) its world?' (p. 18). This passage was added after the *Wake*'s initial publication in *transition*, reflecting again Joyce's expanded engagement with the variety of linguistic forms over the course of the *Wake*'s composition.[57] Aside from the word-world pun, familiar from *Ulysses*, Joyce shows how alphabetical languages, the 'abced' and 'allaphbed', are akin to hieroglyphs, written with a 'rede' or reed on a 'claybook'. For those readers who are 'abcedminded' (absentminded) and believe that language can only be alphabetical (abced), the passage reminds us how today's letters were once based on 'signs' written in clay. Just as the ad in *Ulysses* with its 'triliteral monoideal symbols' calls attention to language's visual form, so Joyce here reminds the reader of the material process of its creation.[58] Furthermore, this passage also alludes to the Koran, thus bringing in the current language of Egypt as well as its ancient one; as Aida Yared has argued, the 'allaphbed' here alludes not merely to the alphabet generally or the first two letters of Hebrew specifically, but also to Arabic, which likewise begins with the letters aleph and bet. Like the modern Egyptian writers discussed in Chapter 4, Joyce brings together hieroglyphs and Arabic, Egyptian languages past and present, through an attention to their visual forms.[59]

Joyce harkens back to a time before the invention of alphabetical languages, but he also demonstrates the coexistence of alphabetical writing and images by tracing the history of the printed word from Gutenberg (Gutenmorg) onwards:

> Gutenmorg with his cromagnom charter, tintingfast and great primer must once for omniboss step rubrickredd out of the wordpress else is there no virtue more in alcohoran. For that (the rapt one warns) is what papyr is meed of, made of, hides and hints and misses in prints. Till ye finally (though not yet endlike) meet with the acquaintance of Mister Typus, Mistress Tope and all the little typtopies. (p. 20)

Even as he alludes to the invention of print and moveable type, or 'Mister Typus' – a giant step towards the dematerialisation of the written word – Joyce continues to look back to the past – to the 'cromagnom' era – and to call attention to the physical material out of which writing is created. Paper becomes 'papyr', or papyrus, returning us to Egypt, and is made of 'hides' or animal skins. 'Rubrickredd' alludes both to the physical substance 'rubric' – 'Red earth, red ochre, ruddle' – and the aspects of printing made possible by that red earth: 'A heading of a chapter, section, or other division of a book, written or printed in red' (*OED*). The process of writing becomes more important than the individual language or technology of inscription.

Joyce here similarly fashions an extended comparison between the creation of text and the fermentation of alcohol – suggested by 'alcohoran' (which combines 'alcohol' with a reference to the printed text of the Koran, or 'alcoran' as it was once called in Europe) and 'Mistress Tope' (tope is a word denoting drinking). This linkage renders writing akin to other processes of transforming the physical world into a useable form. Joyce reminds the reader of the material roots of writing, even when we've reached the age of Gutenberg and of type, or 'Mister Typus'. Writing becomes both more random and enigmatic than it might initially seem – composed of 'hints and misses in prints' – but also more tangible and physical, composed not in a vacuum but out of the actual matter of the world, written on the hides of animals just as later Shem will write 'over every square inch of the only foolscap available, his own body' (p. 185).[60] This linkage is essential for *Finnegans Wake* as a whole, given the way Joyce renders the characters themselves into typewritten characters, in the case of HCE and ALP. If writing derives from the physical world, then it can be re-imbued with physical substance and re-made into characters, just as the words here become 'Mister Typus' and 'Mistress Tope'. As with the H.E.L.Y.S. ad in *Ulysses*, Joyce destroys the boundary between language and identity.

The reference to Gutenberg in the passage above, as well as the many references to hieroglyphs, recall a time when the pictorial and the linguistic were not as separate as they seem to be today. Although the invention of print seems to mark the beginning of the end for visuality in language, Joyce reminds us that, in fact, it did not: the word 'rubrickredd' points to the rubrics or decorated opening letters that were included in many of the Gutenberg Bibles. This form was familiar to Joyce because of his daughter Lucia's work at the same time on what she called 'lettrines' or rubrics for Joyce's poems and for excerpts from the writings of Chaucer. Joyce's extended references to IALs are thus juxtaposed in book I, chapter 5 with a word-for-word parody of Edward Sullivan's commentary on the Book of Kells – one of the most famous illuminated manuscripts, a form which, with its use of rubrics, combines writing and pictures.[61]

In the Book of Kells, Joyce finds a model for his own embellishment and decoration of the English language, his own attempts to call attention to its visuality; he even refers to the *Wake* as 'our book of kills' (p. 482). For the Book of Kells not only includes full pages of pictures, but also features rubrics, as in Figure 5.1, which often combine letters with human forms. The Book of Kells thus provides an antecedent for Joyce's own attempts to turn

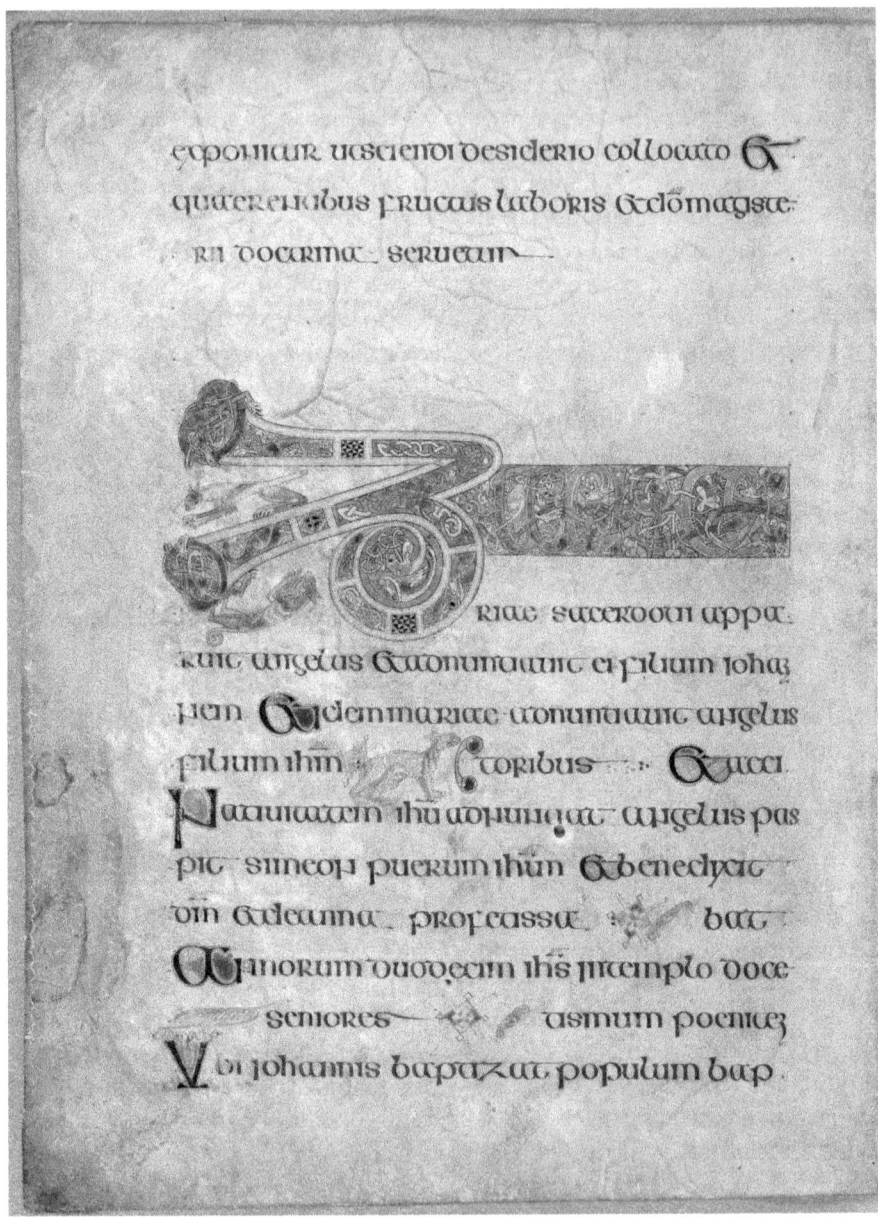

Figure 5.1 Folio 19v from The Book of Kells, TCD MS 58, Trinity College Library Dublin, Courtesy of the Board of Trinity College Dublin

linguistic characters into the personages of his text. Just as the letters H, C and E combine to form the central figure of the *Wake*, so in the Book of Kells the letters turn into bodies. Edward Sullivan, the commentator on the Book of Kells, even points out the similarities between the Book and earlier forms of writing, particularly Egyptian forms: 'We find there the serpentine bands of the Irish ornaments appearing already in the oldest Egyptian and Ethiopian manuscripts, and with a similarity of colour and combination truly astonishing.'[62] As Joyce must have appreciated, given his attempt to forge a transhistorical synthesis in *Finnegans Wake*, Sullivan brings together the two motifs – hieroglyphs and illuminated manuscripts – that are so central to the *Wake*.[63]

But Joyce does not merely look to the past for hybrid forms; rather, he demonstrates that, like an illuminated manuscript, all language, even contemporary language, is 'verbivocovisual'. Near the beginning of book I, chapter 5, he writes, the 'proteiform graph itself is a polyhedrom of scripture. There was a time when naïf alphabetters would have written it' (p. 107). Again Joyce mocks those 'naïf alphabetters' who can only see alphabetical forms of language, and he focuses on more visual, or at least 'proteiform', kinds of language. For proteiform means a changeable – or protean – form (looking back to *Ulysses* and the emphasis on visual perception in 'Proteus') and demonstrates how Joyce desires his 'Work in Progress' to shift and transform itself, perpetually crossing the boundaries of language and media. To confirm the connection to language itself, Joyce's next word is 'graph': 'a visual symbol representing a phoneme'. Such a definition should be familiar, as it is the definition of a letter itself, and, indeed, of a hieroglyph, which, despite the fact that it seems to represent objects, in fact only corresponds to a phoneme. Again, Joyce calls attention to the visuality inherent in language; letters and words have a meaning or a sound that they refer to, but they also have a visual appearance in their own right, one which constantly transforms itself, assuming 'proteiform' significance.

As Joyce describes later in the chapter, ALP's letter is similarly composed of 'changeably meaning vocable scriptsigns. No, so help me Petault, it is not a miseffectual whyacinthinous riot of blots and blurs and bars and balls and hoops and wriggles and juxtaposed jottings linked by spurts of speed' (p. 118). The characters have a purely visual aspect – 'blots and blurs and bars and balls and hoops and wriggles', seemingly without any linguistic function, with Joyce pointing out the ornamental nature, as in the Book of Kells, of the letters. These letters, however, are not purely visual; they are 'scriptsigns' with changeable meanings, like the 'proteiform graphs' mentioned earlier. And like all languages they are 'vocable scriptsigns', possessing an oral meaning as well as a semantic one: verbal, vocal and visual.

Joyce's sigla – the visual symbols, like Ш and Δ, that stand for the characters of the *Wake* – serve a similar function, encouraging the reader not only to remember that writing, in hieroglyphics and illuminated manuscripts, once incorporated visual images but also to become aware that the characters of language remain visual.[64] They function as more radical versions of the ads in *Ulysses*. These sigla, which Joyce used as a form of shorthand, appear in the final published version, most notably on page 299, when they're described by Izzy as the 'Doodle Family'. Joyce even suggests that his sigla actually depict physical objects. The scholarly commentator on the letter writes of 'the meant to be baffling chrismon trilithon sign ⊓ finally called after some his hes hecitancy Hec which, moved contrawatchwise, represents his title in sigla as the smaller Δ, fontly called following a certain change of state of grace of nature alp or delta' (p. 119). Again Joyce looks back to an earlier alphabet, in this case Greek, as the word 'chrismon' implies. As in the passages on ancient Egypt discussed above, he exposes the reader to a more physical form of writing through the meaning of 'trilithon': 'A prehistoric structure or monument consisting of three large stones, two upright and one resting upon them as a lintel' (*OED*). The character Ш itself is connected to the physical object that it almost depicts; language becomes nearly sculptural.

Joyce goes on to write about his sigla Δ, Ш and X, 'why not take the former for a village inn, the latter for an upsidown bridge, a multiplication marking for crossroads ahead' (p. 119). He returns us to the supposed roots of language that Vico described, before the fall from visual depiction into linguistic denotation, the 'change of state of grace of nature'. The character becomes the thing it stands for, moving from denotation to depiction. Ш is 'an upsidown bridge', X 'a multiplication marking'. By estranging the reader from the characters of the Roman language – the sigla are 'meant to be baffling' – Joyce encourages us to see language as a visual marking in its own right, as well as a marking that carries a vocal and written meaning (and in this regard we should note the imitation of stuttering in 'his hes hecitation Hec' above). Rather than looking only at their references, in *Finnegans Wake* we must examine the physical shape and the spoken sound of each word and character. These qualities serve as the point of connection for all of the seventy-odd languages that Joyce incorporates into his text, allowing him to find an origin point for contemporary languages and cultures in ancient scripts.

'The Movibles': Joyce and Cinema

But Joyce is not merely interested in the visual form of writing; rather, he also seeks, like Woolf in 'The Cinema', to claim that visual media like film and photography are simply new iterations of writing itself. By building on the tradition linking film back to hieroglyphs – already well-established by Lindsay and Eisenstein – Joyce folds visual media into the same genealogy that gave rise to alphabetical writing, going back to ancient pictographic and gestural forms. Film emerges not as a more universal alternative to writing – better than alphabetical IALs like Basic English – but merely as a return to the universal and 'verbivocovisual' roots of all writing.

The status of film as a universal language – often bolstered by the imaginative linkage of film with hieroglyphs – was, as we've seen, almost a commonplace in modernism, from Lindsay to Van Zile to Griffith. Given his interest in visual and universal languages, Joyce naturally incorporates countless allusions to film and photography over the course of the *Wake*: Joyce mentions 'Charley Chance' (Charlie Chan) and '"childe" chaplain's [Chaplin's] "latest"', describes a 'dolly pram [. . .] at the movies' and the 'shadows by the film folk. Longshots, upcloses, outblacks', and refers to the 'celluloid art', a 'soundpicture', the 'photoplay' and 'moving pictures' (pp. 65, 166, 221, 534, 570, 516, 565). Joyce compares movies to written text, punning on movies and moveable type; he writes, 'the movibles are scrawling in motions' on the same page as the above passage on Gutenberg and later refers to 'movibile tectu' (pp. 20, 165), explicitly portraying film as a new form of printed language.[65] Indeed, film was an important part of *Finnegans Wake* from its conception. In his early notebook, Joyce includes notes on 'fine pictures (cine)', 'film folk', 'cinema fakes' and 'retake (cine)', among others, and we should remember Joyce's lifelong interest in film and his failed attempt to open Dublin's first movie theatre.[66]

While John Bishop writes that the description of the buried letter as a negative in book I, chapter 5 is proof that Joyce seeks to negate language in the *Wake*, Joyce's references to film demonstrate that we also need to see that 'negative' for what it more obviously is: a photographic negative.[67] Film and photography provide a central metaphor for the visuality of language that Joyce attempts to expose in the novel. ALP's letter, which as Bishop points out serves as a 'meta-commentary on *Finnegans Wake*', is not only composed of words that can be read aloud, but like the Book of Kells is a visual object itself, or, at least, capable of being translated like a negative into a visual object.[68] Joyce becomes the film developer, revealing the visual substance of language. Film must have been even more appealing for Joyce in *Finnegans Wake* because it was able to create 'moving pictures', so fundamental to his 'Work in Progress'. Joyce was writing the novel, at least initially, in the era of silent film, which, through its combination of music, images and intertitles, provided the closest modern equivalent to the illuminated manuscript.[69]

Over the course of the *Wake*, Joyce in fact consistently places references to film in dialogue with references to Egypt, as if bringing together the hieroglyphs of the past with those of the future. These moments are often linked with allusions to America, the country which was most thoroughly associated with the new technology of film, and through Lindsay's work, with the language of ancient Egypt.[70] Despite Joyce's professed aversion to America – Jolas remembers that Joyce 'even showed a certain curiosity about America, although he still adhered to his dogma that the great creative myths of humanity stemmed from Europe' – he seems to see it, because of its association with moviemaking, as the new frontier of representation.[71] America appears in the second sentence of the *Wake* as 'North Armorica' (p. 3) and bundled allusions to film, America and Egypt recur throughout the novel. To take just one example, a reference to 'The new world presses' is juxtaposed with 'mind mand gunfree', a pun on the American screwball comedy *My Man Godfrey*, and both occur on the same page as a mention of the 'Pharoah' of Egypt (p. 387).[72] The linkage between American film and Egypt that Joyce forges in the *Wake* makes of film the art form of the future, the art form of the resurrected world, which, given the Vichian cycle of history that Joyce promulgates, serves as a new form of ancient hieroglyphs.[73]

But just as Joyce's interest in the origins of language encompasses both pictographs and gestures, so film bridges the gap between images and bodies. For while theorists employed the metaphor of hieroglyphs to describe film, they also saw the movies as capturing a primal gestural language. As Marshall McLuhan argues, synthesising this viewpoint, 'If the phonetic alphabet was a technical means of severing the spoken word from its aspects of sound and gesture, the photograph and its development in the movie restored gesture to the human technology of recording experience.'[74] Again bodies and film are contrasted with the 'phonetic alphabet', and this sense of embodiment renders film a universal language; as Laura Marcus writes, 'Silent film, it was argued, had been a universal medium, developing, in Balázs's phrase, "an international universal humanity," and operating in a kind of visual Esperanto, including, for Balázs, a "comparative 'gesturology'".'[75] Just as Joyce traces language back to gesture and hieroglyphs, so Balázs does the same: 'But the language of gestures is the true mother tongue of mankind' (p. 11).[76] By giving us access to these gestures, film will, like Basic English, 'bring together the people and nations, make them accustomed to each other, and lead them to mutual understanding' (p. 44). Hieroglyphs become for Joyce the metaphor for the language of both images and bodies.

Joyce's engagement with film in *Finnegans Wake* need not be ascribed, however, simply to the indirect influence of the widespread discourses on visual media, hieroglyphs and universal languages at the time. For as with Ogden's Basic English, the most famous articulation of the connection between film and visual languages occurred in the pages of *transition*. The nineteenth issue featured a translation of Eisenstein's essay, 'The Cinematographic Principle and the Ideogram', analysed in more depth in Chapter 1. Joyce thus would have been directly aware of the imaginative linkage between Chinese writing and the new medium of film. Indeed, Joyce and Eisenstein had a personal connection, having met in Paris and shared their admiration for each other's work.[77] Eisenstein even uses a quotation from Joyce – naturally, Stephen's remark about his desire for a 'universal language' of gesture – in his essay 'A Course in Treatment', confirming Eisenstein's own interest, probably fuelled by the influence of Griffith, in film as a form of universal language. In Eisenstein Joyce finds an invocation of visual languages that stresses both universalism and difficulty; for Eisenstein the ideogram or hieroglyph can communicate more directly, but only through a series of complex juxtapositions and combinations akin to the famous puns and portmanteau phrases that Joyce incorporates into the *Wake*. It is no wonder that Eisenstein in the same essay includes a footnote saying that 'It has been left to James Joyce to develop in *literature* the depictive line of the Japanese hieroglyphs'.[78]

Eisenstein stresses the visual aspects of Joyce's work – its 'depictive' rather than 'denotative' qualities – emphasising his attempt to create a new, more meaningful language. We might be tempted, given Joyce's interest in film and his seeming belief in hieroglyphics as an older, purer form of language, to take Eisenstein's view and see Joyce as falling victim to the Cratylic fallacy. Joyce, it would seem, is seeking to create a Cratylic language in *Finnegans Wake*, one in which the sign and its referent are, if not the same, then at least more closely related than in alphabetical, phonetic languages. Like Paget and Vico, Joyce seems to believe that if we return to an earlier, more visual form of language, than the pre-Adamic language might be capable of being recaptured. As Beckett says of *Finnegans Wake*: 'Here form *is* content; content *is* form.'[79]

I would argue, in fact, that the opposite is the case. Although Joyce strives to remind the reader of language's visual form, he does not try to bring words closer to the concepts for which they stand. While we as readers may ascribe visual and representative meanings to the shape of words – and Joyce encourages us in this process – he reminds us that we must never lose sight of the fact that these visual meanings are subjective. Seeing words as visual allows us to see just how arbitrary they really are, since even pictures can have multiple meanings. Joyce's siglum 'X', he writes, can be taken for 'a multiplication marking for crossroads ahead', but this explanation already encompasses two separate meanings for the siglum: a multiplication marking, or a 'crossroads ahead'. The dream of a pure language is unreachable, but more than that, the contemporaneous dream that pictures – and particularly film and photography – could somehow supplant words as a better language for communication is revealed as an impossibility. The proponents of universal languages may have had a profound influence on Joyce, but the *Wake* reveals them as misguided. No system of language – even a sign system – can be fixed and made stable, nor can one clearly and unambiguously communicate meaning. Instead meaning resides in the interpretive capacities of each reader, each listener.

Joyce thus exposes as naive Ezra Pound's experiments with Chinese ideograms as a model for a purer form of Imagist poetry, since ideograms, like hieroglyphics, like Joyce's sigla, are not really all that different, or less arbitrary, than regular Latin letters. While Joyce may be drawn towards the idea that hieroglyphs bridge the gap between the particular and the universal, between image and language, he is also aware, far more than Pound, that this belief is largely an illusion. Joyce provides in his own version of a universal language not the solution to the problem of Babel but Babel itself: a radically impure cacophony of different languages that is only an exaggerated form of the polyglot and arbitrary nature of all communication. As is inherent in the double meaning of the word Babel – both the Tower and the babble that results – an attempt to solve the problem of Babel only creates it again. As Hugh Kenner writes, 'Babel is thus both the tower and the fall of the tower, the desire for unity, concentration, and universality and also its inevitable defeat and fall into disunity and chaos' (p. 61).[80] Joyce strives to construct a tower of Babel that does not sacrifice the babble it produces.

TWO-TONGUE COMMON: DISPROVING INDO-EUROPEANISM

Joyce's aim in *Finnegans Wake*, however, is not simply to deconstruct language. Rather, his insights about writing point to the inextricable linkage between his aesthetics and his politics. His simultaneous embrace of cultural and national differences and his universalist desire for a common linguistic origin are woven into the very fabric of the *Wake*'s language. In questioning the idea that there could be a pure language – be it hieroglyphs or film – with a privileged access to the objects it denotes, Joyce appears to endorse a straightforwardly universalist position that undermines one of the most obviously wrong-headed arguments for Irish nationalism. As Umberto Eco writes, linguists throughout the past five hundred years occasionally contended that if there was one language that had survived the curse of Babel, it was Irish: 'the Gaelic language constituted the first and only instance of a language that overcame the confusion of tongues' (p. 16).[81] Linguists claimed that 'no other language, not even English, shows itself to be so close to the first universal language, and to its natural precision and correspondence between words and things'.[82] Irish becomes the pre-Babelic language, both pure and potentially universal. Such a view, one that the Citizen in *Ulysses* might share, Joyce demolishes in *Finnegans Wake* with its polyglot vocabulary and its insistence that all languages – visual and otherwise – are similarly arbitrary. Bloom's description in *Ulysses* of how Molly 'had more than once covered a sheet of paper with signs and hieroglyphics which she stated were Greek and Irish and Hebrew characters' (p. 562) thus removes the primacy of Irish by juxtaposing it with other languages and with hieroglyphics, linking East and West, alphabetical and pictorial.[83] All are interrelated, but all are just as arbitrary and fallen.

Joyce's language seems implicitly anti-nationalist, pointing to the universal connections between cultures and languages. Thus despite his shared focus on the Egyptian past and on the links between cultures, Joyce seems to depart from the nationalist aims of al-Hakim and Mahfouz discussed in Chapter 4.

Derek Attridge provides a clear encapsulation of this universalist interpretation of *Finnegans Wake*, which he opposes: '*Finnegans Wake* is [Joyce's] tower of anti-Babel, [. . .] an artifact which, by making out of the kaleidoscope of languages a new tongue and a new name to hold humanity together, will succeed where the sons of Noah failed' (p. 158). Clearly, as Attridge argues, this view is incorrect; Joyce acknowledges that there can be no 'new tongue' to reunite all languages, and instead he revels in the multiplicity of tongues rather than trying to forge a new one.

Yet the idea of a universal language remains tantalising to Joyce, and his interest in hieroglyphs and other forms of visual language, as well as his note about how the 'phonetic theory is unsound', point to a desire to undermine the emerging consensus of linguists about the Indo-European roots of most Western languages. Instead of a monogenetic theory that all languages derived from a common source, be it Adam or otherwise, the Indo-European hypothesis posited multiple and unrelated language groups. Turning to hieroglyphs and gestural languages, Joyce strives to question the polygenetic hypothesis, to show that even if languages ultimately are still arbitrary, they at least derive from a single source in images or movements that are common to all of humanity. By juxtaposing hieroglyphs with the Latin alphabet, by demonstrating through his sigla that Latin letters are just as visual as ideograms, Joyce seeks to break down the barriers between different language groups and show the similarity between Western and non-Western languages.

Joyce critiques the nationalist idea that there are essential differences between nations, that one country's language or traditions might be privileged above another's, but in so doing he validates Ireland's cultural importance. For in placing Irish and Hebrew and hieroglyphics side by side and by arguing for the universal origins of language, Joyce counter-intuitively circles back towards a kind of nationalism, putting Ireland on an equal footing with the other nations of the world. While certainly Joyce's aims are different, the balance between nationalism and universalism in his look back at the Egyptian past recalls the work of al-Hakim and Mahfouz discussed earlier. Rather than entirely rejecting the very idea of a fixed cultural origin or of a supposedly original language, so central to nationalism, Joyce playfully constructs a more universal original language in hieroglyphs and gestures.[84] Such a view makes sense of Joyce's interest in Jousse, Paget and Vico and their attempts to find a common source in gesture for the world's languages. While Ogden's Basic English and other IALs seek to make up for the loss of monogenesis by imposing a new language on all the nations of the world, Joyce finds, in the hieroglyph, a different way to recapture the possibility of linguistic monogenesis in the distant past.

The political situation in Europe at the time of Joyce's composition of *Finnegans Wake* also helps to explain his attempt to question Indo-Europeanism. For monogenesis opposes Nazism and fascism, specifically the connection forged by the Nazis between the Indo-European language and Aryanism.[85] In *Finnegans Wake*, Joyce even alludes to this cooptation of linguistics when he writes, 'eure sanscreed into oure eryan', punning frequently on 'Eryen blood' (p. 508). As Patrick A. McCarthy points out, this passage 'seems to place Sanskrit and Gaelic – the ancient languages of India and Ireland or Erin – in opposition, but the pun on Erin and Aryan destabilises the opposition, since Sanskrit is one of the Aryan or Indo-Iranian languages.'[86] Linking nationalism and universalism, Joyce posits an originary Irish language ('Eryan'), but in so doing argues for the underlying linguistic links between all cultures. Moreover, in the pun on 'pure' in 'eure' Joyce rejects, again, the idea of a pure language: from Sanskrit, the key to proto-Indo-European, German nationalists have made a 'screed' and transformed it into 'our Aryan'. Joyce would prefer a language '*sans* [without] creed'. This passage was added before the rise of Nazism, but it reflects an early awareness on the part of Joyce of the dangers of Aryan thinking, already widespread in the 1920s. In positing an alternate source of language in image and gesture, Joyce seeks to restore a sense of the commonality among the cultures of the world at a time of increasing nationalist polarisation. Rather than arguing for the equality of the different language groups, however, Joyce unites them without effacing their valuable differences.

The politics of Joyce's aesthetics lie in that liminal space between the particular and the universal, between nationalism and cosmopolitanism, with Bloom both Bloom and the archetypal Ulysses, HCE both a family man in Dublin and the incarnation of myriad figures of world history. The act of translation – both in its primary linguistic meaning and its secondary definition: 'To bear, convey, [. . .] from one person, place or condition to another; to transfer, transport' (*OED*) – thus becomes vital, since translation bridges the literal and metaphorical borders between cultures without attempting to ignore those differences. Marcel Jousse stresses repeatedly the importance of translation: 'This principle enables us to transpose signs into psychological intuitions previously experienced by us, for it is only in ourselves that we find the original text of the human soul; everywhere else we are forced to make use of translations' (pp. 74–5). Translation here is not merely a linguistic act; it is central to interpretation and perception. As Jousse writes, quoting Anatole France in a dialogue invoking hieroglyphs, 'To read, to hear, is to translate. Why is it [. . .] that they admire my books, seeing that it is they who have read into them what they admire?' (p. 76).[87] France's view anticipates Joyce's own proclamation about *Finnegans Wake* that 'It is not I who am writing this crazy book. It is you and you and you and that girl over there and that man in the corner.'[88] There is an act of translation and projection between author and book, just as between individual and individual, between language and language. This emphasis on translation helps to explain Joyce's fascination with translations of his own works – be it Ogden's rendering of *Finnegans Wake* into Basic English or Beckett's French version of the *Wake*, to which Joyce actively contributed.[89] The act of translation allows other cultures to access the novel, but it also emphasises the collaborative nature of the work of art; meaning and communication are always mediated through language and the unique subjectivities of author, translator and reader.

Joyce's purest expression of the importance of translation occurs towards the end of *Ulysses*, in a passage that looks forward to the search for a common linguistic origin point that Joyce undertakes more systematically in the *Wake*. At home in Bloom's house, Bloom and Stephen share with each other the languages of their past, trading lines in Hebrew and in Irish. After asking, 'How was a glyphic comparison of the phonic symbols of both languages made in substantiation of the oral comparison?' Joyce answers, 'On the penultimate blank page of a book [...] with a pencil (supplied by Stephen) Stephen wrote the Irish characters for gee, eh, dee, em, simple and modified, and Bloom in turn wrote the Hebrew characters ghimel, aleph, daleth and (in the absence of mem) a substituted qoph' (pp. 563–4).

Joyce then proceeds to trace the common origins of both languages to 'their antiquity, both having been taught on the plain of Shinar 242 years after the deluge in the seminary instituted by Fenius Farsaigh, descendant of Noah, progenitor of Israel, and ascendant of Heber and Heremon, progenitors of Ireland' and further compares Irish and Hebrew culture through 'their archeological, genealogical, hagiographical, exegetical, homilectic, toponomastic, historical and religious literatures comprising the works of rabbis and culdees, Torah, Talmud (Mischna and Ghemara) Massor, Pentateuch, Book of the Dun Cow, Book of Ballymote, Garland of Howth, Book of Kells: their dispersal, persecution, survival and revival' (p. 564). Soon afterwards, the narrator asks, 'In what common study did their mutual reflections merge? The increasing simplification traceable from the Egyptian epigraphic hieroglyphs to the Greek and Roman alphabets and the anticipation of modern stenography and telegraphic code in the cuneiform inscriptions (Semitic) and the virgular quinquecostate ogham writing (Celtic)' (p. 564).

On one level, these passages clinch the connection between the Irish and the Jews that Joyce builds into Bloom's character, but they also juxtapose cultural and political similarities – 'the restoration in Chanan David of Zion and the possibility of Irish political autonomy or devolution' (p. 564) – with linguistic ones. Joyce compares Hebrew texts with Irish ones, including the Book of Kells, and links the sounds and appearances of both languages. As in *Finnegans Wake*, the Irish and Hebrew characters are described as phonetic 'glyphs', and Joyce again seeks to emphasise not only their sound and sense but also their look. For 'glyphic' of course recalls 'hieroglyphic', particularly since this passage occurs on the page following Molly's comparison of Irish and Hebrew letters with hieroglyphics. Indeed, Hebrew was often considered as a language akin to hieroglyphs in the period; as Terry Ramsaye writes, 'we examine the Hebrew alphabet, one of the several successors to the hieroglyphic [. . .] In the Egyptian the picture became a sound, and in the Hebrew the picture signs for the sound are simplified into nearly arbitrary forms, still with a tinge of the picture in them' (p. liv). While closer to modern alphabets, Hebrew is seen as maintaining its pictographic roots.

This section thus concludes with the creation of a genealogy that links the epigraphic hieroglyphs of ancient Irish and Hebrew with modern alphabetical languages, as well as with stenographic and Morse code. Confirming the connection between old and new linguistic forms, Joyce shows how, after centuries of development, language has looped back, Vico-style, to its origins. In writing down these letters, Bloom and Stephen are engaged in a process of 'verbivocovisual' translation, bringing back dead or dying languages into the light of the present day and spreading them across a cultural divide (albeit a minimal one).[90] The passage that Stephen writes down further emphasises this cross-cultural connection, because the verse derives from the ballad 'Shule Aroon', in which lines of English and Irish are juxtaposed. A process of translation is necessary even within the ballad itself.

This passage is thus a positive vision of cosmopolitanism, of the friendly sharing of different cultures and languages (though, of course, this being Joyce, a heavily ironised one). Through the linkage between ancient Irish writing and Hebrew writing, Joyce forges a universal genealogy of language in which all linguistic forms emerge from a common source. As Don Gifford and Robert J. Seidman note, in mentioning Fenius Farsaigh, Joyce alludes to the apocryphal story of how

> Fenius founded a school of languages on the plain of Shinar exactly 242 years after Noah's flood and 60 years after the 'confusion of tongues' consequent on Nimrod's construction of the Tower of Babel. Fenius sent scholars ('disciples') to learn each of the seventy-two languages of the confusion and based his school among the people on the plain of Shinar who still spoke the one ur-language, Hebrew. Thus, Fenius Farsaigh becomes the legendary ancestral link between Israel and the Milesians – between the Hebrew language and Irish.[91]

Hebrew and Irish ultimately are one, going back to a time before the diffusion of languages with the fall of Babel. However much Joyce knows that these legends are false, he still wants to believe in the monogenesis of language, in the notion that all languages – from the 'cuneiform inscriptions' and 'ogham writing' – were at one point hieroglyphic. While Joyce is of course uninterested in Egyptian nationalism, he, like Mahfouz, likewise looks back to hieroglyphs to construct a cultural origin point, but for Joyce hieroglyphs are the source not of Egypt, but of everything: all languages and nations and media too. Just as Vico argues, language progresses for Joyce from hieroglyphics to alphabetical writing, before the 'ricorso' of modern hybrid forms. Given his interest in a common source for all languages in *Ulysses*, Joyce naturally over the course of his composition of his 'Work in Progress' engages ever more deeply with universal languages, hieroglyphs and films as he imagines what that common language might look like.

Joyce's universalist language theories help to explain his invocation of the 'word known to all men' in *Ulysses*. For *love*, if we trust the Gabler restoration, possesses a meaning that transcends the need for translation. It resists the processes of Babelisation and shines through, despite the distortions of language, to all cultures. If Joyce is at home in a polyglot world of ambiguous and deferred meanings, he simultaneously longs for that word that would be truly universal, that would return to the shared roots of language. Ogden's Basic English, though certainly in a highly debased and literalised form, might have partially fulfilled Joyce's goal; if love were not the word known to all men, then at least it could be one of the eight hundred and fifty words known to all men.

NOTES

1. Ogden, 'James Joyce's Anna Livia Plurabelle in Basic English', p. 259.
2. Joyce, *Anna Livia Plurabelle*.
3. Joyce, *Wake*, p. 116.
4. Richard Paget, *Babel*; C. K. Ogden, *Debabelization*; and Otto Jespersen, *An International Language*. See also Rosiers and Van Mierlo, pp. 55–70; and Milesi, 'Supplementing Babel: Paget in VI.B.32', pp. 75–89. Joyce owned a copy of Ogden's *Debabelization*, personally inscribed to him, and now held at the Lockwood Library at the University of Buffalo.
5. Joyce, *Wake*, pp. 122, 565; Joyce, *Ulysses*, p. 399; Joyce, *Wake*, p. 117.
6. Milesi, 'Joyce, Language, and Languages', pp. 144–61, and 'Vico . . . Jousse: Joyce . . . Langue', pp. 143–62; Rabaté, pp. 51–8; and Sailer, pp. 853–68.
7. Ogden saw English as a possibly universal language partially because, after the addition of sound, film was already spreading it throughout the globe. He also later collaborated with Otto Neurath on the book *Basic by Isotype*, which combined the vocabulary of Basic English with the visual symbols for international communication of Neurath's Isotype.
8. As Liselotte Dieckmann writes, 'Through the building of the Tower of Babel this original, genuine, and "true" language was destroyed and replaced by Plato's language of "convention"' (p. 13).
9. Milesi, Lorraine Weir, and Christy Burns have all explored Jousse's influence on Joyce's use of gestural languages. Weir asserts that Jousse's lectures were a major source for 'The Mime of Mick, Nick, and the Maggies', and Burns claims, more generally, that Joyce's work is characterised by 'an art of gesture, which serves to combine materiality with meaning, body with spirit, sense with essence' (p. 9).
10. Much of the criticism of *Finnegans Wake*, particularly John Bishop's *Joyce's Book of the Dark*, has rejected the visual, with Bishop emphasising how Joyce seeks to cancel language – to blot out daylight modes of communication and create a language that 'resists visualization'. One exception is Sara Danius, who writes in *The*

Senses of Modernism of how his novels 'testif[y] yet again to the preeminence of vision and visuality in Joyce' (p. 174).
11. Joyce, Wake, p. 341.
12. As Edward Clodd writes in *The Story of the Alphabet*, which Joyce read, 'the pictograph is the parent of the alphabet' (p. 25).
13. For an argument that the *Wake* is a full-fledged 'attack on Aryanis[t]' race theories, see Len Platt, *Joyce, Race, and Finnegans Wake*, p. 175. Platt, however, does not discuss the linguistic implications of that attack, seeing the *Wake* as purely deconstructive of the idea of cultural origins, rather than as a search for alternate, universalist origins. For more on the false connection forged between the Indo-European language and Aryan race theories, see Poliakov, *The Aryan Myth*, and J. P. Mallory, *In Search of the Indo-Europeans*.
14. C. K. Ogden and I. A. Richards, *The Meaning of Meaning: A Study of the Influence of Language Upon Thought and the Science of Symbolism*.
15. In fact, Joyce alludes to virtually every language group. See Deane, '*Les Langues du Monde*', pp. 61–75.
16. Attridge, p. 161.
17. As C. K. Ogden writes in *Debabelization*, 'The so-called national barriers of today are ultimately language barriers. The absence of a common medium of communication is the chief obstacle to international understanding, and therefore the chief underlying cause of War' (p. 13). Or, as Richard Paget asks, 'May it not be that much of this unreasonable muddle [of the state of the world] is due to the simple fact that our symbols for thought – language – are not yet set in order' (p. 78). Unfortunately for Ogden, *Debabelization*, written in 1931, includes a message on world peace, translated into Basic English, by none other than Benito Mussolini.
18. The first issue of *transition* even started with the beginning of the *Wake*, and all of the essays about the *Wake* that were collected in *Our Exagmination* . . . were originally published in *transition*.
19. See the sixteenth volume of *transition* on 'The Revolution of the Word' and Jolas et al., *Man from Babel*.
20. For more on the history of *transition* and Joyce's relation to it, see McMillan, *transition: The History of a Literary Era 1927–1938* and Finney, pp. 39–53.
21. McAlmon, p. 130. Or, as Victor Llona writes, 'A new Rabélais, he [Joyce] has tumbled no less than thirteen languages into a smoldering crucible and we are witnessing the birth of a new literary idiom which, being brought into the world by a thorough artist, stands a much better chance of viability than esperanto or volapuck' (p. 169).
22. Jolas, 'Workshop', p. 100. Importantly for his relation to Joyce, the night language Jolas calls for in *transition* is characterised both by its universality and by its embodiment, its ability to 'dance and sing'.
23. Jolas, 'Workshop', p. 100.
24. Jolas et al., 'First Aid to the Enemy', p. 168.
25. Jolas, 'Introduction', p. 137. Indeed, it is as a translator that Jolas is best known today; his translation of Alfred Doblin's *Berlin Alexanderplatz*, published in *transition*, for instance, is still definitive.
26. Basic English was a more easily teachable version of English, with standardised grammatical forms and a vocabulary of only eight hundred and fifty words. It is still in use today as an educational tool.
27. Interestingly, and providing more evidence of *Wake*-ese as a form of universal language, Esperanto was the first language, other than perhaps Irish, that Joyce didn't know that he incorporated into his drafts of the *Wake*. See Milesi, 'Joyce, Language, and Languages', p. 150.

28. Joyce, 'From Work in Progress'; 'Anna Livia Plurabelle: Page Proofs'.
29. Jolas, 'Workshop', p. 104.
30. J. S. Atherton and Aida Yared have traced the engagement with the Koran specifically and the Arabic language in which it is written more generally in the *Wake*. Indeed, references to Islam and Arabic proliferate in Book I, Chapter 5, which opens with a parody of the Koran in 'In the name of Annah the Almaziful' and contains another reference to an 'arabesque' (p. 115). See Atherton, pp. 240–55; Yared, pp. 401–38.
31. Joyce, *Ulysses*, p. 399.
32. For an excellent account of Joyce's engagement with Esperanto specifically and his desire for and distrust of international languages, see Israel, pp. 1–21.
33. Jousse, p. 2.
34. Jolas et al., *Man from Babel*, p. 168.
35. Such a progression was echoed by Jousse. As Stephen Heath writes, 'Like Vico, Jousse postulates three main stages of development, which he calls *style manuel*, *style oral*, and *style écrit*: the first is that of living gesticulation [. . .] the second is that of utterance miming gesture [. . .] the third is that of alphabetism' (p. 130).
36. Jolas, 'Landscape', p. 136; 'Flight into Geography', p. 76; 'Walk through Cosmopolis', pp. 134, 8.
37. Jolas, 'Suggestions for a New Magic', p. 179.
38. Jolas et al., 'The Revolution of the Word', p. 14, and see Fargue, pp. 347–51.
39. Jolas, 'Workshop', pp. 102–3.
40. A new visual language was just what the contributors to *transition* had so long been asking for. As the contributor Bob Brown writes about his own 'Readies', 'For the first time in the History of mental optics there will exist a visual Literary Language sharply separated from the Speaking Tongue' (p. 172). *Finnegans Wake* was even seen by the editors of *transition* as a new universal language precisely because of its seeming visuality; Robert Sage declares, 'His attitude [the reader of *FW*] should be that of a person witnessing a half dozen finely coordinated cinema films being projected together on the same screen while a symphony orchestra expresses the sound complement of the mobile images' (p. 172). The writers in *transition* were also fascinated with film, publishing numerous articles on the cinema, including defences of Charlie Chaplin and stills from films by Man Ray and others.
41. Such views were articulated in *transition* by Samuel Beckett, in his article on *Finnegans Wake*: 'When language consisted of gesture, the spoken and the written were identical. Hieroglyphics, or sacred language, as he calls it, were not the invention of philosophers for the mysterious expression of profound thought, but the common necessity of primitive peoples. Convenience only begins to assert itself at a far more advanced stage of civilization, in the form of alphabetism' (Beckett, 'Dante . . . Bruno. Vico . . . Joyce', p. 247).
42. Paget also agrees with Vico on the development from gesture to hieroglyphics to alphabets: 'But it would have been essential to devise a simple notation for the gestures (as we attempt to do in a roundabout way in our alphabets), or for the ideas which they conveyed (as the Chinese do in their ideographic writing)' (p. 20).
43. These notes are examined in Deane, 'Claybook for *Finnegans Wake*', pp. 21–39.
44. See Thomas Connolly (ed.) *James Joyce's Scribbledehobble*, p. 96. This notebook entry refers to Ernest Fenollosa's 'The Chinese Written Character as a Medium for Poetry', with Joyce referring to Fenollosa by name at another point in his notes. Fenollosa asks if 'we must believe that the phonetic theory is in large part unsound' (p. 59) and answers that we must; Chinese characters, he argues, against the accepted notions of scholars, actually depict the objects they describe, even if those correspondences have been lost with time.

45. Walter Benjamin, in *The Work of Art in the Age of its Technological Reproducibility*, even explicitly compares them, describing how advertising 'tears down the stage upon which contemplation moved, and all but hits us between the eyes with things as a car, growing to gigantic proportions, careens at us out of a film screen.' Benjamin likewise perceives the hybrid nature of ads; he writes of Mallarmé that he was 'the first to incorporate the graphic tensions of the advertisement in the printed page' (pp. 173, 171).
46. Wicke, 'Modernity Must Advertise', p. 603. See also Wicke's *Advertising Fictions*.
47. Moretti, p. 134.
48. Coke even proclaims on its website that 'While local languages may differ, the language of refreshment is universal.' Or, as Otto Jespersen writes in promulgating the universal language Novial, 'Advertising has been hospitable to the international language idea', in Shenton et al., *International Communication*, p. 36.
49. Ads thus become a model of literary symbolism more generally: as Joyce writes, 'Because you see, says Bloom, for an advertisement you must have repetition. That's the whole secret' (p. 265). A symbol only becomes a symbol or motif once, like an ad, it has been repeated, once it has been reproduced or mass-produced and can thus signal its status as especially significant. Bloom's House of Keyes ad – echoed in Stephen's obsession with the 'key' to the Martello tower – is particularly apt, for the 'key' is not only the key to meaning, the key to decipher a map, but also 'To distinguish (an advertisement) by some device which will identify responses to it' (*OED*). Like the symbol 'key', the 'key' in an ad allows the ad to signal its significance to a reader or viewer.
50. The odd interpolated word 'divined' in the above passage renders the ads almost as sacred and mysterious as hieroglyphics, just as the word 'deciphered' points to the efforts to make them legible. Much as Joyce redirects epiphanies from religion to the vulgar world in *Portrait*, in *Ulysses* he makes ads a new form of revelation and inspiration rather than a sign of their loss. As Garry Leonard writes about advertising in Joyce, 'What we should recognize [. . .] is that commodity culture is the new religion' (p. 576).
51. See Behmen.
52. Artaud, p. 94.
53. Artaud's theories similarly have a Cratylic basis: 'I claim [. . .] the right to break with the usual sense of language, to crack the armature once and for all [. . .] in short to return to the etymological origins of speech which, in the midst of abstract concepts, always evoke a concrete element' (p. 101).
54. Beckett, 'Dante . . . Bruno. Vico . . . Joyce', pp. 248–9.
55. Bishop, p. 110. See also Mark Troy's *Mummeries of Resurrection*. Joyce's linkage of Ancient Egypt and writing, particularly physical forms of writing, goes back to *Portrait*, in which he invokes the Egyptian God of writers: 'Thoth, the god of writers, writing with a reed upon a tablet and bearing on his narrow ibis head the cusped moon.' James Joyce, *Portrait of the Artist as a Young Man*, p. 189. Similarly, in *Ulysses,* Stephen thinks of 'Thoth, god of libraries' (p. 159).
56. Beckett, 'Dante . . . Bruno. Vico . . . Joyce', p. 249.
57. This section derives from Edward Clodd's *The Story of the Alphabet:* 'Upon this the characters were impressed by a reed or square-shaped stylus, the clay-books being afterwards baked or sun-dried' (p. 89). Like Clodd, Joyce strives to link words back to their physical origins; Clodd writes of how 'the word "paper" preserves the history of the manufacture of writing material in Egypt from the pith of the papyrus reed' (p. 10).
58. Such an emphasis on language's materiality also crops up occasionally in *transition*, particularly in Sidney Hunt's poem titled, naturally, 'Ideograms': 'BRONZE

PLATES WITH / EXTRA / DEEP CHISELLED / V-CUT / LETTERS / SOLID / BEAUTIFUL / LEGIBLE / PERMANENT' (p. 135).
59. Yared, p. 413. Indeed, a further link between Islam and hieroglyphs may exist in the novel through Joyce's allusion to the Black Stone in Mecca: 'that shebby choruysh of unkalified muzzlenimiissilehims that would blackguardise the whitestone ever hurtleturtled out of heaven' (p. 5). That black stone perhaps evokes another famous black stone: the Rosetta Stone.
60. We should also remember how pressing these issues would have been to Joyce, given his growing blindness. While his eye troubles should not lead us to see Joyce as increasingly forgoing the visual, they do provide incentive for his experimentation with, or at least interest in, more tangible linguistic forms. As Eugene Jolas writes of Joyce, noting how literally material language was for him: 'He felt for the embossed metal letters with the sensitive fingers of defective vision' (Jolas, *Man from Babel*, p. 163).
61. Even as far back as *Portrait*, Joyce sees the illuminated manuscript as providing a privileged access to meaning. Stephen's central epiphany about his name is prompted by his vision of 'a quaint device opening a page of some medieval book of prophecies and symbols' (Joyce, *Portrait*, p. 169).
62. Sullivan, p. 43.
63. Joyce's interest in the visual nature of language and his turn to the illuminated manuscript for inspiration anticipates or is influenced by similar discussions in *transition* at the time. As the contributor Bob Brown writes about his 'Readies', 'The monks in the beginning didn't do it so badly in their illuminated manuscripts, they retained a little of the healthy hieroglyphic, all Oriental books in ideogramatic characters are delights, early colophons splendid' (p. 173).
64. For more on Joyce's sigla, see Roland McHugh, *The Sigla of Finnegans Wake*.
65. Even in *Ulysses*, in a discussion of advertisements, Joyce juxtaposes the materials of print and of cinema, with Bloom commenting, 'Or the inkbottle I suggested with a false stain of black celluloid' (p. 127).
66. See Connolly, pp. 38, 39, 119, 181; Ellmann, pp. 310–18.
67. Bishop, p. 51.
68. Bishop, p. xxi.
69. For more on Joyce's relationship to film, see Briggs, pp. 145–56; Burkdall, *Joycean Frames*; Rice, pp. 161–8.
70. Eugene Jolas saw his adopted country as central to the mission of *transition* (see 'Introduction', p. 137), and *transition*'s greatest impact was due to Jolas's translations of works by European modernists for an American audience. For more on the association of Egypt and America, see Bryant and Eaverly.
71. Jolas, *Man from Babel*, p. 172.
72. Likewise on p. 134 an allusion to *Huck Finn* is followed by a reference to the 'Bug of the Deaf' (Book of the Dead) and 'Silver on the Screen'. Later, Joyce writes of 'that filmacouloured featured at the Mothrapurl skrene about Michan and his lost angeleens' (pp. 134, 443). References to America and movies abound, but Michan, according to Roland McHugh, alludes to preserved corpses or mummies, tying film, seen as an art form preserving the past, to the practices of Ancient Egypt. See McHugh, *Annotations to Finnegans Wake*.
73. John Bishop has argued for how, given the allusions to the Egyptian Book of the Dead, America serves in *Finnegans Wake* as a vision of the New World of the resurrection: 'A reading of the Book of the Dead enables us to see how little contrivance there is in the imaginative transaction by which Joyce transforms America [. . .] into ciphers representative of an other or "New World" like Amenti in the *Wake*' (p. 110).

74. McLuhan, p. 193.
75. Marcus, *The Tenth Muse*, p. 407.
76. Or, sounding like Paget, Balázs writes, 'Modern philologists and historians of language have established that the origins of language are to be found in *expressive movements* [...]. Initially, the movements of his tongue and lips were no more than spontaneous gestures, on a par with other bodily gestures. The fact that he uttered sounds at the same time was a secondary phenomenon, one subsequently exploited for practical purposes' (pp. 10–11).
77. As Eisenstein writes, 'Literature's most brilliant achievement in this field has been the immortal "inner monologues" of Leopold Bloom in *Ulysses*. When Joyce and I met in Paris, he was intensely interested in my plans for the inner film-monologues, with a far broader scope than is afforded by literature. Despite his almost total blindness, Joyce wished to see those parts of *Potemkin* and *October* that, with the expressive means of film culture, move along kindred lines.' Eisenstein, 'A Course in Treatment', in *Film Form*, p. 104. For more on Joyce and Eisenstein, see Costanzo, pp. 175–80.
78. Eisenstein, *Film Form*, p. 96.
79. Beckett, 'Dante ... Bruno. Vico ... Joyce', p. 248.
80. Or, as Len Platt argues, 'In this sense the *Wake* is designed as a monstrous failure, a failure to concoct "pure," original language, to find racial origins' ('"No such Race"', p. 159).
81. This view was promulgated by the linguist Rowland Jones, who also attempted to claim that Roman characters were just as visually motivated, just as depictive, as the Egyptian hieroglyphics. Jones is quoted in Hudson, pp. 83–8, and see Rowland Jones, *Hieroglyfic: or, a Grammatical Introduction to an Universal Hieroglyfic Language*. Interestingly, similar arguments were also made about Hebrew, and I will return to the juxtaposition of Hebrew and Celtic later. As Marcel Jousse writes of Hebrew, 'in each word one fancies one can still detect the echo of the original sensations that first determined the choice of the person who coined it' (p. 48).
82. Eco, p. 102.
83. Likewise, Joyce in his essay 'Ireland: Isle of Saints and Sages' writes, 'Just as ancient Egypt is dead, so is ancient Ireland' (Joyce, *Occasional, Critical, and Political Writings*, p. 125).
84. For more on Joyce's fraught relationship with nationalism and the Celtic revival, see Emer Nolan, *James Joyce and Nationalism*; Pericles Lewis, *Modernism, Nationalism, and the Novel*; and Platt for the linkage 'between Irish and German nationalisms' ('"No Such Race"', p. 163).
85. While there is no necessary connection between Indo-European linguistics and Aryan racial theories, that link was widespread in Joyce's era. As Platt writes in *Joyce, Race, and 'Finnegans Wake'*, 'the idea of an original "Aryan" language [...] became the "scientific" centerpiece of Aryanism' (p. 17).
86. McCarthy, p. 172.
87. See also Anatole France, *Le Lys rouge*, pp. 92–3: 'Lire, entendre, c'est traduire. [...] Qu'est-ce que ça me fait qu'ils admirent mes livres, puisque c'est ce qu'ils ont mis dedans qu'ils admirent?'
88. Jolas, *Man from Babel*, p. 166.
89. See Joyce, 'Finnegans Wake', trans. Beckett et al., pp. 633–46.
90. Both Stephen and Bloom are, of course, mistranslating their sources, but, given Joyce's embrace of jokes and errors, mistranslation would actually also be a positive act.
91. Gifford and Seidman, p. 577.

6

MATRICES AND METAVERSES

In Dan Brown's 2009 bestselling novel, *The Lost Symbol*, a character proclaims in Brown's overemphatic mode, '*This is the missing link between modern science and ancient mysticism!*'[1] Brown in his novel is obsessed with finding that 'missing link', forging imaginative connections between 'Noetic science' and the esoteric wisdom of Masons and alchemists, between cryptographic code and the inscriptions of ancient Egyptians.[2] His novel evinces the widespread cultural and literary fascination with the connections between code and hieroglyphics that keeps appearing throughout post-war American fiction, from Thomas Pynchon to William Gibson, from Neal Stephenson to Ishmael Reed. Like modern novelists who use hieroglyphs to understand new media, these post-war writers use ancient Egyptian scripts to forge a connection between their own writing and digital code.

In the preceding chapters we have seen how hieroglyphics enabled writers to imagine the potential overlaps between their own medium and the new media of film, phonography and photography. And these ways in which hieroglyphics were conceptualised in the early twentieth century – as sharing the qualities of vision, sound and text – get passed down to contemporary understandings of digital code. Theories and imaginative representations of computers in the post-war period emerge out of the historical understandings in the nineteenth and early twentieth centuries of the relationship between hieroglyphs and new media. As one of the prime emblems of intermediality, hieroglyphs served as a natural tool for late twentieth-century writers and theorists to conceive of the newest of new media: digital code. Binary code becomes, like hieroglyphics, a potentially universal language, underlying all the texts and images on a computer screen or mediating between foreign languages through the process of machine translation. In so doing, computers in the post-war American novel come to embody the broader possibilities and dangers of global unity and interconnection, of a linguistic or cultural Pentecost, or moment of sacred communication. While al-Hakim and Mahfouz find in ancient Egypt a way of unifying their contemporary nation and while Joyce in emphasising the material, visual aspects of writing sees in Egyptian hieroglyphs a common origin point for present-day cultures and languages, the connection between digital code and ancient scripts projects that dream of unity into the technological or mythical future. Pentecost is found not simply in the past, but, possibly, in the years to come. For writers like Pynchon, the conjunction of code and hieroglyphs allows for the blurring of the line between writing and digital technologies, with written words and the novel itself coming to embody and subsume the performative and totalising power of the computer. In so doing, however, these writers, unlike the earlier writers discussed in this book, emphasise not the visual or oral form of words but rather the worlds these words can create. The shift from visual media to digital code as the analogy for hieroglyphs thus can illuminate the differing goals of the modern and postmodern novel.

The chance of coherence or meaning associated with new technologies is frequently expressed, as in Dan Brown, through a conjunction of code and ancient mysticism. In Brown's novel, the mysteries of modern science are preserved and anticipated in the Kabbalistic and Hermetic tradition associated with hieroglyphics: they are 'encoded into writings of Pythagoras, Hermes, Heraclitus, Paracelsus, and hundreds of others [. . .] found in dusty, forgotten tomes on alchemy, mysticism, magic, and philosophy. The answer was hidden in the ancient library of Alexandria, the clay tablets of Sumer, and the hieroglyphs of Egypt' (p. 486). Brown blurs the gap between 'alchemy, mysticism, magic, and philosophy', with his hero Langdon commenting, 'history's list of famous Rosicrucians was a who's who of European Renaissance luminaries: Paracelsus, Bacon, Fludd, Descartes, Pascal, Spinoza, Newton, Leibniz' (p. 321). The scientific discoveries of the Renaissance and Enlightenment and the mysticism embodied by the Rosicrucians seem in Brown's novel to go hand in hand, with ancient texts becoming forerunners of modern digital computing. As a character comments, 'A dozen other books in here, including the Kybalion, talk about binary systems and the opposing forces in nature' (p. 59).[3]

Brown's ultimate attempt to link the modern and the ancient – and his most explicit invocation of cryptography and computing – occurs at the end of the novel, in a discussion of the real-life Kryptos statue at the CIA headquarters.[4] In a redacted document that serves as one of the McGuffins for the novel, an online discussion – which turns out to be about the statue – links the coded and seemingly illegible inscriptions on it with a 'portal' to mystical knowledge. This document, and the statue itself, are entirely unimportant to the rest of the plot, yet at the end of the novel Brown returns to them, seemingly only to establish a connection between cryptography and Egyptology. As Brown writes, 'The archaeologist who was quoted on Kryptos, Nola knew, was in fact the famed Egyptologist Howard Carter' (p. 476) who discovered the tomb of King Tut in 1922.[5] Thus the minor character Nola Long concludes, 'In the end, she knew, whatever Kryptos ultimately revealed, the message definitely had mystical undertones' (p. 477). Even an example of seemingly arbitrary cryptography turns out, in Brown's world, to be intimately connected to Egypt and its 'mystical undertones'. Whether or not Brown recognises it, the histories of cryptography and of Western understandings of hieroglyphics go back, as traced in the first chapter, to the same Renaissance sources: to Leibniz and to Kircher.

Robert Langdon's acts of decipherment in the novel similarly follow this pattern of moving from arbitrary cryptographic codes to depictive or mystical hieroglyphic images. Langdon is initially confronted with a grid of unreadable signs, but once he has figured out their key and rearranged them, they form a picture: 'Well, Peter, as you can probably see, this is an allegorical pictogram' (p. 468). Random signs resolve, tellingly, into an image of a pyramid and a staircase. But that meaning is ultimately deceptive. Finally isolating the most important, and seemingly unreadable, aspect of the pictogram, Langdon has a revelation: 'The seven symbols are a transliteration! The simplest of ciphers. The symbols are letters' (p. 483). Rather than esoteric symbols, the signs are merely slightly defamiliarised versions of Latin letters which spell out 'Laus Deo', or 'praise be to God'. Langdon follows the trajectory of Champollion, moving from pictographic meanings to a realisation that the letters resemble, more than he had previously realised, the Western alphabet. Unreadable codes are resolved into the ultimate transcendental and motivated signifier, the word of God.

This equation between modern technology and 'The Ancient Mysteries', between digital or cryptographic code and Egyptian hieroglyphics or alphabetical letters, saturates American popular culture across the boundaries of genre and medium, from high postmodernism to science fiction to Afro-Futurism. America was the site of much of the central post-war work on computing – the pioneering efforts of British mathematicians like Alan Turing notwithstanding – and American writers enthusiastically take up the association between hieroglyphics and code. In *The Crying of Lot 49*, for example, Thomas Pynchon consistently links computers with Egyptian writing. Digital code becomes the modern equivalent of the 'hieroglyphs' of the Trystero – associated with the print medium of letters – that Oedipa Maas sets out to decipher. Pynchon seems to return, like Vachel Lindsay, to the earlier misconceptions of hieroglyphics outlined in the first chapter, emphasising their sacred qualities and potential access to a providential order and to a more primal connection to physical reality. Yet playing off the opposing interpretations of the hieroglyphs throughout history, Pynchon makes Egyptian writing into a figure for the 'binary' of meaning versus not-meaning, of 'one' versus 'zero', and as such a perfect analogue to the digits of computer code. Hieroglyphics represent, on a purely textual level, the essential conflict of Pynchon's novel, embodying both the possibility of pure and primal meaning – of 'a mode of meaning beyond the obvious' – and the reality of disorder and deferral – of 'only death and the daily, tedious preparations for it'.[6] They signify both the promise of revelation that Oedipa longs for in her encounters with the Trystero and the ultimate impossibility of that Pentecostal moment. Indeed, throughout an array of late twentieth-century novels and films, hieroglyphics recur to embody the paranoid possibility – however unreachable – of totalising meaning.

By reading *The Crying of Lot 49* through the lens of two later science fiction novels – William Gibson's *Neuromancer* and Neal Stephenson's *Snow Crash* – which literalise the connection between hieroglyphics and computers, we can understand more deeply why Pynchon seeks imaginatively to link ancient inscriptions and binary code. For all of these writers, digital code ultimately serves as an emblem of how a language – in this case a programming language – can *do* things. And through the connections between hieroglyphs and code, all three writers are able to claim for their own alphabetical writing the same performative ability as the new medium of computers.[7] Gibson and Stephenson both explicitly link hieroglyphs and cuneiform with the capacity of computers to create a fictional world or to influence the real world; for Gibson, hieroglyphs emerge as the building blocks of the computer-generated reality constructed by the AI Neuromancer. And in Stephenson the 'ones and zeroes' of binary code become not merely similar, but actually identical to Sumerian cuneiform, which is represented as a series of formal instructions – as a computer program – capable of influencing the behaviour of machines and humans. The juxtaposition with Gibson and Stephenson reveals how even a writer like Pynchon, less directly concerned with digital technologies, similarly calls attention to how his fictional worlds and characters are created, like a computer program, out of language, out of mere words.

In these novels, the literary fascination with the link between sacred traditions and modern technologies serves to reaffirm the power and resilience of the written word itself. In Gibson, Stephenson and Pynchon, but also in Ishmael Reed – whose Afro-Futurist novel *Mumbo Jumbo* influences both *Gravity's Rainbow* and *Snow Crash* – written words take on the performative and mystical qualities associated with digital technologies. Literary language has the performative capacity, like a computer, to create convincing simulations of reality, to 'project' – to use Pynchon's word – a three-dimensional world from two-dimensional words. In a period in which writers, to a greater degree even than the modernists, faced what Kathleen Fitzpatrick terms the 'anxiety of obsolescence' about their own writing due to the encroachment of new media forms, the conjunction of hieroglyphs and code allowed writers to fold new digital technologies back into the domain of print.[8] Just as Woolf responded to film by claiming that the hieroglyphics of the movies were simply a new iteration of writing, so Pynchon, Gibson, Stephenson and Reed use the metaphor of hieroglyphics to blur the gap between code and writing, emphasising the 'printed' aspects of microcircuits and the performative qualities of language. But while these writers, like the modernists, seek to incorporate into writing the characteristics of the newest of new media, they ultimately do so for different ends. The comparison to digital code, as opposed to visual media like film, emphasises for writers like Pynchon and Stephenson not the visual qualities of their written words, but the power of those words to simulate worlds, a power they simultaneously celebrate and subvert.

For as *The Crying of Lot 49* suggests, hieroglyphics serve not simply as metaphors for other media or for the performativity of written words, but also for the paranoid promise of global unity and interconnection. The linkage between hieroglyphics and the origins of language and race that we've seen in Joyce and Mahfouz becomes associated less with individual nations than with the world itself. Code and hieroglyphics are persistently allied with Pentecost, with the possibility of revelation and worldwide linguistic unity, for good or for ill. This fantasy of 'one worldedness', to use Emily Apter's term, centres on the ontological qualities of digital code itself, rather than specific technologies of media transmission, like television or the internet.[9] Binary code embodies both the dream of a digital Pentecost and the reality of the linkage of code with hegemonic technologies of war and surveillance. Computers and their code may be able to knit the world together into a new whole, to become the simulacrum of a hieroglyphic Book of Nature, but that unity may, like the Trystero, be both revelatory and sinister.

Through the metaphor of hieroglyphics, that ambivalence about 'one worldedness' gets projected from digital code onto the novel itself, with Pynchon, Gibson and Stephenson uncertain about the world-creating, totalising power of the novel as well as the computer. Hieroglyphics emerge as the linguistic microcosm of these fears of 'one worldedness': through their links both to digital code and to written words, they come to embody both the possibility of interconnection and its absence, both in the world of the novel and in the world itself.

THE HIEROGLYPHICS OF CODE

Hieroglyphics have almost nothing in common with digital code. The former is pictographic and phonetic – incorporating both visual and aural content –

while the latter is silent and barely visual, only a repetitive stream of ones and zeroes. Hieroglyphics are carved into stone or written with ink on papyrus by a scribe; binary code is read and programmed using second-order computer languages like Pascal or C++, with even the programmers rarely working with the actual binary digits. Whereas hieroglyphics are a more material form of writing – as we have seen, this was in part what made them so appealing to twentieth-century writers – code in a digital computer is radically *de*materialised (except as it is instantiated in electrical voltages), never even seen by the vast majority of users.

Critics like Katherine Hayles and John Cayley have thus taken pains to insist on the difference between code and writing. What would seemingly be a given needs, in the works of these theorists, to be arduously proved against the persistent misconception, the persistent desire, to see binary code as akin to language, or, indeed, as akin to hieroglyphics.[10] Numerous works of digital or electronic literature play off the equation of visual writing and code: M. D. Coverley's *The Book of Going Forth by Day* juxtaposes hieroglyphs with code in rewriting the Egyptian Book of the Dead, Ted Warnell's 'Lascaux.Symbol.ic' invokes pictography alongside computer languages, and Reginald Woolery's *World Wide Web/Million Man March* sets photographs against backdrops of hieroglyphic inscriptions.[11] There seems to be a deep-seated desire to see code as somehow similar to natural languages, and, particularly, to ancient forms of inscription like hieroglyphs and cave paintings.

Part of this confusion between code and language is terminological. Code refers to binary digits, but the same word is also used for computer languages like C++: a programmer writing code is, by and large, working in one of those higher level languages rather than the actual digital code. As Katherine Hayles summarises, attempting to apply Saussure's model of signifier and signified to code, if 'the signifiers be considered as voltages' – as actual binary digits, charge or no-charge – then 'Programming languages operating at higher levels translate this basic mechanic level of signification into commands that more closely resemble natural language. The translation from binary code into high-level language, and from high-level language back into binary code, must happen every time commands are compiled or interpreted.'[12] And yet these higher and lower levels of programming are assigned the same name – 'code' – with binary digits often falsely associated with the properties of programming languages. Of course, programming language is also different from natural language – as Hayles and Cayley point out, code is addressed primarily to machines and only secondarily to humans – but the distinctions are less stark than between language and binary digits.[13] This confusion between binary code and programming code is exacerbated by the focus on avant-garde writers and digital artists by Cayley, Hayles and Rita Raley, since those avant-garde creators in their effort to 'reveal codes, to make the mechanism of production visible to the viewer', turn to programming instructions rather than to binary digits themselves.[14] Like the critical focus on the use of hieroglyphs and ideograms in poetry and the avant-garde in the first half of the twentieth century, the attention to avant-garde mixed-media experiments with combining code and language has perhaps muddled a precise understanding of the nature of binary code, confusing the differences among ones and zeroes, programming languages and natural languages.[15]

Yet this confusion is understandable: the linkage between code and language, and, particularly, between code and hieroglyphics, transcends specific avant-garde artworks. The same discourses used in the nineteenth and early twentieth centuries to describe Egyptian hieroglyphics are applied in the later twentieth century to digital code. Regardless of whether theorists invoke Egyptian hieroglyphics or other forms of pictographic languages – though they often do – descriptions of code frequently emphasise the same qualities that were invoked in earlier theories of hieroglyphics. In recognising that code is a language that differs in so many respects from alphabetical languages, writers and theorists seem drawn to hieroglyphs, another form of inscription that supposedly is both like writing and different from writing.

From the very beginning, binary code and the digital computer were seen as central to projects for solving the problem of Babel by creating new technologies of translation. Understandings of code thus emerged from the tradition of International Auxiliary Languages discussed in Chapter 5 and, particularly, from C. K. Ogden's Basic English. Just as hieroglyphics promised for many a better, more legible universal language than Basic English or Esperanto, so digital code opened the possibility of greater speed and facility, through the use of computers, in cross-linguistic translation. This desire goes back to the pioneering work of Warren Weaver, who in a 1947 memorandum first proposed computers as a new tool in 'machine translation'. When faced with a new-found problem of Babel – 'modern methods of travel and communication have made the whole world so small that the confusion of tongues, a second time in man's history, becomes a vital issue' – Weaver believed that computers could be 'engaged in erecting a new Tower of anti-Babel. This new tower is not intended to reach to Heaven. But it is hoped that it will build part of the way back to that mythical situation of simplicity and power when men could communicate freely together.'[16] For Weaver, computer translation would be 'very closely related to what Ogden and Richards have already done for English' in their Basic English.[17]

Weaver's purely pragmatic solutions to the problem of Babel – creating new methods of translation – quickly slide into the more mystical possibilities of a universal and perfect language with which, as we have seen, hieroglyphics are so frequently associated. His new 'Tower of anti-Babel' will restore 'a mythical situation of simplicity and power'. Or, even more radically, Weaver wants 'to descend, from each language, down to the common base of human communication – the real but as yet undiscovered universal language'.[18] Through computers, the perfect language of humanity can be discovered and restored.[19] As Marshall McLuhan writes, 'Today computers hold out the promise of a means of instant translation of any code or language into any other code or language. The computer, in short, promises by technology a Pentecostal condition of universal understanding and unity.'[20] The notion of computer codes as creating a 'Pentecostal condition', or the opposite of Babel, recurs in varying forms, as we shall see, in countless literary texts in the last fifty years.

Such associations between computers and universal languages naturally come to be associated with the binary code and the other programming languages that give rise to computing; as Umberto Eco notes, Pascal and BASIC 'are, in one way or another, the heirs of the ancient search for the perfect language'.[21] Regardless of their actual characteristics, digital code and computers have taken over the mantle of hieroglyphics as the dominant metaphor, in the late twentieth century, for a more universally legible language. Indeed, as Hayles notes, contemporary scientists have begun to use binary code to characterise the basic functioning of the universe: 'Recently, however, strong claims have been made for digital algorithms as the language of nature itself. If, as Stephen Wolfram, Edward Fredkin and Harold Morowitz maintain, the universe is fundamentally computational, code is elevated to the lingua franca not only of computers but of all physical reality.'[22] Code takes on even more of the qualities associated with hieroglyphics; whereas Emerson or, before him, Renaissance mystics and Kabbalists saw hieroglyphics as signs of God's book, some contemporary scientists see code as the underlying language of the physical world.

Yet code not only becomes a universal language, but also, again paralleling discourses about hieroglyphs, seems to dissolve the boundaries between visual and textual media. Images and language in a computer become interchangeable information, equally the products of binary code. This collapsing of the distinctions among media provides, for Lev Manovich, the definition of 'new media'; he describes 'the translation of all existing media into numerical data accessible through computers. The result is new media – graphics, moving images, sounds, shapes, spaces, and texts that have become computable; that is, they comprise simply another set of computer data.'[23] Just as Woolf and Joyce saw hieroglyphs as foregrounding the hybrid nature – between text and image – of all language, so for Manovich code enacts a similar blurring of the lines separating media. Thus, as Philip Rosen has pointed out, the 'newness' of digital technologies, which are often seen as supplanting older media like writing, is always characterised by their hybridity: 'The digital demonstrates its radically new capabilities and superior representational powers through its capacity to appropriate the old. [. . .] The ideal of practically infinite manipulability demands a hybridity of old and new.'[24] The digital is just as hybrid as writing or film; indeed, it too is defined precisely by that hybridity.

For critics like Jay David Bolter, this is particularly the case for 'electronic writing', which he argues is 'inclusive, and for that reason it resonated with and reminds us of the earliest forms of writing. Electronic writing is more like hieroglyphics than it is like pure alphabetic writing.' Recalling Joyce, Bolter returns to illuminated manuscripts, which, he claims, like 'computer icons [. . .] functioned simultaneously as text and picture'. These icons 'also remind us of the use of Hebrew letters in the Cabala or the use of alchemical and other signs by Renaissance magi like Giordano Bruno.'[25] As in the theories of code as a universal language discussed earlier, analyses of electronic literature quickly slide into comparisons with hieroglyphics and particularly with the 'alchemical' and magical qualities so often associated with them.

Of course, Bolter and Manovich are not claiming that code literally combines image and text; rather, code produces that hybrid text in the form of electronic writing. As a stream of ones and zeroes, it creates hieroglyphics, and thus serves to make 'any traditional difference among sign-systems even more fuzzy'.[26] And yet because of the confusion between code and coding, between binary digits and programming languages, the characteristics of Egyptian writing are often projected downward from the products of code to the code itself, as we've seen in the juxtapositions of hieroglyphics and code in avant-garde art outlined above. While Rita Raley acknowledges, commenting on 'Lascaux.symbol.ic', that 'there are limits perhaps to the comparison of cave paintings and code', she asserts that:

> Code may be mysterious, cryptic, and in a sense unknowable, but it is, as Warnell's 'Lascaux Symbol.ic' reminds us, made. Analogizing the cave painting to code, 'Lascaux' reminds us that the hand – craft, skill, technical expertise – comes in between code and surfaces of inscription, here the wall of the cave.[27]

Like hieroglyphs and other forms of direct physical inscription, code is a form 'of writing requiring craft and technique'.[28] Even as an entirely dematerialised language, the basic computer language of code needs to be crafted by programmers – by what Hayles refers to as 'priestly' interpreters – just as much as hieroglyphs need to be engraved or copied by a scribe.[29] Code must be made, and yet it remains 'mysterious, cryptic' and 'unknowable', incapable of ultimately being grasped.[30] Of course, in combining the 'crafted' and the 'unknowable' aspects of code, Raley is falling victim to the confusion between code and programming described earlier. In Raley's reading (or misreading), code conforms even more deeply to Western misconceptions of hieroglyphics; as a more tangible but ultimately illegible language, it returns us, once again, to Foucault's and Ginzburg's episteme of conjectural knowledge.[31] Code becomes the unreachable central text, the totally legible Book of Nature that can never quite be reached or read.

As Raley discusses, code is routinely imagined according to a model of surface and depth, a pattern we've already seen in Warren Weaver's attempt to descend through machine translation to the deep structure of a universal language. Or as Raley asks, using the same language as Weaver, 'What the façade of the code surface masks is the deep structure of code, the tower of programming languages that descend from software to hardware. What is the deep structure of computing and are we able to see or otherwise access it?' This surface/depth paradigm of course also corresponds to Western understandings of hieroglyphs. On a surface level, code parallels the hybrid nature of hieroglyphic writing identified by Woolf, Joyce and others, creating 'electronic writing' that blurs the gap between media. But on a deeper level, the stream of ones and zeroes becomes an analogue for the mystical associations of hieroglyphics before the Rosetta Stone, the emphasis on the magical and material properties of Egyptian writing.

The Wachowskis' 1999 film *The Matrix* brings together all of these understandings of code and demonstrates just how much they share with earlier theories of hieroglyphics.[32] On its most obvious level, *The Matrix* corresponds to the surface/depth model of code, with the world itself revealed as merely the surface simulation of a computer program, made from code and created by machines to dupe humans into compliance as they harvest their energy. Code thus becomes the language of the Book of Nature that Neo must read to reveal its sinister authors. If binary code represents the underlying logic behind not only computer programs but nature itself, then in *The Matrix* code naturally becomes the literal hieroglyphics that make up the phenomenal world. And given the CGI technologies used to make the film, the directors reveal how the movie itself is partly made out of code, blurring the gap between film and binary digits.

But code in *The Matrix* does not merely give rise to a simulation of reality; it also becomes figurative. Rita Raley, in discussing the film, laments this 'fallacy' that allows the 'One with special insight [to] render code absolutely legible, even figurative [. . .] It [code] must [. . .] acquire dimensionality and be made to take human shape.'[33] As shown in Figure 6.1, Neo is ultimately able to see through the 'agents' around him in the Matrix world and perceive how they are made out of embodied code. Similarly in the opening sequence of *The Matrix Reloaded* lines of code gradually whirl into the shape of characters and settings, which then dissolve into the medium of film.[34] The simulacrum of the real world is not simply made of lines of code: those lines take on visual form. Given the associations between hieroglyphs and code that I have been tracing, it would be almost impossible to resist the impulse to make code just as seemingly 'figurative' and immediately 'legible' as the supposedly visual language

Figure 6.1 Image from *The Matrix* (dirs. Lana and Lilly Wachowski, 1999, USA)

Figure 6.2 Image from *The Matrix* (dirs. Lana and Lilly Wachowski, 1999, USA)

of hieroglyphics. Code cannot simply give rise to the world, it has to 'body' it forth through images. If code creates the visual world, it needs to have, like hieroglyphs, a visual, pictorial form. Indeed, while it would make sense for the descending streams of data that visually represent the matrix to consist of ones and zeroes, they do not, as illustrated in Figure 6.2. Rather, they look like numbers, but also a wide variety of symbols and sigils that in many cases resemble Chinese ideograms, if not Egyptian hieroglyphics. On a certain level this might make sense, with the symbols representing cryptographic code as opposed to bits (again demonstrating the confusion between programming codes and binary digits), but *The Matrix* demonstrates just how precarious the divide is between code and pictographic writing. Given the persistent associations between code and hieroglyphs, code in *The Matrix* can't remain one and zeroes but must begin to resemble ancient pictorial languages. *The Matrix* literalises the Kabbalistic dream of a world made out of language, out of the spiritual hieroglyphs of Nature, a dream that code as a performative language seems at times to approach.

Rather than focusing on the similarities and differences between code and language, this chapter explores how earlier ways of understanding media as akin to hieroglyphs are projected onto code. The overlap in the discourses used to describe both code and hieroglyphics – as universal languages, etc. – helps to explain why, in so many of the texts I will be discussing, authors routinely seek to bridge the gap between bits and hieroglyphics, between high technology and ancient mystical knowledge. I therefore disagree with the binary between cryptography – associated with digital computers – and hieroglyphics that Shawn James Rosenheim seeks to draw in his *The Cryptographic Imagination*. For Rosenheim, 'As a model of the sign, the hieroglyph is associated with the search for an Adamic universal language; the cryptograph, by contrast is connected with a distinctly modern awareness of the lack of linguistic motivation.'[35] But as this book has shown, these poles are fundamentally interrelated; not only were Leibniz, Kircher and other Renaissance philosophers interested, at one and the same time, in cryptography, universal languages and hieroglyphics, but binary code in the twentieth century is repeatedly described as a universal language. And as Weaver notes, this 'universal language' might even be potentially Adamic. Cryptography and hieroglyphics are, therefore, two sides of the same coin. In *The Matrix* and throughout so much of contemporary literature on computing and cyberspace, writers seek to re-establish the supposedly buried linkages between visual writing and code, to re-invest the arbitrary signifiers of cryptography with Adamic, universal and mystical significance.

Pynchon's 'Hieroglyphic Streets'

Yet the linkage of hieroglyphics and cryptography goes beyond a desire to resacralise the products of contemporary technology by tying them to a lost mystical tradition. If we turn to *The Crying of Lot 49* – which helped to shape the contemporary literary discourse on hieroglyphics – the understanding of Egyptian writing there transcends a mere linkage between ancient and modern media. Pynchon uses hieroglyphs to fold computer codes back into the realm of print, but he also finds in Egyptian writing a way of encapsulating the central binary between order and disorder, between meaning and not-meaning, that structures his novel.

Early in *The Crying of Lot 49*, Pynchon describes how Oedipa

> thought of the time she'd opened a transistor radio to replace a battery and seen her first printed circuit. The ordered swirl of houses and streets, from this high angle, sprang at her now with the same unexpected, astonishing clarity as the circuit card had. Through she knew even less about

radios than about Southern Californians, there were to both outward patterns a hieroglyphic sense of concealed meaning, of an intent to communicate. There'd seemed no limit to what the printed circuit could have told her (if she tried to find out); so in her first minute of San Narciso, a revelation also trembled just past the threshold of her understanding. (p. 14)

In this 'odd, religious instant' (p. 14), hieroglyphics, far more than in Dan Brown, take on their traditional associations with the Book of Nature, even if the clues to the Trystero that Oedipa ultimately discovers are the products of humans rather than of God. The signs of the world become hieroglyphics that carry a 'concealed meaning, [. . .] an intent to communicate' and make of the chaos of the world an ordered, providential pattern. Critics have thus tended to emphasise the religious dimensions of Pynchon's novel, its concern with the possibility, forever deferred, of 'revelation'.[36] Recalling the history of mystical misreadings of Egyptian writing, the references to hieroglyphics become invocations of sacred symbols; indeed, in response to seeing the W.A.S.T.E. posthorn, Oedipa exclaims, 'God, hieroglyphics' (p. 38). The two words occur in apposition to each other, confirming the essential linkage in the novel between spiritual meaning and Egyptian writing. The visual emblem of the post-horn becomes a kind of modern hieroglyph, a potential access point to spiritual meaning that must be deciphered.

But for Pynchon hieroglyphs are not used to stand simply for any symbol or any kind of esoteric knowledge, as many critics suggest, but are specifically tied to Egyptian writing and its history in the West.[37] Pynchon includes a character named 'Mr. Thoth' – the Egyptian God of writing – and Oedipa, remembering her partial epiphany at San Narciso, thinks about 'some promise of hierophany: printed circuit, gently curving streets, private access to the water, Book of the Dead . . .' (p. 20), exposing the Egyptian roots of the hieroglyphs in the 'Book of the Dead'.[38]

Indeed, the final reference to hieroglyphics in the novel most explicitly demonstrates Pynchon's knowledge of the history of Western understandings of hieroglyphics, as he synthesises the two opposing interpretations of Egyptian writing – the sense that hieroglyphs are sacred, illegible symbols and, conversely, the knowledge that they are, in reality, a hybrid form of writing that can serve to mediate between old and new media. In her clearest realisation of the depths of her W.A.S.T.E.-created predicament, Oedipa thinks:

> For now it was like walking among matrices of a great digital computer, the zeroes and ones twinned above, hanging like balanced mobiles right and left, ahead, thick, maybe endless. Behind the hieroglyphic streets there would either be transcendent meaning, or only the earth. [. . .] Ones and zeroes. So did the couples rearrange themselves. At Vesperhaven

> House either an accommodation reached, in some kind of dignity, with the Angel of Death, or only death and the daily, tedious preparations for it. Another mode of meaning behind the obvious, or none. (p. 150)

Looking back to ancient Egypt through the reference to Vesperhaven House – where Oedipa meets Mr Thoth – Pynchon links the 'hieroglyphic' sense of 'transcendent meaning' with new electronic media, in this case 'a great digital computer'. Through hieroglyphs, Pynchon equates the ancient signs of God's providential order with modern technologies; it is no wonder that early in the novel, Oedipa concludes that the only forces capable of calculating the path of a wayward aerosol can are 'god or a digital machine' (p. 25). Just as Oedipa's remark 'God, hieroglyphics' links ancient writing with the sacred, so here she links God with computing.

Katherine Hayles remarks about this tendency to link transcendence and technology, claiming that 'the metaphoric conjunction of a computer with an ineffable religious experience may seem strange; but it is consistent with the tendency of reduction and dissipation to turn themselves inside out at moments of greatest intensity'.[39] But I don't agree that 'a computer' and 'ineffable religious experience' represent a 'tendency of reduction and dissipation'; rather, Pynchon's novel exposes the profound underlying similarities between sacred hieroglyphics and digital computers. Hieroglyphs do not serve arbitrarily to invest computers with spiritual meaning; rather, they represent the 'binary' embodied by the computer and by the novel as a whole.[40] Just as a computer is composed of 'ones and zeroes', so the novel leaves us with the choice between 'transcendent meaning' and 'the earth', between 'another mode of meaning behind the obvious' and 'none'.[41] And this binary is exactly what this book traces in the historical conceptions of the hieroglyphics, which were seen both as an embodiment of pure and unmediated meaning and, post-Champollion, as an everyday language lacking in any esoteric truth. To return to Woolf's story 'The Lady in the Looking-Glass', hieroglyphs at one and the same time symbolise total meaning, everyday meaning and the lack of meaning, with here Pynchon collapsing the two latter possibilities into one. Pynchon's use of hieroglyphs is thus far more sophisticated and appropriate than has previously been noted, as hieroglyphs embody not simply the 'one' of sacred 'meaning', but the binary of 'ones and zeroes'.

Pynchon's novel thus fits with Foucault's sixteenth-century epistemology of the Book of Nature, outlined in the Introduction, in which hieroglyphic marks provide mediated access to an ultimately unknowable central truth or text. While the Trystero post-horn is not truly a part of nature, Pynchon insists that Oedipa's unfulfilled desire to read the man-made clues around her corresponds to the same paradigm:

> Oedipa wondered whether, at the end of this (if it were supposed to end), she too might not be left with only compiled memories of clues,

announcements, intimations, but never the central truth itself, which must somehow each time be too bright for her memory to hold; which must always blaze out, destroying its own message irreversibly, leaving an overexposed blank when the ordinary world came back. (p. 76)

As with Welles and Conrad in Chapter 3, for Pynchon the 'clues' are only indexical; they point to a central truth, which remains apocalyptically unattainable. As Oedipa asks, 'but then she wondered if the gemlike "clues" were only some kind of compensation. To make up for her having lost the direct, epileptic Word, the cry that might abolish the night' (p. 95). The signs of the Trystero can lead Oedipa, like Marlow or Thompson, to conjecture an underlying plot to give meaning and unity to her experience, but that plot remains forever unverifiable and uncertain. It is the signs, the 'clues' themselves, which are valuable in this epistemology, for the direct Word remains lost.[42] Hieroglyphics in the novel signify the possibility of a direct relation to the Word – of the perfect, universal and mystical language that Oedipa craves – but also with the perpetual deferral of that revelation.

This notion of the linguistic nature of the world and the need vainly to interpret its signs returns even more strongly in *Gravity's Rainbow*. Directly invoking the transcendentalist 'pasteboard mask' of *Moby-Dick*, Pynchon describes how Slothrop is left with 'only pasteboard images of the Listening Enemy left between him and the wet sky. Either They have put him here for a reason, or he's just here. He isn't sure that he wouldn't, actually, rather have that *reason* . . .'[43] Like Oedipa, Slothrop longs for meaning even if that meaning is sinister, and he persists in treating the world as a text: Slothrop notices 'giant asterisks on the pavement, inviting him to look down at the bottom of the text of the day, where footnotes will explain all' (p. 207). Later in the novel another character thinks about 'how alphabetic is the nature of molecules' (p. 360), turning the building blocks of the world into text. *Gravity's Rainbow* is more ambivalent about texts and books even than *The Crying of Lot 49*: Slothrop's Puritan ancestors' killing of trees to create paper is characterised negatively, and yet their belief in a textual, potentially legible world is consistently invoked in the narrative, with 'God clamoring to them in every turn of a leaf or cow loose among apple orchards in autumn', 'Data behind which always, nearer or farther, was the numinous certainty of God' (pp. 286, 245).[44] While the 'certainty of God' has become highly uncertain, the epistemology of seeking to decipher the Book of Nature – or the Book of Culture – remains.

Through his invocations of the Book of Nature and by linking, through the hieroglyphs, language with the possibilities of sacred meaning, Pynchon completes a process of radically expanding the significance of visual writing, with hieroglyphics serving as the emblem of the possibility or impossibility of global unity and coherence. Hieroglyphics serve as the linguistic analogue to what

Fredric Jameson calls the 'high tech paranoia' plot, inspired, in many cases, by Pynchon's novel: as Jameson defines it,

> the circuits and networks of some putative global computer hook-up are narratively mobilized by labyrinthine conspiracies of autonomous but deadly interlocking and competing information agencies [...] Yet conspiracy theory (and its garish narrative manifestations) must be seen as a degraded attempt – through the figuration of advanced technology – to think the impossible totality of the contemporary world system.[45]

If in a postmodern world narratives of conspiracy seek to understand, through paranoia, the 'totality' of the late capitalist world system, then hieroglyphics allow that paranoia to infect the level of language itself.[46] As a supposedly more universal and direct form of language, hieroglyphics naturally become associated with the 'circuits and networks of some putative global computer hook-up', both of which promise total, transcendent meaning and interconnection, but are always threatened with the possibility of an ultimate lack of unity, with the possibility that the total meaning lies just out of reach.

The 'ones and zeroes' of meaning and not-meaning at the end of *The Crying of Lot 49* thus become associated with a broader mythical binary in the novel: that between Babel and Pentecost, with Babel signifying the loss of linguistic and cultural unity and Pentecost the future possibility of reintegration. Edward Mendelson has convincingly traced the importance of Pentecost – 'the one traditional miracle most closely involved with communication' (p. 134) – in *The Crying of Lot 49*, which he argues explains the novel's title – as Pentecost occurs fifty days after Easter – and the religious significance of its final scene in the auction house. Babel and Pentecost turn the binary inherent in hieroglyphics – between direct, universal communication and the reality of heteroglossia – and project them into the mythical realm.[47] But even Pentecost itself expresses that same binary, creating a universal, sacred language that remains incomprehensible to ordinary listeners. Just as Babel expresses both the possibility of universal communication and the loss of that possibility, so Pentecost – like Egyptian hieroglyphics – embodies both revelation and the impossibility of revelation. Meaning and non-meaning, order and disorder are – in hieroglyphics, digital code, Babel and Pentecost – inherently interrelated. Like Gibson and Stephenson, Pynchon is thus obsessed with the barriers to communication symbolised by the Babel myth, as well as the imaginative possibility, expressed by Pentecost, of surmounting them and restoring an Adamic unity and legibility to a meaningless world. The hieroglyph – as a symbol of the never-extinguished desire to find a perfect, Adamic language, coupled with the realisation of the hybridity of all languages – operates as a handy linguistic microcosm of both sides of this binary.[48]

If in its concern with Pentecost, *The Crying of Lot 49* seems to reinstate an earlier, sacred sense of hieroglyphs, that notion is inseparable from the twentieth-century association of Egyptian writing and new media. References to the 'binary' digits of computers in the novel do not merely symbolise the possibility of meaning or revelation. Through allusions to hieroglyphs and their links to code, Pynchon seeks to incorporate the qualities of digital code and other new media within the written form of the novel. *The Crying of Lot 49* is of course a novel obsessed with modern mass media, from the 'green dead eye of the television set' on its first page to the computer on its last. Pynchon repeatedly seeks ways to bridge the divide between modern media and ancient writing, between the computer and the 'Word'. For, crucially, in his reference to the 'printed circuit' and its 'hieroglyphic sense of concealed meaning', Pynchon insists on the 'printed' nature of that circuit; even a technology seemingly distinct from text is portrayed as being constituted by the same technologies that produce the printed word. Pynchon's own medium of words and writing brings into being the technologies that are supposedly replacing it, with electronic media emerging as only a new form of print, a 'printed circuit'. As with Joyce's invocation of Vico, Pynchon's references to hieroglyphics create a metaphorical 'circuit' in which new technologies recall and revivify earlier forms of writing.

Pynchon's use of the word 'matrices' in the passage quoted earlier – the 'matrices of a great digital computer' – is central to his understanding of media in the novel. For matrix refers not only to 'an array of circuit elements whose interconnections form a rectangular lattice or grid' – the earlier 'printed circuit' – or 'a single layer of cores in a magnetic core memory'. It also encompasses meanings associated with virtually every other medium: in television a matrix is 'a circuit designed to produce outputs that are linear combinations', in sound recording it is 'a copy [. . .] of an original disc recording, which is used for making other copies', and in photography it is 'a dyed print in relief used for transferring colour to a final colour print'. And, finally, a matrix is 'a metal block in which a character is stamped or engraved so as to form a mould for casting a type' (*OED*). Matrices thus are inextricably linked with print; at least etymologically, the digital matrices of computers are not something new, but rather emerge, like the 'printed circuit', out of technologies of writing. A matrix becomes almost synonymous with the etymological meaning of character, inserting itself into the tradition of the pun on the meaning of character – letters or identity – that is so central to modernism. Through Pynchon's invocation of Egyptian writing, the 'matrices' of computers take on the mixed-media mantle associated with hieroglyphics. If all media are subsumed under the sign of writing, then the digital computer becomes a symbol of the persistence of print and, indeed, for the all-consuming mechanism of the novel itself.

Gibson's 'Unknowable Code'

Before returning to *The Crying of Lot 49*, we need to ask more deeply why Pynchon would be fascinated with hieroglyphs and ancient inscriptions. If through their invocation of hieroglyphics, Western modernist writers like Joyce and Woolf sought to claim for their own alphabetical writing the pictorial and oral qualities that were associated with the new media of film, photography and phonography, then what aspects of binary code does Pynchon find appealing? What claim does he seek to make about his own writing by linking ancient hieroglyphic script with modern digital media?

In order to answer these questions, we can turn to the complex afterlife of hieroglyphics in contemporary science fiction. The works of William Gibson and Neal Stephenson make explicit the implicit connection that Pynchon draws between code and hieroglyphics. Hieroglyphics literally, or almost literally, become not merely analogous to code, but identical, serving as the building blocks of 'cyberspace' or the 'Metaverse'. Gibson's seminal *Neuromancer* – which largely invented cyberpunk fiction – and Stephenson's *Snow Crash* thus can expose what is at stake in the linkage of Egyptian writing and binary digits: a desire to claim for alphabetical writing the performative qualities of digital code. For not only does code, as Katherine Hayles points out, change magnetic or electric charges, it actually does things; code may not be readable, but it forms the building blocks of programs that accomplish tasks and create the 'more representational' upper levels of a computer desktop, a video game or a CGI movie.[49] Binary code is a language that creates a world. By collapsing, through the metaphor of hieroglyphics, the space between the alphabet and code, Gibson and Stephenson lend to their own literary language the same creative potential as computers, and reveal how Pynchon, more subtly, does the same.[50] By looking at Gibson's and Stephenson's novels alongside those of Pynchon, we can see how, in a wide swath of post-war fiction, references to hieroglyphics are used to transform digital code from a technology threatening to supplant writing to merely a new and different form of writing.

Gibson's *Neuromancer* is particularly fascinating given its debt to *The Crying of Lot 49*. Gibson similarly compares electronics to the grid of urban development – 'The pattern might have represented microcircuits, or a city map' – and flirts with the possibility of a Trystero-like underlying order when his hero, Case, repeatedly encounters 'the little sigil, the size of a small coin, woven into the lower left corner of the ad's fabric of light: T-A'.[51] However, the larger link back to Pynchon is not through the Tessier-Ashpool family and their conspiracies – which ultimately depart from Pynchon's concerns in *The Crying of Lot 49* – but rather through different kinds of 'sigil[s]': Egyptian hieroglyphs. Befitting the Asian-inflected world of *Neuromancer*, Gibson frequently mentions 'ideograms', but he also alludes to 'faint glyphs of colored light' and 'the bodies of bathers, tiny bronze hieroglyphs' (pp. 78, 158).[52] At the end of the novel, these references begin to proliferate: waking up unexpectedly in an unfamiliar world, with his dead former lover somehow alive again, Case gradually realises that he is living in an elaborately realistic simulation created by the vast AI Neuromancer. His clue is the appearance of hieroglyphs:

> His vision crawled with ghost hieroglyphs, translucent lines of symbols arranging themselves against the neutral backdrop of the bunker wall. He looked at the backs of his hands, saw faint neon molecules crawling beneath the skin, ordered by the unknowable code. He raised his right hand and moved it experimentally. It left a faint, fading trail of strobed afterimages. (p. 233)

The 'ghost hieroglyphs' reveal that Case is inhabiting a world made out of code, that his reality is simply a product of the 'translucent lines of symbols' – stolen from Gibson's novel by the directors of *The Matrix* – of Neuromancer's programming language. As Case walks along the computer-created beach, 'the hieroglyphs sped across the sand, fled from his feet, drew back from him as he walked', and, rejecting this false world and its comforts, he wakes to 'Maelcum's features [...] overlayed with bands of translucent hieroglyphs' (pp. 235, 237). Hieroglyphs are so deeply linked, throughout history, with the language of nature that they inevitably come to be used to describe any language – including digital code – that seeks to construct a world. Like a good transcendentalist, Case must attune himself to these 'ghost hieroglyphs' in order to fathom the nature of his world and of its author: in this case, to reveal the code created by Neuromancer.[53]

Gibson in his novel thus helps to create the discourse about how data – the bits of binary code – are transformed into physical space or, at least, into the 'consensual hallucination' that Gibson, coining the term, defines as 'cyberspace': 'a graphic representation of data abstracted from the banks of every computer in the human system' (p. 51). If Pynchon fantasises about how digital code could be analogous to the sacred hieroglyphs of nature, then in Gibson that fantasy has been literalised. Cyberspace is a world created by a language – the programming language of computers – which is represented by Gibson through the metaphor of hieroglyphs. Like Dan Brown, Gibson restores the promise of mysticism to contemporary technologies, yet his use of hieroglyphs serves to emphasise the performative power of digital code: its ability to create out of language wholly new cyberspaces like the kind that Neuromancer creates for Case. Just as computer codes can create the illusion of reality, so Gibson's words can bring into being the settings and characters of his novel.

What we have then is a return to the sacred meanings of the hieroglyphs, as the notion of the hieroglyphic Book of Nature prior to Champollion is projected onto digital code and the spaces it constructs. The possibility of mystical revelation, however, has been radically diminished, restricted to the constructed world of cyberspace or fiction, rather than the real 'meat' world, as Gibson calls it. The digital hieroglyphs are the products of men or of computers, not God. But Gibson hedges his bets by suggesting that there is simply a new God: the fusion of the two vast AIs Wintermute and Neuromancer that creates as close to divine providence as the postmodern world can produce. As Case asks Neuromancer at the end of the novel, 'So what's the score? How are things different? You running the world now? You God?' (p. 259). As at the end of *The Crying of Lot 49*, the digital computer itself becomes the repository for good or ill of the possibilities of meaning and coherence in the information age.

While Case ultimately rejects living in a code-created fantasy and returns to the real world, the hieroglyphic codes of Neuromancer promise the possibility of immortality and Pentecost. As Neuromancer says, speaking through the voice of a body, 'I *am* the dead, and their land' (p. 235). And Wintermute, the other AI, is described as 'a voice, out of the babel of tongues, speaking to us' (p. 108). While ineradicably separated from the real world, the world of cyberspace returns us to lost notions of a meaningful, providential order, one which is constructed from a hieroglyphic language and can reveal the secrets of language and of meaning. This dream of transcendent meaning is a common motif in Gibson's fiction, like that of Pynchon. In *Pattern Recognition*, the heroine Cayce Pollard, who almost shares a name with Case, likewise finds in the 'footage' – a series of video clips posted online – a potentially sacred text: the unknown author is referred to as the 'Maker', and upon sending an e-mail to her Cayce says that it's 'kind of like writing a letter to God' (pp. 273, 266).[54] But despite the unwavering power of the 'footage', the author is revealed as simply a person, and one linked to a family of slightly sinister Russian capitalists, with the 'footage' being rendered and processed by prisoners. Indeed, Cayce wonders whether there even is any real meaning in the 'footage': 'what if the sense of nascent meaning they all perceive in the footage is simply that: an illusion of meaningfulness, faulty pattern recognition' (p. 115). The possibility for sacred meaning is just that: a possibility, and one that may not be as liberating or as meaningful as Cayce hopes for.

Indeed, in *Neuromancer* as well that promise of transcendental meaning always remains elusive; as Neuromancer responds to Case's question above about whether he's become a God, 'Things aren't different. Things are things' (p. 259). As in *The Crying of Lot 49*, the linkage of digital machines and hieroglyphics points to the central anxiety about 'oneworldedness' in the postwar novel; on the one hand, computers promise to knit together the scattered world into a new totality, but on the other hand that totality is potentially hegemonic, falsifying and sinister. Gibson seems to long for the transcendent possibility of an authored, meaningful world and to retreat from that possibility. As in Pynchon, references to hieroglyphs allow him to have it both ways, since hieroglyphs in the West are understood both as a mystical language and as simply an everyday form of writing.

Gibson even subtly blurs the line between the constructed world of cyberspace and the actual world. To return to the passage quoted from *Neuromancer* above, the reference to the 'unknowable code' there may refer to the programming language out of which Neuromancer constructs its illusions, but it also suggests DNA, the code that constructs all human bodies. In the same chapter, when Case has sex with the computer-constructed image of his old girlfriend, Gibson describes how 'It was a vast thing, beyond knowing, a sea of information coded in spiral and pheromone, infinite intricacy that only the body, in its strong blind way, could ever read' (p. 232). Gibson equates sex and the body with code itself, with desire reduced to 'a sea of information coded' in the 'spiral' of DNA. He anticipates those theories, discussed above, that see digital code as the building block of all human and natural phenomena. Gibson turns humans into analogues of machines, but simultaneously reclaims a place for the human. The capacity of reading the 'unknowable' sea of bodily information is restricted to the body itself; no machine, and no mind, can capture the innermost workings of human desire. As Shawn James Rosenheim argues, 'Gibson seems to want it both ways, validating the body's quiddity even as that body is revealed as only a sophisticated textual processor, translating information about the world into sensible precepts in ways that computers can only approximate' (p. 56). The body's DNA is analogous to machine code, while at the end of the novel, when Case sees an image of himself inside the matrix – 'at the very edge of one of the vast steps of data' (p. 260) – the strings of ones and zeroes of cyberspace take on human form. As we've seen with Joyce's interest in gestural languages – and with the historical linkage between hieroglyphs and gestures – Gibson's fascination with visual and machine languages naturally leads him to see the human body itself as somehow linguistic, as similarly constructed out of hieroglyphic codes. And by linking the body itself with code and with language, Gibson further cements the connection between his own novel and a computer, calling attention to his ability not only to create through written words a simulated world, but simulated characters as well.

STEPHENSON'S 'LETTERS ON AN ELECTRONIC PAGE'

One of the many novels that Gibson's 'cyperpunk' spawned – Neal Stephenson's *Snow Crash* – reveals even more fully how profound and literal the connection is between discourses about code, hieroglyphs and the body in post-war fiction. In turn, it likewise links the possibility of Pentecost with potentially sinister, hegemonic forces. Through repeated philosophical and historical digressions, *Snow Crash* forges a new genealogy of binary code, one that links digital technologies with the cuneiform tablets of ancient Sumer, emphasising their shared performative capabilities. Computer language, like literary language, like cuneiform, becomes a form of speech or spell-casting, capable of creating 'Metaverses' and transforming the human body itself.

In contrast to Gibson and Pynchon, Stephenson explicitly rejects Egyptian writing as an influence in *Snow Crash*, turning instead to cuneiform as a mythical equivalent to digital code. As the holographic Librarian, who provides much of the historical information in Stephenson's novel, explains to the cheekily named hero Hiro Protagonist:

> 'Egypt was a civilization of stone. They made their art and architecture of stone, so it lasts forever. But you can't write on stone. So they invented papyrus and wrote on that. But papyrus is perishable. So even though their art and architecture have survived, their written records – their data – have largely disappeared.'
>
> 'What about all those hieroglyphic inscriptions?'
>
> 'Bumper stickers, Lagos called them. Corrupt political speech [. . .] Sumer was a civilization of clay. [. . .] So all the data of the Sumerians have survived. Egypt left a legacy of art and architecture; Sumer's legacy is its megabytes.'[55]

Like Joyce, Stephenson looks to the past to find an alternate source for contemporary 'megabytes' and computer languages. But despite their widespread associations with digital technologies, and despite his later use in *Cryptonomicon* of the 'Great Pyramid' as the emblem for the main character's cryptographic program, Stephenson quickly rejects 'hieroglyphic inscriptions', denigrating them as merely banal and fetishised discourse, as 'bumper stickers'.[56] Cuneiform is for Stephenson more appealing because, as his characters say, it is 'the oldest of all written languages' and 'no languages whatsoever are descended from Sumerian' (p. 196). The turn to Sumerian allows Stephenson to project onto cuneiform the properties which were once associated with hieroglyphs – the possibility of mystical knowledge and Adamic legibility – but which, after Champollion's decipherment, were revealed as mere misconceptions. Post-1822, hieroglyphs do become mere 'bumper stickers'. They are legible and thus reduced simply to everyday meaning, to the 'zero' of Pynchon's one and zero binary at the end of *The Crying of Lot 49*. Indeed, in early 2013, Stephenson began a new project, an online forum entitled, naturally, *Hieroglyph:* as he summarises its goals, he wants science-fiction to create more optimistic, fully fleshed-out visions of the future, which will function 'as hieroglyphs – simple, recognizable symbols on the significance of which everyone agrees'. Of course, this is not actually how hieroglyphs function, but Stephenson reveals that, like in *Snow Crash*, he equates Egyptian writing with total legibility. Just as Pound and Eisenstein looked to Chinese because it retained its association with universality and direct legibility, so Stephenson in *Snow Crash* thus turns away from these newly banal and readable hieroglyphs towards a seemingly more mystical form of inscription.

To summarise briefly its complicated mythology, *Snow Crash* proposes that all of civilisation is derived from Sumerian culture and, specifically, from what Stephenson calls '*me*'s – cuneiform inscriptions written by priests. These '*me*'s operate as programs that work directly on the 'deep structures' of the brain and allow the followers of the priests to learn how to hunt, farm, etc. The 'agglutinative' language of cuneiform was thus the original, Adamic language, identical to 'glossolalia', the speaking in tongues associated with Pentecost. As Stephenson summarises:

> We've got two kinds of language in our heads. The kind we're using now is acquired. [. . .] But there's also a tongue that's based in the deep structures of the brain, that everyone shares. [. . .] Glossolalia – speaking in tongues – is the output side of it, where the deep linguistic structures hook into our tongues and speak, bypassing all the higher, acquired languages. (p. 369)

In the future world of Stephenson's novel, the evil capitalist L. Bob Rife is seeking, by recapturing the lost wisdom of the Sumerians, to set himself up as a new priest that will be able to hack into the 'brainstems' of everyone in the world and control their actions. He accomplishes this through Pentecostalist religion and through the Snow Crash drug or computer virus, which, by injection or through exposure to a 'bitmap', infects the brain and restores the Adamic language of Sumer.[57] The hero of civilisation is the Sumerian God Enki who invented a 'metavirus' that prevented the Sumerian subjects from understanding the '*me*'s of their priests. This was the true source of Babel – of the proliferation of languages – which, in Stephenson's mythology, gave rise to creative thinking and to civilisation itself.

Stephenson in *Snow Crash* does not merely align cuneiform and code, the medium of ancient Sumer and that of futuristic America; he imaginatively asserts that they are identical. 'A one and a zero', the Librarian in *Snow Crash* declares, were the Sumerian 'emblems of royal power' (p. 239), and he traces that binary alphabet up through the 'practical kabbalists' who used a system of 'ones and zeroes' (p. 257) that resembled cuneiform. Stephenson thus links the esoteric experiments of the Renaissance – and the inscriptive languages with which they are associated – with the building blocks of digital computers.[58] As he writes, 'Computers speak machine language [. . .] it's written in ones and zeroes – binary code. But it's very difficult to work in machine language because you go crazy after a while [. . .] So a whole Babel of computer languages has been created for programmers' (pp. 260–1). Not only is code the underlying Adamic tongue beneath the 'Babel of computer languages', it also becomes, through the linkage to cuneiform, the primal language of all humanity.

By making binary code the language of the Kabbalists and of the Sumerian priests, Stephenson restores to the products of contemporary technology not only the sacred and magical associations of ancient forms of inscription, but one such association above all: the link between the performative possibilities of oral spells and the materiality of writing. As Stephenson writes of the Kabbalists, 'Early linguists, as well as the Kabbalists, believed in a fictional language called the tongue of Eden, the language of Adam. It enabled all men to understand each other, to communicate without misunderstanding. It was the language of the Logos, the moment when God created the world by speaking a word' (p. 260). For Stephenson in *Snow Crash*, the language of glossolalia, linked to bits and to cuneiform, actually is that 'tongue of Eden, the language of Adam', but what is most important for Stephenson is that 'moment when God created the world by speaking a word'. This connection between word and world, looking back to Joyce's pun in *Ulysses*, foregrounds the performative power of oral discourse; the world, in God's original act of creation, is composed out of language. But while Stephenson seems to be privileging speech above writing here – lending to speech the mystical ability to effect change in the world, even to create a world *ex nihilo* – he consistently characterises cuneiform writing, as well as computer languages and digital code, as akin to speech. He describes the virtual reality world of the 'Metaverse' as 'a fictional structure made out of code. And code is just a form of speech – the form that computers understand' (p. 197). For Stephenson binary code is a 'speech with magical force', both a form of writing and a form of spell-casting. Stephenson subtly shifts the emphasis on hybridity that we've seen in the discourses on hieroglyphs and on digital code. Binary code, like ancient cuneiform, becomes a hybrid language, but Stephenson's emphasis is not on visuality, but rather, as we have seen in Conrad and Welles in Chapter 3, on the combination of speech and writing.

By linking cuneiform to digital bits, Stephenson emphasises code's connection to writing, and, implicitly, his own writing. Like Pynchon's 'printed circuit', Stephenson's invocation of an ancient form of inscription allows him to claim a fundamental similarity between writing and computer code. As Walter Benn Michaels writes about *Snow Crash*, 'the point, in other words, of the analogy between (or the identification of) the biological virus and (or with) the computer virus is the promotion of the model of the code, which is to say, of the idea that languages are codes.'[59] Just as code creates programs that cause computers to run, just as Sumerian priests create cuneiform '*me*'s that control the actions of their subjects, so Stephenson as writer uses his own alphabetical form of writing Kabbalistically to create a world that is composed out of words. As N. Katherine Hayles writes, literature thus 'functions more like simulations than do other discursive forms'.[60]

In the novel, Stephenson conflates the basic language of humans with that of computers, with the Snow Crash virus infecting both computers and their operators, and the 'deep structures' of computers paralleling the 'deep structures' of human thought. Both are ultimately the same 'tongue of Eden'. If language controls both computers and humans, then the novelist emerges as a kind of computer programmer (and Stephenson is in fact a programmer) who creates through language the world – the 'Metaverse' – which his seemingly flesh-and-blood characters inhabit. The programmer, the writer, is the 'really advanced hacker' who 'sees through the language he's working in and glimpses the secret functioning of the binary code – becomes a Ba'al Shem of sorts' (pp. 260–1). The programmer, descendent of the sacred 'Ba'al Shem' of the Kabbalah, 'descend[s] below this surface layer and into the netherworld of code and tangled nam-shubs that supports it, where everything that you see in the Metaverse, no matter how lifelike and beautiful and three-dimensional, reduces to a simple text file: a series of letters on an electronic page' (pp. 327–8). As with Pynchon linking electronic circuitry to print, so Stephenson reduces all of technology – and the entire 'Metaverse' that it produces – into text: 'a series of letters on an electronic page'. Code and its nam-shubs – the cuneiform spells that Stephenson associates with it – become a form of simultaneously written and spoken language, a language capable of producing a world that is 'lifelike and beautiful and three-dimensional'. Stephenson provides the ultimate *mise en abîme* for his novel, and for the role of the novelist in a world of electronic media; beneath the seamlessly mimetic world of the novel lies the invisible linguistic code of 'letters' that creates it. Whether it be the Latin alphabet, cuneiform scripts or digital code, text can, in *Snow Crash*, create a world.

Reed's 'Black Sacred Book'

So far this link between digital code and hieroglyphs, between computing and writing, seems to exist as part of a specific literary genealogy, beginning with Pynchon and continuing through ambitious literary science fiction in his wake. Yet that trajectory is only one manifestation of a much larger desire in contemporary American literature to link ancient hieroglyphic inscriptions with modern technologies. As Pynchon was engaging with hieroglyphs and digital code in the 1960s and 1970s, African-American writers were similarly grappling with the legacy of ancient Egypt; indeed, both Pynchon and Stephenson seem at times to be explicitly engaging with these trends in Afro-Futurism, and, particularly, with one text above all: Ishmael Reed's *Mumbo Jumbo*. For in *Mumbo Jumbo* Reed not only returns to the mythology of ancient Egypt and constructs a network of dueling secret societies akin to the Trystero, but also, like Stephenson, emphasises the performative capabilities of his own text. Tracing the links among Reed, Pynchon and Stephenson can express the complex interplay of literary influence in the post-war period, revealing again the connections among hieroglyphic scripts, the performative possibilities of contemporary technologies and the written word itself.

As discussed in Chapter 4, claims for the connection between ancient Egypt and Africa were essential to Frederick Douglass's attempt to validate black culture and establish links between the races. Scott Trafton in *Egypt Land* has shown how common the motif of ancient Egypt was in nineteenth-century African-American culture, extending beyond the imaginative connection between slaves and the ancient Israelites in Negro spirituals and recurring in the work of George Washington Williams, W. E. B. DuBois and Martin Delaney.[61] Indeed, attempts to align Africa and Egypt have been central to contemporary Pan-Africanism, particularly in Cheikh Anta Diop's *The African Origin of Civilization* and Martin Bernal's *Black Athena*. As Paul Gilroy has argued, 'the appeal of Egypt as evidence of the greatness of pre-slave African cultures, like the enduring symbol that Egypt supplies for black creativity and civilisation, has had a special significance within black Atlantic responses to modernity.'[62] From the nineteenth century up through the present, ancient Egypt has occupied a central place in African-American culture, at the same time as Egyptian modernist writers and filmmakers were attempting to distance themselves from African culture.

This fascination with Egypt extends to the hieroglyphs themselves, which play an important role in African-American writing dating back to Nat Turner's vision of finding 'on the leaves in the woods hieroglyphic characters' and extending up through Zora Neale Hurston, James Baldwin and theorist Barbara Christian.[63] As Aldon Lynn Neilsen has noted, African-American postmodern poets such as Amiri Baraka, Lorenzo Thomas, Stephen Jonas and Julia Fields 'would again turn to ancient African scripts for precedents', seeking in hieroglyphs 'an African genesis for writing against European attempts to strip the African continent of its history of inscription and its history in writing'.[64] These references proliferate in the 1960s and 1970s, particularly due to the rise of Afro-Futurism, which simultaneously looked back to the Egyptian past and forward to the technological future. As Paul Gilroy notes: 'The "traditional" imagery of ancient Egypt was not counterposed to views of "modern" reality but rather presented in a way that emphasised its continuity with contemporary technological and scientific developments.'[65] This juxtaposition of Egypt and technology was most common in music, with myriad album covers and musicians including the funk pioneers Parliament invoking the conjunction of Egypt and space or of Egypt and futuristic technologies (indeed, George Clinton, the leader of Parliament, credited the mythology of his band to the influence of *Mumbo Jumbo*).[66] Most notably, the jazz musician Sun Ra – as his name indicates – created a mythology that linked Egyptian influences with 'cosmic' ones: Sun Ra claimed to have journeyed to Saturn, but he was also affected by his reading of George G.

M. James's *Stolen Legacy*, which argued that Pharaonic Egypt had inspired Greece and Rome.[67] Ra thus incorporated both influences into his stage persona and album covers.

More than any other writer, Ishmael Reed was able to synthesise all of these tendencies in the African-American engagement with ancient Egypt, using Egypt and its hieroglyphs as an access point to an alternative historical genealogy, as an embodiment of the values of African-American culture, and as a symbol of the relationship between the writing systems of the past and the new media of the present. Ancient Egypt is central to Reed's novel *Mumbo Jumbo*, and, indeed, to his views of history and culture more generally: as he writes, 'in the 1960s, the black writers whom I knew were searching for an African civilization that would serve them as Western civilization inspired white writers. Some of us chose Egypt because its ruins seemed to rival those of Western civilization.'[68] In his 1972 novel *Mumbo Jumbo*, Reed, drawing on the African-American invocations of Egypt outlined above, traces all of African culture back to ancient Egypt, and, specifically, to the mythical 'Book of Thoth', written in hieroglyphs. In Reed's account, all of the vernacular traditions of African-American music and dance – embodied in the 'anti-plague' 'Jes Grew' – go back to this 'Black Sacred Book'.[69] As another character proclaims, 'We had returned to our ancient religion just as our ancestors the Egyptians the Nubians the Ethiopians did in times of trouble' (p. 135). Like Douglass, Reed blurs the lines among Egyptian, Nubian and Ethiopian culture, reclaiming ancient Egyptian civilisation as African.

Reed's use of hieroglyphics in *Mumbo Jumbo* thus exposes what has been implicit in all of the writers and directors I have discussed in this project: that the invocation of Egyptian writing is, above all, an act of appropriation. Western modernists wrench hieroglyphics out of their historical and cultural context, using interpretations or misinterpretations of them to comment upon debates about language, media and culture in their own countries and periods. Reed thus seems to mirror the 'international Mu'tafika' in his novel who 'has lifted the sacred Papyri of Ani stored in the British Museum and returned it to "Brothers in Cairo"' (p. 63). Reed reappropriates the hieroglyphics from their British imprisonment and restores them to their African context, to their 'Brothers in Cairo'. And yet given the desire of Mahfouz and al-Hakim to deny their connection to the rest of Africa, those 'Brothers in Cairo' might not be so appreciative, and might see Reed as simply engaged in another act of re-appropriation.

But Reed goes further than simply tying together African and Egyptian civilisation, seeking, like the other writers this chapter has traced, to connect ancient Egypt with the contemporary world. The novel finds in ancient Egypt an explanation for the cultural divisions of present-day society, which began with the co-optation of the 'Book of Thoth, the sacred Work Isis had given to

Moses' (p. 188). In Reed's account, this original text was material and physical, growing out of the dances of Osiris: Osiris 'in the Sudan and Ethiopia [...] became known as "the man who did dances that caught-on," infected other people' (p. 162). These dances were then adapted into a textual form by the scribe Thoth. This first Book of Thoth was written in hieroglyphs, a point made again and again over the course of the novel; Abdul Hamid, the Malcolm X figure who first finds the Book, remarks that 'I even learned the transliteration and translation of hieroglyphics, a skill which has come in handy recently' (p. 37), and a white character describes how 'He says he has this anthology the nigger says has hieroglyphics and strange drawings written all over it' (p. 81). Reed thus draws a connection, familiar to us from Joyce, between hieroglyphs and gesture as more embodied forms of language. Just as in Vico gesture evolves into hieroglyphs and then into the alphabet, so in *Mumbo Jumbo* the dances of Osiris are adapted into the hieroglyphic language of the Book of Thoth.

Osiris's dances are opposed in Reed's history by his brother Set, who substitutes a monotheistic worship of the sun-god Aton for 'paganism', pantheism and 'VooDoo'. This division sets the stage for contemporary cultural battles spearheaded by secret Atonist cabals like the Wallflower League and the Knights Templar: as Reed writes, 'Someone once said that beneath or behind all political and cultural warfare lies struggle between secret societies' (p. 18). That 'someone', of course, might as well be Pynchon, who in *The Crying of Lot 49* similarly traces how the secret society of the Trystero influences the movements of history. Thus at almost the same time as Pynchon, in *The Crying of Lot 49* and *Gravity's Rainbow*, was both looking back to ancient Egypt and presenting a paranoid vision of the nefarious influence of small cliques of the powerful on contemporary society, Reed was doing the same. Indeed, Pynchon even acknowledges the influence of Reed in *Gravity's Rainbow* – 'Well, and keep in mind where those Masonic Mysteries came from in the first place. (Check out Ishmael Reed. He knows more about it than you will ever find here)' (p. 598) – a comment that invokes both Reed's interest in Egypt and in secret societies. The conjunction of Reed and Pynchon thus reveals just how widespread the desire was to construct or reconstruct ancient mythologies and traditions to make sense of the fractures of the present.

Reed also shares with Pynchon an interest in mass media technologies. In all his novels, Reed is fascinated with the overlaps between race and media, and *Mumbo Jumbo* is saturated with references to radio, television and Dictaphones, and even involves a 'Talking Android'. Indeed, as the contemporary critics Michael Chaney and Ron Eglash have noted, race, Africa and new media have always been subtly interrelated: in discussing *Mumbo Jumbo*, Chaney traces 'the extent to which the discourse of technology was and still is imbricated within discourses of race, civil rights, and slavery'.[70] And Eglash, more hopefully, traces the possible influences of African culture – architecture in particular – on Western technologies of cybernetics.[71]

Reed is not simply interested in media; through his invocations of new technologies and ancient forms of inscription, Reed also validates the importance of written words by linking them with spoken and gestural performance. Directly or indirectly, *Mumbo Jumbo* is a major influence on *Snow Crash*, again suggesting the intertwining among science fiction, postmodernism and Afro-Futurism from the 1960s onward. Both novels recount the spread of a new 'plague' or 'anti-plague', whether portrayed negatively or positively, and as with the link between the Snow Crash virus and ancient Sumer in Stephenson's novel, Reed connects the contemporary disease of 'Jes Grew' to an alternative history of Egyptian culture. Jes Grew even involves, like Snow Crash, 'speaking in tongues' (p. 5).

As we've seen, Stephenson uses the conjunction of digital code and hieroglyphs and cuneiform to link the performative possibilities of computing and oral spell-casting to the written words with which he constructs the novel, making his own work into a kind of computing. Likewise, Ishmael Reed's interest in Egypt is not solely about exploring the conflict of African and Judeo-Christian culture, but also, like Joyce or Woolf or Pynchon, in making a claim for the importance of writing against new media technologies. Reed's historical account seems initially to validate spoken words or physical movement over text; once transformed from dance into words, Osiris's 'Work' can be co-opted by Set and those following him. Yet written words are consistently of prime importance in the novel. Crucially, as Reed's hero PaPa LaBas argues, 'Jes Grew' cannot achieve a lasting impact simply in the form of music or dance; it needs to be rendered into words. As he says, 'Being an anti-plague I figure that it's yearning for The Work of its Word', and the future success of Jes Grew is 'up to its Text' (p. 33). Like in Mahfouz's novel, in which Khufu hands down his wisdom in written form, words have the ultimate impact in Reed's world; they ground the cultural phenomena of Jes Grew and allow them to register in the larger world as more than a passing fad. They allow them to be passed into history. And the plot of the novel is the search by the various characters for 'The Work of its Word', which turns out to be the ancient Book of Thoth, written in hieroglyphs. That Book of Thoth thus becomes a hybrid form, between the gestures of performance and the permanence of words. This blurring of the gestural and oral with the textual is characteristic of experimental African-American writing of the 1960s and 1970s; as Neilsen argues, poets of the period emphasise the materiality of their writing in order to oppose the 'continued privileging of orality over the written in the study of African-American writing'.[72] As Neilsen concludes, in a statement that might serve as a motto for modernism: 'orature is not opposed to writing' (p. 30).

Just as Stephenson uses hieroglyphs to equate written words with binary digits, turning computing from a technology threatening to supplant writing to simply another form of writing, so Reed uses the script of ancient Egypt to affirm the importance of text. Given the status of hieroglyphs as a textual form that blurs the lines between visual, oral and digital technologies and writing, by invoking ancient Egypt Reed is able to preserve the foundational importance of writing even in a world of sinister mass communication technologies. 'Text' itself, in the form of the Book of Thoth, sits at the centre of Reed's world.

Projecting a World: Pynchon's Performative Language

Pynchon, similarly to Reed, uses his references to hieroglyphs to affirm the power and performativity of his written words. By folding speech and computing and gesture into writing, Pynchon, like Stephenson and Reed, asserts the all-encompassing power of text. Through the associations between hieroglyphs and code – their seeming ability to combine various media, their status as potentially universal languages, their liminal status between hyperlegibility and mystic inscrutability – Pynchon can blur the gap between electronic languages and more material forms of inscriptions. Like code, language in Pynchon can create a fictional world, with all his novels obsessed with how the alphabetical marks of language are transformed into settings and characters.

While such an insight about language is nothing new, contemporary writers increasingly call attention to how 'a letter of the alphabet' can help to build and do things. As Oedipa asks, twice, in *The Crying of Lot 49*, 'Shall I project a world?', and Pynchon is consistently fascinated with the processes by which a world is projected, in all of the senses of the word. For Oedipa's W.A.S.T.E. world is not only, or possibly, a psychological projection; it is specifically a narrative projection, as the word 'project' implies: 'To devise or design (an action, proceeding, scheme or undertaking); to form a project of.' Pynchon emphasises how a writer or character – like Oedipa – constructs and orders a fictional world out of linguistic or pictorial clues or hieroglyphics. Oedipa thus resembles Pierce Inverarity, who through his Testament perhaps authorises the paranoid conspiracy that so ensnares Oedipa, and Pynchon himself, the ultimate plotter and the God of his creation, who brings a fictional world into existence through language. But this act of construction is fundamentally allied with language and with media, as other meanings of 'project' imply. For 'project' encompasses the oral and the visual – you can project your speaking voice, or you can project a film – as well as the more clearly textual: 'To represent (the earth, sky, etc.) on a plane surface by means of a geometrical or other projection.' For Pynchon, plotting and creation always involve a translation between the reality of the world and the 'plane surface' – the page or screen – on which it is represented and reconstructed.[73] The invocations of hieroglyphs – and the printed circuits and computers with which they are linked – are thus associated with cartography, with the 'ordered swirl' of houses and their 'hieroglyphic streets'. Cartography is, after all, the subject of Pynchon's *Mason & Dixon*. Fiction, like computing, involves this translation from two-dimensional words to a three dimensional 'Metaverse', with, as in Stephenson, the world reduced to a series of letters on a page.

Returning to the final image of *The Crying of Lot 49*, with its 'hieroglyphic streets' and 'matrices of a great digital computer', can now reveal additional complexities in that invocation of a computer. As noted earlier, Pynchon seems through the metaphor of hieroglyphics to be linking the computer with the novel itself. Like code, the written words in a novel call into being a visual world, and the circuits of computers seem to arise from the printed circuits of text. Again, though, Pynchon seeks to have it both ways, just like Oedipa fluctuating between the ones and zeroes of meaning and not-meaning at the end of the novel. For like Gibson, Stephenson and Reed, Pynchon critiques the burgeoning digital world as sinister while simultaneously allying it with the novel itself. Zena Meadowsong has argued that Oedipa misses the point in seeking to choose between the binary possibilities embodied by code and hieroglyphics at the end of the novel; she ignores the fact that there already is a secretive network of information operating in America and in the novel, but that it is not the Trystero, but rather the computer itself. She argues that references to the IBM 7094 – with its sinister alliance with Yoyodyne's military-industrial complex – position digital code as the true new force behind the world.[74] Perhaps Oedipa should have emulated Roger Mexico in *Gravity's Rainbow* in seeking to surmount the binaries of 'zero to one, not-something to something' embodied in that novel by Pointsman and instead embraced 'the middle excluded from this persuasion – the probabilities' (p. 56) or, as Oedipa puts it, the 'bad shit' of 'excluded middles'.

Despite the sinister overtones of the computer at the novel's conclusion, however, I think we can read *The Crying of Lot 49* as also reclaiming the power of digital code by allying it to the written word. For the 'matrices' at the end of the novel refer not only to media technologies but also to 'the womb; the uterus of a mammal' and 'A place or medium in which something is originated, produced, or developed; a point of origin and growth'. Far from being solely an imprisoning, dehumanising new medium, the computer, through the creative capabilities of its code, becomes fundamentally generative, a womb or origin that gives rise to new worlds. Despite its associations with the military, digital code in the novel retains the aura of sacredness of the hieroglyphs with which it is associated. The computer in *The Crying of Lot 49* becomes the framework on which reality is hung, as at the end of *Neuromancer*, when the AI responds to Case's questions with the declaration, 'I'm the matrix, Case' (p. 259).[75] By equating computers and texts – through the linkage of the 'matrix' to print technologies and to hieroglyphs – Pynchon, like Gibson, like Stephenson, like Reed, claims for written words the same procreative powers.

229

While *The Crying of Lot 49* at times finds computers hegemonic and dangerous, and while it reveals the possible corruptions and instabilities in printed texts – as the various versions of the *Courier's Tragedy* make clear – it nonetheless reaffirms the power and creative potential of the 'Word', a power it amplifies through its connection to the sacred and performative power of both hieroglyphs and computers. Similarly, in Don DeLillo's novel *The Names*, the character Vosdanik makes the Kabbalistic claim that 'The alphabet is male and female. If you will know the correct order of letters, you make a world, you make creation.'[76] For Pynchon, as for DeLillo, this is the ultimate goal of fiction; he seeks a language that, like digital code, like hieroglyphics, will 'make creation', even as he constantly seeks to call attention to the process of that making.

Gravity's Rainbow and Postmodernism

This link between computers and texts, and the ambivalence about both the power of code and the power of novels themselves, recurs in the central image of *Gravity's Rainbow*: the Rocket, and, particularly, the unfired 00001 rocket at the novel's end. The Rocket is consistently characterised not just as a machine, but as a text: 'say we *are* supposed to be the Kabbalists out here, say that's our real Destiny, to be the scholar-magicians of the Zone, with somewhere in it a Text, to be picked to pieces, annotated, explicated, and masturbated till it's all squeezed limp of its last drop [. . .] well we assumed – naturlich! – that this holy Text had to be the Rocket' (p. 529). Like Oedipa Maas and the post-horn of the Trystero, the Rocket becomes a 'text' that must be deciphered by Kabbalistic decoders. But the above statement might be construed as a description of *Gravity's Rainbow*, with its readers the 'scholar-magicians of the Zone' ready to pick the Text to pieces. Pynchon thus seems to analogise the rocket with his novel itself.

But the Rocket is not only a rocket, but also a machine, and, perhaps, one linked to digital code. For the identifying number for the rocket pieced together by the Schwartzkommando is 00001: a serial number that also functions as a piece of digital code. And interestingly, given Pynchon's acknowledged debt to Reed in *Gravity's Rainbow*, this invocation of code is explicitly linked to Africa through the presence of the Schwartzkommando, displaced members of the African Herero tribe. The Rocket, like the digital computer at the end of the *Crying of Lot 49*, is thus both computer and novel, both code and Text. Like the computer in *Lot 49*, the Rocket can function both for good and for evil: directly after again comparing the Rocket to a text – 'Kabbalists who study the Rocket as Torah, letter by letter – rivets, burner cup and brass rose, its text is theirs to permute and combine into new revelations, always unfolding' (p. 741) – Pynchon describes both the 'good Rocket' and the 'bad Rocket', the vehicle of destruction and the vehicle for transcendence. These twin possibilities are extended not just to the Rocket, but to computers and to the novels with which they are linked, not just in Pynchon, but in Gibson and Stephenson as well. The novel, like the computer, must be both celebrated for its performative possibilities and exposed for its totalising impulses.

This ambivalence about both the power of computers and the power of novels, this desire to 'make creation' and reveal the mechanics of that creation, rests at the core of postmodern aesthetics. The totalising capability of digital code and the novel to create or control the world is both attractive and dangerously hegemonic, something to be aspired to but also opposed and subverted. *The Crying of Lot 49*, like *Snow Crash* and *Neuromancer*, acknowledges the lure of a seamless fictional or digital world even as it reveals that world as a fiction. This desire both to embrace and resist fiction's world-making power perhaps explains the anti-mimetic tendency in so much of postmodernism. Either through the creation of stylised, absurd or futuristic worlds – as in David Foster Wallace, Don DeLillo and the other writers in this chapter – or by pointing out the constructedness of seemingly mimetic fictional worlds – as in John Barth, Philip Roth, Tim O'Brien or some Toni Morrison – many of the major figures of post-war American fiction acknowledge the fictionality of the novelistic worlds they create. Of course, that acknowledgement cuts both ways – even as they question and potentially undercut the capabilities of writing, they simultaneously call attention to their fiction-making power.

We can even see this tension expressed in the central image of *The Crying of Lot 49*: the muted post-horn. In its shape, the post-horn recalls the 'tundish' or sieve of *A Portrait of the Artist* and 'old Bad Air's horn' in Ralph Ellison's *Invisible Man*, both emblems of the process of artistic creation, of how the raw material of the world is transformed into a novel.[77] In *The Crying of Lot 49* that symbol persists, but in blocked or muted form, with Pynchon both seeking to invoke and interfere with the process of translation between the world and the novel.

Neal Stephenson provides a particularly apt embodiment of these seemingly contradictory impulses in postmodern writing, particularly through the linkage, pointed out by Katherine Hayles, between Stephenson's novel *Cryptonomicon* and his essay *In the Beginning Was the Command Line*, published in the same year.[78] That essay celebrates the Linux operating system against the hegemony of Windows and Apple. As Hayles summarises, 'Linux operates by giving the user direct access to the commands that control the computer's behavior, whereas the Macintosh [. . .] conceals the actual commands within its hidden coding structures.'[79] Linux thus provides the specific model for the kind of novel Stephenson is trying to write, one that through words seamlessly creates a convincing world but simultaneously acknowledges to the 'user' the 'commands' or words that control or give rise to it. The novel, like Linux, both serves as a convincing performance and acknowledges that it is a performance. The title of the essay *In the Beginning Was the Command Line* further links coding and words. This goal of Linux is really the goal of so much postmodern fiction: to have the same fiction-making power as prior modes of fiction – the same figurative computing power – without losing sight of the process of that creation, of how the representational 'upper levels' of a novel, like a computer desktop founded on binary code, are created by words.

Yet despite the similarities – indeed, on many levels, the inseparability – between modernism and postmodernism, this departure from mimesis in calling attention to the processes of writing in some ways counterintuitively stands closer to traditional mimetic modes than to the works of the modernists. As this book has argued, writers, directors and inventors in the early twentieth century turned to hieroglyphs to call attention to the visual, sonic and material properties of their own medium, be it film or written words. In noticing the visual appearance of language or the techniques of 'film grammar', readers or viewers would come to see the medium of writing or of film as the ultimate medium, capable of capturing and incorporating the properties of all other media and even potentially of transcending the boundaries of culture and language. Yet despite the dream of a universal or pure language that might collapse the divide between signifier and signified, the reality of all media, in the writers and directors I have traced, is always hybrid: writing or film can better capture the reality of the world but cannot do so completely. Eye can never quite equal I, Mrs Ramsay's 'sacred tablets' can never quite be read, *Finnegans Wake* cannot totally bring together form and content. Despite their profound desire for mimesis, their constant search for a better form of language and their desire to validate the unique ability of their own media to represent reality, the modernists always insist on the gap between representation and reality, on the unattainability of any pure or primal medium.

By contrast, postmodernists like Pynchon, Gibson and Stephenson seem not as concerned with forging a better language or calling attention to the material properties of their own medium. Rather, even as they may move away at times from traditional mimesis, their concern is less with language or the medium of creation than with the product of that medium: the created or simulated world. That emphasis actually brings High Postmodernism closer to realism than it might initially appear. As Brian McHale has argued, postmodernism shifts to an 'ontological dominant' from modernism's 'epistemological dominant'.[80] The modernist writers I have discussed are indeed concerned with the linguistic and media tools that allow them to know and represent the world. Like realist novelists, however, Pynchon, Stephenson and other postmodern writers are ultimately less interested in the materiality of the written word than the modernists. Even as they point to how their worlds are fictional creations, to how novelists make a world out of words, they largely do not call attention to the visual or sonic form of the words themselves. The imaginative comparison of hieroglyphs to digital code – rather than to film, photography or phonography – involves a shift towards an emphasis on the performativity of language instead of its visual or oral qualities. Just as code remains forever hidden, even in Linux, beneath computer languages and in the unreadable circuits of a motherboard, so language itself is deprived of a visual substance: exactly what modernist writers sought to claim through their imaginative use of hieroglyphs. Instead, what matters is what that code – what those written words – create: the results of language, rather than language itself. And while the modernists find in hieroglyphs a way of imagining the links among nations and races, the hieroglyph in postwar American novels has become potentially sinister, with the possibility of unity consigned to the mythic realm. Thus by tracing the shifting metaphorical uses of hieroglyphs to understand new media we can better understand the subtle distinctions between modernist and postmodernist texts. The imaginative equation, through the emblem of hieroglyphs, between writing and digital code becomes the linguistic embodiment of the larger tendency of postmodern novelists both to laud and to subvert writing's creative potential to 'make a world'.

Notes

1. Dan Brown, p. 57.
2. 'Noetic science' is the speculative pseudo-science about the possibility of thoughts influencing events in the world.
3. Indeed, Brown is so committed to rehabilitating the mystical tradition that he falls into one of the most famous traps of Western thinking about hieroglyphics; in listing famous mystics, he includes 'Ptolemy, Pythagoras, and Hermes Trismegistus' (p. 58). Brown treats Hermes Trismegistus as if he were a real person, and not the god Hermes or Thoth, who, as noted in the first chapter, was the purported author of the forged treatise on hieroglyphics *Corpus Hermeticum*. Brown's understanding of ancient mysticism begins, as in the history of Western theories of Egyptian writing, with a misconception.
4. For background on Kryptos, see John Schwartz, 'Clues to Stubborn Secret in C.I.A.'s Backyard', *New York Times*, 20 November 2010, http://www.nytimes.com/2010/11/21/us/21code.html.
5. Brown repeats the pattern of yoking together present-day America and ancient Egypt, a symbolic juxtaposition going back to Joyce in *Finnegans Wake* and to Vachel Lindsay's invocation of America as a 'hieroglyphic civilization'. Through Masonic symbolism and the Masonic allegiances of the Founding Fathers, America, for Brown, is rooted in ancient Egypt: 'the pyramid builders of Egypt are the forerunners of the modern stonemasons' and 'the Masons transported their secret wisdom from the Old World to the New World' (pp. 129, 131). As the villain of the novel sneers – in a comment with which its hero would agree – 'Egypt is the cradle of your religion' (p. 358).
6. Pynchon, *The Crying of Lot 49*, p. 150.
7. This emphasis on the performativity of writing parallels the rise of theoretical accounts of the role of performance in language, most notably J. L. Austin's *How*

to Do Things with Words. Looking back to the previous chapter, these ideas are also present, in early form, in C. K. Ogden and I. A. Richard's *The Meaning of Meaning*.
8. As Fitzpatrick argues, focusing on the new medium of television, 'What I hope to explore is how the representation of concern about the present and future state of print – a concern that is part of the larger cultural phenomenon I refer to as the anxiety of obsolescence – serves paradoxically to protect print from the death it presumably predicts' (p. 523).
9. Apter, 'On Oneworldedness; Or Paranoia as a World System', pp. 365–89.
10. As Cayley writes, 'In much current codework language is (presented as) code and code is (presented as) language. The utopia of codework recognises that the symbols of the surface language (what you read from your screen) are the "same" (and are all ultimately reducible to digital encoding) as the symbols of the programming languages which store, manipulate, and display the text you read.' This despite the fact that 'code and language require distinct strategies of reading'. (John Cayley, 'The Code Is Not the Text (Unless It Is the Text)'. See also Hayles, *My Mother Was a Computer*, pp. 15–62.
11. The only one of these works currently available online is Ted Warnell's: see http://www.heelstone.com/lascaux/warnell1.html. For further discussion see Milutis, pp. 95–103.
12. Hayles, *My Mother*, p. 45.
13. Hayles, *My Mother*, p. 15; Cayley, 'The Code Is Not the Text'.
14. Rita Raley, 'Code.surface ‖ Code.depth'.
15. As Cayley points out in 'The Code Is Not the Text', contemporary experiments in digital writing – like his own – are often placed in a trajectory going back to Mallarmé and the early twentieth-century avant-garde: 'for example, Marjorie Perloff's *Radical Artifice*, where "reveal code" is revealed as a project of L=A=N=G=U=A=G=E writers such as Charles Berstein, after having been properly and correctly situated in the traditions of process-based, generative and/or constrained literature and potential literature by Modernist, OuLiPian, Fluxus and related writers culminating, for Perloff, in John Cage and the L=A=N=G=U=A=G=E writers themselves.' See Perloff, *Radical Artifice*.
16. See 'Forward', in *Machine Translation of Languages*, ed. by William Locke and A. D. Booth, pp. vi–vii.
17. Locke and Booth, eds, 'Translation', in *Machine Translation of Languages*, p. 23.
18. Locke and Booth, p. 23.
19. As Rita Raley argues in 'Machine Translation and Global English', Weaver thus unconsciously echoes Walter Benjamin's notion of translation as giving rise to a 'true' language:

> He imagines a 'real' universal language at the base of all language. Much as in Plato's *Cratylus* and Walter Benjamin's essay on translation, there are two views of language considered here: functional and mystical. While the more direct route for machine translation – from natural language to natural language – was the more immediately pragmatic and instrumentalist, it was the more mystical route down from the tower to the subterranean, cognitive, authentic language that Weaver offered as both 'true' and efficient. (p. 297)

20. McLuhan, p. 80.
21. Eco, p. 311.
22. Hayles, *My Mother*, p. 15.
23. Manovich, pp. 20, 6.
24. Rosen, p. 325.

25. Bolter, pp. 60, 52.
26. Punzi, pp. 11–12.
27. Raley, 'Code.surface || Code.depth'.
28. In the context of understandings of China and its ideograms in the West, R. John Williams has argued for the idea of 'Asia-as-*technê*': that rather than being opposed to technology, Chinese culture was seen as restoring *technê* – craftsmanship – to technology. Such a view echoes Raley's attempt to see code as similarly 'crafted', like hieroglyphics or ideograms, and the writers I discuss likewise emphasise the craftsmanship inherent in any act of writing or coding. See R. John Williams, pp. 389–419.
29. As Katherine Hayles argues, 'Like esoteric theoretical writing, code is intelligible only to a specialized community of experts who understand its complexities and can read and write it with fluency' (Hayles, *My Mother*, p. 51).
30. As Rita Raley writes in 'Code.surface || Code.depth', 'Whether conceived as "secret," "inaccessible," or an imperceptible background element, the "deep" layers of software [. . .] elude our cognitive reach.'
31. See Ginzburg, *Clues, Myths, and the Historical Method*; Foucault, *The Order of Things*.
32. *The Matrix*, dir. by Lana and Lilly Wachowski (Warner Brothers, 1999).
33. Raley, 'Code.surface || Code.depth'.
34. *The Matrix Reloaded*, dir. by Lana and Lilly Wachowski (Warner Brothers, 2003).
35. Rosenheim, p. 22.
36. Chief among these critics is Leo Braudy in his 'Providence, Paranoia, and the Novel'. Thus Edward Mendelson likewise claims that 'religious meaning is itself the central issue of the plot', and that 'The manifestations of the Trystero [. . .] and all that accompanies it, are always associated in the book with the language of the sacred and with patterns of religious experience' (pp. 120, 117), including the sacred hieroglyphics.
37. As Mark Irwin writes, 'In its broadest definition, the hieroglyph may thus serve to spatialize the sacred through a non-linguistic form' (p. 53).
38. Robert Newman claims, 'The numerous references to Egyptian mythic materials in *Lot 49* – Thoth, the Book of the Dead, hieroglyphs – contribute an infrastructure that links Oedipa's quest with the soul's descent into the underworld as depicted in the Egyptian Book of the Dead' (p. 81).
39. Hayles, '"A Metaphor of God Knew How Many Parts"', p. 109.
40. As Rosenheim argues, at the end of *The Crying of Lot 49* 'We as readers are [. . .] forced to choose between an epistemological skepticism so great that it turns to paranoia [. . .] and an unthinking spiritualization of technology' (p. 191). But this choice between meaning and not meaning is woven into the hieroglyphics themselves that Pynchon uses as analogues for the 'matrices' of digital code.
41. John Johnston notes the 'recurrent either/or grammatical structures' in the text in his *Information Multiplicity*, p. 46.
42. As Molly Hite writes, 'The pattern of the quest is an infinite approach, which brings the seeker closer and closer to a terminal revelation without allowing him to reach it' (p. 121).
43. Pynchon, *Gravity's Rainbow*, p. 441.
44. 'Slothrop's family actually made its money killing trees, amputating them from their roots, chopping them up, grinding them to pulp, bleaching that to paper and getting paid for this with more paper. "That's really insane"' (Pynchon, *Gravity's Rainbow*, p. 562).
45. Jameson, *Postmodernism*, p. 38.
46. As Emily Apter in 'On Oneworldedness' describes the paranoid logic of

'oneworldedness', encapsulated in Pynchon and DeLillo, 'If God is another name for intellectual unipolarity, the paranoid theorist will be God by devising a system of omniscience capable of binding everything into coherence, thereby rendering discrepant orders of signs mutually intelligible or pantranslatable' (p. 371).

47. For background on the rise of Pentecostalist religion in the 1960s and its influence on literature, see Hungerford, pp. 269–98.

48. Following *The Crying of Lot 49*, hieroglyphics become the dominant metaphor in novels or films of paranoia: the embodiment of both the possibility of interconnection, coherence and meaning and of the loss of that possibility. Ancient forms of inscription – juxtaposed with modern media like film – recur in the paranoid world of Don DeLillo's *The Names* and in Jacques Rivette's twelve-and-a-half-hour long film *Out 1* (1971). That film – quite structurally and thematically similar to Pynchon's novel – concerns the possible existence or non-existence of a secret society (based on Balzac's *History of the Thirteen*). The atmosphere of paranoia in the movie finds its linguistic equivalent in the character Colin (Jean-Pierre Leaud)'s comment that he's interested in 'the hidden meaning, what he's trying to express behind the words, behind the gestures, the secondary meaning. It's the language of birds [. . .] a language of rebuses, of hieroglyphs, which enables one who is initiated, a companion, a sage, to be addressed directly in a kind of universal language'. *Out 1*, dir. by Jacques Rivette (Sunchild Productions, 1971).

49. As N. Katherine Hayles writes, 'at the lowest level of code, machine language, inscription merges with incorporation. When a computer reads and writes machine language, it operates directly on binary code, the ones and zeros that correspond to positive and negative magnetic polarities. At this level inscribing is performing, for changing a one to a zero corresponds directly to changing the magnetic polarity of that bit.' Hayles, 'The Posthuman Body', pp. 261–2.

50. Similarly, though not in the context of media or hieroglyphics, Brian McHale in *Constructing Postmodernism* notes how 'cyperpunk tends to "literalize" or "actualize" what in postmodernist fiction occurs as metaphor' and how 'Cyberpunk texts often foreground this metafictional potential of paraspace. For instance, they develop an analogy between the author of the text, who has written the fictional world into being, and the "author" of the cyberspace or paraspace world' (pp. 246, 253).

51. Gibson, *Neuromancer*, pp. 9, 74. Likewise in his later novel *Pattern Recognition*, Gibson describes how 'Eyes closed, she finds herself imagining a symbol, something water-marking the lower right-hand corner of her existence' (Gibson, *Pattern Recognition*, p. 78).

52. Again, in *Pattern Recognition* the logo of the branding company Blue Ant is 'Egyptianate' and 'hieratic' (Gibson, p. 117).

53. As Shawn James Rosenheim argues, 'despite its erotic investment in codes and data, though, the conclusion of *Neuromancer* betrays a nostalgic attachment to the Adamic nature of the hieroglyph' (p. 111). Yet the 'investment in codes and data' and the 'Adamic nature of the hieroglyph', as we've seen, are always intimately interrelated.

54. This idea of the artist as invisible 'Maker' is linked explicitly to Joyce's notion of the novelist as God of creation, as the 'Maker' turns out to be named Nora after Joyce's wife Nora Barnacle (Gibson, *Pattern Recognition*, p. 286).

55. Stephenson, *Snow Crash*, p. 201. Hiro Protagonist's name may be not merely a pun on 'Hero', but also on the 'hiero' of 'hieroglyphics', particularly given Stephenson's fascination with sacred language in the novel.

56. Stephenson, *Cryptonomicon*, p. 25.

57. Given the time period of its publication, *Snow Crash*'s emphasis on viruses brings to mind the AIDS epidemic – mentioned on a couple of occasions in the novel as a

way of understanding the Sumerian 'virus' – though this focus is also determined by a larger history of novels that bring together viruses, language and media, from William Burroughs's *The Ticket That Exploded* through, as we shall see, Ishmael Reed's *Mumbo Jumbo*. For more on *Snow Crash* and AIDS, see Browning, pp. 129–37.

58. Likewise, in his later novel *Cryptonomicon*, Stephenson links cryptography to mysticism, with one character proclaiming, in the context of discussing Liebniz's influence on mid-twentieth century number theory, 'Leibniz was fascinated by the I Ching!' (Stephenson, p. 13).
59. Michaels, p. 69.
60. Hayles, *My Mother*, p. 6.
61. Trafton, *Egypt Land*. See also Williams, *History of the Negro Race in America*; DuBois, *The Negro*; Delaney, *Principia of Ethnology*.
62. Gilroy, *The Black Atlantic*, p. 60. As Stephen Howe has traced, 'For more than two centuries, black scholars and publicists made the claim that civilization was African in origin a centerpiece of their efforts to vindicate the reputation and enhance the self-esteem of African-descended peoples. Identification of Pharaonic Egypt [. . .] or of Ethiopians [. . .] as the originators of arts, sciences, technologies and political organization became a centerpiece of the fight against white aspersion' (p. 32).
63. Turner, *Confessions of Nat Turner*, p. 10. Zora Neale Hurston's claim that the 'white man thinks in a written language and the Negro thinks in hieroglyphics' gets picked up by James Baldwin in his essay 'Many Thousands Gone': 'we find ourselves until today oppressed with a dangerous and reverberating silence; and the story is told, compulsively, in symbols and signs, in hieroglyphics.' For Baldwin, 'The truth concerning the White North American experience is to be deciphered in the hieroglyphic lashed onto the Black man's back.' Likewise, Barbara Christian writes, 'My folk, in other words, have always been a race for theory – though more in the form of the hieroglyph, a written figure that is both sensual and abstract, both beautiful and communicative.' Whether portrayed positively or negatively, these critics see hieroglyphs as a symbolic alternative to the 'written language' of whites, either associated with 'symbols and signs', with 'speech' or with physical marks and traumas. Hieroglyphs become a uniquely African-American hybrid form: material and spoken, communicative and abstract. See Hurston, p. 80; Baldwin, *Notes of a Native Son*, p. 24; Baldwin, *The Evidence of Things Not Seen*, p. 47; Christian, p. 52.
64. Neilsen, p. 21.
65. Gilroy, *Small Acts*, p. 241.
66. Vincent, p. 177.
67. James, *Stolen Legacy*.
68. Reed, *Another Day at the Front*, p. 26.
69. Reed, *Mumbo Jumbo*, p. 194.
70. Chaney, p. 266.
71. See Eglash, pp. 17–28.
72. Neilsen, p. 21. Given the persistent scholarly focus on visual languages and poetry, Neilsen rarely discusses fiction.
73. As Joseph Tabbi argues in *Cognitive Fictions*, Pynchon sees 'the print medium itself as the laminar surface on which the sphere of human and historical consciousness is projected' (p. 26).
74. See Meadowsong, '"Behind the hieroglyphic streets"'.
75. 'Matrix' even etymologically derives from mother, underlying this connection, and *The Crying of Lot 49* is filled with references to mothers, from the parodic Jacobean play to the altered W.A.S.T.E. stamp for the 'mothers of America

issue'. Pynchon's play on 'matrix' thus undermines the traditional associations between computing technology and men, particularly prevalent in Pynchon's time. Katherine Hayles, in the title to her book *My Mother Was a Computer*, plays off the feminine associations of 'computer', which, before the invention of digital machines, meant simply, 'a person who makes calculations or computations', jobs often filled by women. And yet the other term in that equation – 'mother' – is also, through its etymological linkage with 'matrix', connected to computing as well. Appropriately, it is Oedipa Maas – one of Pynchon's few female protagonists – who ends up trapped in this metaphorical matrix.

76. DeLillo, p. 152.
77. Ellison, p. 581.
78. See Stephenson, *In the Beginning Was the Command Line*.
79. Hayles, *My Mother*, p. 127.
80. McHale, *Postmodernist Fiction*, p. 10.

CODA: THE ROSETTA STONE

Hieroglyphs have persisted for so long in the Western imagination because of the malleability of their metaphorical meanings. Emblems of readability and unreadability, universality and difference, writing and film, writing and digital media, hieroglyphs serve to encompass many of the central tensions in understandings of race, nation, language and media in the twentieth century. For Pound and Lindsay, they served as inspirations for a more direct and universal form of writing; for Woolf, as a way of treating the new medium of film and our perceptions of the world as a kind of language. For Conrad and Welles, they embodied the hybridity of writing or the images of film; for al-Hakim and Mahfouz, the persistence of links between ancient Pharaonic civilisation and a newly independent Egypt. For Joyce, hieroglyphs symbolised the origin point for the world's cultures and nations; for Pynchon, the connection between digital code and the novel. In their modernist interpretations and applications, hieroglyphs bring together writing and new media technologies, language and the material world, and all the nations and languages of the globe.

Even as the gap between the reality of Egyptian writing and the reality of new media has grown ever wider – as the example of digital code shows – writers from Reed to Pynchon to Dan Brown keep invoking hieroglyphs. This is no surprise, as the metaphorical use of hieroglyphs has never been about accuracy, but rather about misinterpretation and misappropriation. Hieroglyphs embody this between-ness, this not-quite-ness: not quite image, not quite language, not quite African, not quite European. Whatever new

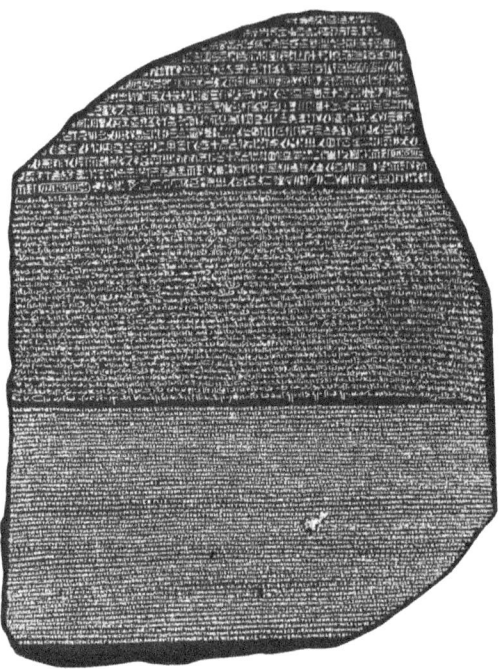

Figure 7.1 The Rosetta Stone

media technologies are developed over the course of the next fifty years, we can trust that, sooner or later, someone will turn to Egyptian writing in an effort to make sense of them. As the twentieth century has shown, we always look to the oldest of old media in our attempt to understand the newest of the new.

For the hordes of visitors at the British Museum snapping smart phone photos of the Rosetta Stone – still the institution's biggest attraction – hieroglyphs have certainly not lost their appeal. Indeed, the Rosetta Stone and its hieroglyphs, pictured in Figure 7.1, are far more popular than the other halls of Egyptian antiquities in the British Museum. That sight – of tourists capturing ancient inscriptions with the newest media technologies – dramatises many of the issues this book has explored. The picture-takers are employing a technology that makes the preservation and dissemination of images far easier than it has ever been before. And yet, the object they are photographing mocks their attempts to capture it – while the digital images will vanish, sooner or later, into the ether, the Rosetta Stone sits there, tangible, material and enduring through millennia. It is no wonder that early film theorists were drawn to the physicality of hieroglyphs, when their own medium, despite its promise of capturing material reality, had been seen from the start as mere shadows.

But the tourists visiting the Rosetta Stone also come face to face with the promise and impossibility of translation. The ultimate emblem of translation, of the transcendence of barriers of language and understanding (as its use as the name of language-learning software makes clear), the Rosetta Stone has also become in its present-day media environment a symbol of universality: one of the most recognised objects in the world. And yet, for all but a handful of Egyptologists, the Stone is, of course, unreadable: the symbol of the triumph of legibility is illegible. Similarly, as this project has shown, the notion of transcending cultural or linguistic barriers always involves an attention precisely to those barriers – to the impossibility of achieving a Pentecostal future, and, often, to the imperialist or capitalist powers that created those boundaries. Like the Rosetta Stone, the digital camera and other new media technologies seem to bring the languages and cultures of the world together, just as they blur the divides between media. Whether focused on the materiality of objects or the Babel of languages, new media technologies, from film and photography up to digital computing, always promise a better form of inscription or communication, as the hieroglyphs did for so long. Yet that promise of pure translatability – either between language and language, or between media and the world, or between one nation and another – remains forever tantalising and unachieved.

BIBLIOGRAPHY

Aarleff, Hans, *From Locke to Saussure* (Minneapolis: University of Minnesota Press, 1982).
Abd al-Salām, Shādī' and Jalal Toufic, 'The Night of Counting the Years (a.k.a. The Mummy)', *Discourse* 21: 1 (Winter 1999), 89–126.
Abdel-Malek, Anouar, 'Orientalism in Crisis', *Diogenes* 11 (December 1963), 103–40.
Abel, Richard, *French Film Theory and Criticism: A History and Anthology, 1907–1939* (Princeton: Princeton University Press, 1988).
Adorno, Theodor, 'The Form of the Phonograph Record', *October* 55 (Winter 1990), 56–61.
—, 'The Schema of Mass Culture', in J. M. Bernstein, ed., *The Culture Industry* (London: Routledge, 1991), 61–97.
Albright, Daniel, *Untwisting the Serpent: Modernism in Music, Literature, and Other Arts* (Chicago: University of Chicago Press, 2000).
Anderson, Benedict, *Imagined Communities*, rev. edn (London: Verso, 1991).
Apter, Emily, *Against World Literature: On the Politics of Untranslatability* (London: Verso, 2013).
—, 'On Oneworldedness; Or Paranoia as a World System', *American Literary History* 18 (Summer 2006), 365–89.
Armbrust, Walter, *Mass Culture and Modernism in Egypt* (Cambridge: Cambridge University Press, 1996).
Armstrong, Tim, *Modernism, Technology and the Body* (Cambridge: Cambridge University Press, 1998).
Artaud, Antonin, *The Theater and Its Double* (New York: Grove Press, 1958).
Atherton, J. S., 'Islam and the Koran in *Finnegans Wake*', *Comparative Literature* 6 (January 1954), 240–55.
Attridge, Derek, *Joyce Effects: On Language, Theory and History* (Cambridge: Cambridge University Press, 2000).

Austin, J. L., *How to Do Things with Words* (Oxford: Clarendon Press, 1962).
Bacon, Francis, *The Works of Francis Bacon*, Vol. 1 (London: A. Millar, 1765).
Badawi, M. M., *Modern Arabic Literature and the West* (London: Ithaca Press, 1985).
Baikie, James, *Peeps at Many Lands: Ancient Egypt* (London: A. & C. Black, 1916).
Balakian, Anna, *The Symbolist Movement: A Critical Appraisal* (New York: New York University Press, 1977).
Balázs, Béla, and Rodney Livingstone, *Early Film Theory: Visible Man and The Spirit of Film* (New York: Berghan, 2011).
Baldwin, James, *The Evidence of Things Not Seen* (New York: Holt, 1985).
—, *Notes of a Native Son* (Boston: Beacon Press, 1955).
Bardaouil, Sam, *Surrealism in Egypt: Modernism and the Art and Liberty Group* (London: I. B. Tauris, 2017).
Barnes, Djuna, *Nightwood* (New York: New Directions, 1961).
Barry, Iris, 'Three Films', *The Adelphi* 1: 10 (March 1924), 926–9.
Bazin, André, *What Is Cinema?* (Berkeley: University of California Press, 1967).
Beardsley, Charles, *Hollywood's Master Showman: The Legendary Sid Grauman* (New York: Cornwall Books, 1983).
Beasley, Rebecca, *Ezra Pound and the Visual Culture of Modernism* (Cambridge: Cambridge University Press, 2010).
Beckett, Samuel, 'Dante ... Bruno. Vico ... Joyce', *transition* 16–17 (June 1929), 242–53.
Beckett, Samuel et al., *Our Exagmination Round His Factification for Incamination of Work in Progress* (New York: New Directions, 1972).
Behmen, Jacob, *Signatura Rerum* (London: John Macock, 1651).
Bell, Alexander Melville, 'Phonetics', *PMLA* 5: 1 (1890), 23–32.
Bell, Clive, 'Art and the Cinema: A Prophecy That the Motion Pictures, in Exploiting Imitation Art, Will Leave Real Art to the Artists', *Vanity Fair* 19: 3 (November 1922), 39–40.
Benjamin, Walter, *The Origin of German Tragic Drama*, trans. John Osborne (London: Nlb, 1977).
Benjamin, Walter and Hannah Arendt, *Illuminations* (New York: Schocken Books, 1969).
Benjamin, Walter et al., *The Work of Art in the Age of Its Technological Reproducibility, and Other Writings on Media* (Cambridge: Belknap Press of Harvard University Press, 2008).
Bernal, Martin, *Black Athena: The Afroasiatic Roots of Classical Civilization* (New Brunswick, NJ: Rutgers University Press, 1987).
Bhabha, Homi, 'Signs Taken for Wonders', *Critical Inquiry* 12 (Autumn 1985), 144–65.
Bishop, John, *Joyce's Book of the Dark, Finnegans Wake* (Madison: University of Wisconsin Press, 1986).
Bolter, Jay David, *Writing Space* (Hillsdale, NJ: Erlbaum, 1991).
Bolter, Jay David and Richard Grusin, *Remediation: Understanding New Media* (Cambridge, MA: MIT Press, 1999).
Bordwell, David, *The Cinema of Eisenstein* (Cambridge, MA: Harvard University Press, 1993).
Brain, Robert M., 'Representation on the Line', in Bruce Clark and Linda Dalrymple Henderson, eds, *From Energy to Information* (Palo Alto: Stanford University Press, 2002), 155–77.
Braudy, Leo, 'Providence, Paranoia, and the Novel', *English Literary History* 48 (Fall 1981), 619–37.
Briggs, Austin, '"Roll Away the Reel World, the Reel World": "Circe" and Cinema',

in Morris Beja and Shari Benstock, eds, *Coping with Joyce* (Columbus: Ohio State University Press, 1989), 145–56.

Brooks, Peter, *Reading for the Plot: Design and Intention in Narrative* (New York: Vintage Books, 1985).

Brown, Bob, 'The Readies', *transition* 19–20 (June 1930), 167–73.

Brown, Dan, *The Lost Symbol* (New York: Doubleday, 2009).

Browning, Barbara, *Infectious Rhythm: Metaphors of Contagion and the Spread of African Culture* (New York: Routledge, 1998).

Brugman, J., *An Introduction to the History of Modern Arabic Literature in Egypt* (Leiden: E. J. Brill, 1984).

Bryant, Marsha and Mary Ann Eaverly, 'Egypto-Modernism: James Henry Breasted, H.D., and the New Past', *Modernism/Modernity* 14: 3 (September 2007), 435–53.

Burkdall, Thomas L., *Joycean Frames: Film and the Fiction of James Joyce* (New York: Routledge, 2001).

Burns, Christy, *Gestural Politics* (Albany: State University of New York Press, 2000).

Burroughs, William S., *The Ticket That Exploded* (New York: Grove Press, 1994).

Bush, Christopher, *Ideographic Modernism* (New York: Oxford University Press, 2010).

Carlyle, Thomas, *Sartor Resartus* (Oxford: Oxford University Press, 1987).

Carringer, Robert, 'Rosebud, Dead or Alive: Narrative and Symbolic Structure in *Citizen Kane*', *PMLA* 91 (March 1976), 185–93.

Cayley, John, 'The Code Is Not the Text (Unless It Is the Text)', *Electronic Book Review* (September 2002), http://www.electronicbookreview.com/thread/electropoetics/literal.

Chaney, Michael A., 'Slave Cyborgs and the Black Infovirus: Ishmael Reed's Cybernetic Aesthetics', *MFS: Modern Fiction Studies* 49 (Summer 2003), 261–83.

Chapman, R. T., '"The Lady in the Looking Glass": Modes of Perception in a Short Story by Virginia Woolf', *Modern Fiction Studies* 18 (1972), 331–7.

Chatterjee, Partha, *Nationalist Thought and the Colonial World: A Derivative Discourse* (Minneapolis: University of Minnesota Press, 1986).

Chow, Rey, *The Protestant Ethnic and the Spirit of Capitalism* (New York: Columbia University Press, 2002).

Christian, Barbara, 'The Race for Theory', *Cultural Critique* 6 (Spring 1987), 51–63.

Clodd, Edward, *The Story of the Alphabet* (New York: Appleton, 1901).

Cohen, Daniel J., *Equations from God* (Baltimore: Johns Hopkins University Press, 2007).

Cohen, Hubert, 'The "Heart of Darkness" in "Citizen Kane"', *Cinema Journal* 12 (1972), 11–25.

Colla, Elliott, *Conflicted Antiquities: Egyptology, Egyptomania. Egyptian Modernity* (Durham, NC: Duke University Press, 2008).

—, 'Counting the Years: Shādī 'Abd al-Salām's Words', *Discourse* 21: 1 (Winter 1999), 127–39.

—, 'Shadi Abd al-Salam's al-Mumiya: Ambivalence and the Egyptian Nation-State', in Ali Abdullatif Ahmida, ed., *Beyond Colonialism and Nationalism in the Maghreb* (New York: Palgrave, 2000), 109–43.

Conley, Tom, *Film Hieroglyphs* (Minneapolis: University of Minnesota Press, 2006).

Connolly, Thomas Edmund, *James Joyce's Scribbledehobble: The Ur-Workbook for Finnegan's Wake* (Evanston: Northwestern University Press, 1961).

Conrad, Joseph, *The Collected Letters of Joseph Conrad*, Vol. 2, ed. Frederick Karl and Laurence Davies (Cambridge: Cambridge University Press, 1986).

—, *Heart of Darkness* (New York: Norton Critical, 2006).

—, *Lord Jim* (New York: Penguin, 1986).

—, *The Nigger of the 'Narcissus'* (New York: Norton Critical, 1979).
—, *The Secret Agent* (New York: Penguin, 1996).
Costanzo, William V., 'Joyce and Eisenstein: Literary Reflections of the Reel World', *Journal of Modern Literature* 11: 1 (1984), 175–80.
Crangle, Sara, 'The Time Being: On Woolf and Boredom', *MFS: Modern Fiction Studies* 54 (2008), 209–32.
Culler, Jonathan, 'Poe and Baudelaire', *Zeitschrift für französische Sprache und Literatur* 100 (1990), 61–73.
Danius, Sara, *The Senses of Modernism: Technology, Perception, and Aesthetics* (Ithaca: Cornell University Press, 2002).
Darwish, Mustafa, *Dream Makers on the Nile: A Portrait of Egyptian Cinema* (Cairo: American University in Cairo Press, 1998).
de Beaumont, Le Comte Etienne, 'Of What Are the Young Films Dreaming', *Little Review* 11: 2 (Winter 1926), 73–4.
Deane, Vincent, 'Claybook for *Finnegans Wake*', *AFWC* 3: 2 (Winter 1987), 21–39.
—, '*Les Langues du Monde* in VI.B.45', *AFWC* 3: 4 (Summer 1988), 61–75.
DeBona, Guerric, 'Into Africa: Orson Welles and "Heart of Darkness"', *Cinema Journal* 33 (Spring 1994), 16–34.
Delaney, Martin, *Principia of Ethnology* (Philadelphia: Harper & Bros, 1880).
Deleuze, Gilles and Richard Howard, *Proust and Signs: The Complete Text* (Minneapolis: University of Minnesota Press, 2000).
DeLillo, Don, *The Names* (New York: Vintage, 1989).
Derrida, Jacques, 'Freud and the Scene of Writing', *Yale French Studies* 48 (1972), 74–117.
Derrida, Jacques and Gayatri Chakravorty Spivak, *Of Grammatology* (Baltimore: Johns Hopkins University Press, 1976).
Dieckmann, Liselotte, *Hieroglyphics: The History of a Literary Symbol* (St Louis: Washington University Press, 1970).
Dimock, Wai Chee, *Through Other Continents: American Literature Across Deep Time* (Princeton: Princeton University Press, 2006).
Diop, Cheikh Anta, *The African Origin of Civilization*, trans. Mercer Cook (New York: L. Hill, 1974).
Donald, James, Anne Friedberg and Laura Marcus, eds, *Close Up, 1927–33: Cinema and Modernism* (Princeton: Princeton University Press, 1998).
Douglass, Frederick, 'The Claims of the Negro Ethnologically Considered', in Howard Brotz, ed., *African American Social and Political Thought: 1885–1920* (New Brunswick, NJ: Transaction Publishers, 1991), 226–44.
Drucker, Johanna, *Figuring the Word: Essays on Books, Writing, and Visual Poetics* (New York: Granary Books, 1998).
DuBois, W. E. B., *The Negro* (Philadelphia: University of Pennsylvania Press, 2001).
Dusinberre, Deke and Ian Christie, 'Episodes in a Lost History of Movie Serialism: Interview with Hollis Frampton', *Film Studies* 4 (Summer 2004), 104–18.
Eco, Umberto, *The Search for the Perfect Language* (Oxford: Blackwell, 1995).
Edison, Thomas, 'The Perfected Phonograph', *North American Review* 146: 379 (1888), 641–50.
—, 'The Phonograph and Its Future', *North American Review* 126 (1878), 527–36.
Eglash, Ron, 'African Influences in Cybernetics', in Chris Hables Gray, ed., *The Cyborg Handbook* (New York: Routledge, 1995), 17–28.
Eisenstein, Sergei, 'The Cinematographic Principle and Japanese Culture', *transition* 19–20 (June 1930), 90–103.
Eisenstein, Sergei and Jay Leyda, *Film Form: Essays in Film Theory* (New York: Harcourt Brace, 1949).

—, *The Film Sense* (New York: Harcourt Brace, 1947).
Eisenstein, Sergei and Herbert Marshall, *Nonindifferent Nature* (Cambridge: Cambridge University Press, 1987).
El Shakry, Omnia, *The Great Social Laboratory: Subjects of Knowledge in Colonial and Postcolonial Egypt* (Palo Alto: Stanford University Press, 2007).
El-Enany, Rasheed, *Naguib Mahfouz: The Pursuit of Meaning* (London: Routledge, 1993).
Ellison, Ralph, *Invisible Man* (New York: Vintage, 1995).
Ellmann, Richard, *James Joyce* (New York: Oxford University Press, 1959).
Emerson, Ralph Waldo, *Emerson: Essays and Poems* (New York: Library of America, 1996).
—, *Nature and Selected Essays* (New York: Penguin, 2003).
Everard, John, trans., *The Divine Pymander of Hermes Mercurius Trismegistus* (London: Robert White, 1650).
Eysteinsson, Ástráđur, 'Notes on World Literature and Translation', *Angles on the English-Speaking World* 6 (2006), 11–24.
Fabian, Johannes, *Time and the Other: How Anthropology Makes Its Object* (New York: Columbia University Press, 1983).
Fargue, Léon-Paul, 'Ecole sortie d'une table tournant', *Les Feuilles libres* 36 (March–June 1924), 347–51.
Farid, Samir, 'The Periodization of Egyptian Cinema', in Alia Arasoughly, ed., *Screens of Life: Critical Film Writing from the Arab World* (Quebec: World Heritage Press, 1996), 1–18.
Fenollosa, Ernest Francisco, Ezra Pound, Haun Saussy et al., *The Chinese Written Character as a Medium for Poetry: A Critical Edition* (New York: Fordham University Press, 2008).
Finney, Michael, 'Eugene Jolas, Transition, and the Revolution of the Word', *Tri-Quarterly* 38 (1977), 39–53.
Fitzpatrick, Kathleen, 'The Exhaustion of Literature: Novels, Computers, and the Threat of Obsolescence', *Contemporary Literature* 43 (Fall 2002), 518–59.
Foucault, Michel and Donald F. Bouchard, *Language, Counter-Memory, Practice* (Ithaca: Cornell University Press, 1977).
Foucault, Michel, *The Order of Things: An Archaeology of the Human Sciences* (New York: Vintage Books, 1973).
—, *This Is Not a Pipe*, trans. James Harkness (Berkeley: University of California Press, 1983).
Frampton, Hollis, *On the Camera Arts and Consecutive Matters: The Writings of Hollis Frampton* (Cambridge, MA: MIT Press, 2009).
France, Anatole, *Le Lys rouge* (Paris: Calmann-Lévy, 1925).
Freud, Sigmund, *The Interpretation of Dreams*, trans. James Strachey (New York: Avon, 1965).
Friedman, Susan Stanford, *Planetary Modernisms: Provocations on Modernity Across Time* (New York: Columbia University Press, 2015).
Géfin, Laszlo, *Ideogram, History of a Poetic Method* (Austin: University of Texas Press, 1982).
Genette, Gérard, *Mimologics*, trans. Thaïs E. Morgan (Lincoln: University of Nebraska Press, 1995).
Gershoni, Israel and James Jankowski, *Egypt, Islam, and the Arabs* (New York: Oxford University Press, 1987).
—, *Redefining the Egyptian Nation, 1930–1945* (Cambridge: Cambridge University Press, 1995).

Gibson, John and Wolfgang Huemar, *The Literary Wittgenstein* (London: Routledge, 2004).
Gibson, William, *Neuromancer* (New York: Ace, 1984).
—, *Pattern Recognition* (New York: Berkley Books, 2003).
Gidal, Peter, 'Interview with Hollis Frampton', *October* 32 (Spring 1985), 93–117.
Gifford, Don and Robert J. Seidman, *Ulysses Annotated: Notes for James Joyce's Ulysses*, 2nd rev. and enl. edn (Berkeley: University of California Press, 1988).
Gilman, Margaret, 'Baudelaire and Emerson', *Romanic Review* 34 (January 1943), 211–22.
Gilroy, Paul, *The Black Atlantic: Modernity and Double Consciousness* (Cambridge, MA: Harvard University Press, 1987).
—, *Small Acts: Thoughts on the Politics of Black Cultures* (London: Serpent's Tail, 1993).
Ginzburg, Carlo, *Clues, Myths, and the Historical Method* (Baltimore: Johns Hopkins University Press, 1989).
Gitelman, Lisa, *Always Already New: Media, History, and the Data of Culture* (Boston, MA: MIT Press, 2008).
—, *Scripts, Grooves, and Writing Machines: Representing Technology in the Edison Era* (Palo Alto: Stanford University Press, 1999).
Goldschmidt, Arthur, Amy J. Johnson and Barak A. Salmoni, eds, *Re-Envisioning Egypt 1919–1952* (Cairo: American University in Cairo Press, 2005).
Greaney, Michael, *Conrad, Language, and Narrative* (Cambridge: Cambridge University Press, 2001).
Greenberg, Nathaniel, *The Aesthetic of Revolution in the Film and Literature of Naguib Mahfouz* (Lanham: Lexington Books, 2014).
Gunning, Tom, 'In Your Face: Physiognomy, Photography, and the Gnostic Mission of Early Film', *Modernism/Modernity* 4 (January 1997), 1–29.
al-Hakim, Tawfiq, *The Prison of Life*, trans. Pierre Cachia (Cairo: American University in Cairo Press, 1992).
—, *Return of the Spirit*, trans. William M. Hutchins (Washington, DC: Three Continents Press, 1990).
Ḥakīm, Tawfīq, *'Awdat al-rūḥ* (Bayrūt: Dār al-Kitāb al-Lubnānī, 1974).
Halmi, Nicholas, *The Genealogy of the Romantic Symbol* (Oxford: Oxford University Press, 2007).
Haman, Iman, 'Al Momia / The Mummy', in Gonul Donmez-Colin, ed., *The Cinema of North Africa and the Middle East* (London: Wallflower Press, 2007), 31–40.
Hankins, Leslie Kathleen, '"Across the Screen of My Brain": Virginia Woolf's "the Cinema" and Film Forums of the Twenties', in Diane F. Gillespie, ed., *The Multiple Muses of Virginia Woolf* (Columbia, MO: University of Missouri Press, 1993), 148–79.
—, 'Virginia Woolf and Film', in Maggie Humm, ed., *The Edinburgh Companion to Virginia Woolf and the Arts* (Edinburgh: Edinburgh University Press, 2010), 351–74.
Hansen, Miriam, *Babel and Babylon: Spectatorship in American Silent Film* (Cambridge, MA: Harvard University Press, 1991).
—, 'Mass Culture as Hieroglyphic Writing: Adorno, Derrida, Kracauer', *New German Critique: An Interdisciplinary Journal of German Studies* 56 (Spring–Summer 1992), 43–73.
Hansom, Paul, ed., *Literary Modernism and Photography* (Westport, CT: Praeger, 2002).
Hartman, Janine, 'Ideograms and Hieroglyphs', *Dalhousie French Review* 54 (Summer 1998), 101–18.

Hayles, N. Katherine, '"A Metaphor of God Knew How Many Parts": The Engine That Drives *The Crying of Lot 49*', in Patrick O'Donnell, ed., *New Essays on The Crying of Lot 49* (Cambridge: Cambridge University Press, 2001), 97–125.
—, *My Mother Was a Computer* (Chicago: University of Chicago Press, 2005).
—, 'The Posthuman Body: Inscription and Incorporation in Galatea 2.2 and Snow Crash', *Configurations* 5 (Spring 1997), 241–66.
Hayles, N. Katherine and Jessica Pressman, *Comparative Textual Media* (Minneapolis: University of Minnesota Press, 2013).
Hayot, Eric, *Chinese Dreams: Pound, Brecht, Tel Quel* (Ann Arbor: University of Michigan Press, 2004).
H.D. [Hilda Doolittle] and Richard Aldington, *Some Imagist Poets: An Anthology* (Boston: Houghton Mifflin, 1915).
H.D. [Hilda Doolittle], *Tribute to Freud* (New York: Pantheon, 1956).
Heath, Stephen, 'Joyce in Language', in Colin McCabe, ed., *James Joyce: New Perspectives* (Bloomington, IN: Indiana University Press, 1982), 129–48.
Hite, Molly, '"Holy-Center Approaching" in the Novels of Thomas Pynchon', *Journal of Narrative Technique* 12 (1982), 121–9.
Hoptman, Laura, 'This Language is Ecstatic Because', *Bulletins of the Serving Library* 3 (Spring 2012), unpaged.
Horapollo, *The Hieroglyphics of Horapollo Nilous,* trans. Alexander Turner Cory (London: William Pickering, 1840).
Howard, Stephen, 'The Lady in the Looking-Glass: Reflections on the Self in Virginia Woolf', *Journal of International Women's Studies* 8: 2 (2007), 44–54.
Howe, Stephen, *Afrocentrism: Mythical Pasts and Imagined Homes* (London: Verso, 1998).
Huang, Yunte, *Transpacific Displacement: Ethnography, Translation, and Intertextual Travel in Twentieth-Century American Literature* (Berkeley: University of California Press, 2002).
Hudson, Nicholas, *Writing and European Thought 1600–1830* (Cambridge: Cambridge University Press, 1994).
Hulme, T. E. and Karen Csengeri, *The Collected Writings of T. E. Hulme* (Oxford: Oxford University Press, 1994).
Humm, Maggie, *Modernist Women and Visual Cultures: Virginia Woolf, Vanessa Bell, Photography and Cinema* (New Brunswick, NJ: Rutgers University Press, 2003).
Hungerford, Amy, 'Postmodern Supernaturalism: Ginsburg and the Search for a Supernatural Language', *Yale Journal of Criticism* 18 (Fall 2005), 269–98.
Hunt, Sidney, 'Ideograms', *transition* 2 (May 1927), 135.
Hurston, Zora Neale, 'Characteristics of Negro Expression', in Angelyn Mitchell, ed., *Within the Circle* (Durham, NC: Duke University Press, 1994), 79–94.
Husayn, Taha, *The Future of Culture in Egypt*, trans. Sidney Glazer (Washington, DC: American Council of Learned Societies, 1954).
Ḥusayn, Ṭāhā, *Mustaqbal al-thaqāfah fī Miṣr* (al-Qāhirah: al-Majlis al-A'lá lil-Thaqāfah, 2013).
Irwin, John T., *American Hieroglyphics: The Symbol of the Egyptian Hieroglyphics in the American Renaissance* (New Haven, CT: Yale University Press, 1980).
Irwin, Mark, 'Hieroglyphs of Revelation: Thomas Browne and Thomas Pynchon', *Pynchon Notes* 22–23 (Spring–Fall 1988), 53.
Israel, Nico, 'Esperantic Modernism: Joyce, Universal Language, and Political Gesture', *Modernism/Modernity* 2: 1 (January 2017), 1–21.
Ivanov, Vjaceslav, 'Eisenstein's Montage of Hieroglyphic Signs', in Marshall Blonsky, ed., *On Signs* (Baltimore: Johns Hopkins University Press, 1985), 221–35.
Iversen, Erik, *The Myth of Egypt and Its Hieroglyphs* (Copenhagen: GEC GAD, 1961).

Jackson, Tony, *The Technology of the Novel* (Baltimore: Johns Hopkins University Press, 2009).
—, 'Writing, Orality, Cinema: The "Story" of Citizen Kane', *Narrative* 16 (January 2008), 29–45.
James, George G. M., *Stolen Legacy* (New York: Philosophical Library, 1954).
Jameson, Fredric, *The Political Unconscious* (Ithaca: Cornell University Press, 1981).
—, *Postmodernism, or the Cultural Logic of Late Capitalism* (Durham, NC: Duke University Press, 1991).
Jespersen, Otto, *An International Language* (London: Allen & Unwin, 1928).
Johnston, John, *Information Multiplicity* (Baltimore: Johns Hopkins University Press, 1998).
Jolas, Eugene, 'Flight into Geography', *transition* 10 (January 1928), 75–85.
—, 'Introduction', *transition* 1 (April 1927), 135–8.
—, 'Landscape', *transition* 4 (July 1927), 134–6.
—, 'Suggestions for a New Magic', *transition* 3 (June 1927), 178–9.
—, 'Walk though Cosmopolis', *transition* 13 (Summer 1928), 133–8.
—, 'Workshop', *transition* 23 (July 1935), 97–106.
Jolas, Eugene, Andreas Kramer and Rainer Rumold, *Man from Babel* (New Haven, CT: Yale University Press, 1998).
Jolas, Eugene, Elliot Paul and Robert Sage, 'First Aid to the Enemy', *transition* 9 (December 1927), 161–76.
Jolas, Eugene et al., 'The Revolution of the Word', *transition* 16–17 (June 1929).
Jones, Rowland, *Hieroglyfic: or, a Grammatical Introduction to an Universal Hieroglyfic Language* (London: John Hughs, 1768).
Jousse, Marcel, *The Oral Style* (New York: Garland, 1990).
Joyce, James, *Anna Livia Plurabelle*, ed. C. K. Ogden (London: K. Paul, Trench, Trubner, 1931).
—, 'Anna Livia Plurabelle: Page Proofs', Ms., Box 5, Folders 100–101, James Joyce Collection, General Collection, Beinecke Rare Book and Manuscript Library.
—, *Finnegans Wake* (New York: Viking Press, 1945).
—, 'Finnegans Wake', trans. Samuel Beckett et al., *La Nouvelle Revue française* 19 (1 May 1931), 633–46.
—, 'From Work in Progress', *Le Navire d'argent* 5 (1 October 1925), 59–74.
—, *Occasional, Critical, and Political Writings* (Oxford: Oxford University Press, 2001).
—, *Portrait of the Artist as a Young Man* (Oxford: Oxford University Press, 2000).
Joyce, James and Margot Norris, *Dubliners: Authoritative Text, Contexts, Criticism* (New York: Norton, 2006).
Kenner, Hugh, *The Pound Era* (Berkeley: University of California Press, 1971).
Kermode, Frank, *Romantic Image* (London: Routledge, 1957).
Kern, Robert, *Orientalism, Modernism, and the American Poem* (New York: Cambridge University Press, 1996).
Kittler, Friedrich, *Gramophone, Film, Typewriter* (Palo Alto: Stanford University Press, 1999).
Kreilkamp, Ivan, 'A Voice without a Body: The Phonographic Logic of Heart of Darkness', *Victorian Studies* 40: 2 (Winter 1997), 211–43.
Lacan, Jacques, *Ecrits: A Selection*, trans. Bruce Fink (New York: Norton, 2002).
Lang, Fritz, 'The Future of the Feature Film in Germany', in Anton Kaes, Martin Jay and Edward Dimendberg, eds, *The Weimar Republic Sourcebook* (Berkeley: University of California Press, 1994), 622–3.
Lant, Antonia, 'The Curse of the Pharaoh: Or, How Cinema Contracted Egyptomania', *October* 59 (1992), 87–112.

Lastra, James, *Sound Technology and the American Cinema* (New York: Columbia University Press, 2000).
Laurence, Patricia, *Lily Briscoe's Chinese Eyes* (Columbia: South Carolina University Press, 2003).
Lawler, James, 'Daemons of the Intellect: The Symbolists and Poe', *Critical Inquiry* 14 (Autumn 1987), 95–110.
Lazarus, Neil, *Nationalism and Cultural Practice in the Postcolonial World* (Cambridge: Cambridge University Press, 1999).
Leonard, Garry, 'Joyce and Advertising: Advertising and Commodity Culture in Joyce's Fiction', *James Joyce Quarterly* 30–1 (1993), 573–92.
Lewis, Pericles, *Modernism, Nationalism, and the Novel* (Cambridge: Cambridge University Press, 2000).
Lewis, Wyndham, *The Essential Wyndham Lewis*, ed. Julian Symons (London: André Deutsch, 1989).
Lindgren, Allana and Stephen Ross, eds, *The Modernist World* (London: Routledge, 2015).
Lindsay, Vachel, *The Art of the Moving Picture . . . being the 1922 Revision of the Book First Issued in 1915* (New York: Macmillan, 1922).
Llona, Victor, 'Foreigners Writing in French', *transition* 2 (May 1927), 169–74.
Locke, John, *An Essay Concerning Human Understanding* (London: Thomas Basset, 1690).
Locke, William and A. D. Booth, eds, *Machine Translation of Languages* (New York: Wiley, 1955).
Long, Bernard Eustace, *Esperanto: Its Aims and Claims* (London: Esperanto Publishing, 1930).
McAlmon, Robert, 'Mr. Joyce Directs an Irish Prose Ballet', *transition* 15 (February 1929), 126–34.
McCabe, Susan, *Cinematic Modernism: Modernist Poetry and Film* (Cambridge: Cambridge University Press, 2005).
McCarthy, Patrick A., 'Making Herself Tidal: Chapter I.8', in Luca Crispi and Sam Slote, eds, *How Joyce Wrote* Finnegans Wake: *A Chapter-by-Chapter Genetic Guide* (Madison: University of Wisconsin Press, 2007), 163–80.
McHale, Brian, *Constructing Postmodernism* (London: Routledge, 1992).
—, *Postmodernist Fiction* (New York: Metheun, 1987).
McHugh, Roland, *The Sigla of Finnegans Wake* (Austin: University of Texas Press, 1976).
McHugh, Roland and James Joyce, *Annotations to Finnegans Wake*, rev. edn (Baltimore: Johns Hopkins University Press, 1991).
McLuhan, Marshall, *Understanding Media* (New York: McGraw-Hill, 1964).
McMillan, Dougald, *transition: The History of a Literary Era 1927–1938* (London: Calder & Boyars, 1975).
Mahfouz, Naguib, *Khufu's Wisdom*, trans. Raymond Stock (New York: Anchor, 2003).
Maḥfūẓ, Najīb, *'Abath al-aqdār [ta'līf]* (al-Qāhirah: Maktabat Miṣr, 1960).
Mallarmé, Stéphane, Mary Ann Caws and Jill Anderson, *Mallarmé in Prose* (New York: New Directions, 2001).
Mallory, J. P., *In Search of the Indo-Europeans* (London: Thames & Hudson, 1989).
Manovich, Lev, *The Language of New Media* (Cambridge, MA: MIT Press, 2001).
Mao, Douglas and Rebecca Walkowitz, 'The New Modernist Studies', *PMLA* 123: 3 (May 2008), 737–48.
Marcus, Laura, '"Hieroglyphics in motion": Representing Ancient Egypt and the Middle East in Film Theory and Criticism of the Silent Period', in Pantelis Michelakis and

Maria Wyke, eds, *The Ancient World in Silent Cinema* (Cambridge: Cambridge University Press, 2013), 74–90.
—, *The Tenth Muse: Writing about Cinema in the Modernist Period* (Oxford: Oxford University Press, 2007).
Matz, Jesse, *Literary Impressionism and Modernist Aesthetics* (Cambridge: Cambridge University Press, 2001).
Meadowsong, Zena, '"Behind the hieroglyphic streets": The Digital Code of Pynchon's *The Crying of Lot 49*', Modernist Studies Association Conference, Las Vegas, NV, 19 October 2012, Panel Presentation.
Melville, Herman, *Moby-Dick* (New York: Norton, 2002).
Mendelson, Edward, 'The Sacred, the Profane, and *The Crying of Lot 49*', in *Pynchon: A Collection of Critical Essays* (Englewood Cliffs, NJ: Prentice-Hall, 1978), 112–46.
Metz, Christian, *Film Language: A Semiotics of the Cinema*, trans. Michael Taylor (New York: Oxford University Press, 1974).
Michaels, Walter Benn, *The Shape of the Signifier* (Princeton: Princeton University Press, 2004).
Milesi, Laurent, ed., *James Joyce and the Difference of Language* (Cambridge: Cambridge University Press, 2003).
—, 'Joyce, Language, and Languages', in Jean-Michel Rabaté, ed., *Palgrave Advances in James Joyce Studies* (Basingstoke: Palgrave, 2004), 144–61.
—, 'Supplementing Babel: Paget in VI.B.32', in Dirk van Hulle and Geert Lernout, eds, *James Joyce: The Study of Languages* (Brussels: Peter Lang, 2002), 75–89.
—, 'Vico . . . Jousse: Joyce . . . Langue', *La Revue des Lettres Modernes* 834–9 (1988), 143–62.
Milson, Menahem, *Najib Mahfuz: The Novelist* (New York: St. Martins Press, 1998).
Milutis, Joe, 'Riddles of the Interface: Hieroglyphic Consciousness and New Experimental Multimedia', *Wide Angle* 21: 1 (1999), 95–103.
Minow-Pinkney, Makiko, *Virginia Woolf and the Problem of the Subject* (New Brunswick, NJ: Rutgers University Press, 1987).
Mitchell, W. J. T., *Picture Theory: Essays on Verbal and Visual Representation* (Chicago: University of Chicago Press, 1994).
Moore, Rachel O., *Savage Theory: Cinema as Modern Magic* (Durham, NC: Duke University Press, 2000).
Moosa, Matti, *The Origins of Modern Arabic Fiction* (Washington, DC: Three Continents Press, 1983).
Moretti, Franco, *The Modern Epic: The World-System from Goethe to Garcia Marquez* (London: Verso, 1996).
Morton, Samuel, *Crania Aegyptiaca* (Philadelphia, PA: John Penington, 1844).
Mulvey, Laura, 'Citizen Kane: From Log Cabin to Xanadu', in James Naremore, ed., *Orson Welles's Citizen Kane* (Oxford: Oxford University Press, 2004), 217–48.
Murnau, F. W., 'Films of the Future', *McCall's* (September 1928), 90.
—, 'The Ideal Picture Needs No Titles', *Theatre Magazine* (January 1928), 72.
Murphet, Julian, *Multimedia Modernism: Literature and the Anglo-American Avant-garde* (Cambridge: Cambridge University Press, 2009).
Musser, Charles, *The Emergence of Cinema* (Berkeley: University of California Press, 1994).
Neilsen, Aldon Lynn, *Black Chant: Languages of African-American Postmodernism* (Cambridge: Cambridge University Press, 1997).
Neurath, Otto, *Basic by Isotype* (London: K. Paul, Trench, Trubner & Co., 1937).
Newman, Robert, *Understanding Thomas Pynchon* (Columbia, SC: University of South Carolina Press, 1986).

Nolan, Emer, *James Joyce and Nationalism* (London: Routledge, 1995).
North, Michael, *Camera Works: Photography and the Twentieth-Century Word* (New York: Oxford University Press, 2005).
—, *Reading 1922: A Return to the Scene of the Modern* (New York: Oxford University Press, 1999).
Nott, Josiah and George Gliddon, *Types of Mankind* (Philadelphia: Lippincott, Granbo, & Co., 1885).
Ogden, C. K., *Debabelization: With a Survey of Contemporary Opinion on the Problem of a Universal Language* (London: Kegan Paul, Trench, Trubner & Co., 1931).
—, 'James Joyce's Anna Livia Plurabelle in Basic English', *transition* 21 (March 1932), 259–62.
Ogden, C. K. and I. A. Richards, *The Meaning of Meaning* (New York: Harcourt Brace, 1923).
Paget, Richard, *Babel* (London: Kegan Paul, Trench, Trubner & Co., 1930).
Perloff, Marjorie, *The Futurist Moment: Avant-Garde, Avant Guerre, and the Language of Rupture* (Chicago: University of Chicago Press, 1986).
—, *Radical Artifice: Writing Poetry in the Age of Media* (Chicago: University of Chicago Press, 1991).
—, *Wittgenstein's Ladder: Poetic Language and the Strangeness of the Ordinary* (Chicago: University of Chicago Press, 1996).
Peters, John, *Conrad and Impressionism* (Cambridge: Cambridge University Press, 2001).
Picker, John M., *Victorian Soundscapes* (Oxford: Oxford University Press, 2003).
Plato, Edith Hamilton and Huntington Cairns, *The Collected Dialogues of Plato* (Princeton: Princeton University Press, 1961).
Platt, Len, *Joyce, Race, and Finnegans Wake* (Cambridge: Cambridge University Press, 2007).
—, '"No such Race": The Wake and Aryanism', in Andrew Gibson, Len Platt and Sebastian D. G. Knowles, eds, *Joyce, Ireland, Britain* (Gainesville: University Press of Florida, 2006), 155–77.
Plotinus, *The Enneads*, trans. Stephen McKenna (London: Faber & Faber, 1956).
Plutarch, *Moralia*, vol. 5, trans. Frank Cole Babbitt (Cambridge, MA: Harvard University Press, 1960).
Poliakov, Leon, *The Aryan Myth* (New York: Basic Books, 1974).
Pound, Ezra, *ABC of Reading* (Norfolk, CT: New Directions, 1951).
—, 'Debabelization and Ogden', *New English Weekly* 6 (28 February 1935), 410–11.
—, 'A Few Don'ts by an *Imagiste*', *Poetry* 1 (March 1913), 200–6.
—, *Gaudier-Brzeska* (New York: New Directions, 1960).
—, *Machine Art and Other Writings* (Durham, NC: Duke University Press, 1996).
—, *Poems and Translations* (New York: Modern Library, 2003).
Pound, Ezra and Harriet Zinnes, *Ezra Pound and the Visual Arts* (New York: New Directions, 1980).
Proust, Marcel, *In Search of Lost Time Volume V: The Captive and the Fugitive*, trans. D. J. Enright, C. K. Scott Moncrieff and Terence Kilmartin (New York: Modern Library, 2003).
—, *In Search of Lost Time Volume VI: Time Regained*, trans. Andreas Major, Terence Kilmartin and D. J. Enright (New York: Modern Library, 1992).
—, *Le Temps Retrouvé* (Paris: Gallimard, 1945).
Punzi, Maddalena Pennacchia, *Literary Intermediality: An Introduction* (Bern: Peter Lang, 2007).
Pynchon, Thomas, *The Crying of Lot 49* (New York: Harper Perennial, 2006).
—, *Gravity's Rainbow* (New York: Penguin, 1973).

—, *Mason & Dixon* (New York: Henry Holt, 1997).
Quigley, Megan, *Modernist Fiction and Vagueness: Philosophy, Form, Language* (Cambridge: Cambridge University Press, 2015).
Rabaté, Jean-Michel, 'Joyce and Jolas: Late Modernism and Early Babelism', in Morton P. Levitt, ed., *Joyce and the Joyceans* (Syracuse: Syracuse University Press, 2002), 51–8.
Raley, Rita, 'Code.surface || Code.depth', *Dichtung-digital* 36 (2006), accessed 22 September 2010, http://dichtung-digital.mewi.unibas.ch/2006/1-Raley.htm.
—, 'Machine Translation and Global English', *Yale Journal of Criticism* 16 (Fall 2003), 291–313.
Ramsaye, Terry, *A Million and One Nights: A History of the Motion Picture* (New York: Simon & Schuster, 1926).
Reed, Ishmael, *Another Day at the Front* (New York: Basic Books, 2003).
—, *Mumbo Jumbo* (New York: Simon & Schuster, 1972).
Rice, Thomas Jackson, 'Ulysses and the Kingdom of Shadows', *James Joyce Quarterly* 41: 1–2 (2004), 161–8.
Richardson, Dorothy, *Pilgrimage 4* (London: Virago, 1967).
Rippy, Marguerite, *Orson Welles and the Unfinished RKO Projects* (Carbondale: Southern Illinois University Press, 2009).
Rivers, Christopher, *Face Value* (Madison: University of Wisconsin Press, 1994).
Rorty, Richard, *The Linguistic Turn* (Chicago: University of Chicago Press, 1967).
Rosen, Philip, *Change Mummified: Cinema, Historicity, Theory* (Minneapolis: University of Minnesota Press, 2001).
Rosenbaum, Jonathan, *Discovering Orson Welles* (Berkeley: University of California Press, 2007).
Rosenheim, Shawn James, *The Cryptographic Imagination* (Baltimore: Johns Hopkins University Press, 1997).
Rosiers, Erika and Wim Van Mierlo, 'Neutral Auxiliaries & Universal Idioms: Otto Jespersen in Work in Progress', in Dirk van Hulle and Geert Lernout, eds, *James Joyce: The Study of Languages* (Brussels: Peter Lang, 2002), 55–70.
Sage, Robert, 'Etc.', *transition* 14 (Fall 1928), 171–8.
Said, Edward, 'Conrad: The Presentation of Narrative', *Novel* 7 (Winter 1974), 116–32.
—, 'Nationalism, Human Rights, and Interpretation', *Raritan* 12: 3 (1993), 26–52.
—, 'Yeats and Decolonization', in Terry Eagleton, Frederic Jameson and Edward Said, eds, *Nationalism, Colonialism, and Literature* (Minneapolis: University of Minnesota Press, 1990), 69–98.
Sailer, Susan Shaw, 'Universalizing Languages: Finnegans Wake Meets Basic English', *James Joyce Quarterly* 36: 4 (1999), 853–68.
Sakkut, Hamdi, *The Egyptian Novel and Its Main Trends* (Cairo: American University in Cairo Press, 1971).
Saussure, Ferdinand de, *Course in General Linguistics* (New York: McGraw-Hill, 1966).
Saussy, Haun, *Great Walls of Discourse and Other Adventures in Cultural China* (Cambridge, MA: Harvard University Press, 2001).
Seeley, Tracy, 'Virginia Woolf's Poetics of Space: "The Lady in the Looking-Glass: A Reflection"', *Woolf Studies Annual* 2 (1996), 89–116.
Shafik, Viola, *Arab Cinema: History and Cultural Identity*, new rev. edn (Cairo: American University of Cairo Press, 2007).
—, 'Egyptian Cinema', in Oliver Leaman, ed., *Companion Encyclopedia of Middle Eastern and North African Film* (London: Routledge, 2001), 23–129.

Shail, Andrew, *The Cinema and the Origins of Literary Modernism* (New York: Routledge, 2012).
Shalan, Jeff, 'Writing the Nation: The Emergence of Egypt in the Modern Arabic Novel', *Journal of Arabic Literature* 33: 3 (2002), 211–47.
Sharp, Dennis, *The Picture Palace* (New York: Frederick A. Praeger, 1969).
Shaw, Walter Hanks, 'Cinema and Ballet in Paris', *New Criterion* 4: 1 (January 1926), 178–9.
Shenton, Herbert Newhard, Edward Sapir and Otto Jespersen, *International Communication: A Symposium on the Language Problem* (London: Kegan Paul, Trench, Trubner & Co., 1931).
Shiach, Morag, '"To Purify the Dialect of the Tribe": Modernism and Language Reform', *Modernism/Modernity* 14 (2007), 21–34.
Sitney, P. Adams, 'Re-Viewing Frampton', *American Film* 11 (April 1986), 67.
Smith, Grafton Elliott, *The Ancient Egyptians and the Origin of Civilization* (London: Harper & Bros, 1923).
Spivak, Gayatri C., 'Unmaking and Making in *To the Lighthouse*', in Sally McConnell-Ginet, Ruth Borker and Nelly Furman, eds, *Women and Language in Literature and Society* (New York: Praeger, 1980), 310–27.
Starkey, Paul, *From the Ivory Tower: A Critical Study of Tawfiq al-Hakim* (London: Ithaca Press, 1987).
Steiner, George, *After Babel: Aspects of Language and Translation*, 3rd edn (Oxford: Oxford University Press, 1998).
Stephenson, Neal, *Cryptonomicon* (New York: Harper Collins, 1999).
—, *In the Beginning Was the Command Line* (New York: Avon, 1999).
—, *Snow Crash* (New York: Bantam, 1992).
Sterne, Jonathan, *The Audible Past* (Durham, NC: Duke University Press, 2003).
Stewart, Garrett, *Reading Voices: Literature and the Phonotext* (Berkeley: University of California Press, 1990).
Sullivan, Edward, *The Book of Kells*, 2nd edn (London: 'The Studio' ltd, 1933).
Swedenborg, Emanuel, *A Hieroglyphic Key to Natural and Spiritual Mysteries*, trans. R. Hindmarsh (London: R. Hindmarsh, 1792).
Tabbi, Joseph, *Cognitive Fictions* (Minneapolis: University of Minnesota Press, 2006).
Thacker, Andrew, 'A Language of Concrete Things', in Edward P. Comentale and Andrzej Gąsiorek, eds, *T. E. Hulme and the Question of Modernism* (Aldershot: Ashgate, 2006), 39–55.
Tiessen, Paul, 'The Shadow in Caligari: Virginia Woolf and the "Materialists" Responses to Film', *Film Criticism* 11: 1–2 (1987), 75–83.
Torgovnick, Marianna, *Gone Primitive* (Chicago: University of Chicago Press, 1990).
Torok, Maria, 'Questions to Freudian Psychoanalysis', *Critical Inquiry* 19: 3 (Spring 1993), 567–94.
Trafton, Scott, *Egypt Land* (Durham, NC: Duke University Press, 2004).
Trotter, David, *Cinema and Modernism* (Malden, MA: Blackwell, 2007).
—, 'Virginia Woolf and Cinema', *Film Studies* 6 (2005), 13–26.
Troy, Mark L., *Mummeries of Resurrection: The Cycle of Osiris in Finnegans Wake* (Uppsala: Almqvist & Wiksell, 1976).
Turner, Nat, *Confessions of Nat Turner* (Baltimore: Thomas R. Gray, 1831).
Tytler, Graeme, *Physiognomy in the European Novel* (Princeton: Princeton University Press, 1982).
Unger, J. Marshall, *Ideogram: Chinese Characters and the Myth of Disembodied Meaning* (Honolulu: University of Hawai'i Press, 2004).
Van Zile, Edward S., *That Marvel – The Movie: A Glance at Its Reckless Past, Its Promising Present, and Its Significant Future* (New York: G. P. Putnam, 1923).

Vatikiokis, P. J., *The History of Modern Egypt*, 4th edn (London: Weidenfeld & Nicholson, 1991).
Vico, Giambattista, *The New Science of Giambattista Vico*, trans. Thomas Goddard Bergin and Max Harold Fisch (Ithaca: Cornell University Press, 1975).
Vincent, Rickey, *Funk: The Music, the People, and the Rhythm of the One* (New York: St. Martin's Griffin, 1996).
Vitalis, Robert, 'Hollywood and Revolution on the Nile', in Walter Armbrust, ed., *Mass Mediations* (Berkeley: University of California Press, 2000), 269–91.
Webster, John, *Academiarum Examen* (London: Giles Calvert, 1653).
Weir, Lorraine, 'The Choreography of Gesture: Marcel Jousse and Finnegans Wake', *James Joyce Quarterly* 14 (1977), 313–25.
Welch, Walter and Leah Brodbeck Stenzel Burt, *From Tinfoil to Stereo* (Gainesville: University Press of Florida, 1994).
Welles, Orson, *Heart of Darkness* script, Welles mss, Box 14, Folders 15–17, Lilly Library, Indiana University at Bloomington.
Welles, Orson and Peter Bogdanovich, *This Is Orson Welles* (New York: Harper Collins, 1992).
Wells, H. G., *The Outline of History: Being a Plain History of Life and Mankind* (London: Cassell, 1920).
Welsh, Andrew, *Roots of Lyric: Primitive Poetry and Modern Poetics* (Princeton: Princeton University Press, 1977).
Wicke, Jennifer, *Advertising Fictions: Literature, Advertisement and Social Reading* (New York: Columbia University Press, 1988).
—, 'Modernity Must Advertise: Aura, Desire, and Decolonialization in Joyce', *James Joyce Quarterly* 30-1 (1993), 593–613.
Wilkinson, Lynn R., *The Dream of an Absolute Language: Emanuel Swedenborg and French Literary Culture* (Albany: State University of New York Press, 1996).
Williams, George Washington, *History of the Negro Race in America* (New York: Arno Press, 1968).
Williams, R. John, 'The *Technê* Whim: Lin Yutang and the Invention of the Chinese Typewriter', *American Literature* 82 (June 2010), 389–419.
Windhausen, Federico, 'Words into Film: Toward a Genealogical Understanding of Hollis Frampton's Theory and Practice', *October* 109 (Summer 2009), 76–95.
Wittgenstein, Ludwig, *Tractatus Logico-Philosophicus* (New York: Harcourt, 1922).
Wittgenstein, Ludwig and G. E. M. Anscombe, *Philosophical Investigations* (Cambridge: Blackwell, 1997).
Wollen, Peter, 'Citizen Kane', in James Naremore, ed., *Orson Welles's Citizen Kane: A Casebook* (New York: Oxford University Press, 2004), 249–62.
—, *Signs and Meaning in the Cinema* (Bloomington: Indiana University Press, 1972).
Woolf, Virginia, 'Class Distinctions. Holograph fragment', Virginia Woolf Collection, Henry W. and Albert A. Berg Collection of English and American Literature, New York Public Library.
—, 'The Cinema', *The Arts* 9: 6 (June 1926), 314–16.
—, *Collected Essays* (London: Hogarth Press, 1966).
—, *The Common Reader* (New York: Harcourt, 1925).
—, *The Complete Shorter Fiction of Virginia Woolf* (San Diego: Harcourt, 1989).
—, *The Death of the Moth* (New York: Harcourt, 1942).
—, 'The lady in the looking-glass. Typescript with the author's ms. corrections. 1929 May 2', Virginia Woolf Collection, Henry W. and Albert A. Berg Collection of English and American Literature, New York Public Library.
—, *Letters of Virginia Woolf, Vol. 3: 1923–1928* (New York: Harcourt Brace, 1980).
—, *Night and Day* (New York: Harcourt, 1948).

—, *Mrs. Dalloway* (San Diego: Harcourt, 1981).
—, *On Being Ill* (Ashfield: Paris Press, 2002).
—, *To the Lighthouse* (San Diego: Harcourt, 1981).
—, *The Waves* (San Diego: Harcourt, 1931).
Yared, Aida, '"In the Name of Annah": Islam and "Salam" in Joyce's "Finnegans Wake"', *James Joyce Quarterly* 35 (Winter–Spring 1998), 401–38.

INDEX

Abd al-Salam, Shadi
   al-Mummia, 16, 131, 151, 153–60
   desire to connect writing and film, 16, 151, 157–60
   use of Pharaonic past, 131, 151, 153–7
Abdel-Malek, Anouar, 162–3n
Adamic language, 25–9, 31–3, 36, 41, 44, 45, 48, 51, 55n, 56n, 60n, 64, 70, 83, 84, 116, 173, 177, 187–9, 196n, 210, 214, 220–2, 234n, 236n
The Adelphi, 66–9
Adorno, Theodor, 58n, 96
advertisements, 84, 87
   for books about ancient Egypt, 1, 5, 65–6, 166–7
   as embodied language, 147, 166–7, 174–81, 184, 196n, 197n
Afro-Futurism, 17, 201, 202, 223, 224, 227
Al-Hakim, Tawfiq, 2, 150–1
   engagement with Pharaonic discourses, 4, 14, 16, 127–8, 129, 139–43, 145–6, 147, 156, 160, 239
   film and, 152–3
   Prison of Life, 153
   in relation to modernism, 128–9, 139–40
   Return of the Spirit, 128, 132, 136, 137, 139–46, 147, 148, 150, 154, 156, 157
   sub-Saharan Africa and, 129, 131, 138–9, 143–7, 157, 163n, 225

Anderson, Benedict, 13, 132, 152
Apter, Emily, 128, 235n
Arabic, 66, 128, 131, 136, 139, 140, 143, 146, 148, 149, 153, 157–8, 161n, 170, 180, 195n
Armbrust, Walter, 140
Armstrong, Tim, 39, 82
Artaud, Antonin, 177–8
Aryanism, 16, 166, 167, 170, 190, 194n, 198n
Attridge, Derek, 168, 189
avant-garde, 6, 15, 16, 18n, 19n, 26, 27, 39, 50, 54, 57n, 161n, 166, 204, 205, 234n

Babel, 13, 15, 16, 21n, 34, 89, 91n, 128, 131, 165, 166–9, 173, 188, 189, 192, 193, 193n, 194n, 214, 218, 221, 241
   new media as solving problem of, 19n, 39, 205, 206
   specific language as transcending, 28–30, 188, 192
Bacon, Sir Francis, 29–31, 200
Baikie, James, 66, 146, 149–50
Balakian, Anna, 32
Balázs, Béla, 7, 11, 21n, 39, 69, 72, 73, 116, 177, 186, 198n
Baldwin, James, 224, 237n
Barnes, Djuna, 4, 81
Barry, Iris, 62, 65, 66, 69

257

Basic English, 16, 30, 38, 165, 167, 169–70, 173, 185–6, 189, 191, 193, 193n, 194n, 205
Bayoumi, Mohamed, 130, 151–2
Bazin, André, 19n, 50, 158–9
Beasley, Rebecca, 17n, 59n
Beckett, Samuel, 177, 179, 187, 191, 195n
Bell, Alexander Melville, 95
Bell, Clive, 65, 69
Benjamin, Walter, 28, 196n, 234n
Bernal, Martin, 224
Bhabha, Homi, 130, 142, 145
Bishop, John, 179, 185, 193n, 197n
Boehme, Jacob, 28, 32, 176
Bolter, Jay David, 3, 207
Book of Kells *see* illuminated manuscripts
Book of Nature, 7, 28–9, 31, 47, 57n, 176, 203, 208, 211–13, 217
Book of the Dead, 139, 153, 179, 197n, 204, 211, 235n
Bordwell, David, 49–50, 59n
Brooks, Peter, 99, 119, 122n
Brown, Dan, 199–201, 211, 233n
  The Lost Symbol, 199–201, 233n

The Cabinet of Dr. Caligari, 64, 68–9, 71
Carlyle, Thomas, 28–9, 33
Carter, Howard, 4, 127, 132, 201; *see also* Tutankhamen
Cayley, John, 204, 234n
Champollion, Jean François, 5, 8, 9, 10, 25–6, 30–1, 33–7, 45–7, 49, 55n, 63, 75, 77, 89, 127, 141, 173, 201, 212, 217, 220
character
  as communicated via speech vs. writing, 98–100
  as constituted by language, 8, 11, 63, 73, 75, 86, 88, 101, 105–6, 115, 175, 177, 178–9, 181, 183, 215, 217, 219, 228
  hieroglyphs and, 8, 15, 33, 63, 64, 73, 75–6
  inscrutability of, 80, 94, 112, 116, 117, 120
  new understandings of media and, 7, 8, 15, 62, 72–3, 104, 108, 112, 116, 121
  as revealed through physiognomy, 116, 120
Chatterjee, Partha, 133, 138, 162n
Chinese *see* ideograms
Chow, Rey, 10
cinema *see* film
Clodd, Edward, 173, 194n, 196n
Close-Up, 15, 57n, 64, 72, 73, 82, 89n, 97
Colla, Elliott, 21n, 146, 147, 156, 161n
colonialism, 12, 13, 108, 109, 130, 133–4, 139, 142, 145, 150, 153, 156, 163n
computing *see* digital code
Conrad, Joseph, 3
  concern with writing and speech, 15, 92–5, 97, 98–108, 112, 118, 120–1, 122n

Heart of Darkness, 15, 92, 94, 98–9, 102–4, 107, 108, 109, 110, 111, 118, 119, 120, 121n, 122n, 144–5, 148
Lord Jim, 94, 97–105, 107, 110, 119, 120, 123
new narrative forms and, 15, 50, 93–4, 103, 105, 108, 109, 118–21, 124n
newspapers and, 105–7, 120, 122n
The Nigger of the 'Narcissus', 94, 98, 106
phonography and, 93, 97–8
The Secret Agent, 102, 105–8, 119–20, 122n
Cratylic language *see* Adamic language
cryptography *see* digital code
cuneiform, 11, 13, 18n, 40, 170, 179, 191–2, 202, 220–3

dance, 32, 88, 167, 178, 225–7
Danius, Sara, 18n, 193n
De Beaumont, Comte Etienne, 66
Deleuze, Gilles, 47–8
DeLillo, Don, 231, 236n
Derrida, Jacques, 10, 20n, 46, 99
Dieckmann, Liesolette, 25, 55n, 193n
digital code
  connection to Pentecost, 203, 214, 218, 221
  as embodied language, 218
  expressing both meaning and non-meaning, 202–3, 210, 212, 229
  hieroglyphs and, 199–211, 217, 221, 229, 232
  as metaphor for writing/novel, 203, 215, 222, 223, 228
  as performative language, 200, 202, 216–17, 222, 228–33
Dimock, Wai Chee, 128
Diop, Cheikh Anta, 162n, 224
Douglass, Frederick, 130, 135, 224, 225
Drucker, Johanna, 6, 19n, 55n

Eco, Umberto, 29, 56n, 188, 206
Edison, Thomas, 2, 11, 18n, 95–6, 103, 121n
Eglash, Ron, 226–7
Egypt
  comparison to America, 1, 4, 186, 197n, 233n
  films in or about, 18n, 130, 151–3, 159–60, 161n, 163n, 164n
  history and independence, 4, 14, 16, 132, 161n
  as inscrutable, 33
  link to Europe, 128–30, 132–4, 137–9
  media and race and, 12, 131, 160, 166, 192, 200, 225, 227–8
  modernism in, 131, 139–40

INDEX

Pharaonic movement in, 4, 14, 16, 21n, 127–31, 133–51, 153–7, 161n, 162n
  relation to Africa, 129–30, 135–7, 139, 143–6, 223–5, 237n
  relation to China, 35, 57n, 138
  Western fascination with, 3–4, 13, 18n, 66–8, 90n, 127, 130, 159, 164n
  see also hieroglyphs; Revolution of 1919
Eisenstein, Sergei
  'The Cinematographic Principle and the Ideogram', 41–2, 44, 186
  connection to Joyce, 49, 186–7, 198n
  influence on Hollis Frampton, 52–4
  interest in narrative, 44, 49–50, 60n, 109
  and London film culture, 57n, 64, 65, 186
  'Nonindifferent Nature', 48–50, 54, 109
  use of ideograms as metaphor for film, 2, 11, 15, 27, 35, 41–2, 44–5, 48–50, 59n, 60n, 187
El Shakry, Omnia, 137, 162n
Ellison, Ralph, 231
Emerson, Ralph Waldo, 29, 31–2, 36, 56n, 87, 206
Esperanto, 12, 20n, 30, 38–9, 57–8n, 165, 167–73, 186, 194n, 195n, 205
Eysteinsson, Ástráđur, 128

Fabian, Johannes, 142, 163n
Fargue, Léon-Paul, 173
female language *see* gender
Fenollosa, Ernest, 32, 35–8, 40, 42, 52, 56n, 57n, 192n
  'The Chinese Written Character as a Medium for Poetry', 26, 35, 36, 38, 42, 56n, 57n, 195n
film, 18n
  America and, 1, 4, 185–6
  as authorless, 78, 123n
  as capturing the passage of time, 70, 78–9, 91n
  character or psychology and, 7, 39, 58n, 62–3, 72–5, 81, 83–4, 87, 90n, 112–15, 117–18, 177, 186
  coming of sound, 49–50, 60n, 82, 113, 193n
  as composed of hieroglyphs or ideograms, 4–5, 15, 19n, 27, 38–43, 49–50, 52, 54, 57n, 58n, 59n, 65–6, 68, 70, 73–4, 90n, 121n, 157, 185–7, 240
  as defined by combinations of still images, 41–2, 44, 52
  as defined by motion, 42–4, 72, 85, 88, 185
  in Egypt, 16, 18n, 130–1, 151–60, 161n, 163n, 164n, 197n
  as expressing the life of objects, 73–4, 79
  as feminine, 82
  gesture and, 38–9, 172, 177, 186
  as hybrid of writing and image, 1–3, 5, 11, 18n, 19n, 21n, 26, 49, 50–1, 53, 58n, 59n, 60n, 62–4, 72, 78, 83, 88–9, 90n, 93–4, 97, 108, 111–13, 115–16, 120, 158, 160, 184–5, 232, 239
  Imagism and, 38, 42–3
  influence of modernism on Hollywood, 110
  interest in among London intellectuals, 64–6, 68–70, 89n
  representation of digital code in, 208
  as universal language, 1, 5, 20–1n, 27, 38–41, 44, 52, 57n, 58n, 62, 69–71, 73–4, 90n, 92, 123n, 172–3, 185–7, 193n, 236n
  visual languages and narrative in, 43–4, 49–50, 54, 60n
Fitzpatrick, Kathleen, 203, 234n
Foucault, Michel, 6–7, 10, 20n, 34, 124n
Frampton, Hollis, 2, 50–4
  Zorns Lemma, 50–4
Freud, Sigmund, 15, 26, 45–9, 59n, 73, 118
Friedman, Susan Stanford, 128, 129, 139, 161n

gender, 64, 80–4, 86, 89
Genette, Gerard, 25, 32, 48, 59–60n
Gershoni, Israel and James Jankowski, 4, 133, 162n
gestural language, 170, 171
  film as, 7, 39, 58n, 72, 167, 171, 172, 186–7
  hieroglyphs and, 29, 88, 167, 171–2, 176, 179, 226
  as original language, 29, 39, 167–8, 170–3, 177, 186, 189, 190, 195n, 198n, 226
  as universal language, 171, 176, 177, 178, 184, 186, 236n
  writing as, 84, 177–8, 193n, 227, 228
Gibson, William, 17, 199, 202–3, 216–19, 220, 229, 231, 232, 236n
  Neuromancer, 202, 216–19, 229, 231, 236n
  Pattern Recognition, 218, 236n
Gifford, Don, and Robert J. Seidman, 192
Gilroy, Paul, 162n, 224
Ginzburg, Carlo, 117, 119, 123n, 207
Gitelman, Lisa, 18n, 121n
Greaney, Michael, 98, 105, 106, 107, 122n
Greenberg, Nathaniel, 152
Griffith, D. W., 2, 11, 39–40, 44, 58n, 59n, 185, 187

Haman, Iman, 156, 164n
Hankins, Leslie Kathleen, 68–9, 89n
Hansen, Miriam, 11, 39–40, 58n, 60n

259

Haykal, Muhammad Husayn, 4, 14, 127, 131, 133–5, 137, 139, 141, 143, 146, 162n
Hayles, N. Katherine, 2, 17n, 204, 206, 207, 212, 216, 222, 231, 235n, 236n, 238n
H.D., 57n, 59n, 64, 65, 73, 90n
Hebrew, 180, 188, 189, 191–2, 198n, 207
hieroglyphs, 1, 2, 4, 8, 10, 33, 40, 41, 42, 45, 47, 49, 56n, 57n, 63, 84, 95, 148–9, 166, 172–3, 188, 191, 197n, 211
  as Adamic, Cratylic, or mystic language, 4, 5, 13, 15, 17n, 19n, 20n, 25–33, 35–7, 40–2, 44, 45, 52, 54, 55n, 56n, 60n, 63–4, 70, 71, 76, 80, 83, 167, 172, 173, 187, 192, 195n, 196n, 198n, 200–2, 205–8, 210–15, 219, 220, 229, 233n, 235n, 236n
  advertising and, 174
  in African-American culture, 224, 225, 237n
  as alternative to male language, 64, 81–2, 83–5, 89
  as appropriated by the West, 13–14, 15–16, 127, 135, 159, 160, 225
  Arabic and, 130–1, 136, 143, 146, 148–50, 157–8, 180, 197n
  avant-garde and, 19n, 26, 37, 50–4, 55n, 172–3, 205
  binary of Babel and Pentecost and, 64, 76, 202–3, 212–14, 218, 228, 235n, 236n
  debates about race or nation and, 13–14, 16, 17, 129, 131, 160, 166, 239
  difficulty of decipherment, 7–8, 33, 46–8, 54, 56n, 59n, 64, 75, 76, 80, 87, 196n, 211, 241
  digital code or computers and, 3, 16–17, 199–210, 211–12, 214–20, 227–30, 233
  as embodied or material medium, 2, 5, 29, 39, 58n, 64, 72, 75, 78, 81, 84, 86, 89, 172, 176–9, 180, 186, 194n, 204, 209, 219, 226, 234n, 240
  film and, 1, 2, 4, 5, 11, 15, 18n, 19n, 26–7, 30, 38–45, 48–54, 58n, 63, 65, 66, 68, 70, 74, 81, 90n, 121n, 158, 159, 160, 179, 184–7, 233n
  gestures and, 7, 29, 39, 88, 167, 171–2, 176–8, 186, 195n, 226
  history of Western understandings of, 2, 4, 5, 13, 14–15, 16, 25, 27–35, 233n, 239
  as hybrid between image, speech, and writing, 2, 3, 5, 8–12, 26, 33–4, 44, 45, 49, 50, 53, 54, 58n, 60n, 64, 78, 84–6, 89, 90n, 97, 115, 159, 167, 174, 179, 181, 183, 207–8, 211, 228
  as language of perception or character, 7–8, 15, 33, 62, 63–4, 72–3, 75, 76–8, 219
  linguistic reform and, 1, 9, 17n, 29–31, 37
  mysticism of new media and, 5, 26, 38–40, 60n, 62–3, 96–7
  narrative and, 6–7, 15, 26–7, 34–5, 46, 49–50, 54, 81
  phonography and, 2, 18n, 93, 95–7, 121n
  photography and, 19n
  physiognomy and the Book of Nature and, 7, 20n, 28–9, 31–3, 47, 59n, 75, 176, 203, 206–9, 211–13, 217–18, 228
  similarity to phonetic scripts, 5, 10, 15, 25–6, 30–1, 36, 45–8, 76, 187, 220
  as source of all languages and media, 166, 167, 168, 189, 192–3
  Symbolism and, 32–3
  as universal language, 9, 12, 16, 29–30, 32, 37–40, 56n, 58n, 90n, 167, 171, 185, 200, 205–6, 210
  used to understand relation between media, 2–5, 17n, 27, 199
  versus ideograms, 6, 26, 30, 35–6, 41–2, 44, 55n, 56n, 138
  Wittgenstein and, 20n, 37
  see also Egypt
Hoptman, Laura, 6
Horapollo, 27, 46
Hulme, T. E., 1, 17n, 32, 38, 55n, 56n, 57n, 72
Hussein, Taha, 134, 137–9, 146
  The Future of Culture in Egypt, 137–9

ideograms, 1, 9–11, 173, 196n, 197n, 209, 216, 235n
  as active, 42–4, 50
  film and, 38, 41–4, 48–50, 52, 57n, 59n, 109, 186–7
  hieroglyphs and, 30, 35–6, 57n, 138
  as hybrid language, 13, 29, 48–50, 55n
  importance to accounts of modernism, 6, 19n, 26, 55n
  as visual language, 10, 13, 20n, 26–7, 35–7, 41, 42, 44–5, 52, 56n, 187, 195n
illuminated manuscripts, 167, 171, 181–5, 191, 197n, 207
Imagism, 1, 38, 42–3
Impressionism, 42, 47, 75–8, 90n
In the Land of Tutankhamen, 16, 130, 151, 160
International Auxiliary Languages *see* universal language
Irish, 167, 170, 188–92, 194n
Irwin, John, 17n, 26, 31, 36, 55n, 56n
Iversen, Erik, 25, 27, 55n

Jackson, Tony, 103, 111, 123n
James, George G. M., 224–5
Jameson, Fredric, 93, 98, 102, 214

Jespersen, Otto, 38, 165, 170, 196n
Jolas, Eugene, 57n, 165–6, 168–73, 185, 194n, 197n
Jousse, Marcel, 171–2, 176, 177, 189, 190, 193n, 195n, 198n
Joyce, James, 2, 3, 4, 10, 20n, 236n
  advertising and, 174–7, 180, 196n, 197n
  anti-Aryanism of, 16, 167, 170, 189–90, 194n, 198n
  Egypt and Arabic and, 148, 170, 180, 195n, 197n
  film and, 39, 49, 52, 167, 184–7, 197n, 198n
  Finnegans Wake, 16, 148, 165–71, 173–5, 177, 178–91, 193, 193n, 194n, 195n, 197n, 198n, 232, 233n
  importance of translation to, 128, 190–2, 198n
  interest in hieroglyphs and gestures as origin point, 4, 16, 150, 160, 166–8, 172–3, 176, 179, 183, 185–6, 188–9, 191–3, 193n, 194n, 195n, 196n, 197n, 198n, 200, 215, 219, 226
  interest in material or embodied languages and media, 8, 166–7, 171, 175–84, 186, 187, 193n, 194n, 196n, 197n, 207, 222
  International Auxiliary Languages and, 16, 165–6, 168–71, 185, 189, 191, 193, 193n, 194n, 195n
  nationalism and universalism of, 129, 160, 166, 169, 188–90, 198n
  A Portrait of the Artist as a Young Man, 196n, 197n, 231
  transition and, 16, 166, 168–9, 172–3, 186, 194n, 195n, 196n, 197n
  Ulysses, 16, 28, 49, 148, 166–7, 170–1, 174–8, 179, 180, 183, 188, 190, 191–3, 196n, 197n, 198n, 222

Kenner, Hugh, 6, 17n, 52, 56n, 57n, 188
Kermode, Frank, 32, 56n
Kern, Robert, 35, 55n, 56n, 57n
Kircher, Athanasius, 28, 30, 35, 56n, 201, 210
Kittler, Friedrich, 19n, 117, 123n
Kreilkamp, Ivan, 97, 102, 121n, 122n

Lacan, Jacques, 46
Lant, Antonia, 18n, 130, 161n
Lastra, James, 18n, 96, 121n
Lazarus, Neil, 133
Leibniz, Gottfried Wilhelm, 13, 29–31, 56n, 200, 201, 210, 237n
letters (correspondences), 73–5, 77, 79, 82, 83–4, 86, 93, 97, 101–2, 104–5, 111, 165, 170, 171, 175, 177, 179, 183, 184, 185, 218
Lewis, Wyndham, 13

Lindsay, Vachel, 1–2, 4, 5, 11, 15, 27, 38–41, 43, 45, 46, 51, 52, 58n, 63, 66, 68, 69–71, 73, 78, 79, 172, 184–5, 202, 233n, 239
  The Art of the Moving Picture, 1, 2, 11, 38–41, 43, 70–1, 73, 79, 233n
Locke, John, 29, 55n, 56n
London Film Society, 15, 64, 69, 70, 91n

McCarthy, Patrick, 190
McHale, Brian, 232, 236n
McLuhan, Marshall, 20n, 186, 206
Mahfouz, Naguib, 2, 3
  connection to European modernists, 129, 131, 148
  film and, 131, 152–3
  hieroglyphs and Arabic and, 10, 16, 130–1, 136, 146, 148–50, 154, 157, 170–1, 227
  Khufu's Wisdom, 130–1, 136, 146–51, 152, 154, 157, 171, 227
  nationalist discourses and, 4, 14, 16, 129, 131, 147, 157, 160, 166, 200, 225, 239
  Pharaonic past and, 14, 16, 129, 146–8
Mallarmé, Stephane, 6, 19n, 32, 177, 178, 196n, 234n
Manovich, Lev, 206, 207
Mao, Douglas and Rebecca Walkowitz, 3
Marcus, Laura, 18n, 19n, 39, 58n, 59n, 60n, 66, 73, 78, 89n, 90n, 186
The Matrix, 208–10, 217
Matz, Jesse, 77–8, 90n
Meadowsong, Zena, 229
media, 1, 12, 17n
  defined in relation to other media, 2–3, 5, 8, 9, 10, 11, 12, 15, 17, 18n, 44, 54, 63, 64, 89, 92, 93, 120, 158, 160, 167, 173, 184, 210, 211, 216, 232, 240
  direct relation to reality, 2, 7, 26, 84, 167, 232, 240
  lack of boundaries between in modernist era, 2, 3, 5, 65, 140
  race and nation and, 4, 12, 14, 16, 17, 129–31, 151–2, 159, 160, 193, 225, 226, 239
  visual languages in relation to, 4, 7, 13, 19n, 26, 27, 35, 50, 54, 64, 92, 157, 172, 186, 199, 232
  writing as, 3, 6, 64, 93–4, 150, 157, 237n
  see also digital code; film; hieroglyphs; phonography; photography
medicine, 117–18, 120, 123n, 124n
Melville, Herman, 4, 33–5, 45, 50, 56n, 57n, 80, 87, 148, 176
  Moby-Dick, 33–5, 56n, 57n
Mendelson, Edward, 214, 235n

Metz, Christian, 11, 20n, 21n, 57n
Michaels, Walter Benn, 222
Mitchell, W. J. T., 3, 8, 11, 12, 20n
modernism,
  global, 128
  importance of media to understandings of, 3, 12, 18n
  importance of visual languages to, 6, 19n, 26, 37, 55n, 57n
  influence on Egyptian writers, 148
  influence on mainstream films, 110
  relation to postmodernism, 231–4
  Western and Middle Eastern conceptions of, 128, 131, 139–40
Moretti, Franco, 174
Morton, Samuel, 135
Murnau, F. W., 39–40
  The Last Laugh, 39–40
Musa, Salama, 4, 14, 127–31, 133–8, 139, 141, 143, 146–7, 162n

narrative
  in avant-garde, 6, 15, 43, 50, 54
  connection to hieroglyphs, 6–7, 26, 34–5, 44, 46, 48–50, 81, 87, 117
  importance to visual languages, 6, 26, 50
  innovative structures of, 15, 92–4, 102–4, 107, 108–10, 118–21, 121n, 123n
  need for world to be deciphered through, 7–8, 46–7, 87
nationalism, 13, 162n
  connection between literature and, 133–5, 161n
  as exclusionist discourse, 136–9, 143–7
  Irish vs. Egyptian, 129, 166, 192
  Joyce and, 188–90, 192, 198n
  link between Aryanism and Irish, 167, 190
  link between Egyptian film and, 152, 157–8, 160
  Orientalism and, 129, 133, 138, 142–3, 145, 156, 163n
  Pharaonic past as contributing to Egyptian, 4, 10, 14, 16, 127, 129, 132–7, 140–2, 146–7, 150, 154–6, 158
  theories of new media and, 2, 12, 14, 16, 17, 129–31, 149–50, 157, 160, 241
  universalism and, 14, 16, 129, 131, 134, 137, 188–90
Neilsen, Aldon Lynn, 224, 227, 237n
newspapers, 1, 18n, 105–8, 111–13, 120, 122n
newsreels, 78–9, 108–13, 120, 130, 158
North, Michael, 8, 17n, 18n, 19n, 20n, 57n
Nott, Josiah and George Gliddon, 135–6

Ogden, C. K., 12, 16, 21n, 38, 57n, 165–71, 186, 189, 191, 193, 193n, 194n, 205, 234n
oral discourse *see* speech
Orientalism, 163n
  adopted and altered by Egyptian writers, 129, 133, 138, 142–3, 156
  Egyptian interest in hieroglyphs as complicating, 14, 16, 127–8
  in film, 130, 160
  interest in hieroglyphs and ideograms as example of, 20, 37, 39, 41, 45, 79, 127, 167, 172–3, 195n
  in modernism, 13, 21n, 110
  sub-Saharan Africa and, 99, 144–5
Out 1, 236n

Paget, Richard, 165, 170, 171–3, 176, 187, 189, 194n, 195n, 198n
Pentecost, 200, 202, 203, 206, 214, 218, 219, 221, 236n, 241
Perloff, Marjorie, 6, 19n, 20n, 55n, 234n
Pharaonicism *see* Egypt
phonography
  Conrad's exposure to, 93, 97–8
  as a form of inscription, 5, 94, 95
  hieroglyphs and, 18n, 95, 121n
  in relation to writing, 3, 15, 18n, 93, 95–7, 98, 100–3, 105–6, 108, 115–16, 120, 121n, 122n
  stenographic shorthand and, 95–6, 122n
photography, 1–2, 5, 18n, 19n, 51, 74, 94, 96, 107, 158–60, 164n, 170, 185, 186, 204, 215, 240
physiognomy, 20n, 28, 33, 39, 58n, 72, 75, 90n, 116–18, 120, 123
Picker, John, 97, 122n, 124n
Pierce, Charles Sanders, 11
Plato, 25, 31, 55n, 193n, 234n
Platt, Len, 194n, 198n
poetry, 1, 6, 10, 17n, 19n, 21n, 26, 33, 42–5, 85, 172, 181, 187, 196n, 205, 237n
Pound, Ezra, 51
  ABC of Reading, 17n, 36–7, 42
  centrality to modernism and visual languages, 1, 6, 17n, 19n, 37, 52, 55n
  film and, 38, 42–5, 57n, 59n
  ideograms and, 10, 13, 15, 17n, 20n, 26–7, 34–8, 41–5, 46, 52, 54, 56n, 57n, 59n, 187–8
primitivism *see* Orientalism
problem of Babel *see* Babel
Proust, Marcel, 4, 8, 10, 15, 26, 27, 32, 45–9, 59n, 62, 77, 111, 148
  Le Temps retrouvé, 46–8, 59n

Pynchon, Thomas
  ambivalence about the novel, 203, 229–31, 233, 237–8n
  Book of Nature and, 203, 211–13
  The Crying of Lot 49, 201–3, 210–15, 216, 218, 220, 226, 228–30, 231, 235n, 236n, 237n
  Gravity's Rainbow, 202, 213, 226, 229, 230, 235n
  influence of, 216, 223, 226, 236n
  interest in hieroglyphs, 8, 17, 199, 201, 203, 210–14, 216, 229, 233, 235n
  performative language and, 17, 200, 202–3, 216, 228–30, 231, 232–3, 237n
  references to digital code and computing, 17, 199, 203, 210–12, 215, 222, 229, 230, 237–8n
  references to other media, 215, 228
  treatment of binary between meaning and non-meaning, 129, 202–3, 210–14, 219, 220, 230, 235n

Quigley, Megan, 20n, 90n
A Quoi Revent les Jeunes Films, 65–6

race
  Aryan theories of, 166, 194n, 198n
  in discourses about ancient Egypt, 135–7, 160, 224
  hieroglyphs used to understand, 12, 14, 16, 17, 129, 131, 166, 169, 203, 237n
  importance to Pharaonicism, 135–7, 145–7, 157, 162n
radio, 70–1, 111, 115, 210–11, 226
Raley, Rita, 204, 207, 208, 234n, 235n
Ramsaye, Terry, 5, 11, 39, 41, 172, 192
Reed, Ishmael, 17, 199, 202, 203, 223–8, 229, 230, 239
  Mumbo Jumbo, 202, 223–8
Revolution of 1919, 127, 130, 132, 138, 139, 140, 142, 143, 146, 162n
rhythm, 77, 85, 88, 91n, 171
Richardson, Dorothy, 57n, 63, 81–4
  Dawn's Left Hand, 82–4
  'The Film Gone Male', 82, 84
Rorty, Richard, 8
Rosen, Philip, 206
Rosenheim, Shawn James, 18n, 210, 219, 235n, 236n
Rosetta Stone, 5, 17, 26, 30, 33, 68, 89, 128, 134, 179, 197n, 208, 239–41

Said, Edward, 93, 98, 134, 150
Saussure, Ferdinand De, 9–10, 116, 122n, 204
Saussy, Haun, 30, 42, 57n, 59n
Shalan, Jeff, 161n, 162n, 163n
Shaw, Walter Hanks, 65

Smith, Grafton Elliott, 136–7
sound recording *see* phonography
speech
  ancient civilisations as lacking, 13
  association of men with, 82
  compared to gestures, 7, 58n, 172, 186, 195n
  difference between Arabic writing and, 157–8
  hieroglyphs as defined by absence of, 9–10, 20n, 36–7, 45, 46, 52
  hieroglyphs as defined by combination of images and, 26, 33, 48–9, 82, 237n
  inner, 60n
  media as hybrid of writing, image, and, 2, 3, 5, 34, 49–50, 66, 80, 83, 88–9, 92–5, 97–105, 107–8, 112–13, 115–18, 120, 158, 171, 174, 183–4, 220, 222–3, 227–8
  phonography as translating from writing into, 95–6, 121n, 122n
Stephenson, Neal, 17, 199, 202–3, 214, 216, 219–23, 227, 229, 231–2, 236n, 237n
  Cryptonomicon, 220, 231, 237n
  In the Beginning Was the Command Line, 231–2
  Snow Crash, 202, 216, 219–23, 227, 231, 236n, 237n
Sterne, Jonathan, 91, 121n, 122n, 124n
Sudan, 129, 139, 143–7, 157, 163n, 226
Sullivan, Edward, 171, 181, 183
Swedenborg, Emmanuel, 28, 31–2

Trafton, Scott, 224
transition, 5, 16, 41, 57n, 65, 165–70, 172–3, 176n, 179, 180, 186, 194n, 195n, 196n, 197n
translation, 21n, 38, 128, 146, 161n, 165–6, 168–9, 194n, 197n, 234n
  between visual or oral and written modes, 35, 46, 59n, 77, 87–9, 93, 94, 97, 98, 103, 108, 118, 120, 122n, 174, 180, 226
  importance to Joyce, 190–3, 198n
  machine, 200, 204–6, 208, 219
  perception or interpretation and, 8, 47–8, 63–4, 66, 78, 81, 94, 120, 190, 228–9, 231
  Rosetta Stone and, 128, 239–41
Trotter, David, 18n, 69, 78, 123n
Turner, Nat, 224
Tutankhamen, 4–5, 16, 26, 28, 66, 127, 130, 131, 132, 161n, 172, 179, 201

universal language, 13, 16, 29–30, 32, 37–8, 56n, 90n, 158, 165–8, 170–1, 178, 179, 188, 193n, 194n, 195n, 196n, 236n
  digital code as, 200, 205–8, 210, 228, 234n

universal language (cont.)
  dreams as, 73
  film and other new media as, 11, 12, 18, 38–40, 59n, 60n, 71, 90n, 95–6, 167, 172–4, 184–7
  gesture as, 39, 171, 176, 177, 178, 184, 186–7, 236n
  hieroglyphs or ideograms as, 5, 9, 12, 16, 27, 30, 36, 37, 40, 45, 54, 59n, 172–3, 186–7, 214
  Joyce's engagement with, 16, 165–8, 170–1
universalism, 2, 13–14, 39, 129, 133–5, 166, 168–9, 188–90, 192–3, 194n, 239, 241

Van Zile, Edward, 39, 172, 185
Vico, Giambattista, 29, 55n, 167, 171–3, 176, 177, 184, 187, 189, 192–3, 195n, 215, 226
virus, 221–3, 227, 236–7n
vocal discourse *see* speech
Vogue, 5, 62, 64, 65, 69, 89n

Weaver, Warren, 205–6, 208, 210, 234n
Webster, John, 28, 30
Welles, Orson, 2
  character and perception and, 108, 112–18, 120–1
  Citizen Kane, 15, 92, 94, 108–13, 115–16, 118–21, 121n, 123n, 158, 160
  concern with relationship between image, sound, text, and identity, 15, 92–5, 97, 108, 111–18, 120–1, 121n, 123n, 160, 177, 222, 239
  Heart of Darkness, 109, 113–15, 118, 121n, 123n
  interest in Conrad, 15, 92, 108–10, 112, 113–15, 117–20, 121n, 122–3n, 123n

new narrative forms and, 15, 50, 93–4, 108, 109, 119–20, 123n, 213
Wells, H. G., 71
Wicke, Jennifer, 174
Wilkinson, Lynn, 32
Wittgenstein, Ludwig, 8–9, 20n, 30, 36–8, 45, 56n, 57n, 81
  Tractatus Logico-Philosophicus, 8–9, 20n, 37–8
Wollen, Peter, 11, 21n, 123n
women *see* gender
Woolf, Virginia
  character or embodiment and, 7, 15, 62–4, 70–6, 79–80, 83–5, 88–9, 90n, 91n, 93, 115, 212
  'The Cinema', 5, 15, 62–75, 77, 78–80, 85, 86, 88, 89, 90n, 91n, 115, 184
  'Craftsmanship', 70–1, 72, 90n
  feminine language and, 64, 80–4, 86, 91n
  film and, 5, 15, 62–3, 64–5, 68–72, 74–9, 84, 87, 88–9, 89n, 90n, 91n
  'The Lady in the Looking-Glass', 62, 63, 72–5, 79–81, 86, 89, 90n, 212
  Mrs. Dalloway, 62, 70, 87–8
  Night and Day, 76, 90n
  'On Being Ill', 63, 65, 66, 81, 91n
  references to hieroglyphs, 4, 15, 63, 66–8, 70–7, 81, 84
  To the Lighthouse, 15, 62, 63, 70, 72, 78–87
  treatment of writing, film, or perception as hybrid, 2, 3, 8, 63–4, 72, 77–8, 83, 85–9, 89n, 90n, 91n, 93, 104, 115, 153, 176, 178, 184, 203, 206, 239
  The Waves, 63, 75–7

Yared, Aida, 180, 195n, 197n

Zaghloul, Saad, 130, 132, 143

EU representative:
Easy Access System Europe
Mustamäe tee 50, 10621 Tallinn, Estonia
Gpsr.requests@easproject.com

www.ingramcontent.com/pod-product-compliance
Lightning Source LLC
Chambersburg PA
CBHW062124300426
44115CB00012BA/1805